CHINA AND THE WRITING OF ENGLISH LITERARY MODERNITY, 1690–1770

This book explores how a modern English literary identity was forged by notions of other traditions and histories, in particular those of China. The theorizing and writing of English literary modernity took place in the midst of the famous quarrel between the ancients and the moderns. Eun Kyung Min argues that this quarrel was in part a debate about the value of Chinese culture and that a complex cultural awareness of China shaped the development of a "national" literature in seventeenth- and eighteenth-century England by pushing to new limits questions of comparative cultural value and identity. Writers including Defoe, Addison, Goldsmith, and Percy wrote China into genres such as the novel, the periodical paper, the pseudo-letter in the newspaper, and anthologized collections of "antique" English poetry, inventing new formal strategies to engage in this wide-ranging debate about what defined modern English literature and culture.

EUN KYUNG MIN is Professor of English at Seoul National University in Korea. Her published work appears in such journals as *The Eighteenth Century: Theory and Interpretation*, *Eighteenth-Century Studies*, *Studies on Voltaire and the Eighteenth Century*, *Social Text*, and *English Literary History*.

CHINA AND THE WRITING OF ENGLISH LITERARY MODERNITY, 1690–1770

EUN KYUNG MIN

Seoul National University

CAMBRIDGE
UNIVERSITY PRESS

CAMBRIDGE
UNIVERSITY PRESS

University Printing House, Cambridge CB2 8BS, United Kingdom

One Liberty Plaza, 20th Floor, New York, NY 10006, USA

477 Williamstown Road, Port Melbourne, VIC 3207, Australia

314–321, 3rd Floor, Plot 3, Splendor Forum, Jasola District Centre, New Delhi – 110025, India

79 Anson Road, #06-04/06, Singapore 079906

Cambridge University Press is part of the University of Cambridge.

It furthers the University's mission by disseminating knowledge in the pursuit of education, learning, and research at the highest international levels of excellence.

www.cambridge.org
Information on this title: www.cambridge.org/9781108421935
DOI: 10.1017/9781108379793

First published 2018

Printed in the United Kingdom by Clays, St Ives plc

A catalogue record for this publication is available from the British Library.

ISBN 978-1-108-42193-5 Hardback

For my parents

Contents

List of Illustrations   *page* viii
Acknowledgements   ix

Introduction: China in English Literary Modernity   1

1   China between the Ancients and the Moderns   15

2   Robinson Crusoe and the Great Wall of China   47

3   The New, Uncommon, or Strange: China in *The Spectator*   89

4   Oliver Goldsmith's Serial Chinaman   125

5   Thomas Percy's Chinese Miscellanies and the *Reliques
     of Ancient English Poetry*   164

Notes   200
Bibliography   249
Index   272

Illustrations

1 Jacobus Houbraken, *Sir William Temple*. Engraving. 1738.
   Harvard Art Museums/Fogg Museum, Gift of William
   Gray from the collection of Francis Calley Gray, G1987.
   © President and Fellows of Harvard College.   *page* 8
2 "R. Crusoe with the Muscovite Caravan pass the Chinese
   Wall from Peking." From Daniel Defoe, *The Farther
   Adventures of Robinson Crusoe*, 4th ed. (London, 1722).
   12614.a.24. © The British Library Board.   68
3 "The Embassadors entry through the famous Chinese wall
   which is 1200 miles long." From Evert Ysbrants Ides, *Three
   Years Travels from Moscow Over-Land to China* (London,
   1706). New York Public Library Digital Collections.   83
4 Front page, *The Public Ledger, or, Daily Register of Commerce
   and Intelligence*, January 24, 1760. Microform. *Early English
   Newspapers*, reel 1020. Photograph courtesy of Firestone
   Library, Princeton University.   126

Acknowledgements

It is a great relief finally to be able to thank the individuals and institutions that supported the writing of this book. This is a book I probably would not have written if I had not chosen to relocate back home after many years of living in the USA. Living and teaching English literature in Seoul propelled me to rethink my relationship to my field of study, as well as the relationship between Asia and English literature. I wrote the book over a long time, in Seoul, Princeton, and Cambridge, thinking continually about issues of cultural translation and transformation. Although the topic of my book departs from my graduate work, I remain indebted to my former graduate advisors at Princeton University, Hans Aarsleff, Claudia Brodsky, Jonathan Lamb, and Esther Schor, who opened up the world of eighteenth-century literature for me. I am particularly grateful to Jonathan Lamb for providing academic life-support at critical junctures and to Esther Schor for always being there – as my mentor, role model, correspondent, and dear friend.

My book was conceived in the air-conditioned rooms of the Clark Library at UCLA where I spent a summer reading William Temple. I am grateful to the Clark Library as well as the Lewis Walpole Library at Yale University for awarding me visiting research fellowships that gave me access to the archival materials that inspired my book. The year I spent at Harvard's Radcliffe Institute for Advanced Study as a Bunting Fellow remains one of the happiest memories of my life. I am deeply grateful to Drew Faust and Judith Vichniac for introducing me to this extraordinary institution and community. The Radcliffe Institute not only gave me a year of lavish freedom to dream up this book but also subsequently awarded me an Exploratory Summer Seminar award as well as a Summer Fellowship, providing continuing support over many years. While at Radcliffe, I had the great pleasure of working with Harvard research assistants Zhenzhen Lu and Victoria Baena, to whom I owe many ideas and insights. I also owe a great debt to institutions in Korea. I am grateful to the SBS Foundation for an Overseas Research Development Grant that funded a year at Princeton University where I wrote the first draft of the book. My home university, Seoul National University in Seoul, provided me with multiple periods of sabbatical leave and, most recently, a College of Humanities Research Fund award that helped me set a deadline for final publication.

It was a great, providential stroke of luck that I met Linda Bree, my editor at Cambridge University Press, during my sabbatical year at Princeton. Her early interest in my project gave me a sense of purpose and fueled my writing. I would like to thank Tim Mason, Sarah Lambert, Clare Owen, and Catherine Hanley for helping me with the final production process. I am also grateful to the anonymous readers for the press who gave me very helpful and encouraging signposts to follow during the final revision process.

Although I cannot name them all here, I would like to thank my past and present colleagues for providing a nurturing home in the English department at Seoul National University. I thank especially Nak-chung Paik and Sungwon Lee, both now retired, for reading parts of the manuscript and showing me how to improve it. I am deeply sorry that I cannot share this book with the late Young-moo Kim. Bumjin Koo, Jongtae Lim, and Youngmin Kim, my friends in East Asian History and Philosophy at Seoul National University, offered convivial support during the writing process. For being much more than just colleagues, I thank Nancy Cho, Mi Jeong Song, and Eun Jung Yoo. My former and current students are more responsible than they know for much of this book. For helping me track down sources and reading materials, as well as for keeping eighteenth-century conversations going, I would like to thank Ja Yun Choi, Yoojung Choi, Kyeong Seo Chung, Inhye Ha, Seongmin Han, Jin Kim, Ungsan Kim, Woochang Lee, and Jane Lim. Beyond Seoul National University, I thank all the members of the Korean Society for Eighteenth-Century Studies and the Korean Society for Eighteenth-Century English Literature – two wonderful intellectual communities where I have found both friends and fun.

It feels as if a whole new field of scholarship has sprung up during the time it took me to write this book. I wrote it in active dialogue with Jeng-Guo Chen, William Christie, Benjamin Elman, Laura Hostetler, Peter Kitson, Robert Markley, Li Ou, Peter Perdue, David Porter, Q. S. Tong, Chi-ming Yang, and Eugenia Zuroski Jenkins, many of whom invited me to attend conferences and contribute to publications. Peter Perdue, Harold Cook, and Wilt Idema kindly answered my questions. Martin Heijdra, Library Director at Princeton's Gest Library, helped me with Dutch sources, and Maggie Powell, former Librarian and Director at the Lewis Walpole Library, sent me much appreciated cards of encouragement for years. John Logan at Princeton's Firestone Library provided succor at the eleventh hour, beaming me a digital image of *The Public Ledger* after all other routes had failed. I am very grateful to all of them.

While working on this book and related projects, I have greatly enjoyed meeting colleagues working at different universities in Asia. Besides those already named, I thank Nahoko Miyamoto Alvey, Stephen Clark, Robbie Goh, Pin-chia Feng, Tianhu Hao, Elaine Ho, Yuko Matsukawa, Anne Thell, Laurence Williams, and Yukari Yoshihara. Their friendship and camaraderie has meant much to me. For taking an interest in my project and encouraging me, I am also grateful to Anne Cheng, Lynn Festa, Claudia Johnson, and Gauri Viswanathan.

Many of my chapters began as conference papers that then developed into journal articles before finally being reworked, in much expanded form, into my book. I would like to thank the National Research Foundation of Korea for funding the writing of some of these articles. Parts of my book were presented in the form of invited talks and conference papers at the Newberry Library, Princeton University, Radcliffe Institute for Advanced Study, Tsukuba University, University of St. Andrews, and University of Sydney. An earlier version of Chapter 1, "China between the Ancients and the Moderns," first appeared in *The Eighteenth Century: Theory and Interpretation* 45.2 (2004). I wrote a version of Chapter 2 for a conference I co-organized with Jongtae Lim for the Institute of Humanities at Seoul National University; it appeared as "Novel/Topograph: Robinson Crusoe and the Great Wall of China" in *Horizons: Seoul Journal of Humanities* 1.2 (2010). A shorter version of Chapter 5 was first published in *Eighteenth-Century Studies* 43.3 (2010). I am grateful to the editors of these journals for granting me permission to use these materials.

Lastly, I would like to thank my close friends in Seoul and elsewhere, near and far, who have buoyed up my daily life: Hyoun Joo Choe, Julie Choi, Eunjin Chung, Anne-Lise François, Borahm Kim, Gina Kim, Jeong Hee Kim, Hye-soo Lee, Margherita Long, Hi Kyung Moon, Hyungji Park, Sunyoung Park, Karin Schutjer, Jane Jeong Trenka, and Hui-sok Yoo. I wish I could have shared this book also with Grace Ko, Ynhui Park, and Allan Silver, three friends who will always remain close to my heart. A very special thank you goes to my dearest friend Talia Bloch for – there is no way to abbreviate it – everything.

This book is dedicated to my loving parents, Byung Kyu Min and Yong Bun Lee, who have always believed in and supported a literary career for me. I thank my dear sister Eun Joo and brother Seung Ki, as well as their spouses, Felipe Lorenzo and Yujin Kim, for bringing familial happiness to us all. My daughter Sue Hwa was a newborn when I embarked on this book and over the years has often taken me to task for *still* writing the *same* book. I will be glad to present it to her at last. Finally, I thank my husband Sang Jun Kim, who has lived with this book as long as I have and never once doubted that I would finish it. This book is for all of them.

Introduction: China in English Literary Modernity

The century between the Restoration and the mid-eighteenth century saw the spread of literacy and readership amid a general expansion and commodification of the literary market. The field of literary production and distribution was dramatically transformed during this period as England emerged from the ravages of the Civil War and began its ascent to a modern imperial world power. We see greater productivity in agriculture and a tremendous growth in trade; a rise in literacy rates; the development of the Post Office and improvements in transportation; the founding of the Bank of England and the rise of the modern financial infrastructure.[1] English literary modernity is indissolubly tied to these rapid social, technological, and commercial changes commonly identified with the dawn of the modern world. However, the kinds of literary changes I am most interested in cannot be attributed to these changing historical conditions in any simple fashion: the rise of the novel, the writing of the first national literary histories, the solidification of a native English literary canon, the burst of review and aesthetic criticism in the periodical press, the spread of serial publication, the flourishing of intercontinental translations, the theorization of a native vernacular antiquity embodied in oral song. Indeed, the historical self-consciousness and national self-awareness that we see emerging in these new genres and modes of literary production engage powerfully with the notion of historical progress vis-à-vis an anterior age but always in multiple, complex, and sometimes contradictory ways.

The story that I wish to tell about English literary modernity is about the unfolding of the idea of the modern in the literature of this period. It is a story about the ways in which the idea of the modern inflects the production of literature as well as reflections on the new literary productions of the time. By no means do I wish to suggest that all literary production in this period is self-consciously 'modern' or that 'modern' works understand their modernity in any one particular way. I do believe, however, that English literature of the long eighteenth century was both interested and invested in defining its timeliness (or untimeliness) in comparative terms. Like Kathleen Wilson, then, I understand modernity not simply as one "unfolding set of relations" with the past but as "a set of relations that are constantly being made and unmade, contested and reconfigured, that nonetheless produces among its contemporaneous witnesses the conviction of historical *difference*."[2] The challenge of my work is to account for the ways in which this idea of historical difference in English literary modernity was always already profoundly intertwined with notions of cultural difference as well. In this book, I track the particular relationship between the growing cultural awareness of China and the emergence of a modern English literary consciousness.

The theorizing and writing of modern English literary identity occurred in the midst of rising awareness of cultural, political, and social alternatives that formed an important part of the new print knowledge. National literary tradition was invented in dialectical relation to other traditions and histories, which operated variously as models to emulate, standards against which to measure oneself, and benchmarks to overcome. A "comparative perspective" was at work when English Renaissance writers struggled to prove that literature written in vernacular English need not languish behind classical texts, or when Restoration writers confronted French cultural hegemony.[3] As Alok Yadav has emphasized, well into the eighteenth century English writers openly aired their anxiety about using a weak language and belonging to a provincial cultural community.[4] With the increasing success of England's overseas ambitions, however, it became fashionable to compare English culture more favorably to other, non-European cultural sites, and English literary culture moved in more confidently to claim a superior position in the world republic of letters.[5] A sense of relative cultural lack would continue to haunt the English, however. It would do so noticeably in English encounters with China.

A growing body of scholarship on the relationship between China and eighteenth-century Britain has recently emerged to tell this story of cross-cultural encounter and influence in different ways.[6] Robert Markley has demonstrated that an economic fascination with the fabled riches of China and the Far East underwrites English literary production in the seventeenth and eighteenth centuries, and David Porter has shown that no discussion of eighteenth-century English taste can be complete without attending to "the semiotic fluidity and transformative potency" of chinoiserie in this period.[7] Expanding on the definition of chinoiserie as "things Chinese," Eugenia Zuroski Jenkins has recently proposed that "Chineseness" is "an English literary effect" crucial to the definition of

English selfhood.[8] Similarly, Chi-ming Yang has shown that ideas about Chinese exemplarity – both economic and moral – modulated eighteenth-century English ideas of virtue. Together, the work of the above critics transforms the discipline of eighteenth-century English literature as we know it, challenging us to place it in a far-reaching global context that few now can afford to ignore. While my book touches on many of the same topics treated in these books, it is more particularly geared toward China's influence on English literary history and form. The central question it raises is: what *literary* difference did China make? In particular, how did an imaginative concern with China shape the invention of new literary forms and genres in this period? My approach has resonances with Yang's in so far as I identify China most of all with a "paradoxical temporality" – "the paradox of its being an ancient yet modern" civilization – but I connect the English interest in Chinese temporality to the formal and aesthetic invention of literary modernity rather than the desire for Chinese exemplarity.[9] Thus, while I share a general field interest in the topics discussed by the above critics, I am less concerned with exploring China as an ambiguous and ambivalent figure of legitimacy/illegitimacy or virtue/vice. And while I share Zuroski Jenkins's interest in Chineseness as a literary effect, I am less specifically interested in "Chineseness as an English literary effect that is ascribed to *objects*" or in a "literary history of *material* things in English life."[10]

My project grew out of my discovery of China's place in an intellectual controversy that permanently affected the course of English literary history: namely, the quarrel between the ancients and the moderns. The quarrel is widely accepted today as a defining moment in the birth of modern consciousness in both the arts and sciences – although it would take a long time before 'modern literature' could overcome the authority and the aura of the ancients. I have previously argued against the standard account that the quarrel was chiefly about the relative merits of ancient (classical) and modern (European vernacular) literature, or the contrasting achievements of ancient and modern European science.[11] What was truly at stake in this quarrel, I proposed, was a fundamental shift in the understanding of world history (or "universal history," as it was then called) which, in light of new information pouring in from the 'new' worlds of the Americas as well as the 'old' worlds of the Near and Far East, could no longer be contained within the boundaries of biblical time and narrative. There was arguably no greater challenge to biblical history than ancient Chinese history, the records of which predated the deluge by many centuries. Jesuit reports marveled at the astonishing continuity of Chinese history and the precision of its documentary record. Ancient Chinese history, they noted, was remarkably free of miracles and punctuated by precise dates and astronomical observations. On the strength of its prodigious, evidentiary documentation, Chinese antiquity threatened not only to throw biblical chronology into question but also to set a new standard in ancientness and thereby become a new origin for universal history.

When William Temple proposed in his 1690 *Essay upon the Ancient and Modern Learning* that the "Seeds" of ancient Greek civilization could be found in ancient Chinese "Learning and Opinions," he was responding to the new histories of China available in his time.[12] His essay demonstrates familiarity with such texts as Alvaro Semedo's *History of that Great and Renowned Monarchy of China* (1655), Martino Martini's *Bellum Tartaricum, or the Conquest of The Great and most Renowned Empire of China, By the Invasion of the Tartars* (1655), Johan Nieuhof's *Embassy from the East-India Company of the United Provinces, to the Grand Tartar Cham Emperor of China* (1669), and Gabriel de Magalhães's *A New History of China* (1688).[13] William Wotton, whose 1694 *Reflections upon Ancient and Modern Learning* launched the English quarrel, took Temple to task for being unsound, unscientific, and most of all, unchristian in his enthusiasm for China. Against Temple's historical and cultural relativism, Wotton asserted the clear superiority of modern European science over Chinese scientific learning, dismissed the records of Chinese antiquity as merely spurious, and scoffed at the pieties of Chinese moral philosophy, which he trivialized as "an incoherent Rhapsody."[14] Wotton conceded that the ancients excelled in the arts in general, as well as in moral and political philosophy, and claimed decisive 'modern' superiority only for natural science. He had nothing good to say about Temple's enthusiasm for China, however. Compared to their relative agreement on the value of classical learning, this disagreement on Chinese history and culture is striking. Reading the English quarrel between the ancients and the moderns as the symptom of a general cultural impasse brought on by the challenge of radically different chronologies and epistemologies, I propose, enables us to place the controversy in a larger, global context, and to interpret it not simply as a struggle to understand English modernity in comparison with the western classical past, but also in connection with other, radically different, pasts, histories, and cultures.

As Douglas Lane Patey puts it, the quarrel continues to mark a "watershed": "in the Moderns' rejection of the authority of the Ancients, their texts, and the rules drawn from them, we can locate the birthplace not only of eighteenth-century criticism but of modern thought."[15] Although it has been pointed out that similar versions of the quarrel can be found much earlier in European history and that the "historical self-consciousness with which the *moderni* have squared off against the *antiqui*" is a "literary constant, as normal and natural in the history of European culture as the alternation of generations is in biology," critics nonetheless agree that, in the long run, the quarrel drew a lasting line between older and newer models of history, science, and taste.[16] The resulting "two most important consequences" of the quarrel, according to Paul O. Kristeller, were as follows:

> First, the Moderns broadened the literary controversy into a systematic comparison between the achievements of antiquity and of modern times in the various fields of human endeavor, thus developing a classification of knowledge and culture that was in many respects novel, or more specific than previous systems. Secondly, a point by point examination of the claims of the ancients and moderns in the various fields led to the insight that in certain fields, where everything depends on mathematical calculation and the accumulation of knowledge, the progress of the moderns over the ancients can be clearly demonstrated, whereas in certain other fields, which depend on individual talent and on the taste of the critic, the relative merits of the ancients and moderns cannot be so clearly established but may be subject to controversy.[17]

Ultimately, it was this 'modern' position that insisted on separating the arts and sciences, and claiming that the sciences were progressive in a way that the arts were not, that would dominate over the 'ancient' position that was much more skeptical about the achievement of modern science. Like most accounts of the quarrel, however, Kristeller's summary glosses over the fact that the "systematic comparison" between the achievements of the ancients and moderns also entailed a systematic comparison not only between the modern Europeans and their ancient, 'classical' forebears, but between Europe and the rest of the world. It is only when this global span of the quarrel is taken properly into consideration that the full political and cultural implications of the quarrel become abundantly clear.

Within Europe, the quarrel led to a lasting division between the progressive sciences and the non-progressive arts in modern European culture. Concurrently, it also gave rise to an aggressive program of comparing the achievements of Europe with those of ancient and modern Egypt, Arabia, India, and China in which this distinction between science and culture would sometimes be forgotten. In Dipesh Chakrabarty's words, the historicism that resulted from the quarrel came to posit "historical time as a measure of the cultural distance (at least in institutional development) that was assumed to exist between the West and the non-West." By the nineteenth century, modern historicism became a key intellectual tool for the imperial conquest of the world by Europe: "Historicism is what made modernity or capitalism look not simply global but rather as something that became global over time, by originating in one place (Europe) and then spreading outside it."[18] Modernity, in short, became a global geopolitical idea and narrative. This, however, is a later development. In its initial phase, the quarrel between the ancients and the moderns was all about looking for a vocabulary and a conceptual framework that would make it possible to compare ancient and modern, eastern and western civilizations, on whose relative values thinkers were hardly in agreement. The intellectual drive to compare different civilizations and cultures along evaluative axes of relative superiority and inferiority is one we have been trained to regard with skepticism, precisely because of the politics of modernity, especially of the kind described by Chakrabarty. When we examine the original quarrel, however, it is evident that the intellectual effort of trying to think of numerous different scientific and cultural achievements together in a global context was in many ways a positive and necessary response to increasing contact between Europe, the Americas, Africa, and Asia. The quarrel shows that intellectuals were actively taking stock of new information about distant civilizations and remapping their knowledge of the world. It was a profoundly worldly quarrel in this sense, a response to real changes and exchanges taking place globally in the realms of trade, diplomacy, religion, and politics. At the same time, however, it was also an imaginative quarrel based on imperfect, second-hand knowledge of distant lands and cultures. It was never clear what kind of commensurability could be established between what seemed to be radically different civilizations. Nonetheless, the quarrel shows us that an emerging global consciousness was beginning to exert pressure on existing, self-contained canons of knowledge in Europe, including canons of literature, forcing thinkers to formulate with much greater precision the criteria of cultural value.

In literature, too, the quarrel effectively introduced ideas of cultural alterity and plurality, ultimately opening up the canon to include a wider spectrum of writers from the vernacular past, encouraging vernacular translations of non-classical literatures, and even turning Homer's characters into "Strangers."[19] According to Patey, the quarrel between the ancients and the moderns "contributed to an understanding of all human works as historical products (cultural constructions) and consequently to a relativization of taste, increased interest in non-classical cultures both past and present, and ultimately to that late eighteenth-century body of thinking we have come to call 'historicism.'"[20] This early form of historicism was explorative, self-critical, and curious about non-European cultures. In the English quarrel it was Temple, not Wotton, who was truly committed to the "relativization of taste" and "increased interest in non-classical cultures both past and present."[21] This is why, if we examine the English quarrel primarily for its impact on English literary history, we realize that the ancients had a much more lasting impact than initially may seem apparent. For this reason, Temple has turned out to be the surprising hero in this book (*Figure 1*). Temple's 'ancient' skepticism about the virtues of the English language notwithstanding, his ideas about the English national character and his theory of genius, as well as his interest in China, provided a fertile groundwork that later writers would turn to again and again. Addison's *A Discourse on Ancient and Modern Learning*, Hume's essays "Of the Rise and Progress of the Arts and Sciences," "Of National Characters," and "Of the Standard of Taste"; and Goldsmith's *An Enquiry into the Present State of Polite Learning in Europe* and "On National Prejudices" all show a keen awareness of the multifaceted dimensions of Temple's writings. In this sense, contrary to his own 'ancient' propositions, Temple ironically was a key contributor to the cultural shift that began to take shape in the aftermath of the quarrel, resulting in a broad transition from the classic to the modern.

In *The Making of the English Literary Canon*, Trevor Ross narrates the background to what he calls the "anti-classicist revolution" of the eighteenth century in terms of major shifts in poetic production.[22] Drawing on the work of J. G. A. Pocock, he notes that, as the older values of civic humanism and republicanism came into conflict with a newer ideology of commercial humanism, the field of literary production became increasingly autonomized as a sphere independent of politics. Whereas the older literary values of eloquence and rhetoric had strong "traditional associations with ritual demonstrations of male valour and productivity in the world of practical affairs," and upheld "a heroic ideal for poetry" that it traced back to the classics, the waning of patronage and the rise of a commerce-based system of publication led to a great diminishment of the political value of writing and, concomitantly, to a redefinition of poetic values. As classicism declined as a model for literary production, a new poetic theory based on "lyrical expressivity, as well as upon feeling, fancy and passion, categories of experience traditionally equated with the feminine" emerged.[23] The force of this cultural change can be gauged in part by the fierce opposition it created. Pope's withering portrait in *The Dunciad* of the modern literary sphere as "a new Saturnian age of Lead" presided over by the Goddess Dulness (Book 1, line 26), "Daughter of Chaos and eternal

Fig 1   Jacobus Houbraken, *Sir William Temple*. Engraving. 1738. Harvard Art Museums/
Fogg Museum, Gift of William Gray from the collection of Francis Calley Gray, G1987.
© President and Fellows of Harvard College.

Night" (Book 1, line 10), is probably the most famous example.[24] For Ross, the decline of classicism amounted to a "poetic revolution" because it "coincided with a reorganization of the cultural field so extensive as to alter the relations and position-takings within the field." In other words, it was not a question of a set of rival positions sorting themselves out within the cultural field. Rather, "whatever the specific values endorsed by writers, the cultural field in general was no longer seen as supporting a set of political relationships and was thus bereft of its former source of legitimacy."[25] Placed in a new context of commercial humanism, and increasingly dissociated from the progressive sciences, the field of culture itself was redefined as, on the one hand, an autonomous field of the imagination and, on the other hand, an object of consumption. It was this ambiguity of the cultural field, caught between autonomy and irrelevance, that prompted the extravagant alarm in Pope's poem.

As the conditions of cultural production underwent a profound change, so did the producers and the products. In literary terms, the period discussed in this book – the late seventeenth to the mid-eighteenth century – marks the transition from an older world dominated by the figure of the classical poet to that of the professional writer, novelist, editor, and periodical author. The eighteenth century made way for eclectic new genres that replaced the high modes of epic and dramatic poetry. The break between the old and the new was more startling yet in prose production. As J. Paul Hunter puts it, there was a "nearly universal perception in England by midcentury that a literary revolution was taking place": "New readers, new modes of literary production, new tastes, and a growing belief that traditional forms and conventions were too constricted and rigid to represent modern reality or to reach modern readers collaborated to mean – in the eyes of both proponents and critics – that much modern writing was taking radical new directions."[26] Hunter defines the new species of writers as "moderns who championed novelty as a major tenet in their program to discover an originality and literary innovation that would appropriately represent 'modern' experience."[27] What the new modern writing would look like was initially far from clear. Hunter proposes that "Claims for novelty in the literary world – claims that a significant interruption of tradition had occurred and that new forms and directions had taken over" came in "two waves two generations apart." He dates the beginnings of the first wave – experimental, audacious, and as yet undefined in terms of literary form – to the 1690s, precisely the decade in which the quarrel between the ancients and the moderns took place. Instancing John Dunton's *Athenian Mercury* as a prime example of this first wave of new writing, Hunter notes that it was singularly unabashed in its call to "lovers of Novelty" as well as inattentive to the question of literary form. Unlike this first wave, which coincided with the careers of the great Augustans such as Pope and Swift, who loved to satirize the moderns, and was formally "unfocused, sprawling across genres and modes more or less indiscriminately," the second wave of the 1740s was centered on a new and "hitherto unattempted" "species of writing" that eventually became synonymous with novelty itself: that is, the novel.[28]

According to Jonathan Kramnick's account of the making of the English canon in the first half of the eighteenth century, the "narrative of progressive and unfolding refinement" in English letters and search after a "polite modernity" were part of a progressive, Whig version of history which celebrated the ascendancy of English literature along with English commerce and national culture. In an ironical reversal, however, this Whiggish view of English cultural history also produced an anxiety about the effects of the market economy on letters as well as a "nostalgia for the literary past," which resulted in the weakening of the narrative of refinement and a rediscovery of the value of the ancients.[29] This time around, however, the ancients in question were the English ancients: Chaucer, Spenser, and Shakespeare. The "battle between the ancients and the moderns, now staged within English culture itself," thus produced an antiquated national canon and a national literary history which could be called 'modern' in one sense (in so far as all English writing written in the vernacular was 'modern' in contrast to literature written in the classical languages of Latin and Greek) and yet also 'classic' (in the sense of establishing a canon of literature that would serve as a standard of greatness for all literature to come).[30] In this way, England's 'modern classics' were born as a new canon of national literature.

When I refer to English literary modernity in this book, then, it is with these different kinds of histories in mind. None of these literary histories simply privileges the dawn of the modern, but situates the birth of the modern in complex and shifting relations to classical heritage, the public sphere, the marketplace, and the nation. The reason why I focus on the works of Daniel Defoe, Joseph Addison, Oliver Goldsmith, and Thomas Percy in this book is because I find their innovations in literary form most relevant for my exploration of English literary modernity.[31] These authors were all active participants in the new literary sphere made possible by the growth of the commercial print market, the spread of commercial humanism, and the receptivity toward novel experiments in literary production. In this sense, they would appear to be good representatives of English literary modernity in the sense discussed by Ross and Hunter. Defoe wrote without regard for classical models of writing, modeling his literary production instead on journalism, criminal biography, and the new sciences. Addison was a champion of vernacular rather than classical literacy and molded a cultural theory for a new commodity culture. Goldsmith began his career as a Grub Street hack and plied his pen for the commercial press, though often reflecting bitterly on the fate of the professional writer in a corrupt republic of letters. And Percy, the gentleman scholar, excavated an alternative set of 'reliques' and marketed them as England's rich and antique literary heritage. Each of these writers has a different use for the concept of the 'modern.' And although they were all important commentators on China, their attitudes toward China likewise differed greatly. They can hardly all be aligned with Wotton's position; in many instances, they show great sympathy for Temple's ideas. What they do have in common, however, is a pressing need to theorize, in their own ways, their position in the ancients-and-moderns debate as a way of reflecting on the value and meaning of their own cultural productions. They are all legatees of the quarrel in this sense. The key argument in this book is that, in all these authors' strategies of self-definition, there is a keen awareness of what I have called the global, and especially Chinese, context of the English quarrel – a context that goes missing, however, in the literary histories I have cited above. Connecting the eighteenth-century discussion of China back to the original English quarrel helps explain why China keeps appearing in multifarious and striking ways in the literature of the first half of the eighteenth century. It also proves that literary history took place in a much wider world than national literary histories would like us to believe.

The quarrel between the ancients and the moderns greatly enlarged the framework of historical inquiry both in space and in time, with the result of defamiliarizing and estranging the present. After the quarrel, Kirsti Simonsuuri writes, the moderns "looked at the culture of antiquity for the first time from the standpoint of a stranger."[32] They also looked at themselves from the eyes of strangers, of whom perhaps the most challenging representative was the Chinese. In her examination of seventeenth- and early eighteenth-century books on China that were marketed in France and England, Laura Hostetler shows that the European "authors framed their works with self-conscious comparison in mind"; "achievements at home became measured in terms of what was known (or imagined) about points of reference abroad." These books thus activated a form of "early-modern exchange, which provided a window onto another world" and "also provided a mirror" in which Europeans might see themselves "through the eyes of the other." Thinking about and thinking through China, in other words, served as a rhetorical way to look objectively at the European self. For Hostetler, this "global awareness of one's own realm in relation to that of the larger world was a hallmark of early modernity reaching into many facets of the period, including trade, technology, diplomacy, and the representation of state power in art."[33] These comments can be used as a poignant introduction to Goldsmith's project in his Chinese letters of impersonating a Chinese philosopher in London. As I shall show, however, this strategy of "self-conscious comparison" with China is not specific to Goldsmith but very widely shared by other writers such as Defoe, Addison, and Percy. For them, China is not simply an object of representation or misrepresentation, but a thinking tool through which they arrive at a self-conscious appraisal of their modern cultural moment. As Eric Hayot, Haun Saussy, and Steven G. Yao write in their introduction to *Sinographies*, " 'China' is not something one thinks about but something one thinks through; it is a provocation; it realizes itself various as subject, process, and end of articulate thinking."[34]

In English literary modernity, China became a means of thinking about the modern in comparative, cultural, and historicist terms, as well as a tool for thinking about the distinctive modality of modern time. As Johannes Fabian has noted, "Time, much like language or money, is a carrier of significance, a form through which we define the content of relations between the Self and the Other."[35] In this book, I follow up on this central insight of Johannes Fabian to ask how notions of time and temporality operate in tandem with notions of identity and difference in the representation of China in English literary modernity. English literary modernity was committed, on the one hand, to a model of decentered, secular, linear time in which universality was understood not in terms of one's incorporation into sacred history but as synchronicity. As Benedict Anderson put it, the modern understanding of simultaneity in time is that of "transverse, cross-time, marked not by prefiguring and fulfilment, but by temporal coincidence, and measured by clock and calendar."[36] Modernity was not quite "an idea of 'homogeneous, empty time,' " however.[37] It entailed, crucially, a comparative and evaluative idea of historical progress. Had China made achievements equal to Europe's in terms of progress in the arts and sciences? This question would never have taken on the importance it did had it not been for the additional evidence of Chinese material culture in the eighteenth century. The technological superiority of many Chinese luxury imports such as porcelain suggested that the Chinese were indeed 'modern' in relation to Europeans, if the word meant outdoing and outperforming them.[38] A growing sense of economic and political competition with China led some writers to employ what Fabian has called "devices of temporal distancing" in order to deny coevalness, and to relegate China to a different historical time – in other words, to claim it had not progressed equally in history.[39] We thus see emerging in English literary modernity a discourse of Chinese difference that writes China in terms of both spatial distance and temporal disjunction, as non-coincidence and non-identity.

China also overdetermined the process through which the concept of beauty became temporalized and relativized – in short, modernized – to become a category of history and time. "It was during the eighteenth century," Matei Calinescu writes, "that the idea of beauty began to undergo the process through which it lost its aspects of transcendence and finally became a historical category."[40] During the eighteenth century, beauty became an idea of "irregularity, asymmetry, variety, surprise" (as opposed to an idea of simplicity, unity, harmony) and an experience of *change in time* (rather than an experience of timelessness and transcendence).[41] In his essay *Upon the Gardens of Epicurus*, Temple famously gave the name "*Sharawadgi*" to "this sort of Beauty," a "Beauty … without order" found commonly "among the *Chineses*" who scorned "Proportions, Symmetries, or Uniformities" in their gardens – a beauty, he noted, that "we have hardly any Notion of." During the course of the eighteenth century, this purportedly Chinese idea of beauty "without order," an artificially disordered beauty calculated to exact the "greatest reach of Imagination," would be widely debated, practiced, and appropriated, to become an important principle of garden design, nature appreciation, and general aesthetic practice in England.[42] Joseph Addison, who in 1712 generalized Temple's comments on Chinese gardens to theorize the pleasure the imagination takes in "Every thing that is new or uncommon," that "fills the Soul with an agreeable Surprise, gratifies its Curiosity, and gives it an Idea of which it was not before possest," cleared the theoretical grounds for the transformation of the supposed Chinese idea of beauty into an aesthetics of repeatedly renewable modernity – namely, novelty.[43] Aligning a particular spatial organization (asymmetry, imbalance, irregularity) with a temporal experience (surprise), and vice versa, novelty honors modernity as an aesthetic experience of constant change and pleasure taken in that change. As an interpretation of modernity, however, novelty also points to a central aporia in the idea of the modern: namely, its epistemological status as a vanishing point in time, for the new is what is so only for an instant before it bows to the next new thing. Modernity, in this understanding, is not an experience of linear time so much as a repeated experience of a permanent transience.

The connection between modernity and the 'gardening' of time helps us understand the relation between modernity and tradition. As Kramnick puts it in his study of English canon-making in the eighteenth century, "Modernity generates tradition." However, I would contest his statement that English tradition and English antiquity were "patterned on the prior notion of the classical age of Greece and Rome" and that "In the initial fray between Wotton and Temple, the period term 'ancient' referred exclusively to Greco-Roman antiquity."[44] The idea of English antiquity, as that of modernity, was increasingly patterned on the non-classical worlds which crowded and changed English cultural consciousness in the early modern era and forced it to re-map itself in the world. A prime instance is the impulse to exoticize the past and to elevate it into a historical curiosity – an impulse apparent in the championing of the traditional ballad and the medieval "Gothic" romance in the eighteenth century – which, in Percy's case, is clearly aligned with the reinterpretation of Chinese culture. The attitude that "the past is a foreign country," a phrase that the historian David Lowenthal borrowed and made famous, was one born in modernity. Lowenthal writes: "Only in the late eighteenth century did Europeans begin to conceive the past as a different realm, not just another country but a congeries of foreign lands endowed with unique histories and personalities."[45] They began to do so, I propose, by transferring their experiences of contemporary foreign lands such as China to their understanding of their native as well as their classical past. English literary modernity, then, is a time that exists in the linear, contemporary 'real' time of the novel and the day-to-day newspaper, but no less in the transient time of the landscape artist, and the suspended, performative time of the printed, elliptical, antiqued, oral ballad. Filtered through a literary lens, modernity is something richer and eerier, much more ambiguous than the scientific time of modernization, ever marching forward. In the readings in this book, I suggest that an imaginative geography of China helped map a distinctively English literary terrain, just as an imaginative history of China helped locate a distinctively English literary moment.

CHAPTER I

China between the Ancients and the Moderns

This Quarrel first began (as I have heard it affirmed by an old Dweller in the Neighbourhood) about a small Spot of Ground, *lying* and *being*, upon one of the two Tops of the Hill *Parnassus*; the highest and largest of which, had it seems, been time out of Mind, in quiet Possession of certain Tenants, call'd the *Antients*; And the other was held by the *Moderns*. But, these disliking their present Station, sent certain Ambassadors to the *Antients*, complaining of a great Nuisance, how the Height of that Part of *Parnassus*, quite spoiled the Prospect of theirs, especially towards the *East*; and therefore, to avoid a War, offered them the Choice of this Alternative; either that the *Antients* would please to remove themselves and their Effects down to the lower Summity, which the *Moderns* would graciously surrender to them, and advance in their Place; or else, that the said *Antients* will give leave to the *Moderns* to come with Shovels and Mattocks, and level the said Hill, as low as they shall think it convenient.

Jonathan Swift, *A Full and True Account of the Battel Fought last Friday, Between the Antient and the Modern Books in St. James's Library* (1704)

In Jonathan Swift's boisterous retelling, the English quarrel between the ancients and the moderns begins as a dispute over real estate. The moderns are imagined as *arrivistes* who move into a highly desired neighborhood and discover to their chagrin that the choicest – "the highest and largest" – spot has been occupied since "time out of Mind" by other tenants called the ancients. Forced to take a lower and smaller piece of ground, the moderns find that their prospect is quite spoiled "especially towards the *East*." Unable to uproot the ancients from their tenancy by lawful means, the moderns resort to verbal thuggery: the ancients will kindly remove themselves from their summit and switch places with the moderns, or else the moderns will come with "shovels and mattocks" to level it. As the ancients gently point out, however, their hill is "an entire Rock" and attacking it will only "break their Tools and Hearts." An easier solution would simply be to "raise" the moderns' "side of the Hill," which the ancients would be happy to "contribute" to. Far from being appeased, the moderns are roused into "much Indignation" by this suggestion and embark on "a long and obstinate War" to oust the ancients from their immemorial seat.[1]

The battle of the books, as Swift tells it, is only the latest and newest chapter of this war, long fought out with quills and "whole Rivulets of *Ink*" (1: 145). The battle takes place in St. James's Library – territory by no means favorable to the ancients, as it is presided over by "a fierce Champion for the *Moderns*" who, "in an Engagement upon *Parnassus*, had vowed, with his own Hands, to knock down two of the *Antient* Chiefs, who guarded a small Pass on the superior Rock." Failing to accomplish his goal, this "*Guardian* of the *Regal Library*" has turned his disappointment into "cruel Rancour to the *Antients*," which he expresses by shelving the ancients' books in the dustiest, most obscure corners of the library (1: 147). At first Swift does not condescend to name this royal librarian, but readers in his day would have had little trouble identifying him as Richard Bentley, classical scholar and Keeper of the Kings' Libraries, who in 1697 had teamed up with William Wotton to argue that the *Epistles* of Phalaris and the *Fables* of Aesop were spurious forgeries. This was an incendiary claim aimed specifically at destroying the credibility of William Temple, who had famously claimed in his 1690 *Essay upon the Ancient and Modern Learning* that "the oldest Books we have, are still in their kind the best," pointing to Phalaris's *Epistles* and Aesop's *Fables* as "the two most ancient, that I know of in Prose."[2] There is no mistaking where Swift stands in this battle. Bentley later reappears as "a Captain, whose Name was *B-ntl-y*; in Person, the most deformed of all the *Moderns*" – a misshapen thing with a "crooked Leg, and hump Shoulder," wearing armor "patch'd up of a thousand incoherent Pieces" and carrying a "Flail" in his right hand and "a Vessel full of *Ordure* in his Left" (1: 160). Wotton, or "*W-tt-n*," is described as the "Darling" of his mother "*Criticism*" who feeds him a monster she has been nursing at the teats of her spleen. This unusual nutriment is said to have "squeez'd out his Eye-Balls, gave him a distorted Look, and half over-turned his Brain" (1: 155–56). In the climactic scene of the battle, Wotton comes upon Temple at the fountain of Helicon. Temple has his back turned toward Wotton and is busy "Drinking large Draughts in his Helmet, from the Fountain" (1: 162). Coward that he is, Wotton throws his lance "with all his Might" at Temple's back: "Away the Launce went hizzing, and reach'd even to the Belt of the averted *Antient*, upon which, lightly grazing, it fell to the Ground. *Temple* neither felt the Weapon touch him, nor heard it fall" (1: 163). The battle ends with the untouchable Temple amply revenged by "young *Boyle*" – Charles Boyle, future earl of Orrery and editor of the 1695 edition of Phalaris's *Epistles* – who, in a contrastive show of lancing skill, impales both Bentley and Wotton with one fell blow. The battle ends cruelly with the image of these two men "transfix'd" like "a Brace of *Woodcocks*" about to be grilled on an "Iron Skewer" (1: 164).

At this point, which is also where the text of Swift's *Battel* breaks down in a final shower of asterisks marking a supposed textual lacuna, the reader may pause and ask what a prospect "towards the East" has to do with this bloodbath. For generations, critics have agreed that the initial quarrel between Temple and Wotton, which later drew in additional ancients such as Boyle and Swift, and other moderns such as Bentley, centered on the authenticity of such 'ancient' texts as Phalaris's *Epistles* and Aesop's *Fables*. The compass of "the East," on this understanding, would reach as far as ancient Rome and Greece, but are they really "East"? It is difficult to know what Swift precisely meant by this phrase, but given his close relationship to Temple, it is likely that he knew very well that the scope of Temple's essay was not limited to ancient Greece and Rome but also touched on such "Eastern regions" as China, Egypt, Chaldea, Persia, Syria, Arabia, and Judea. Temple's most scandalous "Conjecture" in the *Essay* was in fact that much of western learning was derived from "such remote and ancient Fountains as the *Indies*, and perhaps *China*" (1690: 21). It was this hypothesis of Temple, no less than his recommendation of Phalaris and Aesop, that had roused Wotton into action. Swift lived very close to the heart of the controversy during the years it burned hottest. In 1689, he entered the service of William Temple, living with him at Moor Park and serving as his secretary until Temple's death in 1699. It is therefore quite likely that Swift would have registered what posterity seems to have forgotten: namely, the fact that the quarrel grew out of a disagreement over China and other 'eastern' civilizations. Temple's *Essay upon the Ancient and Modern Learning* was first published in his 1690 essay collection *Miscellanea. The Second Part*; William Wotton's rejoinder *Reflections upon Ancient and Modern Learning* appeared in 1694; a second edition with the addition of Bentley's *Dissertation upon the Epistles of Phalaris, Themistocles, Socrates, Euripides, and Others; And the Fables of Aesop* closely followed in 1697. After Temple's death, Swift edited the third, posthumous volume of Temple's *Miscellanea* (1701) which included Temple's *Some Thoughts upon Reviewing the Essay of Ancient and Modern Learning*. Swift's *A Tale of a Tub* and *Battel of the Books* were published in 1704. Within a year, Wotton had brought out another edition of his *Reflections* (1705), including "Observations upon *The Tale of a Tub*," a pointed rejoinder to Swift's attack.[3]

This chapter attempts to recover this lost "Prospect ... towards the *East*" in the history of the quarrel. Recent revisionist accounts of the quarrel note that the quarrel was never simply about the relative merits of classical literature but was always bound up with changing notions of progressive history, historiography, philology, humanism, science, and reading culture.[4] One line of inquiry that has been consistently neglected, however, is the role that China played in this debate about modern European identity. Although many have observed that the discovery of new lands coincided with the philological rediscovery of antiquity, there has been as yet no comprehensive attempt to relate "the fissure ... between imitation and scholarship, rhetoric and philology, literature and history" set in motion by the quarrel to the contemporaneous opening of worlds beyond Europe.[5] Following John Elliott's lead in *The Old World and the New*, scholars have indeed remained skeptical of the real impact of other cultures on European thought through the seventeenth century.[6] However, if the new worlds in Asia, Africa, and America initially made little difference to Europeans because they were rapidly "assimilated" to tradition and written into Christian genealogical narratives about "heathen antiquity," such assimilation became increasingly difficult as the century wore on.[7] This chapter aims to show that the quarrel between the ancients and the moderns usually discussed within the parameters of European tradition was as much about the historical significance of other civilizations. The English quarrel between William Temple and William Wotton, in particular, was to a significant degree a quarrel about the relative cultural achievements of China as an extension of the debate on 'ancient' and 'modern' civilizations. I propose that, in a strong sense, the seventeenth-century debate about China produced the quarrel – i.e. that the numerous published bulletins and reports on China that captured the imagination of seventeenth-century Europe contributed to the historiographical crisis that goes by the name of the quarrel between the ancients and the moderns.[8]

The Ancients of the Ancients

In a seminal essay on the importance of China to the European understanding of history, Edwin J. Van Kley suggests that "Perhaps the most serious challenge to the traditional scheme of world history and the factor most instrumental in changing that scheme was the 'discovery' of ancient Chinese history in the sixteenth and seventeenth centuries."[9] World history – or "universal history" – as traditionally understood was derived from the Bible, covered the ancient Near East, Greece, Rome, and western

Christendom, and began with creation. Ever since the Renaissance, this traditional understanding of world history had come under increasing challenge, as the rediscovery of classical texts led to new conceptions of pagan antiquity and its relationship to sacred Christian history. The dominant intellectual response to the challenge of pagan history was to accommodate new knowledge about the pagans within the structures of traditional history. However, by the seventeenth century it was becoming increasingly difficult to square with Christian doctrine the influx of information not only about the world of western antiquity but also about the non-European world.

Because traditional "universal history" was geographically limited, but chronologically universal, the chief problem posed by pagan history had to do less with remapping the geographical boundaries of the world than redrawing its temporal limits.[10] The problem was that geographical expansion often seemed to lead to chronological expansion as well. The furor caused by Isaac Lapeyrère's 1655 *Praeadamitae* which posited that "pre-adamites" had peopled the world before the biblical Adam illustrates how conjectural prehistory based on pagan records could unsettle the very basis of orthodox Christian history and the historical and theological primacy of the Jews.[11] Accepting the prior existence of pre-adamites on the basis of the greater antiquity of the Chaldeans, Mexicans, Peruvians, and the Chinese meant demoting the history of the Bible to the particular history of a particular people and, in short, challenging the universality of Christianity.

In 1658, three years after the publication of *Preadamitae*, the Jesuit Martino Martini published *Sinicae historiae decas prima*, noting that ancient Chinese chronology predated the Genesis flood and stating his "certainty" that "outermost Asia was inhabited before the deluge."[12] Although Martini, unlike Lapeyrère, refused to comment on the theological ramifications of his Chinese history, stating that it was not his concern to explain how the Chinese had managed to preserve records antedating the Genesis flood when all but Noah's family had been destroyed in the deluge, he ended up casting doubt on the universality of biblical chronology.[13] He also made the question of Chinese antiquity absolutely central to contemporary debates about universal history. The Chinese records as reported in Martini's history could not be easily dismissed because they were of an astonishing continuity, remarkably free of miracles, punctuated by precise dates, and littered with astronomical observations. In short, they seemed to rise much more successfully to the challenge of evidentiary, empirical history than other pagan histories. For this reason, they appeared to challenge the universality of Old Testament accounts of ancient history in a much more radical way than the records of the ancient Near East.[14]

By the 1690s, when William Temple and William Wotton were exchanging spars, extravagant claims had been made on behalf of Chinese history. Isaac Vossius had submitted in *Dissertatio de vera aetate mundi* (1659) that the Flood had been a local phenomenon;[15] John Webb had even opined in *An Historical Essay Endeavoring a Probability that the Language of the Empire of China is the Primitive Language* (1669) that Noah had settled in China after the deluge and that Chinese was the original language of mankind.[16] These speculative treatises were based not only on Jesuit accounts of China such as Martini's *Sinicae historiae*, but also on earlier missionary texts such as Juan González de Mendoza's *Historia de las cosas mas notables, ritos y costumbres del gran reyno de la China* (1586), Nicolas Trigault's *De Christiana Expeditione Apud Sinas* (1615), Alvaro Semedo's *Relatione della Grande Monarchia della Cina* (1643), and Athanasius Kircher's *China Illustrata* (1667), as well as popular histories and geographies such as Richard Hakluyt's *Principall Navigations* (1598–1600), Walter Ralegh's *History of the World* (1614), Samuel Purchas's *Purchas His Pilgrimes* (1625), and Peter Heylyn's *Cosmographie* (1652).[17] The bulk of the evidence supplied by these varied texts suggested that China was the great exception to universal history not only in the sense that its history extended back to pre-adamite, pre-deluge, pre-biblical ages, but also in that China failed to conform to the metanarrative of fall and corruption in most European universal histories. In these accounts, China was a civilization boasting not only astonishing antiquity but also political stability and material prosperity unheard of in Christendom.[18] As David Porter has shown, these ideas about China as an exception to the fall in universal history in turn led to "extravagant fantasies" about the Chinese language as a model of representational clarity and "linguistic legitimacy."[19]

China was very much on William Temple's mind when, at the age of sixty, he wrote his leisurely reflections on the vanity of modern European intellectuals – reflections that the young prodigy William Wotton would take greatly to heart. Temple's immediate impetus for writing his *Essay upon the Ancient and Modern Learning* (1690) was his reading of works such as Thomas Burnet's *Sacred Theory of the Earth* (1684) and Bernard le Bovier de Fontenelle's *Entretiens sur la pluralité des mondes* (1686) as well as *Digression sur les anciens et les modernes* (1688).[20] However, Temple's essay is not so much a specific rejoinder to the "Panegyric of Modern Learning, and Knowledge in comparison of the Ancient" or "the censure of the Old Poetry, and preference of the New" (1690: 5) as a satirical meditation on the "Modern Scholars" (1690: 11) who see themselves as advancing the "mighty Progress" of western European learning unrivalled in all of history (1690: 38). The proper corrective to such modern hubris, as Temple saw it, lay in a broader perspective on world history. The comparison between ancient and modern learning was in his view patently unfair if one did not also take into consideration the relationship between the ancients and those who were "Ancient to them": "But I cannot tell why we should conclude, that the Ancient Writers had not as much Advantage from the Knowledge of others, that were Ancient to them, as we have from those that are Ancient to us" (1690: 6). The problem, of course, was that measuring the advantage the ancients had over those that were ancient to them was an impossible task given the lack of extant records belonging to 'the ancients of the ancients.' Nonetheless, Temple believed that it was possible to conjecture a genealogy of learning that would check the European obsession with ancient Greece and Rome. Judging by the extant records of antiquity, Temple noted that "Those of *China*, are the oldest that any where pretend to any fair Records" (1690: 22); judging by similarity of doctrine, he postulated that "the Seeds of all these *Grecian* Productions and Institutions" could be found in "Ancient *Indian*, and *Chinese* Learning and Opinions" (1690: 24). The fact that Temple makes no serious effort to prove his startling thesis may suggest that he was speaking somewhat tongue-in-cheek, and that his real concern was less to set in motion an historiographical revolution than to instance a proper intellectual humility in contrast to the modern presumption that "we do or shall know, not only all Natural, but even what we call Supernatural Things; all in the Heavens, as well as upon Earth; more than all mortal Men have known before our Age; and shall know in time as much as Angels" (1701: 284).

However, Temple was no doubt familiar with the greater significance of seventeenth-century developments in speculative chronology that attempted to adapt biblical history to non-European pagan histories rather than the other way around. The 1680s had seen an acrimonious debate take shape after John Spencer's publication of *De Legibus Hebraeorum Ritualibus et Earum Rationibus* (1685) in which he asserted that the Jews had arrived at their religion only through a slow process of assimilating and adapting pre-existing Egyptian practices.[21] Burnet's *Sacred Theory of the Earth* (1684) was a similar attempt to naturalize biblical history and accommodate it within a larger vision of geological history. Temple touches on this intellectual context lightly when he notes that "the Fragments of *Manethon* about the Antiquities of *Egypt*, the Relations in *Justin* concerning the *Scythian* Empire, and many others in *Herodotus* and *Diodorus Siculus*, as well as the

Records of *China*, make such Excursions beyond the periods of Time given us by the Holy Scriptures, that we are not allowed to Reason upon them" (1690: 7). The reason Temple refrains from alluding explicitly to the contemporary dispute is probably because he had no desire whatsoever to join "the abyss of Disputes, about Matters of Religion" (1690: 66). His position in the debate about paganism is made clear, however, in his startling postulate of a Chinese origin of European tradition. Temple would have been aware that he was taking the theory of pagan origins of European civilization to a length that would try the patience and religion of many of his contemporaries. In directing attention to China as 'ancient to the ancients,' his primary aim was to show how the very distinction between ancients and moderns could be from a world perspective comically self-undermining. Temple's enthusiasm for China, however, was deeper and more genuine than the overall, gently satirical tone in the *Essay* may suggest.

The references in Temple's *Essay* to "the Missionary Jesuits" who "are content to have Recourse to that [chronology] of the *Septuagint*, and thereby, to salve the Appearances, in those Records of the *Chineses*," to the "Savage Ambition" of a Chinese king who, "desirous to begin the Period of History from his own Reign, ordered all Books to be burnt, except those of Physick and Agriculture" (1690: 22), and to "the Conquests made by the *Tartars*, upon both *India* and *China*" indicate that he was familiar with much of the literature on China available at that time (1690: 26). Alvaro Semedo's *History of that Great and Renowned Monarchy of China* (1655), Johan Nieuhof's *Embassy from the East-India Company of the United Provinces, to the Grand Tartar Cham Emperor of China* (1669), and Gabriel de Magalhães's *A New History of China* (1688) have already been identified as major sources of Temple's information about China.[22] Temple displays his familiarity with Philippe Couplet's *Confucius Sinarum philosophus* (1687), a Latin translation of the Confucian Classics, and he no doubt had read *Bellum Tartaricum*, Martino Martini's influential account of the fall of the Ming empire appended to the 1655 English translation of Semedo's *History*.[23] Unlike the Jesuits, however, Temple was not concerned with squaring biblical chronology with Chinese records, 'accommodating' Confucian to Christian doctrine, or proving the compatibility of science and Christianity. And though he makes passing reference to the bustling economy of China ("so as no Country has so great trade" [1690: 170]), he was, unlike Nieuhof, not so interested in the material details of Chinese life and downplayed the importance of China as a potential market and trading partner for Europe. There are ready explanations for Temple's unusual reticence on the theological and economic significance of European–Chinese relations in the *Essay*. Temple had a horror of religious disputation – "The humour of ravelling into all these mystical or entangled Matters, mingling with the Interests and Passions, of Princes and of Parties, and thereby heightened or inflamed, produced infinite Disputes" (1690: 65) – which he saw as the root cause of the "perpetual Course or Succession, either of Civil or of Foreign Wars" that had "for a Hundred Years past, infested Christendom" (1690: 66). In addition, he was disdainful of the "humour of Avarice and greediness of Wealth" behind merchant and colonial zeal (1690: 69).

In contrast to his sources, Temple's interest in China was neither merchant nor missionary, but moral. In his essay *Of Heroick Virtue*, published together with the *Essay upon the Ancient and Modern Learning* in the 1690 *Miscellanea*, China serves significantly as the first, and by far the most striking, example of a non-Judeo-Christian civilization endowed with natural ethical and political virtues. Temple calls China "the greatest, richest and most populous Kingdom, now known in the World" (1690: 169); a kingdom that "seems to be framed and policed with the utmost Force and Reach of Human Wisdom, Reason and Contrivance, and in Practice, to excel the very Speculations of other Men, and all those imaginary Scheams of the *European* wits, the Institutions of *Xenophon*, the *Republick* of *Plato*, the *Utopias* or *Oceanas* of our Modern Writers" (1690: 192). Temple was especially taken with the "Great and Renowned *Confutius*" (1690: 23) whom he described as a "very extraordinary Genius" and the chief intellectual architect behind the unparalleled excellence of Chinese government (1690: 179). Temple's interpretation of Chinese history, in this sense, is fully in line with the Renaissance tradition of reading history rhetorically, not for "factual completeness and accuracy, but moral guidance."[24] When Joseph Levine comments that "Even in the superficial character of his learning" Temple was "the perfect example of his type," he is pointing to the well-established model of the classical scholar who reads in order to extract from his text "ideal and unproblematic objects for imitation in the present" rather than "exact knowledge about minute details of ancient culture."[25] Temple's hyperbolic praise of Confucius and Chinese government in his essay *Of Heroick Virtue* characteristically relies on the classical demonstrative device of praising singular deeds of heroes and extraordinary achievements. Temple may have culled his information about China from contemporary sources, but in his own writings he treated Chinese history as ceremonial, inventive, imaginative, and epideictic history.[26]

The particular rhetorical approach to China we see in Temple's writings probably grew out of his own disillusionment with English politics. After a distinguished career as a diplomat in the service of Charles II, Temple lived to see his contributions to building peace in Europe come undone in the continuing political struggle between Charles II and his Parliament. In 1681 Temple renounced public service and retired to Moor Park for the rest of his life. Thus, when Temple describes the Chinese king as being simultaneously "the most absolute in the World" and the least autocratic – he passes no laws that are not "first digested and represented by his Councils" so that "no King is better served and obeyed, more honoured or rather adored; and no People better govern'd, nor with greater Ease and Felicity" (1690: 191–92) – it is not hard to read in this flattering description an inverse commentary on the continuing divisiveness of English politics. Temple's true originality does not lie in his use of China as an inverse mirror held up to England, however.[27] It lies, rather, in the subtlety with which he brought Chinese culture to bear on what he considered a self-consuming, narrow-minded quarrel within the western rhetorical tradition. China arguably played the chief role in Temple's belief that "the furthest East and West, may be found to agree in Notions of Divinity, as well as in Excellence of Civil and Politick Constitutions" (1690: 196).

Tracing Chinese Footsteps

William Wotton (1666–1727) was only in his twenties when he published his *Reflections upon Ancient and Modern Learning* in 1694. According to John Evelyn's diary, he was a prodigiously gifted scholar who had been declared "a Miracle" of learning at the age of eleven and a universal genius even beyond Pico della Mirandola.[28] Wotton entered St. Catharine's College, Cambridge, in 1676, at the age of nine; in 1680 he matriculated and graduated at the same time. Having earned his MA in 1683, he became a fellow of the Royal Society in 1687; he became a Bachelor of Divinity in 1691 and was ordained in 1698. Thomas Rhymer writes in *An Essay Concerning Critical and Curious Learning* (1698) that Wotton was "engaged by some Friends, or Patrons, to try what could be said in Defence of Modern Learning, against that of the Ancients," and that, where "Any other Man would have thought it sufficient to have refuted the Arguments in general," "Mr. Wotton had lost his End; it was his Business to attack Sir William Temple."[29] In taking on a figure as well known as Temple, the youthful Wotton knew exactly what he was doing. As he notes in his *Reflections*, "The Opinion which Sir William Temple appears for, is received by so great a Number of Learned Men, that those who oppose it ought to bring much more than a positive Affirmation" (1694: 5). Temple was a well-respected retired statesman with powerful connections in court. A few allusions to Phalaris in his *Essay* had been sufficient to encourage Henry Aldrich, dean of Christ Church at Oxford, to ask the young Charles Boyle to prepare an ill-fated edition.[30] Wotton knew that Temple would be no easy opponent to bring down. But as Wotton saw it, Temple had besmirched all the institutions he believed in: the new learning of the universities, the Royal Society, the Church of England. Whereas Temple's *Essay* is leisurely, detached, and faintly sardonic, written in a tone of gentlemanly retirement and *otium* that suggests its author has seen all the vanity of the world, Wotton's *Reflections* is written with unsmiling gravity. Wotton gets to the quick of the matter in the preface, where he states that his "more powerful Reason" for writing his *Reflections* is that "The fabulous Histories of the *Egyptians*, *Chaldeans* and *Chineses* seem to countenance that Assertion" of "the *Eternity of the World*" – the most dangerously "plausible" of "all the Hypotheses of those who would destroy our utmost holy Faith."[31] Unlike Temple, Wotton thus acknowledges from the very start the acrimonious scholarly debate about rival antiquities and chronologies as the background to his intervention in the quarrel between the ancients and the moderns. Wotton's explicit reference to this debate strongly suggests that the reason why Wotton was riled into a lengthy riposte to Temple was because he was disturbed by the challenge Chinese and other pagan antiquities posed to Christian dogma.

The seriousness with which Wotton regarded the Chinese challenge to Christianity and to western learning is evident in the numerous references he makes to Temple's statements about China as well as in the special chapters he devotes to the topic of Chinese learning. Wotton summarizes Temple's argument in a contemptuous manner in the first chapter of the *Reflections*, claiming Temple argues "That those whom we call Ancients, are Moderns, if compared to those who are ancienter than they: And that there were vast Lakes of Learning in *Egypt*, *Chaldea*, *India* and *China*; where it stagnated for many Ages, till the *Greeks* brought Buckets, and drew it out" (1694: 81). Wotton proceeds to ridicule Temple's "History of Learning" according to which (in Wotton's words), "From *India*, Learning was carried into *Ethiopia* and *Arabia*; thence, by the Way of the *Red Sea*, it came into *Phoenicia*; and the *Egyptians* learnt it of the *Ethiopians*" (1694: 88); "These *Indians*," in their turn,

> had their Knowledge, in all probability, from *China*, a Country where Learning had been in request from the Time of *Fohius*, their first King. It is to be presumed, that they communicated of their Store to other Nations, though they themselves have few Foot-steps of it remaining, besides the Writings of *Confucius*, which are chiefly Moral and Political; because one of

their Kings, who desired that the Memory of every Thing should begin with himself, caused Books of all sorts, not relating to Physic and Agriculture, to be destroyed. (1694: 88)

Despite their scholarly trappings (Wotton references the titles of the works he is referring to, footnotes page numbers, and puts quotation marks around these passages), these supposed citations from Temple's *Essay* present clearly inaccurate, unflattering versions of Temple's ideas. Nonetheless, the distortions manage to strike at the subversive core of Temple's panegyric of China: the preeminent antiquity of China and its unrivalled moral and political exemplarity. Wotton here turns on the unresolved ironies in Temple's account of China where Chinese records are said to be the oldest that exist anywhere even though one of the Chinese kings ordered the burning of all books, and Chinese learning is said to have traveled to India, Arabia, Phoenicia, Egypt, and eventually to Greece although there are no original records or "Foot-steps" of such a transmission. Wotton thus undermines Temple's authority by pointing to the lacunae and logical leaps marring Temple's conjectural history of learning.

To counteract Temple's adulation of China, Wotton devoted the entire twelfth chapter of the *Reflections* to the "Learning of the *Chineses*." Wotton comments on China: "though it is a great Way off, yet it may be easily reached upon Paper, and then will be as easily dispatched" (1694: 144). This is a clear parody of Temple's length account, in *Of Heroick Virtue*, of the prodigious distance at which China lies from the rest of the world. In that essay, Temple notes that China has "continued very long and wholly unknown to the rest of the world" because

> The Great and Ancient Kingdom of *China* is bounded to the East and South by the Ocean, to the North by a Stone Wall of twelve Hundred Miles long, raised against the Invasion of the *Tartars*; and to the West by vast and unpassible Mountains or Deserts, which the Labour or Curiosity of no mortal Man has been ever yet known to have pierced thro or given any account of. (1690: 164)

In addition, Temple adds, "a Custom or Law very ancient among them, of suffering no Stranger to come into their Country, or if they do, not permitting Him to go out, or return any more to His Own" has kept the kingdom veiled in mystery (1690: 166). Wotton's strategy throughout his chapter on the Chinese is to throw doubt on the quality of Temple's sources. In *Of Heroick Virtue* Temple claims he has read the "several Accounts and Relations" of the "several Missionary Friers and Jesuits" who "pierced with infinite pains and dangers thro' these vast and savage Regions" to arrive at Peking, and compares their accounts to the earliest European account of China – that of "Paulus Venetus" (1690: 167). In *Reflections*, Wotton excavates and interrogates Temple's unnamed missionary friars and Jesuits in a spirit that is very different from Temple's imaginative sympathy for their "pains and dangers" in China. Wotton writes: "Sir *William Temple* knows very well, That the whole *Chinese* History depends upon the sole Authority of *Martinius*, and those Missionaries who published *Confucius* lately at *Paris*," naming Martino Martini and Philippe Couplet as two of Temple's primary sources (1694: 144). But given the formidable geographical and cultural obstacles to finding out the truth about China, as well as the Chinese hostility to strangers, can these Jesuits be trusted as a source on China? At what cost to their own conscience and religion had the Jesuits made their way into China? Early versions of the Chinese Rites Controversy in the 1630s had already raised questions about the Jesuits' willingness to 'accommodate' themselves as much as possible to Chinese customs – including Confucian rites and ancestor worship – in order to gain greater inroads into Chinese society.[32] For Wotton, the argument that Confucianism is a philosophy rather than a religion smacks of intellectual and religious bad faith. As far as he can tell, there is pitifully little philosophy in the European reception of Confucius. If Philippe Couplet had published *Confucius Sinarum philosophus* under his own name, Wotton writes, Temple would have been the first to call it "an incoherent Rhapsody of moral Sayings, which good Sense and tolerable Experience might have furnished any Man with" (1694: 145).

Not only does Wotton find Temple's praise of Confucianism dubious at best; he finds Temple's glowing account of the Chinese emphasis on Confucianism over other kinds of learning altogether too naive. Temple noted that "all that which we call Scholastick or Polemick, is unknown or unpractised" in China, and that among the Chinese "Even Astrology and Physick and Chymistry, are but ignoble Studies, tho there are many among them that excel in all these" (1690: 179). It seemed a marvel to him that "all this Learning is ignoble and Mechanical among them, and the *Confutian* only essential and incorporate to their Government" (1690: 180). His point was not to denigrate the natural sciences per se, but to express his sympathy with the Chinese emphasis on political virtue. A brilliant but disappointing career in government behind him, Temple had been favorably impressed by the Confucian doctrine that "no People can be happy but under good Governments, and no Governments happy but over good Men" (1690: 177). Sidestepping this issue of political virtue, Wotton takes direct aim at Temple's description of the Chinese indifference to the natural sciences. Following Temple closely, Wotton queries, "If the *Chineses* think every part of Knowledge, but their own *Confucian* Ethicks, ignoble and mechanical, why are the *European* Missionaries so much respected for their Skill in Medicine and Mechanicks?" (1694: 145). As a fellow of the Royal Society, Wotton had read the letters of Ferdinand Verbiest published in the March–April 1686 number of the *Philosophical Transactions* and found it incredible that the Jesuit had been able to insinuate himself into the Chinese court by "teaching the Emperour to find the Time of the Night by the fixed Stars and an Astrolabe" (1694: 146).[33] In Wotton's eyes, it was risible that the Chinese emperor would be so impressed by such elementary scientific skills as to shower him with honors and keep him close at court; it was also damning that the Jesuits would, for the sake of their mission, act the role of "greatest Scholars" in order to ingratiate themselves to a pagan emperor (1694: 147).

Wotton is willing to allow that the Chinese may be "a sagacious and industrious People," but concludes that "if they had ever applied themselves to Learning in good earnest, and that for near so long a Time, as their History pretends to, there is no Question but we should have heard much more of their Progress" (1694: 146). Having dismissed Chinese astrology on the basis of Verbiest's letters, he proceeds to devote the bulk of his chapter to debunking Chinese medicine, in particular the Chinese "Knowledge of the Pulse" which had attracted considerable attention by then, on the evidence supplied in "the little Tracts of the *Chinese Physick* published by Andrew Cleyer" (1694: 147). The book in question was *Specimen Medicinae Sinicae* (1682), a recently published collection of Chinese medical texts that had been translated by Michael Boym, a Polish member of the Jesuit mission, then later edited and published under the name of Andreas Cleyer, a German-born official and physician of the Dutch East India Company in Batavia. The *Specimen* is in fact an incomplete manuscript that was mired in controversy from the very beginning due to Cleyer's imperfect handling of the material and his failure to acknowledge properly the contributions of other people.[34] On the whole, the document was largely incomprehensible due to the lack of proper commentary, a lack which was recognized and addressed in the 1686 *Clavis medica ad Chinarum doctrinam de pulsibus* – a "key" to the earlier text that did not translate so much as carefully explain the principles behind Chinese medicine for a European audience. Wotton does not mention the *Clavis* and chooses instead to quote directly from the *Specimen* long paragraphs taken from the text of "Nuy Kim" (or *Neijing*) that, lifted out of context, read like pure gibberish: "Out of the Eastern Region arises the Wind, out of the Wind Wood or Plants, out of Wood

Acidity, from thence the Liver, from the Liver the Nerves, from them the Heart," and so on, for several pages.[35] Wotton's point is to show how unreadable these supposedly scientific texts are ("they are not very pleasant to read," he tersely comments) and how "whimsical" Chinese science is. Whatever merit Chinese medicine may have, he believes, can be reduced to "not unhappy Guesses" (1694: 153). There may be "excellent Empiricks" in China, he notes, just as among the "*West-Indian* Salvages," but that does not make them philosophers (1694: 153).[36] Levine's verdict that of all the English and French works on the ancients and the moderns, Wotton's "was easily the most complete and the most juidicious," and that Wotton had "made a deliberate effort to assess the whole question fairly and to sort out the possibilities on both sides" may be a fair assessment of Wotton's achievement in comparing ancient and modern western European learning.[37] Wotton conceded that the ancients excelled in the arts in general, as well as in moral and political philosophy, and claimed decisive modern superiority only for natural philosophy. However, Levine's characterization of Wotton's work is difficult to apply to his discussion of China in which he consistently adopts an ironic, condescending, and mocking tone. Considering the fascination in Europe at that time with Chinese as a 'universal' language,[38] it is indeed surprising that a man who was famous for having mastered "Hebrew, Greek, Latin, Arabic, Syriac, and most of the Modern Languages" at the age of eleven shows no interest in the Chinese language at all.[39] Indeed, Wotton goes as far as to mock Martini for having spent "Eight, or Ten of the best Years of a Man's Life" in learning "Sixty Thousand independent Characters before he could read the Chinese Authors with Ease" (1694: 145).

The fact that Wotton revised the chapter on China with considerable care in the second edition (1697), adding a discussion of India and changing the title to "Of the Learning of the Ancient *Indians* and *Chineses*," suggests that his treatment had met with resistance. Softening his assault on Temple, Wotton points out in the revised chapter that "Sir *W. T.* is not the only Man who has asserted great things concerning" China, and that "Other Men, to strengthen their particular Hypotheses, have exalted it as much as he" (1697: 165). Tellingly, he chooses as his example Thomas Burnet who, like Temple, took a relativistic and naturalistic view of biblical history but, unlike Temple, was committed to progressive learning and ultimately to the universal truth of Christianity. In *Sacred Theory of the Earth* (1684), Burnet had anticipated Temple in declaring that, "as to the *Greeks*, their best and Sacred Learning was not originally their own; they enrich themselves with the spoils of the East, and the best remains we

have of that Eastern Learning, is what we pick out of the *Greeks*" (1: 279).[40]
Burnet had also alleged that the ancients' "account of the Chaos, though
it seem'd to many but a Poetical Rhapsody, contain'd the true mystery
of the formation of the Primitive Earth" (1: 280). However, Burnet had
gone on to conclude that "what was made known to the Ancients only
by broken Conclusion and Traditions, will be known (in the later Ages
of the World) in a more perfect way, by Principles and Theories" (1: 287).
Wotton seizes on Burnet's description of "the Philosophy of the Eastern
Nations" as "*Traditionary*," contrasting the philosophic learning of the
Greeks who pursued "Enquiries in the Causes of the *Phaenomena* which
daily occur" to the "*Barbaric Philosophy*" of the Chinese, built only on
tradition (1697: 165–66).
   The following is critical:

> If, indeed, the Traditions of the East had comprehended a System of
> Natural Knowledge, had given an Account of the leading *Phaenomena* of
> the Universe, had, in short been anything else but bare Memorials, and
> those short, imperfect and obscure, of what the World once was, and what
> it should hereafter be, they would be much more valuable for the present
> Purpose, than any Conclusions made by the exactest Reasoning possible.
> They would then, as they ought, be esteemed as Revelations made by Him
> that made the World, and consequently, could best tell in what Manner,
> and for what Ends and Purposes he has created, and does preserve this
> Planetary System in which we live. But since this is not pretended to, and
> if it were, could not be made good, I cannot possibly see how those who
> allow the *Greeks* to have been the chief Advancers of *Science* as opposed to
> *Tradition* among the Ancients, can deny that Natural Learning, in every
> Particular, was carried to a greater height by them, than by any of the
> Oriental Nations. (1697: 167–68)

This passage illustrates the important role "the Oriental Nations" played in
the definition of western modernity characterized, in stark contrast to the
"Traditionary" east, by the advancement of science and natural learning.
In positing that the ancient Greeks were more learned than "any of the
Oriental Nations," Wotton suggests that the ancient Greeks were indeed
moderns to the ancient Chinese. Wotton makes this point through the
most cursory kind of survey of both ancient and modern Chinese scientific
achievement, eliding the difference between ancient and modern Chinese
learning. Whereas Burnet (who in fact did not include China in his list of
eastern nations) had lamented at length Caesar's sacking of the "famous
Library at *Alexandria*" where there had been "a Collection, besides *Greek*
Books, of *Aegyptian, Chaldaean,* and all the Eastern Learning" (1: 277–78),

Wotton does not express any regret at the burning of Chinese books at the hands of Qin Shi Huang (259 BCE – 210 BCE) or admit his inability to judge Chinese learning fairly. Wotton's stance in many ways exemplifies the logic according to which China increasingly came to be represented as an antique nation mired in pre-scientific traditions – a view that would gain ascendancy in the eighteenth century. It also importantly registers the unresolved conflict between historicism and universalism in modern learning.

As Robert Markley has pointed out, the discourses of natural philosophy in the seventeenth century are never very far from "the narrative forms of teleological history" and theological concerns.[41] The quarrel between the ancients and the moderns indeed shows that moderns were never simple progressivists, and that they had to take seriously the achievements of the ancients precisely because the ancients were central to understanding the moderns' proper place in history. Even such an apparent 'modern' hero as Isaac Newton, who was "first chosen as the paradigm of the sort of progress achieved by the Moderns within the context of Royal Society apologetics," was in fact a firm believer in prophetic history, with wide-ranging interests in ancient chronology, geography, religious ritual, ruins, and prophecy.[42] Newton, a committed anti-trinitarian, held that modern scientific progress in fact consisted only of a revival of an original Noachian wisdom lost and corrupted in history.[43] In this sense, although his achievements in modern science turned him into a hero for the 'moderns,' Newton was in many ways an "extreme proponent of the Ancients," especially in his unpublished writings.[44] In comparison, Wotton, who took Newton's *Opticks* to be one of the exemplary modern achievements, held much more orthodox religious views.[45] In his 1694 *Reflections*, he marvels that in *Of Heroick Virtue* Temple chose to "give us an Account of *Mahomet*'s Life, and that so minutely" but took "no notice of *Moses* and *Jesus Christ*" (1694: 18). He found Temple's politics no less suspect than his religion. Wotton's objections to the Treaty of Utrecht outlined in *Observations upon the State of the Nation, in January 1712/3* show him in all his patriotic, Protestant colors, battling against "the secularizing tendency in political ideology," so well represented in Temple's diplomatic work, that made an alliance with France thinkable.[46] As he put it, "Popery" was inimical both "to the *Protestant Religion*, and to *British Liberty*."[47] Wotton's overriding concern for the Protestant succession, so evident in the *Observations*, is the political corollary to his commitment to stabilizing history around Christian teleology in his *Reflections*. Wotton was equally against making "a precipitate Peace" with France, the Jesuits in China, and their sinophilia.[48]

The Fall of Parnassus

Temple never published a retort to Wotton in his lifetime, but he did pen one, which Jonathan Swift published under the title *Some Thoughts upon Reviewing the Essay of Ancient and Modern Learning* in the posthumous *Miscellanea. The Third Part* (1701). No doubt provoked by Wotton's scathing rhetoric, Temple altered his tone. We see him rising to the occasion when he starts discussing modern "critics," whom he characterizes alternately as stockbrokers and levelers:

> I must confess that the Criticks are a Race of Scholars, I am very little acquainted with; having always esteemed them but like Brokers, who having no Stock of their own, set up and trade with that of other Men; buying here and selling there, and commonly abusing both sides, to make out a little paultry Gain, either of Money or of Credit, for themselves, and care not at whose Cost. (1701: 256–57)
>
> There is, I think, no sort of Talent so despicable, as that of such common Criticks, who can at best pretend, but to value themselves, by discovering the Defaults of other Men, rather than any Worth or Merit of their own: A sort of Levellers, that will needs equal the best or richest of the Country, not by improving their own Estates, but reducing those of their Neighbours, and making them appear as mean and wretched as themselves. (1701: 259–60)

Temple's choice of metaphors speaks volumes about his pride in his social set – an estate owner among "the best or richest of the Country" – whom he defends against the "despicable" encroachments of Wotton's "Race" of unlanded, unmoneyed, unpropertied men eager to raise their "value" at the expense of others. The language is deliberately unkind, meant to rub in the wide social distance separating him from Wotton, who is likened to a stockbroker whose only way to make money is to play havoc with other people's money, and to a leveler whose social vision amounts to razing other people's rich estates. We can easily see how Swift's satirical salvos in the *Battel of the Books* were authorized and launched by such passages as these. In particular, Temple's image of the levelers not "improving their own Estates, but reducing those of their Neighbours," is precisely echoed in Swift's image of the "*Moderns*" threatening "to come with Shovels and Mattocks, and level the said Hill" of Parnassus (1: 144).

Swift's intervention, however, had the unfortunate consequence of narrowing the quarrel between Temple and Wotton to a quarrel between ancient and modern authors – or, more precisely, the writers of ancient Greece and Rome, and modern European writers. As we have seen, the quarrel originally had a much more expansive historical and geographical reach, as Samuel Johnson recalls in the telescopic opening lines of his 1749 *Vanity of Human Wishes*: "Let Observation with extensive View, / Survey Mankind, from *China* to *Peru*." These lines, clearly an echo of Temple's description of his speculative method – "passing at one leap from these of *China* to those of *Peru*" (1690: 196) – in his 1690 essay *Of Heroick Virtue* map an intellectual and imaginative terrain that Swift managed to shrink considerably.[49] Even in *Some Thoughts upon the Essay*, Temple had stood his ground on the issue of China: he had insisted he knew not "why, the Regions of *Assyria, Phoenicia, Aegypt*, the Lesser *Asia, Greece, Rome*, and especially *China*, may not be allowed to produce naturally greater force of Wit and Genius, of Invention and Penetration, than *England, Holland*, or the Northern Parts of *France* and *Germany*, to which all our Modern Learning seems to have been confined" (1701: 278). Temple had also noted that "the *Chineses* have had the Knowledge and Use of Gun-powder, many Ages before it came into *Europe*" (1701: 280). Swift's treatment of the quarrel, however, confines it quite literally to a European library, reducing it to a battle between books within Europe.

The lineup in Swift's battle consists of such select 'ancients' as (loosely in the order of appearance) Aesop, Homer, Pindar, Euclid, Plato, Aristotle, Herodotus, Livy, Hippocrates, and Virgil, with their "Allies" Vossius and Temple. As to the 'moderns,' the list is generously long (again, loosely in the order of appearance): Tasso, Milton, Dryden, Wither, Cowley, Despreaux, Descartes, Gassendi, Hobbes, Paracelsus, Harvey, Guicciardini, D'Avila, Polydore Virgil, Buchanan, Mariana, Camden, Regiomontanus (Johann Müller), Wilkins, Scotus, Aquinas, Bellarmine, L'Estrange, Scaliger, Davenant, Denham, Wesley, Perrault, Fontenelle – not to forget the "lovely, loving Pair" Bentley and Wotton (1: 161). A large portion of Swift's expansive list was original to him, but he had no doubt consulted and enlarged upon Temple's own lists of modern writers in his 1690 *Miscellanea* essays *Essay upon the Ancient and Modern Learning* and *Of Poetry*. According to Temple, "*Homer* was without Dispute, the most Universal *Genius* that has been known in the World, and *Virgil* the most Accomplish't"; the two poets together had "so much excelled in their kinds, as to have exceeded all Comparison, to have even extinguished Emulation, and in a manner confined true Poetry, not onely to their two Languages, but to their very Persons" (1690: 297). All 'modern' poetry, or poetry produced after the fall of the Roman Empire, was only a ghost of its former state: it had been "introduced after the Decays, or rather Extinction of the old, as if true Poetry being dead, an Apparition of it walked about" (1690: 311–12).

The extended barbarian invasions that brought down the Roman Empire had so "Corrupted the Purity of the *Latin* Tongue" (1690: 312), in Temple's view, that "the antient Poetry was wholly lost" (1690: 315). In its place, a barbarous new poetry of "*Gothick Runes*" – "a raving or rambling sort of Wit or Invention, loose and flowing, with little Art or Confinement to any certain Measure or Rules" (1690: 318), mostly devoted to the subject of war, conquest, and superstition – had taken hold, and "the Composure of such Feet and Measures, as were in use among the *Greeks* and *Latins*" had been lost (1690: 324). Even after the "dawn of a New Day, and the Resurrection of other Sciences, with the Two Learned Languages" in the Renaissance (1690: 323–24), Temple believed, the best efforts of modern poets such as Ariosto, Tasso, and Spenser had failed to reach the heroic heights of their classical forefathers, and poets had thereafter largely abandoned epic and "turned to other Veins, as if, not worthy to sit down at the Feast, they contented themselves with the Scraps, with Songs and Sonnets, with Odes and Elegies, with Satyrs and Panegyricks, and what we call Copies of Verses upon any Subjects or Occasions" (1690: 325).

Swift's animosity toward not only the champions of modern science and philosophy, such as Descartes, Gassendi, and Hobbes, but also modern British writers such as Milton, Dryden, Cowley, Davenant, and Denham, was motivated by his antipathy for radical republicanism, political and religious apostasy, as well as the culture of literary triumphalism and shameless self-advertising that he saw rampant around him. In the "Apology" prefacing *A Tale of a Tub*, Swift skewers "Dryden, L'Estrange, *and some others I shall not name*" for "*having spent their Lives in Faction, and Apostacies, and all manner of Vice*" and for having "*pretended to be Sufferers for Loyalty and Religion*" (1: 7). In the main body of the text, he goes on to lampoon Dryden's manner of sententiously promoting his own work in the form of "*Prefaces, Epistles, Advertisements, Introductions, Prolegomena's, Apparatus's, To-the-Reader's*" (1: 85), just as, in the *Battel*, he heaps scorn on the likes of Cowley and Davenant who defiantly claimed their right to stray from, leave out, and add what they pleased to the ancient examples.[50] And yet, from today's perspective, Swift's list of moderns would seem overly inclusive, to his own detriment. Does Swift leave enough room in the space of the modern to justify his own literary productions? What is his answer to Temple's distaste for "Ridicule," which Temple had characterized as a "Vein which was entered and helpt to Corrupt our modern Poesy" (1690: 327)?

The defense of the ancients as exemplified by their spokesmen such as Temple and Swift in fact would meet increasing resistance in the eighteenth century. The mantle of classical humanism would never be entirely thrown off; no modern writer, not even one of those singled out by Swift for derision, operated entirely outside the literary parameters long established by classical learning. Their differences notwithstanding, Temple and Wotton were basically in agreement about the value of classical learning and the literature of western antiquity. As Levine puts it, both of them were products of "a single common culture, the neoclassical culture that had been reborn in the Italian Renaissance and slowly but steadily taken root in England."[51] Long after the quarrel, the classical languages would continue to operate as "a badge of class and, like a set in the country or in Parliament, the mark and property of a gentleman."[52] And Temple's notion of the barbaric, Gothic quality of the English vernacular language, in contrast to the purity and smoothness of the classical languages, would also continue to live on as a cultural commonplace. Yet a growing number of writers would seek to revise the terms on which they would engage with their classical forebears.

Wotton's chapter "Of Ancient and Modern Eloquence and Poesie" in his 1694 *Reflections* charts some of the directions in which the defense of modern literary production would move. Wotton notes that, although the reverence for the ancients could be suspected of being a product of education rather than independent judgment ("being accustomed from our Childhood to hear them commended"), it is clearly based on "more than Prejudice" since "Their Works give us a very solid Pleasure when we read them" (1694: 23). He grants that Greek has "a vast Advantage above any other Language that has ever yet been cultivated by Learned Men" (1694: 26), having "a vast Variety of long Words, wherein long and short Syllables are agreeably intermixed together, with great Numbers of Vowels and Diphthongs in the Middle-Syllables, and those very seldom clogged by the joining of harsh-sounding Consonants in the same Syllable" (1694: 24). However, he ascribes this "peculiar Smoothness of the *Greek* Language" to natural accident rather than to native genius, as Temple does (1694: 26). If "*Homer* and *Virgil* had been *Polanders* or *High-Dutch*-Men," Wotton asks, would they have written "Heroick Poems"? His point is that "the Language it self has so great an Influence" that genius becomes almost incidental (1694: 34).[53] Wotton agrees that it is unfortunate that "Length of Syllable" is no longer a "Guide of Verses" in the modern European languages, but "only Number of Feet, and Accent" (1694: 34). It is also true that the English language "abound[s] in Consonants"; for this reason, in comparison to French and Italian that have fewer consonants and more vowels, English is admittedly "more unfit for some Poems" (1694: 34). However, Wotton avers that there can be an advantage to writing in one's mother tongue rather than in a dead language. Hence "that Pleasure which Men take in *Milton, Cowley, Butler,* or *Dryden,* who wrote in their Mother-Tongue, and so were able to give that unconstrained Range and Turn to their Thoughts and Expressions that are truly necessary to make a compleat Poem" (1694: 29). As to rhetoric, Wotton submits that "the Humour of the Age" among the moderns is "exceedingly altered" from that of the ancients, since eloquence is no longer the chief criterion to enter government (1694: 38). In the modern age, "Men apprehend or suspect a Trick in every Thing that is said to move the Passions of the Auditory in Courts of Judicature, or in the *Parliament-House.*" "Even in the Pulpit," he notes, "the Pomp of Rhetorick is not always commended." "And therefore, when Men have spoken to the Point, in as few Words as the Matter will bear, it is expected they should hold their Tongues" (1694: 38). To say that the value of rhetoric and the classical standards of eloquence are subject to "the Humour of the Age" and a particular culture of politics is to suggest that eloquence ultimately has not a transhistorical but a contingent value. Wotton does not go so far as to say, as Sprat did in *The History of the Royal-Society of London* (1667), that "*eloquence* ought to be banish'd out of all *civil Societies,* as a thing fatal to Peace and good Manners," but his comments clearly support the "plain style" favored by the Royal Society – the language of objectivist, rather than rhetorical, thinking.[54]

Wotton's writings form a part of what Howard Weinbrot has called the "weaning" process that took place over the long eighteenth century: in "the slow process of weaning themselves from the Greece and Rome that still nourished them," English writers would gradually learn to pit English modernity against classical antiquity, defining English and later British national identity in contrast to an increasingly "suspect classical past."[55] What Wotton called the new "Humour of the Age" would look progressively askance at "the malice of Roman conquest, the insufficiencies of Roman trade, the brutal nature of the Greek epic hero, and the necessary limitations even of the ablest minds – like Aristotle's – of the ablest past."[56] The new spirit of the age was defended not only by men of science and learning such as Wotton, but by modern writers of the ilk of Charles Gildon, who believed the ancients had been "Masters of but little Reason, when they made their Gods such *limited* and *criminal* Beings," and John Dennis, who proclaimed in *The Advancement and Reformation of Modern Poetry* (1701) his desire "*to set the Moderns upon an equal foot with even admir'd Antiquity.*"[57] Representatives of the self-made entrepreneurs of the age likewise declared their distance from the ancients. Pierre Motteux wrote in the early issues of the *Gentleman's Journal* in 1692, "Nothing hinders more the progress of Learning, nor so much confines Minds as an excessive admiration of the Ancients."[58] As the word 'modern' took on a luster in its own right, it would cease to be a term of condescension or a mark of automatic inferiority. Instead of being doomed forever to the fate of being, as Temple put it, "imperfect Copies … of so excellent an Original" (1690: 59), the moderns would learn to take pride in their advantages: revealed religion, the refinements of politeness and civility, a robust political culture of Liberty, scientific advancement, and the rise of the British empire.[59] Even the English language itself would be eventually hailed as a unique modern achievement. Denham claimed "the *English* is more strong, more full, more sounding, more significant, and more harmonious than the *French*"; Henry Felton declared in his *Dissertation on Reading the Classics and Forming a Just Style* (1713) that "Our English, of all *Modern* Languages that have been cultivated, is upon Experience and Comparison justly thought most capable of all the Beauty, Strength, and Significancy of the *Greek* and *Latin*."[60]

In his 1711 *Essay on Criticism*, Pope could still confidently intone:

> Hear how learn'd *Greece* her useful Rules indites,
> When to repress, and when indulge our Flights:
> High on *Parnassus'* Top her Sons she show'd,
> And pointed out those arduous Paths they trod,
> Held from afar, aloft, th'Immortal Prize,
> And urg'd the rest by equal Steps to rise;
> Just *Precepts* thus from great *Examples* giv'n,
> She drew from *them* what they deriv'd from *Heav'n*. (lines 92–99)[61]

However, by the mid-century the view of the great classical writers as "great *Examples*" located "High on *Parnassus'* Top," so close to "Heav'n," had shifted considerably. As the modern, progressive outlook gained ascendancy, the ancients were cloaked in a different kind of aura – not the aura of perfection and unreachable heights implied by Pope's invocation of Parnassus, "th'Immortal Prize," and "Heav'n," but the aura of a foreign culture. As Kirsti Simonsuuri puts it, the moderns "looked at the culture of antiquity for the first time from the standpoint of a stranger."[62] The Homeric epics so lauded by Temple, Swift, and Pope were brought down from Parnassus and repositioned in a human rather than a quasi-divine historical past; they became "the product of a particular area in a particular epoch" and the preeminent example of pagan, "primitive literature";[63] possibly the creation of multiple authors rather than the singular creation by "the vastest, the sublimest, and the most wonderful *Genius*" of Homer, as Temple had claimed (1690: 297). Modern critics such as Wotton held in such contempt by Temple, Swift, and Pope certainly had a big hand in this shift.[64] The great historical irony, however, is that although the "Humour of the Age," as Wotton correctly diagnosed, would eventually move literature away from strict classicist imitation and toward a much more estranging view of the classics, it would also end up affirming critical tendencies inimical to Wotton and characteristic of Temple instead. In particular, Temple's wide-ranging interest in non-classical cultures, so vividly exemplified in his enthusiasm for China, would become a strong mark of the modern aesthetic. Hans Robert Jauss describes this "unexpected conclusion" of the quarrel as a joint insight, on the part of both ancients and moderns, that the "gradual dismantling of classical aesthetic norms" led to "a historical understanding of ancient art": the view "that alongside the eternally beautiful there was also the historically or conditionally beautiful."[65] This was, in effect, a later compromise solution worked out between the moderns who denied the peerless, universal exemplarity of the classical authors and that of the ancients who, as we can confirm in Temple's writings, harbored a "nascent historicism" in their interest in geographical and historical context.[66] Douglas Lane Patey similarly writes that the quarrel led to "a new understanding of history: one that contributed to an understanding of all human works as historical products (cultural constructions) and consequently to a relativization of taste, increased interest in non-classical cultures both past and present, and ultimately to that late eighteenth-century body of thinking we have come to call 'historicism.' "[67] What I shall call English literary modernity – English literature produced in the wake of the quarrel between the ancients and the moderns, imbued with a strong sense of its distance from the classical models, and burdened by a strong need to theorize its own historicity – evolved out of these complex negotiations between ancient and modern positions. Understanding English literary modernity as the gradual working out of the central questions raised by the quarrel between the ancients and the moderns, I propose, helps us understand why the seemingly quirky fad for China in the eighteenth century can be read as the expression of a cultural turn that was central to the English experience of modernity. Here, again, it helps to turn to Temple.

China and the Plurality of Worlds

J. E. Spingarn noted more than a century ago that, although Temple can be said to have "provoked" the quarrel between the ancients and the moderns, he is "inadequate as a representative of the 'ancients.' Despite his nominal leadership on this side, his tastes were markedly modern, and he represents …

a trend of criticism in complete opposition to ancient rules."[68] As Clara Marburg comments in *Sir William Temple: A Seventeenth Century "Libertin"* (1932), Spingarn's insight into Temple as a "man of letters" has tended to take second place in critical studies that have focused on the scientific or philological aspect of the quarrel.[69] The best way to follow up on Spingarn's suggestive comment, I propose, is to return to Temple's *Essay upon the Ancient and Modern Learning*. At the beginning of his essay, Temple writes:

> Two Pieces that have lately pleased me ... are, one in *English* upon the *Anti-deluvian* World; and another in *French*, upon the *Plurality of Worlds*; one Writ by a Divine, and the other by a Gentleman, but both very finely in their several Kinds, and upon their several Subjects, which would have made very poor work in common hands: I was so pleased with the last (I mean the Fashion of it, rather than the Matter, which is old and beaten) that I enquired for what else I could of the same hand, till I met with a small Piece concerning Poesie, which gave me the same exception to both these Authors, whom I should otherwise have been very partial to. (1690: 4–5)

Temple is setting up Thomas Burnet and Fontenelle, the authors here mentioned, for a considerable fall when he begins by praising them, for he quickly goes on to accuse them of a dangerous preference for the "Modern" and the "New" (1690: 5). It is noteworthy, however, that he provides a detailed account of the initial pleasure he took in Fontenelle's *Entretiens sur la pluralité des mondes* (1686).[70] In fact, he was "so pleased" with it, he reports, that he "enquired" for more "of the same hand." His investigations led him to a "small Piece concerning Poesie." Although Temple does not name the work, this was clearly Fontenelle's short *Digression sur les anciens et les modernes* published in his *Poésies pastorales* (1688). Temple adds that, contrary to his expectations, he was more than disappointed with this work. The discrepancy in Temple's response is curious. What was it that gave him pleasure in Fontenelle's earlier work? What took that pleasure away in the later one?

Temple's remark that he liked the "Fashion" of the *Plurality of Worlds* "rather than the Matter, which is old and beaten," shows that he had read Fontenelle's text as literature rather than as science, missing its main "Matter." He goes so far as to suggest that *Plurality of Worlds* does not contain any scientific ideas original to Fontenelle; its excellence lies rather in its delivery. If Temple's misleading dismissal of what he describes as the "old and beaten" scientific content of the work reminds us of Temple's dislike for the modern sciences, his esteem for its literary presentation speaks to his literary taste. To this day hailed as a "brilliant popularization of Descartes' cosmological theory" and "the first classic in the popular literature of science," *Plurality of Worlds* offers the reader a speculative cosmology of the universe not in the form of a dry philosophical tract but in the eminently sociable form of flirtatious conversations between a scientist narrator and a beautiful Marquise of ***, who has no prior knowledge in science but who proves herself an able student and witty conversation partner.[71] The setting is worthy of a romance: conversations take place over five different evenings, as the two speakers take a private night walk through a garden under a starry sky. As Herbert Dieckmann puts it, Fontenelle takes the established literary genre of the *entretien* or dialogue to a different level in this text: "A light and fine irony" permeates Fontenelle's style and "eliminates all oratory, pomp, solemnity, and grandiloquence from his style, even when it is elevated." He uses apologue, allegory, images, analogies, dramatizing and poeticizing his scientific ideas, and placing them in an attractive social milieu.[72] Fontenelle's manner of placing ideas in a worldly, sociable context was no doubt congenial to Temple. In addition, his lack of philosophical bombast, his naturalistic understanding of the limitless, plural universe, and his moral implication that, despite scientific advance, humans are ultimately deeply limited beings who do not have access to the whole truth would have appealed to Temple's skeptical bent of mind. As Fontenelle put it, "if we could really see things as they are, we would really know something, but we see things other than as they are."[73]

In the preface to the *Plurality of Worlds*, Fontenelle claims that the "idea of the infinite diversity that Nature has placed in her works" "governs the whole book" (6). The narrator of *Plurality of Worlds* takes this idea to an extraterrestrial level, postulating the existence of life-forms beyond human imagination, first on the moon and then elsewhere in the universe. In order to explain this idea of life-forms beyond our ken in the vast universe, the narrator resorts to an analogy between the diversity of life in the universe and on planet earth. It is not clear what Temple made of the postulate of extraterrestrial life, but Fontenelle's vision of a limitless diversity or plurality of existence on earth in all likelihood strongly appealed to him. We can imagine him delighting in a passage such as this:

> I sometimes imagine that I'm suspended in the air, motionless, while the Earth turns under me for twenty-four hours, and that I see passing under the maze all the different faces: white, black, tawny, and olive complexions: At first there are hats, then turbans; wooly heads, then shaved heads; here cities with belltowers, there cities with tall spires with crescents; here cities with towers of porcelain, there great countries with nothing but huts; here vast seas, there frightful deserts; in all, the infinite variety that exists on the surface of the Earth. (20)

This bird's-eye, or God's-eye, view of the earth presents a remarkable thumbnail gallery of contrastive images – diverse complexions, headwear, hairstyle, architecture, natural vistas – that illustrate the "infinite variety" that rules over the earth. The image of a three-dimensional globe turning before our very eyes puts a dramatic spin on the modern map – which, as Temple notes, has greatly improved on the world map of the ancients. In *Of Heroick Virtue*, Temple observes that the moderns have managed to map a much larger portion of the world than the ancients: "if we consider the Map of the World, as it lies at present before us, since the discoveries made by the Navigations of these three last Centuries, we shall easily find what vast Regions there are, which have been left out of that ancient Scene on all sides" (1690: 161). However, he claims that the moderns have failed to reap the full benefits of these advances and remain ignorant of vast areas of the world, in large part because of cultural prejudice. *Of Heroick Virtue* does not take the reader on a tour of the universe as *Plurality of Worlds* does, but it does take the reader on a "little known or traced" path of earthbound exploration, surveying the "vast Extent, and variety of Soiles and Clymats, with their natural Productions," and "Laws and Customs" in these "out-lying Parts of the World" – in particular, China, Peru, Tartary, and Arabia (1690: 161–62).

Reading Temple's essay *Of Heroick Virtue* alongside *Essay upon the Ancient and Modern Learning* and *Of Poetry* enables us to see that Temple's appreciation of the classical writers of ancient Greece and Rome was significantly tempered by his sense that these "great Empires, so much renowned in Story" (1690: 149), constituted "but a limited compass of Earth that leaves out many vast Regions of the World ... accounted barbarous, and little taken notice of in Story, or by any celebrated Authors" (1690: 159). Indeed, what is so remarkable about Temple is his unusual ability to balance his appreciation of classical civilization with a genuine and generous curiosity about "these remote (and, as we will have it, more ignoble) Regions of the World" (1690: 162). Grouping ancient Greece and Rome together with Egypt and Persia, Temple notes:

> These Four great Monarchies, with the smaller Kingdoms, Principalities and States, that were swallowed up by their Conquests and Extent, make the Subject of what is called Antient Story, and are so excellently related by the many *Greek* and *Latin* Authors, still extant and in common vogue, so commented, enlarged, reduced into order of time and place, by many more of the Modern Writers, that they are known to all Men, who profess to study or entertain themselves with Reading. The Orders and Institutions of these several Governments, their progress and duration, their successes or decays, their events and revolutions, make the

common Theams of Schools and Colledges, the Study of Learned, and the Conversation of Idle Men, the Arguments of Histories, Poems, and Romances. (1690: 157)

Temple's startling charge against "the Modern Writers" is that they continue to go over the same, worn ground already covered by the ancient Greek and Latin authors, continuing in their prejudice against the so-called "barbarous" and "ignoble" parts of the world, and making no progress in this regard over the ancients. Modern writers continue to draw their examples of virtue, vice, honor, justice, and liberty from the histories of these ancient empires; deeming "the discoveries made by the Navigations of these three last Centuries" not "worth the Pens of any good Authors," they leave it to the "Traders, Seamen, or Travellers" to come up with their "common and poor Relations" (1690: 161–62). In this way Temple characterizes the moderns as narrow-minded, unimaginative, and paradoxically out of tune with the modern world. Culturally, politically, and ethically, they remain chained to "a limited Compass," whereas, in his opinion, some of the "vast Regions" of the world, "left out of that ancient Scene" (1690: 161), "upon enquiry, will be found to have equalled or exceeded all the others, in the wisdom of their Constitutions, the extent of their Conquests, and the duration of their Empires or States" (1690: 159).

What Temple demanded from the moderns, in short, was a cultural and moral humility – an acknowledgement that their intellectual and moral universe was a limited one. This was, for him, the lesson provided by modern navigation. Encountering Fontenelle's vision of a plurality of worlds (albeit largely in the form of extraterrestrials), Temple may have thought that he had found a kindred spirit. The *Digression* would have proved a rude awakening, however. For in this self-congratulatory piece, Fontenelle does away with all humility and lauds modern French culture as an achievement that will one day rival that of ancient Greece. Fontenelle writes almost as if he were openly courting outrage from the ancients' camp. The ancient Greeks, he finds, were not capable of "reasoning to the last perfection" in philosophy (1707: 114); indeed, "Aristotle had never been a true philosopher" (1707: 123).[74] It might be true that the Greeks had reached a "point of perfection" in the literary arts, but there was a big difference between saying they could not be "surpassed" and they could not be "equalled" (1707: 118). Many centuries from now, he predicts, when his time will seem as remote as that of the ancient Greeks, the tragedies of Sophocles, Euripides, and Aristophanes will "hold nothing up to" those of Pierre and Thomas Corneille and Molière; the romances of Honoré d'Urfé, Voltaire, Madame de Scudéry, and Madame de Lafayette will not even invite comparison with those of Heliodorus (1707: 122).⁷⁵ In short, there is no reason to assume that the ancients were more naturally gifted than the modern French. The modern French would have been more than able to do what the ancients had done had they been there in their place (1707: 111); there is no reason to indulge in an "excessive admiration of the ancients" (1707: 123).⁷⁶

As to other regions of the world, Fontenelle does not have much to say, except that the "perfect equality" between "the Ancients and Moderns, Greeks, Romans and French" cannot be assumed to extend to all parts of the world (1707: 110). He explains why through a horticultural analogy: "even if the trees of all centuries are equally tall, the trees of all countries are not equally tall" (1707: 109). The reason he gives is primarily climactic, although he adds that "external circumstances" such as history, government, the state of general affairs can cause additional variations (1707: 111). Fontenelle instances China once in this brief essay as a negative example of how "prejudices and fantasies" can prevent men from fully exercising their natural talent. Drawing apparently on the *Lettres édifiantes et curieuses*, he claims the excessive "respect for cadavers" in Chinese culture has prevented the Chinese from performing dissections on dead bodies and hence from developing any mastery of the human anatomy (1707: 118).⁷⁷ It is striking that Temple, who actually shared Fontenelle's belief that climate, geography, and both natural and political "accidents" had a great impact on the course of civilizations, derives conclusions very different from Fontenelle's (1690: 36–37). Nature may essentially be the same everywhere, but that is no reason to rule out exceptions which are everywhere in evidence. Elaborating on Fontenelle's image of trees growing equally in ancient and modern times, he asks, "Because there is a Stag's-head at *Amboyse* of a most prodigious size, and a large Table at *Memorancy*, cut out of the thickness of a Vine-stock, is it necessary, that there must be, every Age, such a Stag in every great Forest, or such a Vine in every large Vineyard" (1690: 34)? Let us say " 'Tis very true and just, All that is said of the mighty Progress, that Learning and Knowledge have made, in these *Western* Parts of *Europe*, within these hundred and fifty Years," he says, "but that does not conclude, it must be at a greater Heigth, than it had been in other Countries," either past or present (1690: 38). Temple reads a chastening message in nature and history; the very idea of progress is an intellectual and moral presumption.

What feels so modern in Temple's thought, I propose, is precisely this resistance to a single model of history, or to a single set of cultural norms. In lieu of a theory of progress culminating in the triumph of modern European culture, Temple espoused a theory of genius which he elaborated in both his essay *Of Heroick Virtue* and *Of Poetry*. Genius, which he deemed responsible for greatness in both politics and poetry, was "the pure and free Gift of Heaven or of Nature," "a Fire kindled out of some hidden spark of the very first Conception" (1690: 293). Temple writes that "elevation of genius … can never be produced by any Art or Study, by Pains or by Industry," and "cannot be taught by Precepts or Examples" (1690: 292–93). Like the Stag's-head at *Amboyse* and the thick vine of *Memorancy*, genius is an irregular natural phenomenon, an exception to all rules and examples. Western culture has no monopoly on it. If genius is universal in the sense that it can occur in any part of the world, for Temple it is also plural because it can appear in so many different shapes and guises. Just as "many circumstances concur" to "the stupendious growth of a Tree or Animal" – "the native strength of the seed," the "propriety of Soyl," "accidents of Water and of Shelter," "the kindness or unkindness of Seasons," "joined with the propitiousness of Clymat" – many accidents can concur to produce "prodigies of Invention and Learning" with "unparalleled and inimitable excellencies" (1690: 34–35). Examples can be found in China, as in the "very extraordinary Genius" of Confucius (1690: 179). Temple uses China again in a very striking way in his essay *Upon the Gardens of Epicurus*, where he again demonstrates his willingness to acknowledge the possibility of alternative cultural standards – in this case, the standard of taste. Noting that the Chinese are "a People, whose way of thinking, seems to lie as wide of ours in *Europe*, as their Country does," he reports that he has heard "from others, who have lived much among the *Chineses*" of their strikingly different way of planting gardens – not according to "certain Proportions, Symmetries, or Uniformities," as the English do, but "without any order or disposition of parts, that shall be commonly or easily observ'd" (1690: 131–32). Temple does not go so far as to recommend that English gardens be redone in this fashion. Quite the opposite. He writes: "I should hardly advise any of these Attempts in the Figure of Gardens among us; they are Adventures of too hard achievement for any common Hands" (1690: 132). Yet his brief mention of a Chinese "Beauty … without order" (1690: 132) would, in Arthur Lovejoy's words, "have consequences of such unforeseen range" that the course of British aesthetics would be changed forever.[78] The new aesthetics of "irregularity, asymmetry, variety, surprise" championed by Addison, Walpole, and Chambers would return, time and time again, to Temple's ideas.[79] Even later champions of modern literature such as Edward Young would betray their debt to Temple in their theorizations of originality and genius.

As we shall see in the following chapters, Temple provides an acute entry-point to many of the central debates in modern English literature. Temple was a defender of the ancients and left many caustic remarks on English literature, but he did not merely belittle modern English literature. In the concluding pages of *Of Poetry*, he proposed that the English had a unique genius for comic drama: "the Native Plenty of our Soyl, the unequalness of our Clymat, as well as the Ease of our Government, and the Liberty of Professing Opinions and Factions," he proposed, had produced a unique English humor, or "Medly" of humors (1690: 337), and turned England into a nation of "Originals" (1690: 333). In a passage brimming with comic wit, he writes:

> There are no where so many Disputers upon Religion, so many Reasoners upon Government, so many Refiners in Politicks, so many Curious Inquisitives, so many Pretenders to Business and State-Imployments, greater Porers upon Books, nor Plodders after Wealth. And yet no where more Abandoned Libertines, more Refined Luxurists, Extravagant Debauches, Conceited Gallants, more Dablers in Poetry as well as Politics, in Phylosophy, and in Chymistry. I have had several Servants far gone in Divinity, others in Poetry, have known in the Families of some Friends, a Keeper deep in the *Rosycrucian* Principles, and a Laundress firm in those of *Epicurus*. (1690: 336–37)

The English are paradoxically alike by being utterly unlike one another: "We are not only more unlike one another, than any Nation I know; but we are more unlike our selves too, at several times, and owe to our very Air some ill Qualities as well as many good" (1690: 334). According to Temple, this is why English drama has "in some kind excelled both the Modern and the Antient" (1690: 332) – namely, in the "greater variety of Humor in the Picture" (1690: 333) – and why Shakespeare can be counted a great dramatic genius unequalled in history. Temple considers Shakespeare a modern writer (for Temple, all literature produced after the fall of the Roman Empire is basically modern), but in later generations Shakespearean drama would be held up as an example of "an alternative, non-classical literary tradition – a new *ancienneté*" within English literary tradition itself.[80] The story of how the quarrel between the ancients and the moderns was imported into the canon of modern English literature, forcing a distinction between 'modern' English writers and such 'ancients' as Chaucer, Spenser, and Shakespeare, who were first denigrated for their primitive roughness and then later praised for their antique sublimity, has been so well told by such critics as Jonathan Kramnick, Douglas Lane Patey, and Trevor Ross, that it would hardly be necessary to retell it here. By the mid-eighteenth century, the rediscovery of the medieval and Gothic traditions, the development of antiquarian interest in native 'ancient' poetry, and the elevation of romance were well-established, irrevocable literary trends. Temple would have disagreed with many of these developments, for he had a poor opinion of the "*Gothick Runes*" and romances in general (1690: 318). And yet, by mapping out a pluralized world, Temple had made many of these developments possible. Indeed, his interest in non-classical cultures, his theorization of alternative antiquities, his ideas about English national character and the singularity of genius in his *Miscellanea* essays had arguably laid the essential groundwork for these very changes. The quarrel between the ancients and the moderns started out as a "battle over the locations and sources of authority, with its consequences for the legitimacy of established religion and the state and for the intellectual role of the scholar."[81] After the initial *quid pro quo* between Temple and Wotton, however, it would branch out in directions that neither writer could have possibly foreseen. In this sense, the quarrel was not at all a battle with a clear victor like Swift's battle of the books. It was a far messier affair marred by blurred boundaries and categorical confusion. In my opinion, however, this should not lead us to dismiss the controversy as "unserious, trivial, and disingenuous," as Kristine Louise Haugen does in her recent book on Richard Bentley, or as "memorable only as furnishing a theme for the energy and brilliance of Swift's satiric genius," as Homer Woodbridge writes in his biography of William Temple.[82] As the following chapters will show, the quarrel would serve as an important and fecund reference point in literary developments long after the Temple–Wotton debate.

CHAPTER 2

Robinson Crusoe and the Great Wall of China

Unlike Temple, whose name appears often in texts written in the century after the Temple–Wotton debate, Wotton is a name seemingly all but forgotten. As the previous chapter has shown, however, the debate did not result in an easy or lasting victory for Temple and the ancients. Wotton's interest in scientific and material culture, as well as his confidence in modern English literary production, were widely shared by writers who sought to break away from the dominance of classical models in their bid for success in the literary marketplace. The career of Daniel Defoe is a case in point. Dissenter, projector, hack-writer, criminal-biographer, propagandist, and pilloried-satirist, Defoe produced late in his life a slew of adventure stories set in what Temple called "the Map of the World, as it lies at present before us" (1690: 161). These stories featured adventurers and wagerers who, like Defoe, staked their lives on the mobility made possible by the modern world. Defoe's characters know no geographical boundaries: they are the "Traders, Seamen, or Travellers" mentioned by Temple as the suppliers of the "common and poor Relations" of "the discoveries made by the Navigations of these three last Centuries" (1690: 161). Had Temple lived to read Defoe's *Life and Strange Surprizing Adventures of Robinson Crusoe, of York, Mariner* (1719), *The Farther Adventures of Robinson Crusoe* (1719), *The Life, Adventures, and Pyracies, of the Famous Captain Singleton* (1720), or *A New Voyage round the World* (1725), he might have been impressed by Defoe's geographical reach that spanned the African continent and South America, as well as the West and East Indies. However, he would have been appalled by what he recognized as the "humor of Avarice and greediness of Wealth" in these texts (1690: 69). What motivates Defoe's characters is never simply the pursuit of wealth, but it cannot be denied that they become tangled up in peculiarly modern forms of trade and material exchange. What alarmed Temple was precisely what fired up Defoe's imagination: the "pursuit of insatiable gains" unleashed ever "since the Discoveries and Plantations of the *West-Indies*," and the arrival of "those vast Treasures that have flowed into these *Western* parts of *Europe* almost every Year, and with such mighty Tides for so long a course of time" (1690: 69).

Like Wotton, Defoe was interested in modern science and technology, and believed that the moderns had far surpassed both the ancients and other contemporary cultures in terms of key innovations. For Wotton, the most impressive modern achievements lay in "*Geography, Astronomy*, and *Navigation*" (1694: 247) as well as scientific instrumentation: "*Telescopes, Microscopes*, the *Thermometer*, the *Baroscope*, the *Air-Pump, Pendulum-Clocks, Chymistry*, and *Anatomy*" (1694: 170). Defoe shared not only Wotton's enthusiasm for these modern innovations but also his belief that progress in the natural sciences went hand in hand with the growth of commerce. As Wotton put it in the 1694 *Reflections*:

> If these Sciences have brought to us the Wealth of the *Indies*, if they have enlarged the Commerce and Intercourse of Mankind, it is so far from being a Disparagement to the Industry of the Moderns, who have cultivated them to such useful Purposes, that it is the highest Character that could be given of those Men, that they pursued their Inventions to such noble Ends. (1694: 247–48)

In *A General History of Discoveries and Improvements, in useful Arts, Particularly in the great Branches of Commerce, Navigation, Plantation, in all parts of the known World* (1725–26), Defoe treats navigation, commerce, and learning as basically synonymous and coeval. When "the World ... was in but a poor Condition, as to Trade or Navigation," he writes – when "All the discover'd inhabited World ... was prescrib'd within very narrow Limits; that is to say, France, Britain, Spain, Italy, Germany, and Greece, the Lesser Asia, the West parts of Persia, Arabia, the North parts of Africa, and the Islands of the Mediterranean Sea" – in that "Green-headed Age," "every useful improving Thing was hid from them" and "they were confin'd and narrow'd in their Understandings, as they were in their Dwellings." Back then, Defoe argues, Europeans lived mostly in a general, confounding lack: they had "Philosophy without Experiment," "MATHEMATICS without Instruments," "GEOGRAPHY without Scale," "ASTRONOMY without Demonstration"; "They made War without Powder or Shot, Cannon or Mortars," "They went to Sea without Compass, and sailed without the Needle," "They view'd the Stars without Telescopes," "Learning had no Printing Press," "They were cloath'd without Manufacture," "They carry'd on Trade without Books, and Correspondence without Posts," "They had Chirurgery without Anatomy." "How surprising is it," he writes, "for us to look back so little away behind us, and see, that even in less than two hundred Years all this (now so Self-wise) part of the World did not so much as know whether there was any such Place as a Russia, a Muscovy, a China, a Guinea, a Greenland, or a North-Cape." These pre-moderns had never heard of America, had no knowledge of "the Gold and the Grain Coasts, on the West-side of Africa … from whence since that time such immense Wealth has been drawn," and "All the East-India and China Trade, tho' a Mine of Gold, was not only undiscover'd, but out of the reach of all Expectation." To think that, back then, "Coffee and Tea, those modern Blessings of Mankind, were never heard of"![1]

Given Defoe's view of the vast improvements that had been made in the sixteenth and seventeenth centuries, and his belief in the essential role that trade, navigation, and commerce had played in those improvements, there can be no doubt as to where he stood on the issue of the ancients and the moderns.[2] It is quite clear that he meant his writings to contribute to the debate, as is evident in his use of the metaphor of the moderns standing upon the shoulders of the giants. In the preface to *A General History of Discoveries and Improvements*, he writes:

> *We have infinite advantages beyond what the Antients could pretend to, and vast helps in the search after Knowledge, which they were utterly destitute of; for we stand upon the shoulders of three thousand Years application, and have all the benefit of their Discoveries, and Experiments handed down, gratis, to improve upon, and encourage our Enquiries.* (1: iv)

Defoe celebrated the modern world and its modern inventions and com-forts, and found little reason to look back in history with piety or longing. "Looking into Antiquity, is a Dry, Empty, and Barren Contemplation," he wrote, "any farther than as it is brought down to our present Understanding, and to bear a steady Analogy of its parts, with the Things that are before us" (1: 4–5). The world was now bigger, vaster, and full of opportunities that, only generations ago, would have been unimaginable. There was no question for him as to which world or age he would prefer to live in.

As to Temple's famous views of China, Defoe evidently thought they were worthy of a joke. *The Consolidator: Or, Memoirs of Sundry Transactions from the World in the Moon* (1705), a satire on English history between 1660 and 1705 written in the form of an allegorical voyage to the moon, begins with an extended excursus on China that Defoe might have imag-ined issuing from Temple's lips.[3] After beginning rather obliquely with an encomium to the Russian tsar Peter the Great, whom he praises for having "Improved his Country" both by entering into commerce with "the Politer

Nations of *Europe*" as well as a "prodigious Trade" with China (1705: 3–4), the narrator launches into a discussion of China proper:

> And as the *Chineses* have many sorts of Learning which these Parts of the World never heard of, so all those useful Inventions which we admire our selves so much for, are vulgar and common with them, and were in use long before our Parts of the World were Inhabited. Thus *Gun-powder*, *Printing*, and the use of the *Magnet* and *Compass*, which we call Modern Inventions, are not only far from being Inventions, but fall so far short of the Perfection of Art they have attained to, that it is hardly Credible, what wonderful things we are told of from thence. (1705: 5)

The phrase "that it is hardly Credible" is the giveaway here. A similar clue is given later, when the narrator declares his plan to take, in his "next Journey that way," "an Abstract of their most admirable Tracts in Navigation, and the Mysteries of *Chinese* Mathematicks; which out-do all Modern Invention at this Rate, that 'tis Inconceivable" (1705: 7). In both passages, China stands for an alternative modernity that puts to shame the European modernity that "we admire our selves so much for." China is the obstacle to European self-love; it is where what "we call the European Modern Inventions" were really invented – so long ago, in fact, that they do not count as inventions at all in China, but only "vulgar and common" things. Clearly, Defoe was conversant with both Temple and Wotton, and understood the importance of China in the quarrel between the ancients and the moderns. Defoe was aware that the very definition of European modernity was challenged by the reputation of the Chinese as "an Ancient, Wise, Polite, and most Ingenious People" whose civilization had improbably first "invented much of mankind's basic technology" (1705: 4).[4] In his *Reflections upon Ancient and Modern Learning*, Wotton had not stooped even to consider the claims that the Chinese had first invented gunpowder, printing, and the magnet – claims that had been circulating in such texts as Tommaso Campanella's *La Città del Sole* (1623) and Samuel Purchas's *Hakluytus Posthumous, or Purchas his Pilgrimes* (1625).[5] By the late seventeenth century, however, even those who acknowledged the Chinese origin of these inventions were beginning to criticize the Chinese for failing to understand their meaning fully. The moderns would take a harsh view of Chinese science, increasingly claiming that the Chinese had repeatedly proven themselves to be incapable of speculative science.

By impersonating a moony character who spouts over-the-top compliments to China and then claims to have traveled to the moon and conversed with lunar scientists, Defoe brings the joke down on both Chinese antiquity and science. Defoe's narrator, whose gullibility and enthusiasm for scientific curiosities anticipates Gulliver's, repeatedly marvels at the "hardly Credible," "Inconceivable" prodigies of Chinese history and learning (1705: 5, 7). Referencing "the 365 Volumes of *Angro-machi-lanquaro-zi*, the most ancient Mathematician in all *China*," the narrator retells the story of how the Chinese predicted the "General Deluge" and built "a Fleet of Ships of 100000 Sail" which they "fastned by wonderful Arts to the Earth" and loaded with "120 Days Provisions" so that, "when the Waters abated, the People had nothing to do, but to open the Doors made in the Ship-sides, and come out, repair their Houses, open the great *China* Pots their Goods were in, and so put themselves in *Statu Quo*" (1705: 7–8). Not only did the Chinese in this way put Noah's ark to shame, they are said to have preserved their ancient history and learning in books "Printed in Leaves of Vitrify'd Diamond" (1705: 6). The narrator of *Consolidator* is awestruck by the prodigious "Publick Library at *Tonquin*" (1705: 6) where "wonderful Volumes of Antient and Modern Learning" are collected (1705: 11), including those "written many Ages before we pretend the World began," such as the book of "Ancient Comments, upon the Constitution of the Empire" which lists "a most exact History of 2000 Emperors" (1705: 13); a book of "*Chinese* Navigation" printed "2000 Years before the Deluge," containing a "Chapter of Tides" that lists "the Reason of all the certain and uncertain Fluxes of that Element," including the "exact Pace ... kept between the Moon and the Tides" and "the Power of Sympathy" between the heavenly and earthly bodies – a book that, the narrator believes, would have caused Aristotle to drown himself "because he could not comprehend this Mystery" (1705: 16–17); and "an exact Description of the Circulation of the Blood" discovered long before the time of King Solomon (1705: 15). With this list of prodigies, Defoe mocks the Jesuits' fascination with numbers in their accounts of Chinese antiquity,[6] while taking to task claims that the Chinese had long enjoyed advanced knowledge in navigation and had also long known about the circulation of the blood, recently hailed in England as a modern discovery of William Harvey.[7]

As it turns out, the reason why "the *Chinese* are such exquisite Artists, and Masters of such sublime Knowledge" is that they were visited in antiquity by a "wonderful Philosopher" who "was Born in the *Moon*" and who, "by a strange Invention arrived to by the *Virtuosoes* of that habitable World," landed in China, where he was persuaded to stay and impart the "most exquisite Accomplishments of those *Lunar* Regions" (1705: 17). It is hard not to read this argument as a satirical jibe at Temple's argument in *Essay upon the Ancient and Modern Learning* that the ancients themselves had those who were "Ancient to them" (1690: 6). The question Defoe is asking is, if all the modern inventions of Europe all came from China, where did China get her inventions? Why should China be accepted as a final origin of history? Perhaps China derived her inventions from the moon! As Narelle Shaw has pointed out, Defoe's strategy here ironically mimics that of Swift in *A Tale of a Tub*: "As Swift's persona 'thro' the Assistance of our Noble *Moderns*' investigates 'the weak sides of the *Antients*' and unwittingly sabotages his allies' arguments, so Defoe's persona applauds ancient Chinese ingenuity in terms which inevitably vindicate his antagonists, the moderns."[8] Defoe appears to have derived his idea of the Consolidator, the "Engine" that is responsible for transport between the earth and the moon (an "Engine formed in the shape of a Chariot, on the Backs of two vast Bodies with extended Wings … compos'd of Feathers so nicely put together, that no Air could pass" [1705: 36]), partly from the satire on modern learning in Swift's *Tale of the Tub* (1704) and partly from the description in John Harris's *Lexicon Technicum: Or, An Universal English Dictionary of Arts and Sciences* (1704) of the steam-driven machines used to remove water from mines.[9]

In taking up the subject of China in this Swiftian exercise, Defoe signals his positionality in the Temple–Wotton debate by simultaneously paying homage to and subverting Swiftian satire. At the same time, as a modern Defoe shows a clear investment in debunking the myth of China as an ancient rival to modern England. Defoe's most brilliant, and most problematic, engagement with China, however, arguably is to be found not in *Consolidator* and its unwieldy satirical machinery and heavy-handed allegory, but in his Robinson Crusoe trilogy: *The Life and Strange Surprizing Adventures of Robinson Crusoe, of York, Mariner* (1719), *The Farther Adventures of Robinson Crusoe, Being the Second and Last Part of His Life, and Strange Surprizing Accounts of his Travels Round three Parts of the Globe* (1719), and *Serious Reflections during the Life and Surprising Adventures of Robinson Crusoe: With His Vision of the Angelick World* (1720).[10] In this trilogy we see Defoe attempting to write China into a new kind of narrative that he helped invent – the novel of formal realism, written in a non-classical, plain and simple idiom, offering a supposedly authentic account of the modern world as experienced by an ordinary man. Here Defoe was treading on very uncertain ground. Although there were numerous Jesuit and other continental sources in circulation at that time documenting travels in China, these were based on the experience of a very limited number of missionaries and diplomats. No eyewitness accounts of Englishmen in China existed at the time that Defoe was writing. Peter Mundy's story of his voyages to India and China with the English East India Company existed only in manuscript form and was not published until the twentieth century, and Lord Anson's account of China would only appear in 1748.[11] Defoe's choice of character – a brooding, self-righteous middle-class English man with a taste for adventure and a knack for colonial business in the New World, as well as a limited set of imaginative and intellectual tools to deal with cultural difference – heightened the challenge of writing China into English modernity. Crusoe does not inhabit the bookish, classical world of Temple; he travels through the world with the sole textual mediation of the Bible. His experience of China, like all his experiences of the world beyond England, is deprived of the luxury of contemplative distance. He is thrust into China at the brink of disaster and has to find his way out with very little guidance other than his own native wits. In the process, he is forced to make sense of his own position vis-à-vis a culture that he understandably finds threatening and foreign. Defoe's decision to extend his "multinational thought-experiments" beyond the fixed confines of the Caribbean island in this first volume of the trilogy to the uncharted territory of China in the second volume is an index of the continuing centrality of China to definitions of English modernity in a world Defoe understands, above all, in terms of unprecedented maritime expansion, commercial opportunity, and racial and cultural conflict.[12] Charles H. Parker has recently described the early modern period as a "a period in world history characterized by intense cultural, political, military, and economic contact," where "a host of individuals, companies, tribes, states, and empires clashed and competed" without any region standing "at the apex of world dominion." Defoe's novel, I suggest, is an acute response to the "integration of global space" produced by the early modern forms of global exchange, and attests to his far-ranging interests in the global processes of his time.[13] By focusing on these economic and political aspects of the early modern world, Defoe moves effectively away from the scholarly Temple–Wotton debate to take up pressing practical questions about how to deal with the mounting trade imbalance with China and combat the English weakness for Chinese manufactured goods. For Defoe, these were the real issues – not whether Confucius could be counted as a significant political philosopher or Chinese medicine was any good. In this sense, Defoe's work is prescient. With him, China emerges decisively out of the land of legend and speculation to become a modern economic, political, and cultural problematic.

Building on the pioneering critical work done by Robert Markley and Hans Turley on the *Farther Adventures*, in this chapter I contextualize

Defoe's engagement with China specifically within the quarrel between the ancients and the moderns. Defoe's quarrel with China was, as Markley and Turley note, fundamentally economical and religious. However, it was also a quarrel about the merits of Chinese military science and the utopian image of China as a naturally protected, self-sufficient and self-enclosed island. Defoe's 'modern' approach to China was basically Wottonian in outlook and a pointed rejoinder to Temple; it aimed at debunking stories of Chinese scientific and technological superiority, while pointing to problems of heterodoxy posed by Chinese culture and religion. And yet, as I will show, his Crusoe trilogy remains imaginatively imbricated in China in self-contradictory ways. Lucinda Cole has recently shown us that Crusoe's island is not so much 'realist' as 'apparitional' in presenting "not an open, dynamic ecosystem but a closed, zoomorphic world in which Crusoe hunts, gathers, farms, and stores under metaphysically secured conditions."[14] Correlatively, I suggest, Crusoe is haunted by an ideal of a perfectly fortified and independent self that hyperbolically mimics the political fantasy of China's Great Wall.

A "Poetics of Fortification"

Of the three inventions that were routinely invoked as proof of modern superiority over the ancients (and, ironically, as examples of ancient Chinese ingenuity) – gunpowder, printing, and the compass – it is most of all gunpowder that visibly dominates the imagination of *The Life and Strange Surprizing Adventures*. Gunpowder is the *sine qua non* of Crusoe's island survival, the instrument that raises him safely above the threat posed by savages of all kinds. If there is a dream of science that suffuses Defoe's novel, it is a dream of the gun's safe and civilizing power. In the lengthy account of Crusoe's tumultuous early career before his shipwreck, when he is first a Guinea trader, then a white slave in Barbary, and finally a Brazilian colonist, Crusoe uses the gun in an admirably controlled way. Crusoe only admits to trading in "Toys and Trifles" such as "Beads, Toys, Knives, Scissars, Hatchets, bits of Glass, and the like" in exchange for "Gold Dust, *Guinea* Grains, Elephants Teeth, &c." as well as "*Negroes*" with the Africans in Guinea – even though we know, from historical records, that guns were routinely exchanged for slaves in western Africa (1: 68, 85). When Crusoe escapes from his Moorish slave master with the help of a Moor he calls Moely and a Maresco slave named Xury, he points a gun at Moely (and, presumably, later also at Xury) only to make Moely jump into the sea and swim back to shore and to persuade Xury to escape with him. No manslaughter occurs during his voyage along the African coast with Xury; Crusoe uses his gun only to kill a lion and a leopard, mostly for the narrative effect of proving his modernity before the astonished African natives. As to Crusoe on his Caribbean island, he is so outlandishly over-armed that the net effect is comical. He initially walks about with a gun on his shoulder, as well as a saw, hatchet, and pouches for gunpowder and shot in his belt; after he finds remainders of a cannibal feast on the island, he doubles his armor, adding "a great broad Sword" and two pistols to his armor, but the effect is still mostly droll (1: 180). If anything, his excessive armor makes his hunting skills seem all that less impressive. Crusoe fantasizes about digging a hole under the place where the cannibals make their fire and blowing them all up in one stroke with a massive dose of gunpowder, or alternatively lying in ambush with "three Guns, all double loaded," and letting the guns "fly at them," then "falling in upon them" with his pistols and sword so that "if there was twenty I should kill them all" (1: 181). But too many scruples about "the Lawfulness of it" as well as the prudence of such an action stop him in his tracks (1: 203). The first shot he takes at a man is in clear self-defense, when one of the cannibals aims an arrow at him in the episode where Friday runs practically into his arms. Real gunfire comes only very late in the novel, when Crusoe discovers the cannibals on the brink of butchering "a white Man" (1: 229). This is a scene of infamy that finally overpowers his qualms and makes him lead Friday into battle. Even then, he is curiously hesitant. Friday is said to be the better marksman ("*Friday* took his Aim so much better than I, that on the Side that he shot, he kill'd two of them, and wounded three more; and on my Side, I kill'd one, and wounded two" [1: 230]). And he gladly arms the Spaniard he rescues with a pistol and sword, delegating more killing to him while he watches ("I kept my Piece in my Hand still, without firing, being willing to keep my Charge ready; because I had given the *Spaniard* my Pistol, and Sword" [1: 231]). Likewise, in the climactic scene where he rescues an English captain whose sailors have mutinied against him, Crusoe delegates most of the killing (which in any case is kept to a bare minimum) to the captain and his faithful followers and instead uses intelligent tricks, including theatrics, to subdue the mutineers and secure the ship that finally takes him back to England.

In light of these scenes, we could say that *The Life and Strange Surprizing Adventures* mounts an implicit and ambiguous defense of gunpowder as "a humane and beneficial instrument." As Roy Wolper notes, gunpowder posed a challenge for the apologists of modern inventions. Printing was generally championed for spreading learning; the compass for saving lives, opening the world to modern geographical discoveries, and making the world one commonwealth.[15] Gunpowder, however, was obviously a violent invention, capable of wreaking great destruction and taking numerous lives. Various lines of argument were developed in the service of what Wolper calls "the rhetoric of gunpowder." George Hakewill argued, rather unconvincingly, in *An Apologie or Declaration of the Power and Providence of God* that the terror of gunpowder would prevent battle: "But sure it seemes that *God* in his providence had reserved this Engine for these times, that by the cruell force and terrible roaring of it, men might the rather be deterred from assaulting one another in hostile and warlike manner."[16] Others were more open about their faith in the role of gunpowder in advancing colonial enterprise. Joseph Glanvill, for one, waxed rhapsodic when he noted how the new "*Thunder* and *Lightning*" had reduced the West Indies to "*easie prey.*" He optimistically intoned, "And now by the gaining of that mighty *Continent*, and the numerous *fruitful Iles* beyond the Atlantick, we have obtained a *larger* Field of *Nature*, and have thereby an *advantage* for *more Phaenomena*, and *more helps* both for *Knowledge* and for *Life*"; "And so these *Engines* of *Destruction*, in a *sense* too are *Instruments* of *Knowledge.*"[17] However, these arguments were dropped by later apologists of modern progress such as Thomas Sprat, Thomas Blount, William Wotton, and William Derham. Wotton's own catalogue in the *Reflections* of "Instruments invented by the Moderns, which have helped to advance Learning," consists of printing and engraving on the one hand (as instruments that are "useful to all Parts of Learning" [1694: 169]) and, on the other hand, "*Telescopes, Microscopes,* the *Thermometer,* the *Baroscope,* the Air-Pump, Pendulum-Clocks*" (1694: 170).[18] As to the magnet, he concedes Temple's point that the loadstone was "anciently known." However, Wotton argues that it was "a Stone which the Ancients admired without ever examining to what Uses it might be applied" (1694: 246, 245). The compass, he declares, is the "Original" of "noble, pleasant and useful Propositions in *Geography, Astronomy* and *Navigation*" (1694: 247). Answering Temple's charge that the new geography in the service of "endless Gains and Wealth" has mapped out "many original Nations, which we call Barbarous, and I am sure, have treated them, as if we hardly esteemed them to be a Part of Mankind" (1690: 49), Wotton retorts, "If these Sciences have brought to us the Wealth of the *Indies,* if they have enlarged the Commerce and Intercourse of Mankind, it is so far from being a Disparagement to the Industry of the Moderns" (Wotton 1694: 247–48). However, Wotton refrained from claiming gunpowder for modern science, even though he did claim it for the Christians.[19]

Defoe, on the other hand, clearly lists gunpowder as a modern invention in *A General History of Discoveries and Improvements*. He dates it precisely to the fifteenth century, when (according to his history) printing and the compass were also invented. Noting that "Powder and Ball, at once put a new Face, not upon the Armies only, but upon the very War" (3: 229), Defoe gives "Improvements in the Art of War" a legitimate place in his "Discourse" (3: 229). He even makes the bizarre argument that, whereas premodern war had men marching up to battle behind "the burnish'd Iron" of "Greaves and Helmets," modern war made men "shew the true Courage and Gallantry of a Soldier" by making them "quit their retreat behind their Iron Walls" and march "boldly" into "the Mouth of the Cannon and Musquet" (3: 230). He also notes that the "fatal Invention" of gunpowder has necessitated "modern Improvements of Fortifications," in the "manner of approaching and attacks in Seiges and Stormings," and new forms of " *Tormentarii*, or Artillery of several kinds, besides the mere Invention of Cannon; such as *Mortars, Patereroes, Hawitzers, Chambers, Bombs, Carkasses, Stinkpots, Hand Grenades, cum multis aliis*, all perfectly new" (3: 231). As to the theory that "almost all our nicest Discoveries were found out, and in practice in China before they were discover'd here," Defoe pointedly says, "This I believe nothing of, and give less credit to what they talk of having several Arts which we have not." He will admit that "Japanning, or Lacquer, cannot be imitated, nor their China Ware." However, he is convinced that "it is want of the Materials" or "want of Climate," rather than "want of the Skill or Knowledge" that has left these "Arts" out of European reach (3: 226).

By describing Crusoe's modernity as empowered by the gun, Defoe clarifies the larger political ramifications of the ancients-and-moderns debate in an age of empire. In the Robinson Crusoe trilogy, science matters because it translates into better navigation, greater gun power, easier settlement and conquest. However hard he tries to smooth over the colonizing process, Defoe is very straightforward about the essential linkage between "guns and sails."[20] This is particularly true of *Farther Adventures*, which depicts gunpowder in a much more troubling light. Whereas Defoe shields Crusoe from the nastiest aspects of maritime expansion while he is confined to his Caribbean island, in *Farther Adventures* Crusoe is thrown into a much more forbidding, hostile, and violent world. The second Crusoe novel features rape and massacre in Madagascar, a mutiny in the Indian Ocean, a pirate chase in the South China seas, and wild skirmishes with Tartars in the Siberian hinterlands. It is as close to a blockbuster action movie as one can get in the eighteenth century.[21] It is not so surprising, then, that when Crusoe arrives in China he continues to think in terms of guns, fortresses, and walls. The scene in which he confronts the Great Wall of China, I propose, is a climactic moment that lays bare the militaristic aspects of global expansion. It is a scene that also parodies the dream of military impregnability that bears up Crusoe's island "Fortress" (1: 101) and "Wall" (1: 107). To clarify this point, let us backtrack and examine his buildings on the Caribbean island.

When Robinson Crusoe is shipwrecked on his island, his terror of being "devour'd by wild Beasts" leads him to spend his first night in a tree (1: 91). After canvassing the shipwrecked ship for supplies, he sets about finding himself "a proper Place for my Habitation" (1: 96), and eventually finds "a little Plain on the Side of a rising Hill" with "a hollow Place worn a little way in like the Entrance or Door of a Cave" (1: 100–01). Crusoe's description of his new home is painstakingly detailed. On this "little Plain" he builds a "Fence" in the shape of "a half Circle," driving "two Rows of strong Stakes" "into the Ground till they stood very firm like Piles." In between the rows, he piles up "Pieces of Cable … in Rows one upon another, within the Circle," eventually building a "Fence … so strong, that neither Man or Beast could get into it or over it" – discounting himself (1: 101). Inside this fence, he builds himself a "double" Tent ("*viz.* One smaller Tent within, and one larger Tent above it"), and then, working his way into the rock, also a "Cave" that serves as a "Cellar" or "Kitchin" to his "House" (1: 101–02). Crusoe does not install a door in his fence. Instead, he uses a "Ladder to go over the Top," so that he can be "compleatly fenc'd in, and fortify'd … from all the World" (1: 101), and so "that there might be no Sign in the Out-side of my Habitation" (1: 116). Later, "being still jealous of my being attack'd by some Body," he fortifies this "Fence or Wall" (1: 113) – this "compleat Enclosure" (1: 116) – by raising "a kind of Wall up against it of Turfs, about two Foot thick on the Out-side" (1: 107). Crusoe comments on this "Wall": "I thought I should never be perfectly secure 'till this Wall was finish'd; and it is scarce credible what inexpressible Labour every Thing was done with, especially the bringing Piles out of the Woods, and driving them into the Ground, for I made them much bigger than I need to have done" (1: 113). "When this Wall was finished," he adds, and "the Outside [was] double fenc'd with a Turff Wall rais'd up close to it," he persuaded himself he was finally in safety (1: 113). No sooner does he complete this wall, however, than "a terrible Earthquake" almost buries him alive in the cave, sending him scampering "over my Wall for Fear" (1: 116). Crusoe is sorely tempted to "remove my Habitation," but soon falls ill and gives up his project (1: 118). Later, however, he supplements his wall with "a double Row" of trees that provide "fine Cover" as well as "Defence" for his habitation (1: 135). When Crusoe discovers a footprint on the beach, he launches into yet another building fury, erecting "a second Fortification, in the same Manner of a Semicircle, at a Distance from my Wall, just where I had planted a double Row of Trees." He eventually ends up with "a double Wall" – an outer wall thickened with "every Thing I could think of, to make it strong," and an inner wall "above ten Foot thick" made by "continual bringing Earth out of my Cave, and laying it at the Foot of the Wall, and walking upon it." He fits his cannon into this wall so that, if need be, he can "fire all the seven Guns in two Minutes Time." This is still not enough, however. He plants his double wall round with "Stakes or Sticks of the *Osier* like Wood" that soon grows into a "thick Grove" and then "a Wood ... so monstrous thick and strong, that it was indeed impassable; and no Men of what kind soever, would ever imagine that there was any Thing beyond it, much less a Habitation" (1: 175–76). Call it compulsion, obsession, mania, or neurosis. The furious building going on in these passages bespeaks psychic pain. Crusoe's architecture is structured in terms of repeating doubles: a double tent (sheltering its shadowy double, the cave) surrounded by a double row of stakes, soon thickened into a double wall, outside which he plants a double row of trees, which in turn is fortified as another double wall protected by an impassable wood. Emphatic and yet endlessly insufficient, his doubled and redoubled structures paradoxically signal his agony of insecurity, his terror of encountering a human double. Crusoe's fortification is an architecture of fear and self-erasure – a perfect disappearing act.

In a suggestive essay entitled "No Man's Land: The Novel's First Geography," Joan DeJean reads "a poetics of fortification" behind this imaginative architecture.[22] Noting that Robinson's activities on his West Indian island essentially boil down to different versions of one paradigmatic and obsessive activity, she suggests that the birth of the novel is coeval with the rise of the "Vaubanian vision of the enclosed self."[23] DeJean is referring here to Sebastian Le Prestre de Vauban (1633–1707), Louis XIV's chief military engineer, who designed, refurbished, and rebuilt fortresses around France in pursuit of a completely fortified nation with impregnable borders. The key questions DeJean raises are: why does "defensive architecture" play such an important role in the work that critics have called the first modern English novel? What function do Crusoe's fortifications serve, and how are they related to the project of the realist novel? DeJean proposes that Crusoe's architecture "reveals that the original space of that novel, the space at the novel's origin, is the fortress." The fortress "marks the limits of Crusoe's self," setting up a "demarcation between inside and outside, Self and Other, civilized and cannibal that is in turn the foundation of his self-definition."[24] In other words, the modern novel imagines a "defensive" and "exclusionary" self that defines itself in dichotomous, oppositional terms, against its "potential enemies, barbarian, Other." At the same time, however, DeJean suggests that Defoe's novel "reveals an awareness of the limitations of this Vaubanian vision of the enclosed self as the self intact."[25] No wall or fortification can shut out Crusoe's exorbitant fear of God's avenging angel or man-eating humans. As she points out, when Crusoe dreams that he is visited by an angel "with a long Spear or Weapon in his Hand, to kill" him for his sins, he is "sitting on the Ground on the Out-side of my Wall" (1: 122). The dream reveals "that every fortress inevitably creates its no man's land" – that "spatial paradox," that space just beyond the wall that is "defined by its lack of definition," "unowned and under no one's jurisdiction."[26] In England, DeJean notes, the term referred to the area just outside the wall of the city of London, a space historically reserved for executions. She then proceeds to make a most interesting point:

> The expression 'no man's land' enters English literature in the work often referred to as its first modern novel, *Robinson Crusoe*, when Defoe's hero speaks of "a kind of Border, that might be called no Man's Land" (*OED*). Its appearance there was perhaps inevitable, for in his narrative of man's struggle against nature Defoe assigned a central role to an activity never mentioned in the actual accounts of shipwreck victims that served as model for Robinson's other activities, namely the construction of fortifications.[27]

It is not clear from this brilliant and yet oddly underdeveloped passage whether or not DeJean is fully aware of the beauty of her remarks, for she limits them to Crusoe's island experience. Her reference to the *OED* and the generic title *Robinson Crusoe*, as well as her complete silence with regard to *Farther Adventures* in her article, would suggest that she was writing with only *The Life and Strange Surprizing Adventures* in mind. But it is only when we see precisely where and when this passage appears in the trilogy that we can appreciate its full power.

The passage in question occurs *not* in *The Life and Strange Surprizing Adventures* where Crusoe builds so many fortifications after shipwreck, but in *Farther Adventures* where Crusoe, his long Caribbean sojourn behind him, has left England once more to satisfy his rambling desires and traveled all the way to China. Crusoe is here departing from China, surprisingly not by sea but by land. He has just "pass'd the great *China* Wall, made for a Fortification against the *Tartars*," and entered into "a vast great wild Desart" in the company of a Russian caravan (2: 183, 185).

> I ask'd whose Dominion this was in, and they told me, this was a kind of Border, that might be called *no Man's Land*; being a Part of the Great *Karakathie*, or Grand *Tartary*, but that however it was all reckon'd to *China*; but that there was no Care taken here, to preserve it from the Inroads of Thieves, and therefore it was reckon'd the worst Desart in the whole World, tho' we were to go over some much larger. (2: 185)

This desert, this no man's land, is a kind of second border – a border that supplements "the great *China* Wall" in that its expanse is "all reckon'd to *China*." But it is a place of anarchy rather than order. Indeed, it appears to be a safe haven for thieves – so much so, that it is "reckon'd the worst Desart in the whole World." The Chinese do not care to police it, for it is officially Tartar territory; Tartars do not care to populate and police it, either, for it lies too close to the Chinese border. When DeJean refers to Crusoe's island fortifications as a "miniature Great Wall," however, it is not to amplify on this surprising Chinese connection between *The Life and Strange Surprizing Adventures* and *Farther Adventures* but to draw an allegorical lesson about "the hysteria and violence accompanying the philosophical and political foundations of all Great Walls." The Vaubanian fortification, DeJean notes, was intended as a metaphor for "a king seeking ever more absolute control over his domain," as well as a spatial definition of the "concept of enmity": all those inside the Vaubanian complex were French and civilized; all those outside were defined as "enemies, barbarian, Other." However, any Great Wall is also necessarily a failed metaphor for the dialectical reason that, in order to create a space of safety, it also preserves a space of danger; in drawing the line between civilization and barbarism, it attests to the fragility of the former. In attempting to map and allocate space, it creates "territory defined by its lack of definition" – the no man's land.[28] Thus, DeJean reads Crusoe as a Vaubanian subject who obsessively builds his fortifications not because of any actual danger but because they are necessary for his self-definition.

To use the architect Robin Evans's formulation, Crusoe's "miniature Great Wall" is an example of "the war against information," of the "strange way in which human beings render their world inhabitable by circumscribing and forgetting about those parts of it that offend them." All walls,

Evans notes, equate "the flow of information with psychic disintegration and danger."[29] Walls attempt to erase and forget the environment by becoming a substitute environment. Evans, who interprets the Great Wall of China as "the principle of information exclusion writ large," thus takes it as an example of the "recrudescent fear of the unassimilable" mobilized into "retreat" on an unprecedented and unrivalled scale.[30] Although walls may look like a defensive solution to an onslaught of unacceptable reality, however, they may not be "simple barriers to energy-transfer," but embody "the martial declaration of the intent to repel all delinquent perception and all illicit communion" by "eliminating that part of the other more disparate world which fails to conform to it." On this reading, Crusoe's fortifications are visual translations of his "military metaphysics."[31] They are extensions of the numerous guns, swords, and knives that encumber his every outing.

Another suggestive context for Crusoe's wall-building and wall-gazing can be found in Patricia Seed's work on European "ceremonies of possession" in the New World. As Seed points out, whereas the Spanish turned to ritualized speech and the French undertook elaborate processions, the English used the remarkably mundane acts of building houses, pitching fences, and planting gardens to claim ownership of their new territories. Crusoe's stakes, fences, piles that mark his "compleat Enclosure" (1: 116) are clearly related to the "hedgerows, fences, and paling" that were the preferred property boundaries of the English occupants in the American colonies. The New World houses, gardens, and fences that inscribed ownership on the land were a natural extension of the peculiarly "English preoccupation with boundaries and boundary markers as significant markers of ownership" that characterized the earliest English property transactions, as well as the enclosure movement that was rapidly converting the English commons into private property.[32] Once territory was marked in this fashion, it took on legal and political significance. Seed's analysis helps us identify the wall, or the overblown fence, in the Crusoe trilogy as a nexus between English property rights, colonial settlement, and military technology. At the same time, Crusoe's "poetics of fortification," which clearly links the first two books of the Crusoe trilogy, limns life beyond the pale of the English nation state, in locations construed as no man's lands, where the individual's most lasting resources are exposed as fear, retreat, and a war against the environment.[33] For this reason, Crusoe's encounter with the Great Wall begs to be read, at least in part, as a commentary on his own technology of the self.

"This Mighty *Nothing* Call'd a Wall"

Farther Adventures picks up where *The Life and Strange Surprizing Adventures* leaves off, in the year 1694 to be precise. Born in 1632, he is "61 Years of Age" at the start of *Farther Adventures* (2: 5). A preview of the sequel is given at the end of *The Life and Strange Surprizing Adventures*, thus: "my Wife dying, and my Nephew coming Home with good Success from a Voyage to *Spain*, my Inclination to go Abroad, and his Importunity prevailed and engag'd me to go in his Ship, as a private Trader to the *East Indies*: This was in the Year 1694" (1: 284). Since Crusoe returns to England in 1687 after thirty-five years of absence, he has just spent seven years in Europe when his wanderlust hits again. This time around, the novel is more forgiving of Crusoe's "Distemper of Wandring" (2: 10). His wife has died and he feels depressed and lost, "like a Ship without a Pilot"; all his former taste for "the pleasant innocent Amusements of my Farm, and my Garden, my Cattel and my Family, which before entirely possest me, were nothing to me" (2: 10). This suggestion of former conjugal and domestic bliss with a woman whose name we never even learn is not entirely convincing. As Christopher Hill has pointed out, his marriage and his wife's death occur "unceremoniously" in the very same sentence in *The Life and Strange Surprizing Adventures*; she does not survive beyond the first few pages of *Farther Adventures*.[34] Indeed, Crusoe's claim that "the World look'd aukwardly round me; I was as much a Stranger in it, in my Thoughts, as I was in the *Brasils* … and as much alone … as I was in my Island" suggests that it is not the memory of his wife, but the memory of his life prior to his marriage that is uppermost in his mind (2: 9).

A convenient opportunity to pursue his passion for travel presents itself to Crusoe when his nephew, a "Commander of a Ship" recently returned from "a short Voyage to *Bilboa*," invites him to come with him on "a Voyage … to the *East Indies*, and to *China*, as private Traders" (2: 10). It is not so much the idea of China, however, but the thought of being able to stop by his island, he says, that makes him take up the offer. Crusoe is very insistent about his lack of interest in trade per se. It is not the lure of trade but rather his need for "an active Life" that sets him voyaging again, he claims, and he initially refuses to "promise to go any farther than my own Island" (2: 10–11). It is only when his nephew tells him that his merchants would never allow him to take a detour that might take an additional three or four months and pose numerous dangers to "a loaden Ship of such value" that Crusoe is persuaded to undertake the full journey (2: 11). A full half of

Farther Adventures features Crusoe back on his island and dealing with the messiness of colonial business for about twenty-five days. Once he is finally "done with my Island" (2: 125), he sails on to "the *Brasils*," "to the *Cape de bon Esperance*, or as we call it, the *Cape of Good Hope*," then "the Island of *Madagascar*" (2: 127) where the shipmen become embroiled in a violent "massacre" of the natives (2: 136).[35] This massacre leads to a breach between Crusoe and the shipmates. When Crusoe, who is outraged by the bloodshed, takes to "frequent Preaching" (2: 140) about how "God would blast the Voyage" for "all the Blood they shed that Night," the shipmates mutiny against Crusoe and the captain (2: 139). Thus, despite the fact that Crusoe's investments make him is a "considerable Owner of the Ship" (2: 141), his nephew is forced to leave him in Bengal, "the remotest Part of the World," "near three thousand Leagues by Sea farther off from *England*, than I was at my Island" (2: 143). In Bengal, he luckily finds "good Lodging in the House of an *English* Woman" and meets an English merchant who persuades him to invest in "a Trading Voyage to *China*" (2: 143–44). Crusoe is again careful to state that "Trade was none of my Element" (2: 144). It is, rather, "Rambling," the "Proposal for seeing any Part of the World which I had never seen before," that makes him embark once again on a shipping journey (2: 144). Yet when they manage at last to procure a ship and gather together a motley crew of seamen, they do not immediately sail off to China but, surprisingly, spend six years engaging in maritime inter-Asian or "country" trade. They travel to Sumatra, Siam, Suskan, and back, trafficking in arrack and opium; they also visit the Spice Islands (Crusoe mentions "*Borneo*, and several Islands, whose Names I do not remember") and bring back cloves and nutmeg, which they sell to Persians (2: 146). Buoyed up by their success, they then buy a Dutch ship, a "Coaster, not an *European* Trader" (2: 146), with which they make many successful journeys "backward and forward," before finally sailing to China by way of "the *Philippine* and *Mollucco* Isles" and Siam (2: 146–47). Crusoe's actions suggest that his repeated disclaimers regarding his economic motives need not be taken at face value. After all, he manages to make a whopping profit out of this journey to the East Indies, just as he conveniently discovers after his twenty-eight years of island life that his Brazilian plantation has brought him more wealth than he knows what to do with. However, Crusoe's description of his arrival and stay in China suggests that he is not merely deflecting our attention away from what Watt calls his "economic individualism" when he disavows money as his primary motive. By denying trade as his real interest, Crusoe dissociates himself from the English East India Company, about which he has few good things to say. When Crusoe lands in Bengal, he notes that he "came hither without any Concern with the *English East-India* Company" and that the Company is therefore very unlikely to offer him any help in returning to England (2: 143). The East India Company officers, he later comments, grow exceedingly rich during their stay in India (they "get such very great Estates as they do, and sometimes come Home worth 60, to 70 100 thousand Pound at a Time") because they are doing so much illegal private trading on the side (2: 145). Crusoe is also a private trader, but he has no company backing him up, and for all intents and purposes is indistinguishable from a pirate, as his ensuing troubles quickly demonstrate.

It is while Crusoe and his fellow English merchant are embarked in "the River of *Cambodia*" that they learn to their chagrin from "a Gunner's Mate, on board an *English East-India* Ship," that the men they bought their Dutch ship from were mutineers turned pirates; that their ship is in fact a pirate ship and will surely be seized; that Crusoe and his partner are liable to be mistaken for pirates, tortured, and killed (2: 148). This information terrifies Crusoe, who is well aware of the fate met by Englishmen at the hands of the Dutch at Amboyna in 1623. Crusoe therefore decides to steer clear of all ports where Dutch ships may be embarked and to sail directly on to China. In a surprising twist, the ships that eventually give him chase turn out to be English. Despite all the signs he makes with a "Gun without Ball," "a Flag of Truce," and a "speaking Trumpet," Crusoe is unable to stop their threatening approach and ends up firing guns at them (2: 151–52). Mistaken for a pirate, Crusoe ends up acting like one, and sails "quite out of the Course of all *European* Ships" (2: 153). In this inauspicious manner, effectively turned into an outlaw, Crusoe and his company sail on to "the Bay of *Tonquin*" (2: 155), then to "the Island *Formosa*" (2: 159), and finally to "a little port call'd *Quinchang*" in "the Great Gulph of *Nanquin*" where, with the help of an old Portuguese pilot who acts as their guide to China, they manage to sell the ship off to a Japanese merchant (2: 163). It is at this point, nearly 300 pages into the 1719 edition of *Farther Adventures*, that Crusoe finally finds himself in China proper, shipless, unable to trade (they need to wait four months for the next trade fair to take place), uncertain of the route home, and finally in a position to satisfy that "restless Desire of seeing the World" of his of which the reader has heard so much (2: 145). Crusoe does not show much desire to see China, however. The two cities he chooses to visit – "*Nanquin*" and "*Peking*" – fail to impress him in any way. Indeed, his stay in China only proves to him that China is "not … worth naming, or worth my while to write of, or any that shall come after me to read" (2: 173). He has spent barely a week in Peking when he is told about "a great Caravan of *Muscovite* and *Polish* Merchants in the City" proposing to travel by land from China to Europe (2: 178). Crusoe decides that this is a godsend and quickly joins the caravan. Thus, whereas China is identified as the ostensible destination of *Farther Adventures*, it takes a death threat to push Crusoe into China, and he is no sooner in China than he finds a way to leave it.

The sections of *Farther Adventures* that deal with the Great Wall occur at this juncture when Crusoe, having seen a little of China but nothing much to his liking, opts to follow a multi-national caravan back to Europe.[36] The caravan reaches the Great Wall, extolled as "the Wonder of the World" by the Chinese caravan guide, a few days after departing from Peking. Crusoe makes an unusual pause in his narrative, twice declaring that he "stood still an Hour" to look at the wall "on every Side, near, and far off":

> In two Days more, we pass'd the Great *China* Wall, made for a Fortification against the *Tartars*; and a very great Work it is; going over Hills and Mountains in a needless Track, where the Rocks are impassible, and the Precipices such, as no Enemy could possibly enter, or indeed climb up, or where if they did, no Wall could hinder them; they tell us, its Length, is near a thousand *English* Miles, but that the Country is five hundred in a strait measur'd Line, which the Wall bounds, without measuring the Windings and Turnings it takes; 'tis about four Fathom high, and as many thick in some Places. (2: 183)

When the guide, "mighty eager to hear my Opinion of it," asks Crusoe's opinion of the Wall, he tersely comments that it is "a most excellent Thing to keep off the *Tartars*" (2: 183). Initially, the Chinese guide is taken in by this apparent compliment, but is later struck "dumb all the rest of the Way" when he learns Crusoe's true opinion of "his fine Story of the *Chinese* Power and Greatness":

> do you think it would stand out an Army of our Country People, with a good Train of Artillery; or our Engineers, with two Companies of Miners; would not they batter it down in ten Days, that an Army might enter in Battallia, or blow it up in the Air, Foundation and all, *that there should be no Sign of it left*? (2: 183, my emphasis)

Far from being impressed by this "Wonder of the World," Crusoe sees it as a most superfluous and "needless" addition to an already fortified *natural* border. The Wall is also "needless" in the sense that, though it might keep out a pathetic troop of Tartars, it would hardly stand a chance against the artillery of a properly equipped European army. In this way, Crusoe blows up the Wall as an empty sign. This "mighty *Nothing* call'd a Wall" is, for

Crusoe, "something like the *Picts* Wall, and so famous in *Northumberland*, and built by the *Romans*" (2: 183). It is a futile signifier of a ridiculously overestimated military might – an antiquated thing, a relic, whose time has long run out.[37] Crusoe's grudging acknowledgement that he spent a full hour surveying this "Wonder of the World," however, suggests that his fantasy of blowing it "up in the Air, Foundation and all," is a response to something grander, something closer to the sublime, than Hadrian's Wall. Unfortunately, the woodcut illustration of this scene included in the third edition of *Farther Adventures* (1722) captures none of the repressed anxiety and attraction at work in this rare moment in which Crusoe engages in what looks very close to aesthetic contemplation (*Figure 2*). Crusoe's main point that the wall stretches over a vast link of impassable rocks, precipices, and mountains is entirely lost in the flat and level plain; the wall is reduced to a bathetic stage prop with a passageway that looks more like an inviting frame than a mighty military boundary. As an illustration it is appallingly inattentive to Defoe's text, yet its interpretation of the Great Wall does capture something of Crusoe's near comical inability to process it in realist terms. What Crusoe offers instead is a polemic.[38]

Like the immediately preceding scene in which Crusoe is made "curious indeed to see" a porcelain house that turns out to be "nothing but ... a Timber-House ... plaister'd with the Earth that makes *China* Ware," the Great Wall scene sets up a paradigmatic encounter with Chinese achievement only to puncture its claims to greatness (2: 181). What Crusoe learns from these encounters is only that the Chinese "excel in their Accounts" and tell "incredible Things of their Performance" (2: 181), to the "Contempt of all the World but themselves" (2: 176). Crusoe's passage through China is throughout set up as a conflict between hearsay and, to use Anthony Pagden's term, "autopsy" – "the authority of the eye witness" who possesses the "privileged understanding which those present at an event have over all those who have only read or been told about it."[39] Crusoe's own experience in China, however brief, has convinced him that his experience explodes the existing canon on China:

I must confess, it seem'd strange to me, when I came home, and heard our People say such fine Things of the Power, Riches, Glory, Magnificence, and Trade of the *Chinese*; because I saw and knew that they were a contemptible Hoord or Crowd of ignorant sordid Slaves; subjected to a Government qualified only to rule such a People ... As their Strength and their Grandeur, so their Navigation, Commerce, and Husbandry is imperfect and impotent, compar'd to the same Things in *Europe*; also in their Knowledge, their Learning, their Skill in the Sciences; they have Globes and Spheres, and

Fig 2   "R. Crusoe with the Muscovite Caravan pass the Chinese Wall from Peking." From Daniel Defoe, *The Farther Adventures of Robinson Crusoe*, 4th ed. (London, 1722). 1264.a.24.
© The British Library Board.

a Smatch of the Knowledge of the Mathematicks; but when you come to enquire into their Knowledge, how short-sighted are the wisest of their Students! they know nothing of the Motion of the Heavenly Bodies; and so grosly and absurdly ignorant, that when the Sun is eclips'd, they think 'tis a great Dragon has assaulted it, and run away with it, and they fall a clattering with all the Drums and Kettles in the Country, to fright the Monster away, just as we do to hive a Swarm of Bees. (2: 174)

Seeing is believing, Crusoe insists. Nothing he has seen in China matches up to the reports he has heard about "their Strength, and their Grandeur." On the contrary, everything he sees proves the very opposite. And yet, as this passage amply illustrates, Crusoe's claims always outstrip his own autoptic testimony, which he constantly undermines. To support his argument about the untruthfulness of all favorable reports about China, Crusoe does not hesitate to appeal to incidents and histories that he has never witnessed.[40] And in order to account for his inability to describe China in any detail, he makes a very lame excuse: he purports to have fallen into the water as he was crossing a river on a horse, and spoiled a "Pocket-Book, wherein I had set down the Names of several People and Places which I had Occasion to remember" (2: 177). In lieu of the "descriptive and denotative use of language" which, according to Watt, characterizes the modern novel, then, what we have in these China episodes is a flagrant violation of that

> premise, or primary convention, that the novel is a full and authentic report of human experience, and is therefore under an obligation to satisfy the reader with such details of the story as the individuality of the actors concerned, the particulars of the times and places of their actions, details which are presented through a more largely referential use of language than is common in other literary forms.[41]

In lieu of submitting a detailed description of China undertaken in his own name, Crusoe presents the reader with scenarios lifted out of other people's accounts and imaginary battles where pan-European armies take down Chinese cities and walls.

If Crusoe, as DeJean puts it, defines himself first and foremost an enclosed and fortified self on his Caribbean island, the Great Wall of China is in some ways a monumentalized, public, political version of his ideal self. Both Crusoe's miniature Great Wall and China's Great Wall project images of the enclosed self – in Crusoe's case, his embattled, marooned, private British self; in the Chinese case, the perfectly fortified state. As Susan Stewart says, "We find the miniature at the origin of private, individual history, but we find the gigantic at the origin of public and natural history."[42] The gigantic, spectacular nature of China's Great Wall signals to the gigantic nature of the state; Crusoe's comically miniaturized, self-concealing Great Wall expresses his feeling of smallness and vulnerability on his island. Both the miniature and the gigantic Great Walls aim at creating an illusion of an enclosed space, a space of safety, which creates in turn "a tension or dialectic between inside and outside, between private and public property, between the space of the subject and the space of the social," between the self and the other.[43] If Defoe identifies this same dialectic in Crusoe's walls and the Great Wall of China, however, the reasons he gives for their breakdown are very different. As Evans might say, at the end of *The Life and Strange Surprizing Adventures* Crusoe manages to lower his "barriers to energy-transfer," and to end his "the war against information" by inviting select strangers on his shore into his fort and conferring his civility on them.[44] His walls, fences, houses, and gardens transform the wilderness of the island into a domestic home. As Cole notes, by the time he returns in *The Farther Adventures* to his island, its mixed population of Englishmen, Spaniards, and Caribbean natives has reinvented his island fortress with beehive-like wicker-ware houses, complete with outer and inner walls. These apian houses signal the successful re-engineering of basket-weaving artisanry (whose native Caribbean roots Defoe predictably denies, just as he turns the Carib barbecue and canoe into Crusoe's own inventions) into a grand "architectural apotheosis of the agro-colonial ideal."[45]

In contrast, in *Farther Adventures* the Chinese Great Wall functions as an antiquated reminder of a fruitless and stagnant enmity that paradoxically has not separated the Chinese from the Tartars so much as blurred their difference. As Crusoe says while observing "Troops of *Tartars* roving about," "I wonder'd more that the *Chinese* Empire could be conquer'd by such contemptible Fellows; for they are a mere Hoord or Crowd of wild Fellows, keeping no Order, and understanding no Discipline, or manner of Fight" (2: 184). This pointed reference to the Qing conquest shows that Defoe was clearly aware that the Manchu Tartars had overtaken China, and that his sense of the "needlessness" of the Great Wall was informed by its inefficacy against the Manchu invasion. Crusoe's own understanding of the "military metaphysics" of walls gives him insight into the passivity and "recrudescent fear" behind the Great Wall's "martial declaration," so well proven by the fall of the Ming dynasty.[46] However, Defoe's intention in making Crusoe take on the Great Wall is not simply to make an allegorical point about walls in general or to point to its historical failure in Chinese history. With regard to China, Defoe's real aim, I suggest, is two-pronged. On the one hand, he uses the Great Wall to unmask China as a mythical European construct – as a product, in other words, of ideological mystification on the part of Europeans themselves. His particular target is the European image of China as a self-contained *"absolutum mikrokosmon,"* a "being independent and totally separated from the rest of the world," perfectly fortified by natural and man-made boundaries, a kind of utopian island.[47] The realist aspect of Crusoe's quick passage through China has to do with this negative project of demystification. At the same time, by making his hero pointedly pass through the Great Wall, Crusoe locates China in a highly specified, larger geopolitical landscape, proving it is not the impregnable island that it seems but a nation that, like all other nations, must struggle to define itself through political and economic transactions with the outside world. This becomes especially clear when we examine Defoe's choice of sources for Crusoe's unprecedented, madcap trek home through Siberia.

*"*This Back-Door Trade to *China*"

The image of China as an unreachable destination, hidden behind impassable mountains, deserts, and seas, is a constant in much of the literature on China that would have been available to Defoe at the time he was composing the Crusoe novels. Temple's description of China as a "Great and Ancient Kingdom" bound to the east and south by the ocean, to the north by the Great Wall, and to the west by "vast and unpassible Mountains or Deserts, which the Labour or Curiosity of no mortal Man has been ever yet known to have pierced thro or given any account of" is perfectly conventional (1690: 164). Jesuits and Dutch merchants had joined their voices to admire China's unique and enviable topography. Kircher marveled that "Nature in a manner hath contriv'd all this complex of Kingdoms inaccessible unto all others" by means of "scarcely Navigable" oceans, mountains admitting "no passage," deserts of "an immense vastness," and a Wall that the ancients would have "reckon'd ... amongst the seven Wonders of the World."[48] Likewise, Nieuhof wrote:

> *China* is not a little secure in regard of the adjacent Kingdoms, and the natural and strong Forts whereby this Kings Realm stands so intirely protected against all violence from without, that the like is hardly to be seen elsewhere; neither are there any Avenues found leading to this Monarchy, insomuch that it is so well provided and guarded, that it seems to be a World within it self, and separated from all the rest.[49]

These passages prove that the medieval image of China as a great isle, as illustrated in Mandeville's well-known phrase, "Cathay est vne grande ylle, belle et bonne, riche et bien marchande," continued to shape the Europeans' image of China even as they made new inroads into its interior.[50] As Timothy Billings points out, the image of China as a self-enclosed, naturally fortified island links it to the utopian imaginary. More's Utopia, too, is famously an island whose "totality, self-containment, and immutability" is a function of both natural and manmade geographical isolation.[51] China's status as a distant and impregnable world unto itself would not have excited such inordinate interest, however, if it were not for the reports of its almost unimaginable riches. Even the latest reports coming out of China were full of stunned testimony. Semedo marveled that "nature seems there to have laid upon heapes, what shee but scatters through the rest of the world"; China

> hath within its owne doors all that is necessary for mans life, together with all superfluity of delicacies: whence it hath, not only no need to take almes of other Countries; but, with what it is able to spare (which is both much and very good) it satisfieth the desires of the neighbouring and remote kingdoms, who have always a longing desire to see and enjoy it.[52]

Magalhães reported that there was so much gold in the Chinese mountains that "instead of Coining it into Money, to buy Necessities; it is it self a Commodity"; there was so an "inexhaustible Plenty of Silk," he exclaimed, that "the very Footmen that run by their Masters Horses, are clad in Sattin and Damask"; as to "Flesh, Fish, Fruit, and other Provisions," the Chinese "have all which we have in *Europe*, and many more Varieties that we have not," and "all so cheap, that I could never have believ'd it, had I not been convinc'd by my own Experience for Two and twenty years together that I liv'd at Court."[53]

By the time Defoe was composing *Farther Adventures*, however, the centuries-old image of China as a utopian and paradisal land of unimaginable wealth and plenty was beginning to give way to a more wary understanding based on the realities of the China trade in which the Europeans had a distinct disadvantage. As his later economic writings make abundantly clear, Defoe perceived China first and foremost as a European economic problem. As he writes in the 1729 *Advantages of Peace and Commerce; With Some Remarks on the East-India Trade*, the Chinese are trading "with *Europe* infinitely to its Loss, and to their own Gain," such that "all the ready Money of the other three Parts of the World, all the Gold and Silver of *Africa* and *America*, would be hardly able to serve for Returns."[54]

The balance of trade, in particular, could not be worse for Britain which has a lamentable weakness for things Chinese:

> We see the Produce of their Land is coveted by all the *Europeans*, and by us in Particular; witness, especially, their Tea, their *China* Ware, and several of their Drugs and other Growth of their Soil: And as for their Manufactures, they were not only brought hither in vast Quantities, but they became, as it were, the Terror of *Europe* in Trade, and of *Great Britain* in particular. (1729: 16–17)

Defoe is yet more succinct in the 1728 *Atlas Maritimus & Commercialis; Or, A General View of the World So far as relates to Trade and Navigation*, where he writes:

> *Europe* calls for a vast Variety of Goods from *Asia*:
> *Asia* calls for little or nothing from *Europe* but money.[55]

Unlike Crusoe who, most uncharacteristically for an East-Indies trader, shows little interest in Chinese markets or manufactures and spends all his time bad-mouthing Chinese cities, buildings, furniture, junks and barks, husbandry, sciences, clothing, horsemanship, food, and eating habits, Defoe adopts an even, measured tone in these economic and geographical writings where he notes that it is not only an overwhelming natural abundance that makes China economically strong but also "the prodigious Numbers, and inimitable Diligence and Application of its Inhabitants" (1729: 100). Lydia Liu may argue that Defoe disavows Chinese porcelain in *The Life and Strange Surprizing Adventures*; in the *Atlas Maritimus & Commercialis*, Defoe is very ready to concede the "Ingenuity and Art of the China Manufacturers" whose "wonderful Variety of their Work" is "such, as really is not only without Imitation, but in some Cases not to be attempted, or at least perform'd by any but the same People," particularly "their Lacquer and their China, and their Tea" (1728: 221). There are barbs, however. Defoe attributes the outstanding competitiveness of Chinese products to the "constant Application and Diligence" of the Chinese workers who labor "under the Hardship of so mean a Fare, and so hard a way of living" (1728: 221–22). If Chinese products are "made cheap to a surprise," it is because the workers have "neither strengthning or heartning Diet, or Money to purchase it, but who live upon Herbs, chewing the *Betele*, and such other Plants, with Roots and Fruits." Whereas even the English poor live heartily on "Beef and Mutton," and drink "Wine, Ale, Beer or Brandy," "Articles that eat deep" into their pockets, the Chinese consider their "highest Treats" to be "boil'd Rice and the like Vegetables"

(1728: 221). Though skilled in many arts, the Chinese are "the most effemi-
nate, weak-hearted People in the Universe" and "not the most accurate
Managers of their Ships and Barks" (1728: 222). This is a lucky stroke for
the "rest of the World," though, for "Were the *Chineses* a hardy, bold,
adventurous Nation at Sea, and a brave well-disciplin'd Nation at Land;
in a word, were they as good Sailors and Soldiers as the *English* or *Dutch*,
and with such a Number of Ships and Seamen as they have, what a Terror
to the rest of the World would they be?" (1728: 222–23). By repeatedly
linking "Terror" with "Trade," Defoe interprets global maritime trade as
a potentially violent conflict between different national states. Although
he argues for the advantages of "peace and commerce," he correlates commercial and naval power very clearly. Trade, and only trade, he argues,
keeps seamen "nourish'd, increas'd, and in Time of Peace employ'd"; creates
"Naval Strength" that makes them "terrible at Sea, as well as formidable on
Shore"; and allows them to "carry the War home to their Enemies Coasts,"
"look into every Port, knock at every Door, command Peace or War; and,
in a word, awe the World" (1729: 4). Trade is, in every sense, a loaded ship.

Defoe obviously had little time for the mythical image of China as a
secluded isle. Perhaps he saw this image as an imaginative compensation
for the difficulty Europeans had encountered in their efforts to open up
trade with China. No doubt he was well aware that, whereas the Portuguese
and the Dutch had repeatedly sent embassies in the latter half of the seventeenth century in the hope of setting up regular diplomatic relations and
trade treaties with China, their efforts had foundered amid the intricacies
of the Chinese tribute system and the Chinese lack of interest in European
trade items. China was, in this sense, a challenging frontier. Defoe knew
that it was not an aversion on the part of the Chinese to commerce per
se that was causing trade problems for Europe. His image of the Chinese
was that of a highly commercialized, industrious people who engaged in
a "prodigious Course" of inland trade and also enjoyed a bustling, "open
and free Trade" with other Asians along the Chinese coast (1728: 222–23).
As a journalist and political historian long interested in Russia's involvement in European politics, Defoe was also acutely aware of the growing
Sino-Russian trade along China's northern border. In *The Advantages of
Peace and Commerce*, he shows a keen interest in the 1727 Kyakhta Treaty
between Russia and China, which, following upon the Nerchinsk Treaty of
1689, cemented diplomatic relations between the two states and opened up
frontier trade in addition to caravan trade between Moscow and Peking.
When it came to China, Defoe took the position of conservative mercantilism rather than *laissez faire* and free trade.[56] As far as Defoe was concerned,

the only remedy for the hopelessly skewed trade imbalance with China was to "prohibit that Commerce, except what is absolutely necessary for the supply of *Europe*'s Wants" – i.e. "Salt-petre, Pepper, Spices, needful Drugs and Dye-stuffs, and the like." As to tea and coffee, "the two great Articles so much in Demand" in England, Defoe recommended that the British "transplant those Vegetables, and many more" to Africa and raise them in "our own Factories on the Coast of *Guinea*" (1729: 18–19). For this reason, he is alarmed rather than encouraged by the Kyakhta Treaty, which he construes as a "free Trade" treaty between "the two Empires" of China and Russia (1729: 29). The implications of such a treaty for Europe, as he sees it, are dire. When "Trade between *China* and *Russia* will be as safe and easy as it is or can be in *Europe* between one Province and another" (1729: 30), he warns, all of Europe's efforts to stem the China trade will come to naught, and a "Back-Door" will open up "by which all the most hurtful Part of the East-India Trade is like (and very quickly too) to break in upon them like a Flood" (1729: 19). In reality, the Nerchinsk and Kyakhta treaties were basically diplomatic treaties that included fairly minimalist provisions for trade as incentive and compromise rather than any full-fledged guarantees for free trade. China's chief motivation for signing the Nerchinsk Treaty was to resolve border skirmishes in the Amur River valley in Eastern Siberia and to enlist the Russians as allies against a rising Mongolian power (the Zunghars) to the northwest of China.[57] For Russia, the commercial motivation was strong, but even with the greater concessions won by the Kyakhta Treaty all trade with China remained strictly limited to two frontiers posts and triennial caravans from Moscow to Peking.[58]

In this context, Crusoe's caravan journey back to Europe from China via Russia reads as a simulation of this dangerous "back door" to Europe. Crusoe's dates match the dates of the Russian treaties. Since Crusoe sets out from England in 1694, and spends a full six years engaging in the country trade in south Asia, his caravan trip takes place after 1700 and is a clear beneficiary of the Nerchinsk treaty.[59] *Farther Adventures* is in line with the Treaty of Nerchinsk in other ways as well. Just as the Treaty of Nerchinsk functioned to enable "the suppression of groups who did not fit into the imperial definitions of space"[60] – for instance, such Mongol tribes as the Zhungars, the Tungusics, and the Khalkhas – Crusoe names and legitimizes only China and Russia as empires, relegating all the other nomadic peoples he encounters beyond the Great Wall as Tartars as "the worst, and most ignorant of Pagans," and "the most barbarous, except only that they did not eat Man's Flesh, as our Savages of *America* did" (2: 190, 192). In addition, the trading items that Crusoe picks up in China and in Russia accurately reflect the Sino-Russian trade at this time. Mark Mancall states that the caravan trade was based primarily on exchanging Russian fur for Chinese cloth.[61] Before departing from Peking, Crusoe loads up his camels with "ninety Pieces of fine Dasmasks, with about two hundred Pieces of other very fine Silks, of several Sorts, some mix'd with Gold," as well as "a very large Quantity of raw Silk" in addition to tea, calicoes, nutmegs and cloves (2: 179). In Siberia, he buys "a considerable Quantity of Sables, black Fox Skins, fine Ermines, and such other Furs as are very rich" (2: 212) and is able to find "very good Sale" for them in Europe (2: 217). Why, then, does Defoe have Crusoe act out his nightmare vision of the private East India trader breaking in upon Europe by its back door? What is the difference between Crusoe (and his caravan loaded with Chinese cloth and Russian sables) and the "Thieves ... to carry away our ready Money" mentioned in *The Advantages of Peace and Commerce* (1729: 36)? After all, his camels are loaded not only with "absolutely necessary" goods such as spices but also calicoes and tea – precisely the goods Defoe accused of ruining Britain (1729: 18). A partial defense of Crusoe is supplied by his insistence that he is merely an accidental merchant – "a Man on the wrong Side of threescore, that was rich enough, and came abroad, more in Obedience to a restless Desire of seeing the World, than a covetous Desire of getting it" (2: 145). Besides, by the time he makes it back to England, Crusoe is seventy-two years old, hardly in a condition to repeat his journey, and sufficiently disenchanted by the difficulty of the caravan journey "to know the Value of Retirement, and the Blessing of ending our Days in Peace" (2: 217). It is true, as Aparna Dharwadker points out, that all this is too "mechanical."[62] Crusoe protests too much while he manages to make profits out of all of his adventures. Yet it is also true that Crusoe's travels fail singularly to provide a clear blueprint for commercial or political action, either on the part of the state and the commercial institutions it backs up, or that of adventurous individuals.

Defoe's inspiration for the Siberian leg of Crusoe's journey home have been identified as two accounts of a Russian embassy that traveled to China in 1692–95 as a follow-up to the Nerchinsk Treaty: Adam Brand's *A Journal of the Embassy From Their Majesties John and Peter Alexievitz, Emperors of Muscovy, &c. Over Land into China* (1698) and Evert Ysbrants Ides's *Three Years Travels from Moscow Over-Land to China* (1706).[63] Ides, a German born in Hamburg to Dutch parents, had prospered as a merchant in Archangelsk but, falling upon commercial losses, had petitioned the Russian court for permission to trade with China when he was unexpectedly asked to serve as ambassador.[64] Leading a diplomatic team of twelve

Germans (including Brand, who served as secretary) and nine Russians, Ides undertook a treacherous three-year journey to Peking and back. On account of a diplomatic *faux pas* in the documents he was carrying, he was unfortunately unable to make any significant political negotiations.[65] Nonetheless, Ides was treated to banquets and was given a free run of the city, which allowed him to collect information about the China market. Historian Mark Mancall, who deems the Ides embassy a "commercial success," estimates that Ides made a 48.1 percent profit on the state's investment in his caravan, proving to Moscow that trade with China would be both possible and profitable.[66] In a letter to Nicolaas Witsen, the publisher and editor of Ides's book as well as pioneering Dutch cartographer of Tartary, published in the 1691 *Philosophical Transactions* of the Royal Society, Robert Southwell had written of this area of the world that it had "from the beginning" of history "layn in the Dark," seemingly "condemned to an everlasting Solitude" on account of its "impenetrable Desarts, the endless Boggs and Marshes, the inaccessable Mountains and those mighty Tracts, which by their Climate are rendered uninhabitable."[67] Using the narratives of Brand and Ides, Defoe opens up a new vista on China and maps it in relation to this relatively unknown, frozen Siberian land mass adjoining Europe. Whereas both Brand and Ides take pride in being the first Germans to have traveled through "great *Tartary* to *China*," however, Crusoe makes no similar claims to distinction.[68] Neither does he disclose the ethnographic zeal so characteristic of their books.

Although Defoe follows the geographical signposts in Ides and Brand very closely in order to plot a credible itinerary across Siberia, he veers wildly from the main thrust of their accounts in depicting Crusoe's caravan as being constantly attacked by huge bands of traveling "Tartars" numbering in the tens of thousands: "ten thousand in all" appear on the outskirts of "*Naum*," "a Frontier of the *Chinese* Empire" (2: 188); another "ten thousand" ominously follow them as they move from Nerchinsk to Jarawena (2: 199).[69] No such confrontations occur in the accounts of Brand and Ides, who are warned about the raids of specific Tartars – the Kalmuks and the Mongolian Tartars, for instance – but who end up having no military confrontations. The closest Brand and Ides come to these feared enemies is in the form of rumors of past raids, fires set on the plains by some Mongol Tartars, and by their messengers who return to them "robb'd and stript."[70] In the main, however, to their "no small astonishment," they are greeted by the Siberian locals with "extraordinary Liberality and Hospitality" and their three-year-long journey is challenged much more by harsh weather and terrain than by the Tartars. As Brand candidly admits, their "kind treatment among such Barbarous Nations" took them by surprise, "they being generally of the *Tartarian* Race."[71] Ides's book, which is especially invested in supplying new ethnographical information about the different nomadic peoples of Siberia, makes clear distinctions between the different people inhabiting Siberian tracts, such as the Muslim Tartars, the Tungus, the Buryats, and the Daurians. Crusoe instances several of these people – the *"Mongul Tartars,"* *"Tongueses,"* "the Sable-Hunters," the *"Ostiachi,* a Kind of *Tartars* or wild People on the Bank of the *Obi,"* and the *"Tartars* of *Kalmuck"* – but he is generally "at a Loss to know" the difference between them, unlike Ides who obsessively details their different physique, dress, hairstyle, marriage and burial customs, food, housing, and especially religious practice (2: 191, 200, 213). For Crusoe, they are a mass of nondescript, cowardly "Hoord or Crowd of wild Fellows" (to use his favorite phrase for them), armed only with bows, arrows, and scimitars and riding on "poor lean starv'd" horses (2: 184). What Defoe appears to have taken most from Ides and Brand is their horror of the Siberians' heathen religions. Ides, however, was despite himself utterly fascinated by the varieties heathenism could take: he notes that the Siberian Tartars worship the sun, moon, and stars and pray only once a year, at which time they make a sacrificial offering of a horse or tiger, which they skin and hang on a tree; the *"Mahometans"* of Tobolsk worship in mosques; the "Ostiacks" of the River Obi have "gods made of Wood and Earth, in several humane shapes," which are dressed in "silken Cloaths" and daily fed with "Milk Pap"; the Tungus keep wooden idols in their huts and rely on male shamans for divination; the Buryat Mongols worship dead bucks and sheep which are impaled on pools before their dwellings; and the Daurians have *"Diabolical Ministers"* who conjure up the dead in drum-beating ceremonies.[72] Defoe lumps all these practices together, describing "the Inhabitants of the Country" as "meer *Pagans,* sacrificing to Idols, and worshipping the Sun, Moon, and Stars, or all the Host of Heaven" (2: 191–92). Nor is there any parallel in Brand or Ides for the grotesque but generic wooden idol, blown up to an absurd height of "eight Foot" and dressed with sheepskins and a Tartar bonnet, that enrages Crusoe so much that he blows it up with gunpowder in front of several hostage Tartars (2: 192–97). Crusoe himself links this disturbing scene to the Madagascar massacre.[73]

The concluding section of *Farther Adventures* is dissatisfying not only in its portrait of these faceless Tartar hordes but also of an aged Crusoe who increasingly shows off a trigger-happy, fundamentalist Christian mentality. More alarmingly still, in *Serious Reflections During the Life and Surprising Adventures of Robinson Crusoe: With His Vision of the Angelick*

World (1720), Crusoe proposes that the "Christian Princes of *Europe*, however few in Number," being "so superior to all the rest of the World in martial Experience and the Art of War," should unite to "beat Paganism out of the World" (3: 207). With the help of the northern European powers, he declares, the "*Czar* of *Muscovy*" "would not find it impossible to march an Army of 36000 Foot and 16000 Horse, in Spite of waste and unhospitable Desarts, even to attack the *Chinese* Empire" (3: 208). Crusoe's dream of having "the military Power reduce the Pagan World, and banish the Devil and Mahomet from the Face of the Earth" is a disturbing coda to the first two books of the trilogy (3: 209). Crusoe wants to take a trade route and convert it into a path for Christian crusaders. As Hans Turley has put it, by the end of the trilogy Crusoe's "resistant passion for travel and dissatisfaction with middle-class domesticity" is transferred into "a system that allows him to 'play God' and impose his 'true Christianity' on the rest of the world."[74] It is not easy to gauge Defoe's own relation to Crusoe's zealotry, but it is clear that he intended to put to rest the notion that the Chinese religion consisted of anything other than idolatry. The violent triangulation of trade–war–religion interests that we see casting a dark shadow on the last two books of the Crusoe trilogy undermines much of the subtlety and power of the earlier *The Life and Strange Surprizing Adventures*.

The final climactic scene in *Farther Adventures* consists of Crusoe waylaid by a troop of Tartars on his way to the port of Archangelsk, where he will embark on a ship home. Crusoe and his party hide in a "little Wood" where they "cut down great Arms of the Trees, and laid them hanging *not quite cut off* from one Tree to another," to make "a continued Fence" around themselves (2: 214). Thus "barricado'd that they could not break in," they fire at the Tartars who are "terribly surpriz'd with our Fire and retreated immediately" (2: 214–15). Then, leaving a fire burning in their camp so "that the *Tartars* might conclude we were still there," they steal off in the night with their numerous horses and camels laden with goods (2: 216). This is a tried – and tired – scene, made yet more implausible by the utter unworthiness of the Tartars as an enemy, but it leaves us with an unmistakable and very diminished Great Wall.

Mapping China in the Early English Novel

Although Crusoe reads the Great Wall as a great Chinese lie, evidence suggests that the mythical magnification of the Great Wall came from European rather than Chinese sources. In *The Great Wall of China: From*

History to Myth, Arthur Waldron traces the beginning of the myth to the mid-seventeenth century, when the accounts of Jesuits Martini and Kircher put into wide circulation exaggerated accounts of the newly constructed Ming walls. The earliest stories linking Asia with a wall can be traced back to the biblical story of Gog and Magog and the legend of Alexander the Great enclosing them behind walls.[75] When the Great Wall began appearing in travelogues, histories, and maps, it was in relatively modest form in comparison to the seventeenth-century aggrandizements. Thus, in *A Treatise of China and the adjoining Regions* (1559), the first European book devoted to China since Marco Polo, the Dominican friar Gaspar da Cruz (ca. 1520–1570) reported "a Wall of an Hundred leagues in length" or possibly "more than a hundred leagues"; Benedict Goes (Bento de Góis, 1562–1607), a Portuguese Jesuit who successfully traveled from India to China under the cover of an Armenian merchant, unfortunately only to die at China's closed borders, observed that much of the Great Wall was 200 miles long and "naturall of rockes or hils"; Juan González de Mendoza (ca. 1540–1617) reported a longer wall of 500 leagues in *Historie of the Great and Mightie Kingdome of China* (1588) but similarly noted that "foure hundred leagues, of the saide wall is naturall of it selfe, so that they be high and mightie rockes verie nigh together; but the other hundred leagues is comprehended the spaced or distance that is betwixt the rockes."[76] The earliest European maps of China reflected this understanding of a wall that was a composite of natural and man-made matter.[77] The Portuguese mapmaker Luis Jorge de Barbuda's map of China included in Abraham Ortelius's 1584 *Theatrum Orbis Terrarum* shows a three-dimensional wall, drawn as a discontinuous structuring combining tower and wall and adjoining mountains. The inscription read: "The Wall rises high from a platform base, is 400 leagues long, between the mountains, erected to enclose the Chinese empire against the Tartars, but crumbling in places."[78] A qualitatively different note is sounded, however, in Martini's 1655 *Novus Atlas Sinensis* in which the wall is monumentalized as "the most stupendious work of works."[79] Martini claimed to be an eyewitness, but went on to describe the wall in terms that his empirical experience could not have possibly supported: he claimed that it "fortifies the borders" of all of China in a "long series" that "continues without any gap," except in "the North part … which is supplyed with the inaccessible part of a Mountain." Martini noted that the wall was studded with gates and towers, and fortified additionally with neighboring castles and garrisons. The wall stretched out almost interminably in his imagination, not only through space but also through time. Conflating the Ming walls still standing in the seventeenth century with the legendary walls of Qin Shi Huang (259 BCE–210 BCE), he claimed that the wall had been built "two hundred and ten years before Christ" by "*Xius* Emperour of *China*, and Founder of that Imperial Family … who excelled all the *Chinesian* Princes in the Magnitude of his Works, and the Glory of his Martial Atchievments." This emperor, according to Martini, managed to complete "the whole Fabrick" of the Great Wall in the astonishing "space of five years" by "impressing three Men out of ten through that world of *China*, amounting to many millions."[80] The general map of China included in Martini's *Atlas*, which was published as part of Joan Blaeu's *Theatrum orbis terrarum sive novus atlas* (1655), visualizes this new understanding of the Great Wall as a continuous, solid structure interrupted only at one point by mountains. Martini's 'little map' of China, also included in the *Novus Atlas Sinensis*, depicts it more yet schematically and symbolically, as a continuous structure of extremely even masonry, crowned with crenellated battlements and moving in an improbably straight line across the northern borders of China.

Martini's account of a wall of mythic proportions and incredible longevity was repeated by almost every subsequent seventeenth-century account of China.[81] It appeared verbatim in Kircher's 1667 *China Illustrata* and close to verbatim in Nieuhof's *Embassy from the East-India Company of the United Provinces, to the Grand Tartar Cham, Emperor of China* (1669).[82] Brand's and Ides's accounts are important contributions to this tradition. They combine accurate empirical description, clearly based on their eyewitness sighting of the wall, with an uncritical acceptance of Martini's mythical history. Thus, Brand notes that "The famous Chinese Wall" is "four Fathoms high, and of such thickness that eight persons may ride upon it a-breast," in parts "much decay'd" and built upon "Hills and vast Mountains," but also states that it "was begun to be built in the year 215 before Christ's Birth, and was finished in 5 years," in a clear reference to Martini.[83] Similarly, Ides claims that "This prodigious Wall … was built some Centuries before Christ's time by the *Chinese* Emperor, *Chien Chu Voang*, in order to prevent the Incursions of the Western *Tartars*."[84] Ides's account stands out from all previous accounts, however, in its textual as well as visual detail.

> This really seems to be one of the Wonders of the World. About 500 Fathom from this famous Wall is a Valley, each side of which was provided with a Battery of hewn Stone, from one of which to the other a Wall about three Fathom high is erected, with an open entrance, as the Print expresses it. Passing through this fore Wall, we came to the entry of the great Wall, through a watch Tower, about eight Fathom high, arched over with hewn

Stone, and provided with Massy Doors strengthened with Iron; the Wall runs from East to West, across the Valley up the extraordinary high Rocks, and about 500 Fathom distant from the other, hath on the Rocks on each side of it a Tower built on it, as our Print represents it.[85]

The beautiful print that accompanies this description shows towering mountain ridges billowing like clouds (*Figure 3*). The wall climbs fantastically and improbably up these "extraordinary high Rocks" on top of which towers perch like birds, while down in the valley two more gigantic watch towers enclose a rectangular garrison that controls all passage through the wall. The human figures who grow increasingly more diminutive as they move from the foreground of the print to the center, where they are entirely dwarfed by the towers, speak to the print's complex negotiation of perspective, scale, and movement. The horizontal vector of the mountain range is matched by a strong vertical axis in the towering mountains; the wall undulates as it almost bisects the range, while the embassy caravans move in a long line that cuts a perpendicular path to the wall. The wonderful dynamism of this print, whose horizontal length imitates the endless stretch of the wall, dramatizes the reader's own entry into a fabled land made accessible by a distancing vision. The Great Wall, transformed into an aesthetic object, is a target for visual pleasure – rather than, as in Crusoe's imagination, an object of military destruction.

It is likely that Martini's image of the Great Wall was influenced by its iconic representation in Chinese maps such as Luo Hongxiang's map of China in *Guang Yutu* (1579/99), which was known to the Jesuits.[86] The prominent pictorial rendering of the wall may look naturalistic, but is actually in service of its traditional function as a symbolic marker of an ideal and transhistorical, rather than a real, Chinese border. Already in the earliest surviving maps of Song China dating to the twelfth century, such as the 1136 *Huayi tu*, the wall is rendered as a continuous and regular structure marking its ideal, 'natural' borders, even though the Song walls were in fragments at that time and many of the northern provinces within the wall had fallen to the Jurchen Jin.[87] Whereas the Chinese map had long functioned in this manner as a symbol of an idealized Chinese empire and often as "a marker of loss" or hope rather than "reality on the ground," in its European renditions it morphed into a hyperreal sign of Chinese cultural and physical impregnability.[88] For this reason, it became a standard gesture to claim special knowledge of China by prying open, or even magically waiving away, the Great Wall. The painted frontispiece to Martini's *Novus Atlas Sinensis*, for instance, features a muscular, Atlas-like man who mutters "I open that which was closed" ("Clausa Recludo") as he strains to

Fig 3 "The Embassadors entry through the famous Chinese wall which is 1200 miles long." From Evert Ysbrants Ides, *Three Years Travels from Moscow Over-Land to China* (London, 1706). New York Public Library Digital Collections.

hold open a heavy door in a ponderous structure that clearly represents the Great Wall. The newly opened door reveals the new world of China optimistically represented by a blue sky and verdant fields, in front of which naked angels frolicking with scientific instruments (Jacob's staff, compass, armillary sphere) cluster excitedly before a scroll map and a globe on which China is prominently marked as well as a celestial globe. China has evidently been discovered by the angels. Above, Christ, seated on a chariot-shaped cloud, is apparently engaged in a scientific experiment: using an immaculate, heavenly mirror ("speculum sine macula"), he reflects God's heavenly beams to light a Christian torch of enlightenment.[89] The frontispiece to Kircher's *China Illustrata* adopts a slightly different strategy by representing Matteo Ricci and Adam Schall holding up a textile map of China in which the wall, the most stylized marker on the map, has clearly become a metonym for China itself. It is a wall, however, that can be scrolled up and packed away to reveal the open path between the temples behind them – a path that we imagine leads gloriously to China. In this sense, both Martini's and Kircher's texts subvert the myth of the Great Wall even as they propagate it, arguing that everything the Great Wall represents – "Isolation from the outside world, the assertion of superiority, the idea of China as the 'Middle Kingdom'" – is an ideological construct that can be overcome by the burning light of Christianity.[90] The message in these prints is clear: the wall of China will be opened by Christianity, represented by Ricci, Schall, and the painted "swift angels" ("Angeli veloces") called upon in Martini's frontispiece, to bring science, learning, and the Christian faith to the hitherto walled-in populace of China.

The prominent display of maps in these frontispieces points to the centrality of cartography in the Jesuit missions in China. The Jesuits used maps to their advantage as part of their negotiations with both China and Europe, offering new world maps to the Chinese court while compiling detailed maps of China for a rapt European audience. Before Martini, Ricci compiled his famous *Kunyu Wanguo Quantu* (A Map of the Myriad Countries of the World) at the request of the Wanli Emperor in 1602, carefully placing China at the center of the map; he also created a map of China which was published by Nicolas Sanson, the French royal geographer, in 1656. As intermediaries between China and Europe, Jesuits plied their knowledge on multiple fronts, using their rare and privileged access to geographical knowledge to claim both diplomatic and scientific distinction. As geographical knowledge of China grew in Europe, however, it was claimed that the Chinese themselves had very limited geographical knowledge of the outside world. Semedo wrote that the Chinese, "not being acquainted with remote Countries and Kingdomes, they have not been able to distinguish their bounds; nor to assign them their proper confines," even though they had "very perfect *maps*" of their own country.[91] Magalhães also observed that "In their Maps they allow a vast Extent to *China*, but represent all other Kingdoms round about it, without any good Order, Position, or any other Mark of good Geography; small, contracted, and with Title Ridiculous and Contemptible"; "Of latter times having understood something of *Europe*, they have added it to their Maps, as if it were the Island of *Tenariff*, or some Desert Island."[92] Such comments formed part of a larger tendency in the early modern European discourse to instance cartographic science as "a crucial marker of difference between Europeans (the knowing Self) and non-Europeans (the unknowing Other)" – a tendency identified by Matthew Edney as part of an "imperial formation."[93] In this particular sense, the Jesuits were as guilty as others in propagating their own scientific modernity over the Chinese.

Defoe's decision to use a world map as the frontispiece to *Farther Adventures* should be understood in this wider context of a cartographic understanding of the world that had emerged as a preeminent modern strategy of "managing the world's complexity."[94] Christian Jacob points out that the map is "an instrument for overcoming the fear of the unknown by slowly integrating the outer regions into the visual schema of the world." The origins of cartography in the "domestication of remote regions" and the effort to bring unknown lands into "a single homogeneous space" with "familiar territories" signals its profoundly "performative" dimension as a tool of representational, intellectual, and psychological mastery.[95] Maps embody a "gesture of spatial appropriation" that "expands the perceptual field" to "articulate geographical data in terms of a cultural and political script."[96] In *The Compleat English Gentleman*, Defoe celebrated the new knowledge of "the geography of the Universe in the maps, atlases, and measurements of our mathematicians," declaring it to be "delightfull and pleasant too to the last degree":

He may travell by land with the historian, by sea with the navigators. He may go round the globe with Dampier and Rogers, and kno' a thousand times more in doing it than all those illiterate sailors. He may make all distant places near to him in his reviewing the voiages of those that saw them, and all the past and remote accounts present to him by the historians that have written of them. He may measure the latitudes and distances of places by the labours and charts that have survey'd them, and know the strength of towns and cityes by the descripcions of those that have storm'd and taken them, with this difference, too, in his knowledge, and infinitely to his advantage, viz., that those travellers, voiagers, surveyors, soldiers, etc., kno' but every man his share, and that share but little, according to the narrow compass of their owne actings. But he recievs the idea of the whole at one view.[97]

For Defoe geography implied a powerful and liberating relationship between the reader and the earth, or the inhabited world as a whole. He emphasized that, in the modern age, geography was no longer a province of the landed gentleman with a vast inherited estate. Even the Englishman who had not been "sent to school, as he ought to have been, in his childhood, and been made master of the learned languages," or had "not made the grand tour of Italy and France," could in his own time become "the master of the geography of the Universe," a "studious geographer and the well read historian."[98] In Defoe's mind, maps and geographies were powerful, democratic instruments of knowledge that could open doors onto a vastly expanded world. They provided their readers with the ability to see "the whole at one view" and to go beyond the "narrow compass" of first-hand empirical experience to achieve a more comprehensive understanding of the earth's physical and historical bounds.[99] The entanglement we see here between map and text – between "charts" and "descripcions" – is symptomatic of the understanding of geography in Defoe's time. Geography implies "a particular spatial scale, that of the earth in general," which distinguishes it from cosmography (description of the world in general, including the universe), chorography (description of a particular country or region), and topography (description of cities and towns).[100] Defoe's map thus signals the *geographical* scale as well as ambition of the novel to come, foreshadowing and encapsulating Crusoe's circumnavigation of the world.

A profound interest in and strategic use of modern maps is a recurring characteristic of Defoe's work, evidenced not only in *Farther Adventures*, but also in *A Tour through the Whole Island of Great Britain* (1724–28), which was embellished with Herman Moll's fold-out maps of England, Wales, and Scotland, and the work he did for the *Atlas Maritimus & Commercialis* (1728). The eighteenth-century connoisseur of travel narratives would have recognized that the "MAP of the WORLD, on wch is Delineated the Voyages of ROBINSON CRUSO," which prefaces the 1719 edition of *Farther Adventures* and was always reprinted in later editions, was a replica of maps printed in other narratives of English circumnavigations: "A Map of the World Shewing the Course of Mr Dampiers Voyage Round it: From 1679 to 1691" published in William Dampier's 1697 *A New Voyage round the World* and "A Map of the World with the Ships Duke & Duchess Tract Round it from 1708 to 1711" in Woodes Rogers's 1712 *Cruising Voyage*

Round the World. Like the other two maps, Crusoe's map is adorned with a dotted line that transforms the static cartographic space into an interactive medium and opens it up temporally for narrative movement. The map of Crusoe's circumnavigation is not signed by Moll, as the other two are, and generally has fewer textual markings on it.[101] These may be subtle clues to the real nature of the narrative to follow: a history that is and is not a history, and a geography that is and is not one. With the map, *Farther Adventures* allies itself with these earlier texts that undertake the "two totalizing or planetary projects" identified by Mary Louise Pratt: first, circumnavigation, "a double deed that consists of sailing round the world then writing an account of it," and second, "the mapping of the world's coastlines."[102] It also suggests, I believe, that whatever heroism Defoe may have intended to endow Crusoe with was a highly ambiguous one, not unrelated to the piratical errancy of Dampier and Rogers. The map, in other words, serves to produce an evaluative distance toward Crusoe, even as it links his travels to the new sciences, the mercantilist exploration of the globe, and the developing imperial state – all of which powerfully inform the geographical imagination. Crusoe's trajectory in *Farther Adventures* suggests that one of Defoe's aims in the novel was to import China into a narrative of English circumnavigation and to map it, by narrative and cartographical means, thereby bringing it under representational control. In this sense, his aim was not so different from Martini's – to open up China's doors and to pave way for the penetration of European knowledge, powerfully symbolized by the opening of the Great Wall.

Recognizing the ways in which Defoe understood maps and novels as co-constitutive, correlative ways of managing a modern world with vastly expanded geographical boundaries helps us place our finger on the unresolved formal tension in *Farther Adventures* between the mapmaker's (or geographer's) impulse to spatialize and the novelist's impulse to narrate, between the global and the local. One reason why Defoe's narrative experiments with globetrotting protagonists did not issue in a long tradition of geographical novels is probably the same reason why *The Life and Strange Surprizing Adventures* is so much more satisfying a read than *Farther Adventures*. In the latter novel, the narrative grows thinner as it spreads farther, until Crusoe is left declaring absurdly that he will "make no more Descriptions of Countrys and People," even though the primary motive for his ceaseless mobility is said to be a desire to see the world, chiefly so that the novel can come to a reasonably quick close (2: 174). And yet it is also true that the enduring power of the Crusoe story comes from Defoe's ability to tap into and mobilize a correspondent desire in the reader to reach out to and experience a world beyond the small confines of individual existence – to travel, at least in one's imagination, to the farthest reaches of the world. Defoe imagined a reader with Crusonian desires to ramble – a reader whose taste for the strange and surprising, for adventures that went 'farther,' was not at odds with a craving for the latest scientific and factual knowledge; a reader at home in the intense imbrications of modern commerce, science, and geography; one who drank Chinese tea and perhaps owned a few Chinese or imitation-Chinese goods. This reader was someone at home in an economy in which global commerce played a key part, as well as the new culture of print-capitalism and the mediations it facilitated between individuals and nations. Defoe's Robinson Crusoe novels respond vigorously to these changes by defining the modern space of the novel as nothing less than the entire globe, and by staging a paradigmatic encounter with China as a quintessential moment of European modernity.

CHAPTER 3

The New, Uncommon, or Strange: China in The Spectator

In his *Essay upon the Cure of the Gout by Moxa*, an amusing piece written at the behest of his friend Constantijn Huygens (1596–1687), Temple provides an account of how, to his great chagrin, he became the talk of the town by submitting to a "new experiment" while he was living in the Hague (1680: 189).[1] The story goes as follows. During his stay in the Hague, Temple suddenly felt a sharp pain in his right foot while dining in company but "thought it was with some sprain at Tennis" and, pulling off his shoes, sat through dinner. Thinking no more of it, he went to bed, but the pain proved so bad that he was not able to "sleep a wink." In the morning, he discovered that the foot was "very red and angry." The frequent application of "common Poultives to it" over the course of the next two days helped "the violence of my pain to asswage," and though he found his foot too sore to move about with ease, he was again "content to see company" (1680: 202–03). His visitors' reaction to his illness, however, left him thoroughly depressed:

> Every body that came to visit me, found something to say upon the occasion; some made a jest of it, or a little reproach; others were serious in their mirth, and made me Compliments as upon a happy accident and sign of long life. The *Spaniards* ask me *Albricias* for telling me the news, that I might be sure 'twas the Gout; and in short, none of the company was in ill humour but I, who had rather by half have had a Fever, or a worse disease at that time, where the danger might have been greater, but the trouble and the melancholy would I am sure have been less. (1680: 203)

Temple was deeply embarrassed by the traditional associations of gout with intemperate drinking and sexual indulgence. He himself had "always scorned it as an effect commonly of intemperance; and hated it" (1680: 203). It was of little consolation to him that gout tended to fall upon "persons engaged in publick affairs, and great imployments" or persons "born of Families Noble and Rich," since he believed that it was a combination of age, "ease and luxury," and "the plenty of their fortunes," that engaged "men in the constant use of great Tables, and in frequent excesses of several kinds" that eventually saddled them with the disease (1680: 193–94). His visitors, on the other hand, jocosely congratulated him on his rich man's disease, treating it alternately as a benign sign of Temple's secret excesses or as a "happy accident and sign of long life" (1680: 203). They were alluding to the common belief that diseases were mutually exclusive. Temple's gout, they suggested, was as good as insurance against worse diseases.[2] Temple, however, was not amused.

Deeply oppressed by the thought that he was now saddled with a disease without cure, Temple gave himself up to "sullenness enough to use no Remedy of a hundred that were told me." Then he was paid a visit by his distinguished Dutch friend Huygens, who "never came into company without saying something that was new." Huygens informed him about "the *Indian* way of Curing the Gout by *Moxa*," a treatment that Temple had never heard of before (1680: 204). Temple emphasizes that he would never have imagined himself as "the first that should try a new experiment," much less "be Author of any new invention, being little inclined to practice upon others, and as little that others should practice upon me" (1680: 189–90). But as he "hated the very name of the *Gout*, and thought it a reproach" (1680: 206), and could not bring himself to place any faith in any of the common remedies, he was drawn to Huygens's account of "this new Operation" (1680: 205) – an account that Huygens, in turn, had found in "an ingenious little Book … by a *Dutch* Minister at *Batavia*, who being extremely tormented with a Fit of the Gout, an old *Indian*-woman coming to see him, undertook to Cure him, and did it immediately by this *Moxa*" (1680: 205–06). This was a book by Hermann Busschoff, who had served in Taiwan as a Dutch minister of the Reformed Church, where he had tried the treatment by moxibustion as a remedy for his gout with so much success that he had published a short treatise on it in Utrecht in 1674.[3] Temple sent his family doctor to Utrecht to procure and "learn the exact method of using" the "*Indian*" moss and the perfumed match from Busschoff's son; upon the doctor's return, Temple had him perform the operation, setting the moss on his toe and lighting it with the match until the moss burned down to the skin (1680: 213–14). After three burnings, Temple was able to walk "half a dozen turns about the room without any pain or trouble" (1680: 215), and though the blister from the burn took several weeks to heal entirely, he was able to walk every day "without the least return of pain" (1680: 215, 217). The story of Temple's cure by moxa became a sensation: "The talk of this Cure run about the *Hague*, and made me the conversation in other places" (1680: 217). Huygens told the story to "his Friends at *Gresham*-Colledg," whence the Royal Society promptly had Busschoff's book translated into English and undertook a scientific investigation of this East Indian cure.[4]

Much of the humor in this story comes from Temple's portrait of himself as a private man. He may have been one of the greatest statesmen of his age, but he confesses that he was "at all times caring little to appear in publick" and mortified by the thought of becoming a topic for gossip (1680: 220). Protesting against Huygens's demand for a public account of his trial, Temple humorously complains, "I confess, your engaging me first in this adventure of the *Moxa*, and desiring the story of it from me, is like giving one the torture, and then asking his confession, which is hard usage to an innocent man, and a friend" (1680: 191). An additional source of comedy lies in Temple's alleged suspicion of "new inventions or experiments" (1680: 220). His "adventure" with moxibustion, a novelty in seventeenth-century Europe, reads like a story of the conversion of an unbeliever. For all his protestations, however, it is likely that Temple's high regard for Chinese civilization made him receptive to the idea of moxibustion. One cannot blame him for nonetheless feeling squeamish about setting fire to his own skin. There are many ways to read this enjoyable essay: as proof that, unlike Wotton, many 'modern' scientists of Temple's day were intrigued by and interested in Asian science; as an illustration of the conversations and collaborations that took place between the English and the Dutch; and as an indication of how objects and practices indigenous to Asia were impacting and transforming Europeans in rather sensational ways. As Rajani Sudan has pointed out, in early English encounters with Asian science we see a marked tendency to sublimate Asian techne as "marvelous, wondrous, or magical" – a tendency that is later reversed as British imperial ideology intentionally forgets Asian technology in order to claim British scientific and cultural superiority.[5] Here, however, I want to focus attention on the stylistic merits of Temple's essay on moxibustion, which both indulges in and ironizes the hyperbolic reaction to Asian medicine. Temple's essay is an important precursor to the kind of writing that would be perfected in the early English periodical: an essay employing a chatty, conversational tone; navigating a tricky line between gossip and public account; gently satirizing social mores; documenting and reflecting on the latest, the novel, and the new. As Homer Woodbridge points out, a particular type of personal and moral essay written in an easy, accessible style is realized in Temple's writing, which clearly "prepares the way for the periodical essay." "Temple hands on the torch of the essay from Montaigne

and Bacon to Addison and Steele": the combination of personal remin-
iscence, humorous self-revelation, and social commentary, delivered in a
conversational tone in service of a general moral and didactic aim, are
characteristics of Temple's writing that Addison would inherit and perfect
in *The Spectator*.[6]

The early periodical, J. Paul Hunter reminds us, was virtually synonymous
with curiosity and novelty. John Dunton, the publisher of *The Athenian
Gazette: Or Casuistical Mercury, Resolving all the most Nice and Curious
Questions Proposed by the Ingenious* (1691–97; after the first few issues, the
title was soon changed to *The Athenian Mercury*), defined Athenianism as
"a search after Novelties" and referred to his readers as "lovers of Novelty."[7]
The originality of *The Athenian Mercury* lay in its question-and-answer
format which invited readers to mail in "nice and curious questions proposed by the Ingenious," the answers to which would be published by
anonymous respondents.[8] Thus, the word 'novelty' encompassed eccentric,
trivial, and amusing questions as well as their answers, while also referring
to the most current – the most up-to-date as well as fashionable – objects
of inquiry. In other words, *The Athenian Mercury* made it clear that novelty was an experience created by, as much as for, a reading public whose
"*Athenian itch*"[9] was allegedly conditioned by the social "shame or fear of
appearing ridiculous by asking Questions."[10] By providing a safe public
forum for this "itch," and naturalizing it as a justifiable though potentially
gauche response to a rapidly changing world, *The Athenian Mercury* low-
ered barriers to knowledge, and made it piquant, chatty, and entertaining.
In his autobiographical *Life and Errors of John Dunton*, Dunton claimed
that Temple was not only an enthusiastic reader but also contributor to his
popular journal: "The late Sir *William Temple*, a Man of clear Judgment,
and wonderful Penetration," he wrote, "was pleas'd to Honour me with *frequent Letters* and Questions, very Curious and uncommon; in Particular,
that about the *Talismans* are his."[11] It makes good sense that Temple, who
for all his avowed *ancienneté* was keenly interested in the widening world
of the moderns, was an avid reader of *The Athenian Mercury*. It is no
more surprising that his worldly, non-academic, low-key approach to the
issues of his time and his gently self-deprecating, easy style made a lasting impression on Addison and Steele's *Spectator* in which Temple appears
many times as an important source, inspiration, and authority.

There exists, of course, an important difference. Whereas Temple
portrays himself humorously (and to some extent disingenuously) as a
reluctant inductee into the modern world and its new experiments, *The
Spectator* as a whole exudes an "acceptance of modernity" and an "Appetite

for the new and the different, for fresh experience and novel excitements."[12] Mr. Spectator, who calls "Curiosity" his "prevailing Passion, and indeed the sole Entertainment of my Life," delights in the world of gossip, private letters, and clubhouse talk, which he prefers to the agitations of political news (2: 111).[13] The *Spectator* papers can indeed be interpreted as a project aimed at the reinvention of what may count as new or newsworthy. While proudly asserting his aversion to party politics by declaring that his "Paper has not a single Word of News" in it (2: 517), Mr. Spectator fills his papers with alternative novelties in fashion, social mores, tastes, and manners. As Scott Black points out, novelty rules *The Spectator* both in subject and style: "Representing the contingent and the new, the essay was the means by which the modern, as such, could apprehend itself."[14] On the one hand, *The Spectator* is invested in making the presentation of contemporary life a subject diverting and rewarding for reflective thinking. At the same time, *The Spectator* promotes an easy, rambling style – an anti-methodical method – to match its expanded subject matter.[15] The essayistic style is, in Addison's words, all about setting down thoughts "not met with in other Writers" in precisely the way they naturally and freshly occur, "without being at the Pains to Connect or Methodise them" (2: 351), "without any Order or Method" (2: 465). In this way, the "new," which Temple humorously pinpoints as a source of personal anxiety as well as a productive cure in his essay on gout, is enshrined in *The Spectator* not only as a new subject but also as a new method of writing.

The aim of this chapter is to investigate both the sympathy and the divergence between Temple and Addison, particularly with regard to China as one of the most important manifestations of the new, rather than the ancient, in early modern English culture. As we have seen, while Temple explored the idea of China as a new standard of ancientness, he also recorded its palpable entry into modern European culture as a curious novelty in areas as diverse as medicine and aesthetics. How does Addison use Temple's legacy in developing the category of the new as the central aesthetic category for an emergent civil society? What happens to the idea of China as it is increasingly transported into England in the tangible form of commodity and cultural practice? Using Temple as a guide, I propose, we can trace the process by which China came to have a founding role in a new cultural discourse centered on what Addison called the *new*, the *uncommon*, and the *strange*. As I shall show, these aesthetic concepts developed most fully in Addison's *Spectator* papers on the pleasures of the imagination show how a vibrant mercantile culture built on global trade gave rise to powerful redefinitions of English landscape and literary history.

The story of China's subtle, yet transformative role in these transformations connects back to the quarrel between the ancients and the moderns, but also moves beyond the quarrel, into the realm of popular taste and culture where Chinese influence was registered in even more wide-ranging ways.

In the sections that follow, I will trace the fertile process by which a Chinese "sort of Beauty" of which "we have hardly any Notion," according to Temple, becomes the basis for Addison's aesthetics of the "new, uncommon, or the strange" – in short, a differential aesthetics marked by the experience of novelty, curiosity, and alterity. Here I am in agreement with Tony Brown's helpful remarks that for Addison "Aesthetics and the agent of aesthetic experience find their necessary conditions of enunciation to be global" and that "it is by thinking through the exotic figure of China" that Addison theorizes the aesthetic. However, I do not share Brown's view that "the *typosis* of Chinese aesthetic experience suggests an attenuation of temporality" or that Addison empties out the figure of China to use it merely as an abstract "allegory of the aesthetic" in general.[16] In turning to China to theorize his aesthetics of novelty – which occupies a very specific, third space between the aesthetic space of beauty and that of the sublime – Addison foregrounds, rather than attenuates, the temporality of aesthetic experience and affirms the particular aesthetic value of the experience of transience, change, and epistemic uncertainty. These experiences constitute and color a specific kind of aesthetic encounter rather than enveloping all aesthetic encounters whatsoever. As Brown points out, Temple regards the Chinese ideal of beauty as "relative, objective and foreign," whereas Addison uses it to illustrate "a universal aesthetic experience." Brown uses this distinction to argue that Chinese taste is important for Addison because it "exemplifies aesthetic experience in its immediacy, on the one hand, and its indifference to cognition, on the other."[17] However, I wish to propose that Addison equates Chinese taste with a mediated, self-conscious experience of mental endeavor. Another way to put this is to say that, whereas Temple references Chinese taste as a curiosity, with Addison a putative Chinese aesthetic ideal becomes constitutive of the aesthetic experience of novelty and curiosity in general. As Hans Robert Jauss points out, "*Modern* in the aesthetic sense of the word is to be distinguished … from the classic or the classical, the eternally beautiful, that which holds for all time."[18] Addison's modern aesthetics consecrates a differential aesthetics of modernity, marking a shift from "a time-honored aesthetics of permanence, based on a belief in an unchanging and transcendent ideal of beauty, to an aesthetics of transitoriness and immanence, whose central values are change and novelty," and giving it a Chinese name.[19] As

Stacey Sloboda has pointed out, chinoiserie, the aesthetic taste that went by the name of China, was not a mere reflection of "an emergent global culture" but "a critical visual and material language" that "worked both to celebrate and critique eighteenth-century cultures of commerce."[20] In my view, however, what is most striking about Addison's move away from an aesthetics of symbolic and static beauty to what I will call an aesthetics of temporality is that in the process he broadens the significance of Chinese taste, using it in inventive ways to develop nothing less than a theory of the imagination and, ultimately, modern literary genius. This is why, I suggest, we need to read Addison's discussion of Chinese porcelain and gardens not just within the context of chinoiserie, but also in connection with his broader aesthetic, cultural, and literary theory.

Philosophy at the Tea Table: Addison's Aesthetics of Mercantilism

Let us return, for a moment, to Defoe and think back on the goods that Robinson Crusoe brings back to Europe from Peking. The "ninety Pieces of fine Damasks, with about two hundred Pieces of other very fine Silks, of several Sorts, some mix'd with Gold," as well as "a very large Quantity of Raw Silk," "together with Tea, and some fine Callicoes" make up an accurate catalogue of the Chinese commodities that swelled the British markets and dominated European consumer culture in the eighteenth century. At the end of *The Farther Adventures of Robinson Crusoe*, Defoe plays a complex game with his readers, simultaneously invoking these Chinese goods to mobilize the readers' desire, while finding a convenient narrative excuse to make Crusoe dispose of the goods before he returns to London. In keeping with Defoe's economic policy, Crusoe thus sells all his goods in Hamburg and does not implicate himself in the damaging China trade – though Crusoe himself attributes this not to any policy of his but rather to the fact that a boat from Hamburg happens to arrive before any English ships at Archangelsk, where he spends six weeks waiting for a ship. The novel's incoherence with regard to China – Defoe turns Crusoe into a China trader at the beginning of the novel, only to make him deliver polemics against "the Power, Riches, Glory, Magnificence, and Trade of the *Chinese*" (2: 174), then promptly load his "26 Camels and Horses" full of Chinese merchandise to take back to Europe (2: 180) – is a symptom of the difficulties Defoe had reconciling his importation of China into "the peculiar, present-centered form of narrative" we today call the novel and his ideological need to keep Chinese manufactured goods out of it.[21] His mode of writing played to the contemporary "preoccupation with novelty" and "contemporaneity," as well as "the new cultural consciousness based on human curiosity" in which China played such a central role, and yet he wanted his literary modernity to dovetail with his vision of British foreign trade in which the novelties of China would be kept out as much as possible.[22] This is why Defoe registers, but also adamantly downplays, the association of China with the newness and novelty of Chinese luxury goods.

Tracking and taking stock of the cultural meaning of the influx of Chinese goods in the English marketplace and its domestic spaces was a literary job tackled more enthusiastically in the English periodical that, like Defoe's novel, capitalized on "the whole sprawling context of attention to the new, strange, and surprising," but located this taste for novelty in England's fashionable new public and domestic spaces rather than in the overseas adventures of a born rambler.[23] As early as the sixteenth century, moralizing critics had singled out the English weakness for foreign commodities or "new fangledness," connecting it to various social and religious vices such as pride, ambition, and fickleness. The Puritan Philip Stubbes, for instance, claimed that "new fangles and toies, are occasions, why all nations mocke, and flonte us," identifying the British penchant for novelties with a particular national shame.[24] Unlike Defoe, however, these critics were not primarily interested in calling into question a foreign trade imbalance, but rather in using a consumerist trend to propound that the British were an inherently unstable and fickle people, prone to social and political instability, due to causes that were primarily geographical and climactic rather than economical. A very different note is sounded in the famous *Spectator* paper no. 69 where a burgeoning market full of novelties culled from the far corners of the world brings hyperbolic tears of joy to Mr. Spectator's eyes. "I cannot forbear expressing my Joy with Tears that have stolen down my Cheeks," he declares, as he surveys the Royal Exchange with "a secret Satisfaction" and gratified "Vanity" at being an Englishman (1: 294, 292). Mr. Spectator understands foreign trade as a beneficial "mutual Intercourse and Traffick among Mankind, that the Natives of the several Parts of the Globe might have a kind of Dependance upon one another, and be united together by their common Interest" (1: 294–95). Sugared tea, or "The Infusion of a *China* Plant sweetened with the Pith of an *Indian* Cane" (1: 295), becomes one example of the blessed junctures of global trade. Although *Spectator* no. 37 satirizes Lady Leonora's "Pyramid" of porcelain vessels, in this paper "Pyramids of *China*" are recuperated as a pleasurable sign, among others, of England's enlarged "natural Prospect" through "the Benefits and Advantages of Commerce": "Our

Tables are stored with Spices, and Oils, and Wines; Our Rooms are filled with Pyramids of *China*, and adorned with the Workmanship of *Japan*: Our Morning's Draught comes to us from the remotest Corners of the Earth: We repair our Bodies by the Drugs of *America*, and repose our selves under *Indian* Canopies" (1: 295).

Addison manages this turnabout by refiguring Britain's role in this global commerce. It is not that Britain is overrun with foreign novelties that threaten its national integrity. Rather, as Mr. Spectator's merchant friend Sir Andrew Freeport puts it, the world itself has turned into Britain's garden, kitchen, and playground: "My Friend Sir ANDREW calls the Vineyards of *France* our Gardens; the Spice-Islands our Hot-Beds; the *Persians* our Silk-Weavers, and the *Chinese* our Potters" (1: 296). In this scenario, where the entire world is re-imagined as a British possession at its service, the products of the world play a both "Convenient and Ornamental" role, adding "Variety" and imparting new pleasures to British "Palates" (1: 296).

Placed against the backdrop of a full range of responses to Britain's growing trade in luxury products from the East that irrevocably changed its material culture, Mr. Spectator's response stands out as a remarkably – and improbably – sanguine vision. Especially when juxtaposed with Defoe's much more critical reaction to the influx of East Indian goods, it may even seem intentionally forgetful of the economic problems structurally embedded in the China trade. Mr. Spectator can weep with joy at the sight of the Royal Exchange, we suspect, because he is not a merchant and has no business at stake there. For him, the Royal Exchange is simply a pleasing and entertaining aesthetic spectacle, a stage on which "so rich an Assembly of Country-men and Foreigners" commingle. As he puts it: "This grand Scene of Business gives me an infinite Variety of solid and substantial Entertainments" (1: 294). Addison's well-known papers on the pleasures of the imagination (*Spectator* nos. 411–21) can be read, in part, as a defense of this aestheticizing stance toward the market as an example of the "innocent" pleasures of the imagination, equally freed from the strains of "serious Employments" and the "Negligence and Remissness" of mere idleness (3: 539). Addison's point is not that aesthetic pleasure has to be freed from the workings of the global market. On the contrary, it is that global trade gives rise to aesthetic pleasures that can transform basic physical activities open to all – such as drinking, eating, and sleeping – into minor acts of art.

The acute pleasure Mr. Spectator takes in his vision of English men and women eating food cooked in oils and spices imported from far corners of the globe, drinking beverages of foreign provenance such as coffee, tea, and wine, living in rooms furnished with lacquered furniture and porcelain objects from Japan and China, and covering themselves by day and night in the exotic printed fabrics of India suggests that Addison's critique of women's collections of chinaware was not at all meant as a wholesale attack on the new consumer habits of his days. The particular anxiety that is registered in the *Spectator* papers especially with regard to Chinese porcelain, in other words, adds complexity to but does not change the basic tenor of Addison's attitude toward mercantile ethos and practice. Defoe's well-known description of Queen Mary's china collection in Kensington Palace serves as an instructive point of contrast. In *A Tour Through the Whole Island of Great Britain* (1724–26), Defoe noted several customs introduced to the British Isles by William and Mary after the Glorious Revolution. To King William he attributed "the strange passion, for fine gardens, which has so commendably possess'd the English gentlemen of late years," while pointing to Queen Mary as the source of two much less praiseworthy "fatal excesses": "the love of fine East-India calicoes, such as were then call'd masslapatan chints, atlases, and fine painted calicoes" and "the custom or humor, as I may call it, of furnishing houses with china-ware, which increased to a strange degree afterwards, piling their china upon the tops of cabinets, scrutores, and every chimneypiece, to the tops of the ceilings, and even setting up shelves for their china-ware, where they wanted such places." Defoe absolves Queen Mary of "designing any injury to the country where she was so entirely belov'd," suggesting that her status and wealth gave her a private right to these objects. Had she known that she would be so widely emulated to the economic detriment of her nation, he avers, she would have reformed her manners.[25] However, it is clear that he did not absolve the general populace of succumbing to the same taste. Defoe dates the consumer revolution in East Indian fabrics and Chinese porcelain very precisely, to the last decade of the seventeenth and the early decades of the eighteenth century, and suggests that the larger economic repercussions of a lately introduced fashion only began to make themselves felt after Queen Mary's death. Her preference for eastern rather than domestic fabrics, he charges, "afterwards descended into the humours of the common people so much, as to make them grievous to our trade, and ruining to our manufactures and the poor," prompting Parliament to pass two acts to prohibit their importation and to protect the domestic woolen trade.[26] As to women's mania for amassing chinaware, he remarks that "it became a grievance in the expence of it, and even injurious to their families and estates."[27]

While Addison appears to accept Defoe's theory that the consumption of Indian calicoes and Chinese porcelain is a gendered phenomenon that has been dangerously generalized, he is interested in appealing to the active female agency behind these scenes of "strange" clutter. In early numbers of *The Spectator* (nos. 4, 10), he had already declared that he would "take it for the greatest Glory of my Work, if among reasonable Women this Paper may furnish *Tea-Table Talk*" (1: 21) and was "ambitious to have it said" of him that he had "brought Philosophy out of Closets and Libraries, Schools and Colleges, to dwell in Clubs and Assembles, at Tea-Tables, and in Coffee-Houses" (1: 44), making it humorously clear that he sought a fashionable, female readership. Asking that his papers be "looked upon as Part of the Tea Equipage" and consumed "every Morning," along with "Tea and Bread and Butter," in particular, was his way of teasingly courting women as well as declaring his right to intrude upon the diurnal rhythms of the domestic sphere that he deemed an equally legitimate site for his writerly ambition (1: 44). Addison could not have been blind to the fact that both the tea and the tea equipage that he chose as the proper stage and accompaniment for his papers were of Chinese origin and that tea and porcelain were two of the most important items in the overseas trade.[28] This suggests that Addison carefully reserved his critique for what Anna Somers Cocks calls the "nonfunctional use of ceramics," while quietly accepting their functional use and their intimate reformation of dietary practice and manners, as well as their association with women.[29] Defoe, in a very different move, stops Crusoe from bringing any chinaware whatso-ever back to Europe and makes him dump all his Chinese tea, damasks, silks, and calicoes in Russia before allowing him to return to England's shores. The contrast between Addison's unobtrusive naturalization of two of the most important Chinese imports and Defoe's insistence on keeping them, as much as possible, out of England underscores Addison's interest in assessing the social and aesthetic values of Chinese products over and above their economic worth and meaning. When we consider the fact that tea, primarily considered a medicinal or luxury drink for the elite, "took off" as a major commodity for the mass market only in the first decade of the eighteenth century, and that the visual representations of families organized in polite ensembles around tea tables date mostly to the 1740s, we can see that Addison is responding presciently to patterns of consump-tion that would in the long run redefine Britishness itself in terms of a taste for exotic imported goods.[30] By acknowledging a material history and culture of Chinese goods in British society, as well as their links to gen-dered sites of domestic femininity, Addison proposes a model of national cultural identity that opens it up in significant ways to both women and global commerce, especially women's use and appropriation of the fruits of global commerce.[31]

Needless to say, this apparent openness in *The Spectator* to models of national identity deeply inflected by gender as well as cultural difference has its limits. Feminist scholarship has been especially wary of giving Addison too much credit for his showy wooing of women readers. Kathryn Shevelow criticizes Addison's appeal to a polite female readership for propagating a rigid and less than emancipating domestic ideology under the mantle of a progressive gender outlook; Elizabeth Kowaleski-Wallace glosses the repeated invocations of the spectacle of women at the tea table as a "sign of an ongoing process of the disciplining and normalizing of the upper-class female body."[32] For Amanda Vickery, the staging of tea drinking in Georgian England can be read as a story of "ornamental femininity" whose primary purpose is to adorn and beautify a social sphere dominated by men.[33] And yet, as Vickery reminds us, "the pervasiveness and appeal of a gendered language of furniture" and furnishings in the eighteenth century, which in its initial stages did not so much reflect as perhaps create an economic atmosphere for gender-typed consumption, suggests that one motivation for the repeated couplings of femininity and Chinese imports may have derived from an awareness of the new forms of female independence such couplings enabled. In particular, Vickery proposes that the anxiety surrounding the tea table and its satirical associations with malign gossip may be a reaction to the increase in "female visiting," which opened up the domestic interior to independent, homosocial forms of female entertainment that rivaled the male coffeehouse public sphere.[34] The ritual of drinking Chinese tea, in other words, may have disciplined and ornamentalized the female body but it also reconfigured domestic space and amplified social life for women in significant ways.

On the one hand, Addison's rather conventional satire on the female fad for chinaware subordinates an aesthetic evaluation of these immensely popular objects to a social and largely gendered critique of consumption. On the other hand, as we see in *Spectator* no. 37, Addison's defense of British mercantilism shows that his gendered critique of this fashionable taste goes hand in hand with an acknowledgement of a fundamental change that was occurring in British material culture. By granting a new cultural dignity and meaning to all that is *new*, the papers on the pleasures of the imagination authorize the appeal of these foreign objects and clear a cultural space for their appropriation and appreciation. Addison's famous papers on the pleasures of the imagination (nos. 411–21) indeed can be read as a defense of what James Bunn has called the "aesthetics of British mercantilism." Bunn interprets this mercantile aesthetics as primarily an aesthetic of superfluity, of "accumulating exotic goods materialized as a side effect of mercantilism," of bric-à-brac and clutter.[35] Taking Bunn's argument a step farther, I wish to suggest that Addison understands the aesthetics of mercantilism in broader terms, connecting it not only to a love of collecting but also to novel ways of consuming, eating, drinking, and enjoying – to use his own terms – the new, uncommon, and strange in an enlarged social and public sphere. While Addison does not explicitly connect his defense of what Ronald Paulson calls "stigmatized or marginalized areas of enjoyment," formerly associated with base, dangerous, unnatural, and generally aberrant objects and doctrines, to the consumption of exotic imports, the central meaning of novelty as foreign import (already current, as we have seen, in the sixteenth century) strongly suggests that globalized mercantile trade is the unspoken condition for the aesthetics he is espousing.[36]

The reason why this backdrop is easy to miss is that Addison later chooses to explain and authorize the appeal of these new, foreign objects by disembodying taste, as it were. In these papers, Addison restricts the question of taste to the faculty of vision, the supposedly most rational of all the senses, conveniently sidestepping the messier associations of taste with bodily enjoyment. Nonetheless, a lingering alimentary or consumptive metaphor can be detected in his discussion of the pleasures of the new, uncommon, or strange in *Spectator* no. 412:

> Every thing that is *new* or *uncommon* raises a Pleasure in the Imagination, because it fills the Soul with an agreeable Surprise, gratifies its Curiosity, and gives it an Idea of which it was not before possest. We are, indeed, so often conversant with one Sett of Objects, and tired out with so many repeated Shows of the same Things, that whatever is *new* or *uncommon* contributes a little to vary Human Life, and to divert our Minds, for a while, with the Strangeness of its Appearance: It serves us for a kind of Refreshment, and takes off from that Satiety we are apt to complain of in our usual and ordinary Entertainments. It is this that bestows Charms on a Monster, and makes even the Imperfections of Nature please us. It is this that recommends Variety, where the Mind is every Instant called off to something new, and the Attention not suffered to dwell too long, and waste it self on any particular Object. (2: 541)

Here it is the "Mind" or "Soul" rather than the body that is "refreshed" by an unusual "entertainment," in keeping with Addison's visual definition of the pleasures of the imagination as deriving from "visible Objects" (2: 536–37). However, the scene he conjures up here could equally be read as a dining or even a tea-drinking scene in which an unfamiliar taste in both edibles and collectibles creates new appetites in palates glutted by boredom. Addison's overall strategy is to downplay these appetitive and economic connotations of taste as consumption, etymologically linked to disease and destruction. Addison's interest in the mercantile world, however, should not lead us to conclude that "within his model, novelty pleases only as a kind of refreshing surprise, a momentary diversion from the insipidity of the familiar and commonplace."³⁷ What is at stake here, I suggest, is nothing less than a newly temporalized understanding of aesthetic enjoyment that explains much more than the appeal of an imported Chinese or chinoiserie object. Indeed, by highlighting the *new* as a specific kind of experience of time that can also explain the appeal of the strange, new and uncommon, Addison takes mercantile aesthetics to another philosophical level.

Garden, Landscape, and the Aesthetics of the New

It is Temple who supplies the clue to the theoretical link between Addison's aesthetics of mercantilism and the theory of landscape and gardening that occupies a central place in his papers on the pleasures of the imagination. In the *Essay upon the Gardens of Epicurus*, Temple proposed that the Chinese had a way, quite unknown in Europe, of contriving beauty out of "Forms wholly irregular." While Europeans abided by an idea of beauty dependent on regular forms, he stated, the Chinese proved that it was also possible to shape "disagreeing parts into some Figure, which shall yet upon the whole be very agreeable."

> And though we have hardly any Notion of this sort of Beauty, yet they have a particular Word to express it; and where they find it hit their Eye at first sight, they say the *Sharawadgi* is fine or is admirable, or any such expression of Esteem. And whoever observes the Work upon the best Indian Gowns, or the painting upon their best Skreens or Purcellans, will find their Beauty is all of this kind (that is) without order. (1690: 132)

Much ink has been spilled on whether or not *sharawadgi* is a genuine Chinese word, as if it held the key to Temple's theory of the Chinese garden, but Temple clearly admits that he is going by second-hand reports from "others, who have lived much among the *Chineses*" (1690: 131), as well as his first-hand observations of "the Work upon the best Indian Gowns, or the painting upon their best Skreens or Purcellans" (1690: 132).³⁸ It is striking that Temple opens up the experience of *sharawadgi* to "whoever" has had any contact with these sumptuous objects that offer, as it were, their own trip to China. While there is little reason to assume that by the phrase

"the Work upon the best" gowns, screens or porcelains Temple was referring to a particular type of decoration, we should note that objects decorated with gardens and landscape motifs were one of the most popular and
prized items of the China, and more generally East Indian, trade. In 1682,
John Evelyn described a visit to the mansion of Christopher Boone, a com-
mittee member of the governing board of the East India Company: "We
went after to visite our good neighbor Mr. *Bohune*, whose whole house
is a Cabinet of all elegancies, especialy *Indian*." Evelyn was especially
impressed by "the Contrivement of the *Japan* Skreenes instead of Wainscot
in the *Hall*," which he found "very remarkable"; "so are the Landskips of
the screens," he noted, "representing the manner of living, & Country of
the *Chinezes* & c."³⁹ The "China Trunke" mentioned by Dorothy Osborne
in her February 19, 1654 letter to Temple during their protracted courtship
was probably similarly decorated. According to Osborne, it was a gift from
her brother and "the finest of the kinde that ere I saw."⁴⁰ It is likely that the
analogy Temple draws between the art of the Chinese garden and the decorative arts of the China trade was significantly facilitated by such decorations that were often read as accurate representations of and windows onto
the culture and manners of a distant and impenetrable country.

As we can see from Evelyn's comments, a general confusion between
India, Japan, and China reigned in seventeenth-century England. These
countries were identified with their major exports – calico and chintz,
lacquer, and porcelain, respectively – to such an extent that their names
denoted both a type of decorative object and a geographical origin, leading
to understandable confusion. When Temple assumed that a common aesthetic, traceable back to China, ruled all three kinds of objects, however, he
was not being simply confused. Centuries before the Europeans had insisted
on making their entry, cotton, lacquer, and porcelain had been some of the
most important items in a wide network of global trade between India,
the Middle East, and East Asia. Chinese porcelain was widely traded in the
Middle East long before the Portuguese first brought it to Europe in the
sixteenth century;⁴¹ Indian cotton was introduced to China in the ninth
century;⁴² and lacquerware, featuring an ancient decorative technique first
developed in China during the Shang dynasty (ca. 1600 BCE–1100 BCE),
was an important part of the inter-Asian trade as well as the long-distance
trade between China and the Arab world from the tenth century on.⁴³
Naturally, these interactions gave rise to cross-fertilizations and collaborations, not only in terms of shared technical information but also aesthetic
practice. For instance, blue-and-white porcelain was in fact the product
of a "remarkable collaboration" between Chinese and Middle Eastern

ceramic traditions. The processed cobalt oxide that was responsible for the blue tint was an import from Persia to China, where undecorated Song whitewares and greenwares were the norm before the Persian-influenced decorative wares gained wide popularity in the early Ming period.[44] The decoration of Chinese blue-and-white ware thus combined elements from both traditions: the "symmetry, mathematically organized space, rectilinear patterns, and detailed enrichment of surface" in the Islamic tradition and "asymmetry, a flowing sense of space, naturalism, curvilinear patterns, and rotating directional designs (such as cloud, wave, and lotus scroll)" in the Chinese.[45]

In the case of landscape-decorated Asian export art, it is especially easy to see a stylistic convergence and mutual influence between different object types. Temple probably saw and owned two varieties of Chinese porcelain available on the seventeenth-century European market: *Kraak* and transitional ware, both of which were well-represented in the Dutch East India trade. *Kraak* porcelain, which was produced in Jingdezhen in southwestern China for the export market during the late Ming dynasty (between 1580 and the mid-seventeenth century), was handpainted in underglaze blue, had alternating narrow and wide panels on its rims and sides, and featured deft sketches of river scenes and landscapes with birds, insects, deer, and trees placed near rocks or a flower vase.[46] Between the fall of the Ming in 1644 and the reopening of the imperial factory at Jingdezhen in the 1680s, production dropped drastically and only small quantities of privately made "transitional" porcelain made their way to Europe. "Transitional" ware dropped the foliated radial panels of *Kraak* and adopted a looser, more informal design, often depicting running landscapes or river scenes that resembled Chinese woodblock prints that accompanied novels, plays, and romances.[47] The tremendous popularity of these porcelain landscapes in Europe exerted a significant influence on the production of other kinds of export art ranging from wallpaper, lacquer, and chintz. The ubiquitous conceit in Indian chintz of an exotic flowering tree emerging from a stylized, irregular rocky mound, then branching out into a rich texture of flowers, was partly based on motifs found on Chinese porcelain.[48] Decoration on Japanese export lacquerware, in sync with European taste in Chinese porcelain, increasingly featured asymmetric pictorial scenes depicting landscapes drawn from literary classics such as the eleventh-century Japanese classic *Genji monogatari*.[49] Temple does not mention wallpapers, perhaps because they were first brought to England only in the 1690s after the publication of his second *Miscellanea*, but they follow the same trend. Of the three general types of wallpaper decoration – flowering tree with fantastical rocks and birds, flowering tree with people, and people in a Chinese landscape – it was the third that was most popular and prized.[50] It was only a matter of time before these popular decorative motifs were taken up by European chinoiserie products. The most obvious example is the blue-and-white soft-paste Staffordshire porcelain decorated with Josiah Spode's willow pattern, which culled different compositional elements from landscape depictions on Chinese porcelain and recomposed them in a standardized format – a bridge with persons crossing it, a willow tree, a boat, a tea house, two birds, and a fence across the foreground of the garden – for the mass market at the end of the eighteenth century.[51] By the nineteenth century, as Elizabeth Chang points out, porcelain imprinted with the blue-and-white willow pattern was so ubiquitous as to become "one of the most centrally recognizable touchstones of Britishness, and particularly domestic middle-class Britishness."[52] No self-respecting British middle-class family could do without it. This imprinting of a Chinese landscape design on modern British consciousness and mores took place via a process of industrial standardization that had little regard for authenticity. Its success, however, would have been neither possible nor predictable without a longer history of consumer preferences that privileged the landscape over other decorative motifs.

When Temple spoke of Chinese gardens organized according to an idea of beauty "without order," then, he was probably referring to stylistic commonalities detectable in these decorations on Chinese export art items. Without any knowledge of China's painting or design conventions, Temple had an impoverished vocabulary to analyze the kind of beauty he was talking about. He could only describe it, at best, as the negation or the absence of the mathematical, rectilinear, and geometric principles governing western European aesthetic practices ranging from architecture to gardening. As B. Sprague Allen points out in his important study of changing norms in English taste in the seventeenth and eighteenth centuries, "Just as classical motives and the symmetry and axial emphasis of their arrangement indicate the organizing influence of the Renaissance, so the stylized landscapes, the naturalistic representation of insects, flowers, and plants, and their asymmetrical disposition identify Oriental design whether the object decorated be porcelain, lacquer, or wallpaper."[53] The "naturalistic disregard of uniformity," "absence of perspective and proportion in the representation of landscapes," and highly stylized treatment of clouds, water, and mountains with an emphasis on irregular shape formations challenged classicist norms of beauty.[54] Although Temple demonstrates an acute sensitivity to this alternative aesthetics, he is very far from recommending it in English gardening. His *Essay upon the Gardens of Epicurus* serves, on the one hand, as a personal *apologia* as well as philosophical defense of his choice to spend the remainder of his life cultivating his garden, far from the public eye. It is, at the same time, a pragmatic guide to such practical questions as how big a garden should be (Temple deemed "four or five to seven or eight Acres" sufficient), what its essential elements are ("Flowers, Fruit, Shade, and Water"), what plants and fruit trees one ought to plant in one's garden (he was very partial to peaches and grapes), and how to lay it out (1690: 112, 119). "The best Figure of a Garden," Temple specified, was "either a Square or an Oblong, and either upon a Flat or a Descent," with preference given to the descent, since it provided a better "View" (1690: 126). Other layouts were obviously possible, which made him curious to know how the Chinese, with their different taste, organized theirs. However, he believed that he had hit upon the right form for practicing gentleman gardeners in his own country. While the "Figure" of the garden, which determined the quality of its view, obviously added to the pleasure to be found in gardens, it was far from being the most important aspect for Temple. For Temple, the psychological and health benefits of owning a garden appear to have been paramount: the peace, exercise, air, and the good "Sallads or Fruits" to be had from it (1690: 140).

Picking up on Temple's reference to the Chinese garden in his *Spectator* papers on the pleasures of the imagination, Addison approached the garden from a very particular vantage point – namely, from the perspective of what Temple calls the *view*, and what was also known as the *prospect*. Addison's papers made an important contribution to the cultural shift from what Horace Walpole, in his *History of the Modern Taste in Gardening* (1780), derisively called Temple's "fruit-garden" or "kitchen-garden" to the eighteenth-century "pleasure-garden" and landscape.[55] This change, which emphasized the visual properties of a rural scene and treated it like a decorative object intended first and foremost to please the eye, was reflected in several overlapping phenomena that can be observed over the course of the century: the increasing enclosure of the land that led to the conversion and consolidation of arable farmland into pastoral vistas; an intense interest in landscaping and visual "improvement" of the land, especially in the great country estates; the birth of a picturesque aesthetic; the birth of domestic tourism to rival the Grand Tour; and, in cities, the growth of immense pleasure gardens such as Vauxhall that offered variable and entertaining landscapes for the urban masses.[56] These changes mark the birth of what Peter de Bolla calls the "culture of visuality" – "a *culture* based on the visual, on modalities of visualization, the production and consumption

of visual matter."⁵⁷ Addison, an early spokesman for this culture, explains
the supremacy of vision in the following way. "Our sight," he says, "is the
most perfect and most delightful of all our Senses." Describing it as "a
more delicate and diffusive kind of Touch" that can extend itself to the
most distant objects, he claims it as the most powerful, far-reaching, and
informative of all the senses. Thus, by the phrase "pleasures of the imagination," he clarifies,

> I here mean such as arise from visible Objects, either when we have them
> actually in our view, or when we call up their Ideas into our Minds by
> Paintings, Statues, Descriptions, or any the like Occasion: We cannot
> indeed have a single Image in the Fancy that did not make its first Entrance
> through the Sight; but we have the Power of retaining, altering and com-
> pounding those Images which we have once received into all the varieties of
> Picture and Vision that are most agreeable to the Imagination; for by this
> Faculty a Man in a Dungeon is capable of entertaining himself with Scenes
> and Landskips more beautiful than any that can be found in the whole
> Compass of Nature. (3: 537)⁵⁸

What is original in Addison's theory of the imagination is not the
preeminence of vision in this empiricist account of images making their
"Entrance" into the theater of the mind through the sensory apparatus,
nor the Lockean model of the mind that then stores them up, changing
and combining them into new forms. It is, rather, the penchant he displays
for what I shall call illusionary aesthetic practices – practices that depend,
in other words, in creating illusions of the real. The scene depicted here
strikingly reverses Plato's monitory allegory of the cave, which subordinates the material world to an ideal world of forms. Far from admonishing
the "man in a Dungeon," it credits him for his ability to entertain himself
with "Scenes and Landskips" more beautiful than any real ones. Addison's
alternative allegory, and his ensuing aesthetic theory, thus defend what he
calls the "Secondary Pleasures of the Imagination" – pleasures taken in
"agreeable Visions of Things that are either Absent or Fictitious" (3: 537).

In Addison's theory, there are, broadly speaking, three kinds of landscapes, either real (visible) or imagined, which correspond to three different aesthetic categories: the great, new, and beautiful.⁵⁹ The landscape
that Addison uses to redefine aesthetic pleasure as an alternative kind of
"Possession" or "Property" is the visible, "great," or sublime landscape.

> A Man of a Polite Imagination, is let into a great many Pleasures that the
> Vulgar are not capable of receiving. He can converse with a Picture, and find
> an agreeable Companion in a Statue. He meets with a secret Refreshment in
> a Description, and often feels a greater Satisfaction in the Prospect of Fields

and Meadows, than another in the Possession. It gives him, indeed, a kind of property in every thing he sees, and makes the most rude uncultivated Parts of Nature administer to his Pleasures. (3: 538)

Whereas Temple clearly spoke as the proprietor of a garden that he enjoyed as his private, secluded, and assiduously cultivated property, here Addison speaks of relishing "uncultivated" "Fields and Meadows" without possessing them. In fact, he goes so far as to say that the ability to take pleasure in the "Prospect" of a natural landscape is a higher, more "Polite" form of possession than mere economic proprietorship. As Carole Fabricant has remarked, while Addison does not do away entirely with the social connotations of the "prospect viewer's lofty position," he "de-emphasizes their link to privileged positions of ascendancy and eminence."[60] This "rude uncultivated" landscape that is the property of all who know how to take pleasure in it is connected in Addison's theory specifically to what Addison calls the "Great" and what is more commonly theorized as the sublime. It is defined, most of all, by "wide and undetermined Prospects," a "rude kind of Magnificence," and "a spacious Horison," all of which produce in us "a pleasing Astonishment," "delightful Stillness and Amazement" (3: 540–41).

The beautiful landscape, on the other hand, is the cultivated landscape or the garden, which Addison associates with "the nice Touches and Embellishments of Art" (3: 549). Given Addison's definition of beauty as consisting "either in the Gaiety or Variety of Colours, in the Symmetry and Proportion of Parts, in the Arrangement and disposition of Bodies, or in a just Mixture and Concurrence of all together" (3: 544), one might infer that he has in mind a highly organized garden, but he is in fact very critical of the geometric English garden "laid out by the Rule and Line," with trees rising "in Cones, Globes, and Pyramids" (3: 552). Such a garden, he believes, cannot give much pleasure to the imagination because it makes for a static, unchanging scene that can only make us feel bored. We are apt to grow inured to our familiar, unchanging surroundings, Addison writes, so "that whatever is new or uncommon contributes a little to vary Human Life, and to divert our Minds" (3: 541). Addison goes on to interpret nature itself in terms of perpetual change, motion, and novelty, with such examples as meadows in spring bloom, "when they are all new and fresh, with their first Gloss upon them, and not yet too much accustomed and familiar to the Eye," and the "Prospect" of "Rivers, Jetteaus, or Falls of Water, where the Scene is perpetually shifting, and entertaining the Sight every Moment with something that is new" (3: 542).

The Chinese trick in gardening, according to Addison, has everything to do with organizing, directing, and "humouring" nature in such a way that gratifies this restless curiosity of the eye and keeps it moving. The Chinese, he declares, "shew a Genius in Works of this Nature, and therefore always conceal the Art by which they direct themselves" (3: 552). Chinese gardens thus strike "the Imagination at first Sight, without discovering what it is that has so agreeable an Effect" (3: 552). Addison's phrase here closely follows Temple's description of Chinese *sharawadgi* as a powerful aesthetic impact ("strike the Eye," "hit their Eye at first sight") linked to an imperceptible, unfamiliar order ("without any order or disposition of parts, that shall be commonly or easily observ'd") (1680: 132). What interests Addison most in Temple's discussion, I propose, is not so much the immediacy of aesthetic experience or its indifference to cognition, but the imaginative play between seeing and not-seeing, between the primary and the secondary pleasures of the imagination.[61] This gap or lag between what is and what is not seen, what appears and what is concealed ("without discovering") rewards the imagination while simultaneously deferring imaginative gratification. In this way Addison modifies Temple's notion of the Chinese garden's beauty "without order," theorizing it as an example of the "*new* or *uncommon*," and aligning it crucially with curiosity and "agreeable Surprise," an experience *in* and *of* time (3: 541). Chinese gardens are gardens of the new, he implies.[62] Addison takes Temple's spatial idea of irregular form, in other words, and temporalizes it, psychologizing the Chinese garden as an experience of novelty.[63]

The category of the new in Addison's aesthetic theory has troubled critics from the start. Not only is it lumped unceremoniously together with the uncommon and the strange, ideas that have meanings quite distinct from the new, it seems to have much more to do with the perceiving subject and his apprehension of the object rather than any characteristic intrinsic to the object itself.[64] On the one hand, Addison's use of the concept of novelty has seemed too close to that of earlier thinkers such as Descartes, Hobbes, and Dryden, who also spoke of novelty, wonder, and admiration, to be considered original.[65] At the same time, his "semantic laxness" in using the word 'new' to cover such diverse objects as monsters, camera obscuras, and Chinese gardens has seemed lacking in rigor. As Robin Dix has convincingly pointed out, however, what is original to Addison and what unites the categories of the new, uncommon, and strange is his conception of an object that has taken on (and continues to take on) a form never realized before.[66] This could be an object that is "ever in Motion, and sliding away from beneath the Eye of the Beholder," constantly moving and changing, such as a waterfall, or simply something we have never seen before (3: 542). Strikingly, Addison both naturalizes and temporalizes this concept of the new, tying it to an idea of nature understood as an object in constant growth and change. As Neil Saccamano puts it, for Addison "nature is a hypostatization of perpetual motion."[67] Addison's favorite image for nature in motion is "a Tree in all its Luxuriancy and Diffusion of Boughs and Branches" – precisely the image of the flowering tree, branching out luxuriously, that is so common in Chinese wallpaper and Indian chintz in eighteenth-century England (3: 552). Without this idea of perpetual motion, it is difficult to see why Addison would refer to a landscape in a camera obscura in the same paper in which he discusses Chinese gardens. The continuity arises, most of all, from the notion that the most exact representation of nature is that which can produce a "near Resemblance to Nature, as it does not only, like other Pictures, give the Colour and Figure, but the Motion of the Things it represents." Hence the beauty of Addison's remark that the "prettiest Landskip" he ever saw was one drawn on the walls of a room camera obscura in which he was treated to a vision of an undulating river, a ship that traveled from one end of the room to another, "Green Shadows of Trees, waving to and fro with the Wind, and Herds of Deer among them in Miniature, leaping about upon the Wall" (3: 551). Addison's point is that we experience nature not as a still picture but in and through time. This cinematic image of nature as a series of moving pictures informs Addison's Chinese garden, which also creates visual images of nature by artificial means, but with a view to exciting surprise and preserving a sense of nature's movement in time. In the *Spectator* papers on the pleasures of the imagination, we thus see Addison moving away from the cult of chinaware as the representative (and static) Chinese object to an exploratory appreciation of the Chinese garden as a novel aesthetic program. Recognizing this turn from Chinese object to Chinese practice helps us identify Addison's move away from a beauty-centered aesthetics to one more attuned to the temporal experience of the viewer.[68]

Addison's theory of the pleasures of the imagination explains not only why our enjoyment of nature always involves an experience of time, but also why our very idea of nature is always already profoundly cultural. Although all aesthetic experience for Addison depends on an initial immediate impact (a sense impression), imagination mediates that experience by mobilizing it in time. Nothing is more characteristic of the imagination, in fact, than movement. The imagination is always on the move, going somewhere. In his rhetoric, Addison is constantly turning the imagination into a runner and a rover: "The Beauties of the most stately Garden or Palace lie in a narrow Compass, the Imagination immediately runs them over, and requires something else to gratifie her" (3: 549). The imagination runs both backward and forward in time, responding to visual impressions by comparing them to objects formerly seen, seeking out new pleasures, looking for resemblances, representing them "to our Minds, either as Copies or Originals" (3: 550). This is why Addison is so interested in doubles and doubling effects. The pleasures of the imagination, he asserts, arise "from a double Principle: from the Agreeableness of the Objects to the Eye, and from their Similitude to other Objects" (3: 550). Hence Addison's fascination with objects that blur the boundary between nature and art.[69] Rather than limning the line between art and nature, Addison points to their mutual confusion and collaboration. Thus, nature is for him not simply an "aesthetic norm" in the sense of an object to be imitated, an ideal or generic type, but an experience irrevocably mediated by art.[70] We think of nature as a painter working in "bold and masterly" scenes with "rough careless Strokes" (3: 549), and "we find the Works of Nature still more pleasant, the more they resemble those of Art" (3: 549). This is both the corollary and the inverse of the more generally accepted principle that art pleases when it resembles nature. As Addison puts it, "artificial Works receive a greater Advantage from their Resemblance of such as are natural" (3: 550). The interplay between nature and imagination creates, as David Marshall puts it, "a double landscape" – a landscape that is both visual impression and imaginative mindscape, straddling the border between the real and the unreal, vision and illusion, design and chance.[71] The Chinese garden, in this regard, is an emblematic realization of the double principle, where "the Curiosities of Art" (3: 551) meet that which is "more Grand and August" in nature; where the imagination goes looking for a concealed art "without discovering what it is that has so agreeable an Effect" (3: 552), where art wears the garb of nature and the viewer cannot tell the difference. When we place the Chinese garden within this larger context of Addison's writings, it becomes clear that, while he was interested in the idea of art imitating nature in its original, uncultivated state, he approached this idea both as a contradiction and an illusion. The Chinese garden, as he saw it, embodied the contradictory program of "producing the illusion of untouched natural scenery in an artificial way, even if with natural means."[72] The problem with the formally designed European garden is not that it is artificial – all gardens are necessarily artificial modifications of nature – but that it cannot sustain the kind of imaginative play named by the "double principle."

The greatest difference between Addison's account of the Chinese garden and later, widely read versions such as Jean-Denis Attiret's *Description
of the Emperor of China's Gardens and Pleasure-Houses Near Pe-king* (1752)
and William Chambers's "Of the Art of Laying Out Gardens among the
Chinese" (1757) and *Dissertation on Oriental Gardening* (1772) is that
this delicate balance between art and nature is lost in the later accounts,
although the concepts of novelty, variety, and irregularity continue to play
a key role.[73] In its place, we find a repeated emphasis on artifice, whether
in the form of an exaggerated grandeur in scale, as in Attiret's account, or
sheer inventiveness and contrivance, as in Chambers's *Dissertation*. Both
Attiret, who was a painter in the service of Emperor Qianlong's court, and
Chambers, who had briefly visited Canton while working as an assistant
supercargo for the Swedish East India Company, are intent on piquing
their readers' interest in China as a land of spectacular luxury and splendor, as well as despotic power. In their rendering of the imperial garden of
Yuanming Yuan, they play up the exotic, erotic, and excessive dimensions
of a nature theme park constructed at huge expense for a single, omnipo-
tent man. The dominant image is not that of a rural landscape but rather
an urban pleasure ground offering expensive and exclusive thrills. Attiret
speaks of entire mountains, raised sometimes to the height of sixty feet, and
artificial valleys, canals, rivers, lakes, and meres surrounding a miniature
city built solely to entertain the emperor.[74] Chambers, who has clearly read
Addison, asserts that the Chinese gardeners use "three separate classes" of
scenes distinguished by "the appellations of the pleasing, the terrible, and
the surprising," which they mix up to create complex theatrical effects.
Always "upon the stretch in search of novelty," they resort to "a thousand
artifices" to "excite a great variety of passions in the mind of the spectator." These range from water-works, buildings, sculptures, paintings, trees
in the "pleasing" scenes; artificially ruined buildings and trees, birds and
animals of prey, even instruments of torture in the "terrible" scenes; and
subterraneous vaults, complete with special lighting and musical effects,
and "pale images of antient kings and heroes, reclining on beds of state"
in the "surprizing, or supernatural scenes."[75] Chambers's construction of
the Chinese garden as a theatrical, even cinematic experience where the
viewer is guided through a succession of surprising tableaux clearly alludes
back to Addisonian aesthetic principles, but overdramatizes them to the
point of grotesquerie. Novelty becomes an idea of artificial stimulation
rather than imaginative play, and Chambers ends by suggesting that the
Chinese emperor, for all his pleasure pavilions stocked with the "fairest and
most accomplished concubines," "entertaining books, amorous paintings,

musical instruments, implements for gaming, writing, drawing, painting and embroidering; with beds, couches, and chairs, of various constructions, for the uses of sitting and lying in different postures," must be a rather bored man.[76] As Walpole quips in *The History of the Modern Taste in Gardening* (1780), "Methinks this is the childish solace and repose of grandeur, not a retirement from affairs to the delights of rural life."[77]

The transformation of the figure of the Chinese garden in the eighteenth century from a complex and productive concept of irregular beauty, novelty, and nature-as-artifice in the early decades of the century to an idea of sheer contrivance and strange, despotic theater in the second half of the century was part of a larger process in which the image of China was increasingly politicized in negative terms as "despotic, excessive, fantastic, incoherent, illogical, and exotic."[78] Addison's grouping together of the new and uncommon with the strange and monstrous in his aesthetic theory may have indirectly authorized this conceptual slippage. In Addison's *Spectator* papers, which, as we have seen, inherit and update Temple's sympathetic interpretation of a differential Chinese aesthetics, we see emerging an image of China that clearly departs from Temple's 'ancient' notion of China as a land of exemplary political virtue and veers much closer to Defoe's 'modern' idea of the Chinese as an alien people. Like Defoe, Addison appears to have relied on Le Comte as an important contemporary source, though his tone is usually much lighter than Defoe's or Le Comte's. A brash defender of Jesuit policy, Chinese antiquity, and ancient Chinese religion, Le Comte was much more ambivalent about modern Chinese culture, which he accused of being both inferior and idolatrous. His *Memoirs and Observations* (1697) is peppered with derogatory comments on Chinese architecture, writing, and science. Addison, who names "Father *Le Comte*" as a source in *Spectator* no. 189, uses him often for comical or ironical effect, comparing and contrasting Chinese customs with the equally odd and outlandish English ones. In a paper (no. 73) that compares fashionable women to idols, for instance, Addison alludes to "the *Chinese Idols*, who are Whipped and Scourged when they refuse to comply with the Prayers that are offered to them" to make the facetious point that the English have their own irrational ways of treating their idol-like women (1: 313). In another paper on disobedient children and their overpunishing fathers (no. 189), he recalls the Chinese custom of punishing the son who "should be known to kill or so much as to strike his Father" by razing the house, even the village where such an infamy has occurred to make the point that unnatural sons do not justify the violence of unnatural fathers (2: 242–44).

Although Addison uses these quirky anecdotes drawn from Le Comte's book mostly to make satirical points about English culture, he also shows a tendency to turn them back on Chinese customs and mores. This tendency, already plain in the story about the zero tolerance shown to filial disobedience in Chinese culture, is especially evident when Addison discusses gender relations. In *Spectator* no. 511, Addison retells a story found in Le Comte about how the Tartars, during their invasion of China, would round up the women, throw them in sacks, and put them on the market for sale.[79] In Le Comte's story, a man picks out a sack marked with a high price but discovers that the woman he has chosen "sight unseen" is an old hag. Enraged with disappointment, he comes close to killing her, but she persuades him to spare her on the basis of her wealthy family connections and in the end proves to be "an excellent Wife." Although this story makes the ostensibly universal point that feminine beauty should not be the most important criterion in a man's choice of wife, Addison's allusion in the same paper to "the Manner among the *Persians* to have several *Fairs* in the Kingdom, at which all the young unmarried Women were annually exposed to Sale" makes it clear that, under the guise of a lighthearted joke about women's 'value,' he is making a serious contrast between English liberty and eastern despotism (4: 314–15). In *The Freeholder*, a Whig party paper he published in 1715–16 during the Jacobite rebellion, Addison advances the argument that British women are an exemplary and fortunate lot who enjoy, along with their male cohorts, a political culture of liberty realized nowhere else in the world. Nothing can make this point clearer than a comparison of British women with the women of the 'East,' including China:

> In those Countries the Men have no Property in their Wives, who are the Slaves to Slaves; every married Woman being subject to a domestick Tyrant, that requires from her the same Vassalage which he pays to his Sultan. If the Ladies wou'd seriously consider the evil Consequences of arbitrary Power, they would find, that it spoils the Shape of the Foot in *China*, where the barbarous Politicks of the Men so diminish the Basis of the Female Figure, as to unqualify a Woman for an Evening Walk or a Country Dance. In the *East Indies* a Widow, who has any Regard to her Character, throws her self into the Flames of her Husband's Funeral Pile, to shew, forsooth, that she is faithful and loyal to the Memory of her deceased Lord.

The examples go on: in Persia women have the same status as "a Bale of Silk, or a Drove of Camels"; in "all the Dominions of the Great Turk," "a Woman thinks her self happy if she can get but the twelfth Share in a Husband" for whom she matters little more than a slave. In all these countries where

"Arbitrary Government" rules, Addison argues, women lead "uncomfortable lives," to put it mildly, and practice "Passive Obedience" to its "utmost Perfection." Women living in European countries where "Popery" rules do not fare much better. Pointing specifically to the plight of women in Spain, Italy, and France, whom he likens to the unfortunate women of the despotic East, Addison drives his message home: women should be "no less averse to Popery than to arbitrary Power." Calling upon his "fair Fellow-Free-holders" who "have all the Privileges of *English*-born Subjects, without the Burdens," he urges them to participate in national politics by winning over their men to the right party.[80] What interests me here is not the problematic expedience that accompanies the use of women's status as a gauge of political liberty so much as the difficulty created by this political understanding of China for Addison's elaboration of a Chinese aesthetics of novelty. While Addison was clearly indebted to Temple's aesthetic ideas, his political understanding of China was much closer to Defoe's. For a writer who aligns aesthetic pleasure with political freedom and claims that "a spacious Horison is an Image of Liberty" (3: 541), the idea that the Chinese have access to a profound understanding of nature aesthetics but live politically straitjacketed lives should have posed a thorny intellectual problem. There is little indication, however, that Addison attempted to work out a genuine solution to the contradiction between China's aesthetic modernity and its purported political premodernity. The same problem, as we saw, plagues the accounts of the Chinese gardens by Attiret and Chambers who inherited Addison's dilemma and, far from solving it, ultimately abetted rather than complicated the clichés circulating about China.

It was perhaps inevitable that Addison's attempt to develop a mercantile aesthetics of novelty into a full-fledged aesthetics of temporality or modernity would fail. Addison's concept of the new was always too much of a mixed bag that tried to unite everything from monsters and camera obscuras to springtime meadows and prospect gardens. In his haste to award surprise with aesthetic value, Addison did not sufficiently sort out the different varieties of sudden wonder. Furthermore, although Addison's idea of novelty honored modernity as an aesthetic experience of constant change and pleasure taken in that change, it failed to grapple seriously with the paradox that the new is a vanishing point in time. What is new is so only for a moment before it becomes part of that overly familiar "Sett of Objects" that tire and bore us (3: 541). This infallible and self-destructive logic that lies at the heart of novelty explains why and how, over a relatively short period of time, China's paradigmatic novelty ultimately condemned it to obsolescence. The more China was absorbed into the culture of consumption, the more quickly it became a predictable sign of an out-moded idea of the fashionable. The transformation of Temple's idea of an undefinable *sharawadgi* into the programmatic decorative garden struc-tures such as pagodas – what Walpole condescendingly calls "the fantastic sharawadgis of the Chinese"[81] – had little to do with the real China, and everything to do with this aporia in the internal logic of novelty. Although Addison attempted to overcome this aporia by making the surprising move of defining nature as the ultimate novel object, avoiding the more obvi-ous theoretical problems associated with the novel as mercantile commod-ity, his effort to meld these different examples of the novel would prove unconvincing. Later theorists would drop novelty as an aesthetic category altogether.[82]

And yet Addison's redefinition of aesthetic pleasure in terms of "agree-able Surprise," "Curiosity," "Strangeness," and "Variety" – the key words that define both the experience of the "*new* or *uncommon*" and the Chinese garden (3: 541) – had a lasting influence on eighteenth-century literary his-tory, where new ideas about landscape gardening shaped the very terms in which literary works would be discussed. As John Dixon Hunt comments, the landscape garden became "an increasingly prominent and crucial fea-ture of the century's aesthetic patterns," such that "the literary history of the eighteenth century could partly be written in terms of the development of precisely those genres that were identified with the landscape garden."[83] Does Temple's idea of *sharawadgi* or Addison's notion of the double (arti-ficially natural) Chinese garden bear any relevance to the shifting terms of literary criticism? Where does Addison stand on the issue of the ancients and the moderns, and does his position relate in any way to his position on China?

Poetic Genius, or the Garden in Time

Landscape is Addison's favorite metaphor for poetry. The strong poet, he says, "seems to get the better of Nature; he takes, indeed, the landskip after her, but gives it more vigorous Touches, heightens its Beauty, and so enlivens the whole Piece" that nature itself appears "weak and faint, in Comparison" (3: 560–61). The weak reader, in contrast, is "As a Person, with a weak Sight," who "may have the confused Prospect of a Place that lies before him, without entering into its several Parts, or discerning the variety of its Colours in their full Glory and Perfection" (3: 561). Addison's choice to discuss the imagination primarily as a visual and visualizing faculty, as well as his notion that the landscape is a temporal as well as spatial object, goes some way toward explaining his choice of metaphor. Just as the chief concern in his discussion of Chinese versus English gardening was to advocate a method of artfully ordering nature while taking care to "conceal the Art" in order to preserve a sense of nature's spontaneity, Addison's main interest in discussing different poetic landscapes is to distinguish between the more natural and irregular works and the more artificially ordered ones (3: 552). Nonetheless, the metaphor is not a perfect fit. As Neil Saccamano has pointed out, poetry simply does not relate to nature in the same mimetic way that painting does. "One cannot see the mimicry of a description; one can only read poetic description."[84] Addison's visual metaphors for writer and reader, who are both described as agents of visualization, clue us into the strain behind the circular logic of his definition of art. By requiring "visible objects to function as at least the virtual or possible referents of poetic description," Addison ends up having to use the same metaphors for both writer, reader, and the work of art.[85] The poetic landscape thus refers to both the writer's vision, the poetic work itself, and the reader's experience of poetry. What, then, would count as irregular, natural, and wild in the linguistic medium of poetry?

Addison's visual metaphors require circumspect reading precisely because they make it look like he is advocating a return to 'original nature,' or nature in all her original wildness, whereas his aesthetics in fact privileges the role of the imagination in our experience of nature. Addison firmly argues that the aesthetic appreciation of nature is conditional upon the mediation of nature by our own imaginative activities. This is why we need to exercise caution with Addison's thesis that the ancient writers are the closest to rough, untamed nature, while the more refined and polished modern writers lie farther from it. Constrained by his own visual metaphors, Addison vacillates between the concept of poetry as the imitation or ordering of nature and a theory of the author as himself a force of nature, between the poet as the painter of landscape and as the landscape itself. The idea of genius as a force of nature, already adumbrated in Temple's reflections on genius, appears in *Spectator* no. 160, published almost a full year before the papers on the pleasures of the imagination, where it is used to differentiate the "great natural Genius's that were never disciplined and broken by Rules of Art" from "a Genius refined by Conversation, Reflection, and the Reading of the most polite Authors." Addison submits that "Many of these great natural Genius's" who, "by the meer Strength of natural Parts, and without any Assistance or Art of Learning," had "produced Works that were the Delight of their own Times and the Wonder of Posterity," are "to be found among the Ancients, and in particular among those of the more Eastern Parts of the World." The works of the great natural genius are characterized by "something nobly wild and extravagant," something "infinitely more beautiful than all the Turn and Polishing" of the "*Bel Esprit*" or the refined and polite author (2: 127). Using Homer as his prime example of this unbroken and undisciplined genius, Addison states that such a genius is "like a rich Soil, in a happy Climate, that produces a whole Wilderness of noble Plants rising in a thousand beautiful Landskips *without any certain Order or Regularity*" (2: 129, my emphasis). This rhetoric of a beauty without order, reminiscent of Temple's description of the Chinese garden, subtly aligns the great "Eastern" "Genius of the first Class" with an idea of Chinese aesthetics. Meanwhile, Addison discusses another kind of genius of "a second Class," exemplified in authors such as Virgil and Milton, whom he likens to a contrastive garden "laid out in Walks and Parterres, and cut into Shape and Beauty by the Skill of the Gardener." These second kind of geniuses, he says, "are those that have formed themselves by Rules, and submitted the Greatness of their natural Talents to the Corrections and Restraints of Art" (2: 129). While Addison associates the first kind of genius primarily with the ancient authors, he does not limit it to them. "Our Countryman *Shakespear*," for instance, is held up as "a remarkable Instance of this first kind of great Genius's," while the ancients Plato, Aristotle, and Tully are held up as examples of the secondary kind (2: 218–19). The categories of genius, in other words, cut across the ages, and fail to conform to the ancient-modern divide.

In the papers on the pleasures of the imagination, Addison makes it clear that he believes that wild and irregular gardens are, aesthetically speaking, superior to the gardens decorated with topiaries and "Little Labyrinths of the most finished Parterre" (3: 552–53). This does not mean that geniuses of the first class are in every instance superior to the second, however. Addison is much more measured in his discussion of literary genius. The geniuses of the second class, he says, are not "inferior to the first, but only … of a different kind" (2: 129). In making clear the difference between his view of real gardens and poetic gardens, Addison introduces an incommensurability between seeing and reading. The crucial difference, I propose, is time or history. Just as his theory of the double principle explains how an imaginative surplus can accrue from the gap between the original and the copy, which always comes after it in time, reading always involves an awareness of a temporal difference between the original composition and the act of reading. In addition, Addison postulates a historical rupture between the ancients and the moderns whose difference is likened to that between nature and culture, between the wild landscape and the manicured gardens. Nature, in this sense, is also our name for that which we are historically and culturally distanced from, that which we have lost. Addison's famous landscape analogies for Homer, Virgil, and Ovid ask to be read in this light.

> Reading the *Iliad* is like travelling through a Country uninhabited, where the Fancy is entertained with a thousand Savage Prospects of vast Desarts, wide uncultivated Marshes, huge Forests, mis-shapen Rocks and Precipices. On the contrary, the *Aeneid* is like a well-ordered Garden, where it is impossible to find out any Part unadorned, or to cast our Eyes upon a single Spot, that does not produce some beautiful Plant or Flower. But when we are in the *Metamorphosis*, we are walking on enchanted Ground, and see nothing but Scenes of Magick lying round us. (3: 564)

This account of three representative authors who embody the three different aesthetic categories of the great, the beautiful, and the strange represents Addison's attempt to reconcile the divergent historiographies of the ancients and the moderns: namely, the 'ancient' view that "the classics should be imitated because they had imitated nature so well," with the 'modern' view that the march of history has brought about undeniable progress.[86] The reason why Virgil's beautiful gardens cannot be regarded as simply inferior to Homer's "Savage Prospects" is the same reason why literary or poetic modernity cannot be merely demoted to a faint copy of the ancients. This passage in fact performs a virtuoso balancing act: Addison accepts historical progress and poetic refinement while also acknowledging loss. At the same time that he follows the 'ancients' in instancing Homer as the most sublime genius, Addison also hints at the savagery of ancient times; while affirming that Virgil is a belated and less inspired poet than Homer, he also indirectly praises him for making leaps forward in judgment and refinement. Ovid, who represents the new, uncommon, or the strange, represents yet another kind of temporality – a suspended, radically self-renewing temporality – that is distinct from the regressive and the progressive models of history: "he every where entertains us with something we never saw before, and shews Monster after Monster, to the end of the *Metamorphosis*" (3: 566). Ovid's conception of time suggests a way out of the impasse between the ancient and modern models of history, as well as an alternative model of poetic creativity that is not modeled on the faithful mimesis of nature. Here is a different concept of originality that reconstructs poetic genius as an estranging and inventive rather than a merely imitative power.

Even as Addison inherits Temple's theory of genius, then, he veers decisively away from Temple's unequivocal favoring of the ancients. Temple had pronounced modern literature a ghost standing on the ruins of the ancient "Empire of Wit." In his words, it was "as if true Poetry being dead, an Apparition of it walked about" (1680: 310, 312). While Addison stands steadfast by his argument that we must "allow a greater and more daring Genius to the Ancients," he also notes that "the greatest of them very much failed in, or, if you will, that they were much above the Nicety and Correctness of the Moderns" (2: 127). Tracking this failure of decorum or *bienséance* in works no less august than the Old and New Testament and Homer's *Iliad*, Addison argues that the modern reader who reads these works across a vast time divide necessarily brings his own cultural standards to bear on them. From a different time and place, what is sublime can look like an "Indecency." It may be that the "little Wits," themselves incapable of any sublimity, will always be the first to find "a large Field of Raillery" in "Cavelling against the Ancients." However, Addison reserves his sharpest ridicule for those who make the mistake of believing that they can copy geniuses of the first order, "singular in their Kind and inimitable" (2: 128–29).[87] Discovering breaches of decorum in the ancients is itself indecorous but nowhere as ridiculous as "Men following Irregularities by Rule." For this reason, writing modern Pindaricks counts as a much graver offense for Addison than scoffing at ancient Homeric similes (2: 218). Being creatures of our own time, to some extent we cannot help feeling alienated by ancient TEXTs, even in the best case of Homer. If one does not inhabit one's own history in one's writing but goes searching after ancient models without fully coming to terms with historical difference, one is left with a lifeless caricature of an original rather than a lively copy. For Addison, modern writers face the task of "giving the full Play to their own natural Parts" rather than trying to imitate ancient geniuses who by definition are beyond imitation. To "cramp their own Abilities too much by Imitation, and form themselves altogether upon Models," in his view, is precisely the wrong way to become "a good Original." Observing that "very few Writers make an extraordinary Figure in the World, who have not something in their Way of thinking or expressing themselves that is peculiar to them and entirely their own," he cautions against an unhealthy subservience to ancient models and defends the possibility of original genius in modern literature (2: 129–30).

Clearing space for modern English literature is in fact a task Addison took on for himself early on in his career. We see this interest both in early poems and essays such as "To Mr. Dryden" (1693), "An Account of the Greatest English Poets" (1694), and *A Discourse on Ancient and Modern Learning* (c. 1695; published posthumously 1739).[88] Addison takes steps unimaginable to Temple in these texts where he praises Dryden for 'improving' a whole host of classical authors.

> Thou mak'st the beauties of the *Romans* known,
> And *England* boasts of riches not her own;
> Thy lines have heighten'd *Virgil*'s Majesty,
> And *Horace* wonders at himself in *Thee*.
> Thou teachest *Persius* to inform our isle
> In smoother Numbers, and a clearer Stile;
> And *Juvenal*, instructed in thy page,
> Edges his Satyr, and improves his Rage.
> Thy Copy casts a fairer Light on all,
> And still out-shines the bright Original. (*MW* 1: 3; lines 11–20)

The language of progress ripples through these lines where it is further glossed as a heightening, instructing, and sharpening of ancient texts into "smoother Numbers, and a clearer Stile." Reading Dryden becomes a double experience of appreciating both the "bright Original" and its still "fairer" "Copy." Translated "in the *British* tongue" (line 22), the ancient authors undergo a metamorphosis more marvelous than any told by Ovid; Dryden's Ovid, "thus transform'd, reveal[s] / A Nobler Change than he himself can tell" (lines 35–36). In *A Discourse on Ancient and Modern Learning*, Addison elaborates on this notion of the ancient languages forming a barrier for the modern reader who must necessarily translate them into his or her own language. A skilled classicist in his own right, Addison locates this necessity of translation in "the Death and Disuse of the Languages in which the Ancients compil'd their Works." His main point is not so much that literacy in the classical languages is on the decline, but that "Time has quite worn out, or decay'd several Beauties of our ancient Authors" (*MW* 2: 459). Lacking access to "the secret History of a Composure: What was the Occasion of such a Discourse or Poem, whom such a Sentence aim'd at, what Person lay disguis'd in such a Character," the moderns can only guess at the multiple meanings an ancient text harbors, whereas its first readers who shared the time and space of the original poem must have been able to "see their Author in a Variety of Lights" (*MW* 2: 449). Simply by being contemporaries, and living "as it were upon the Spot, and within the Verge of the Poem," they must have had an insuperable advantage over the moderns for whom the ancient authors necessarily lie "at so great a Distance of Time" (*MW* 2: 449). It is thus axiomatic for Addison that "the Ancients took a greater Pleasure in the Reading of their Poets than the Moderns can" (*MW* 2: 457). The flipside of this argument is that the moderns should make better use of their own historicity and extract greater delight from their contemporary writers rather than merely looking up to the ancients. Because "their Language is dead," he argues, "and no more us'd in our familiar Conversations," moderns tend to cloak the ancients "in the Splendour and Formality of Strangers" (*MW* 2: 460). But the aura the ancients have taken on is a product of temporal distance and a function of the moderns' inability to hear all the rich tones and meanings of what was originally a vernacular and now only a dead language. Addison thus implies that the view of English as a coarse and vulgar language in comparison with the ancient languages is at least in part a function of a loss of hearing: we no longer recognize the "natural Homeliness and Simplicity" of the ancients (*MW* 2: 460). If the ancient languages appear free from the "Meanness" contracted by "common Use," it is because they are no longer living languages (*MW* 2: 460).[89]

For Jonathan Kramnick, the most decisive example of the "striking overcoming of the classical by the vernacular, the ancient by the modern" in Addisonian aesthetics is Milton.[90] Rather than reading Addison's criticism of Milton as a triumphalist account of 'modern' aesthetics, however, I wish to view it as his attempt to counteract simplistic versions of either 'ancient' or 'modern' historiography. As an example of a modern writer who had honed his skills by reading the ancients but had taken the ancient models to a new level of inventiveness and translated them in a vivid vernacular, Milton proved to Addison that it was possible to unite the great, the strange, and the beautiful in a single work of art and to honor the ancients while also achieving a freedom from them. For Addison, Milton represents "a perfect Master of all these Arts of working on the Imagination." *Paradise Lost* embodies the great in its depiction of the Messiah, Satan, and the angels; the beautiful in its representation of "*Pandaemonium*, Paradise, Heaven, Angels, *Adam* and *Eve*"; the strange in the Creation, "the several Metamorphoses of the fallen Angels, and the surprising Adventures their Leader meets" (3: 566). The very idea that a modern writer can be a "perfect Master" of the imagination and hold his own before his classical predecessors comes with a caveat, as if Addison wished to tone down the boldness of his claim. Modern English, he admits, is "of a coarser Nature" than classical Greek, likening Milton's epic to "a stately Palace built of Brick." If Milton's "*Paradise Lost* falls short of the *AEneid* or *Iliad* in this respect," he writes, "it proceeds rather from the Fault of the Language in which it is written, than from any Defect of Genius in the Author" (3: 566). Yet what modern English loses in musical quality, we know, it can gain in vivacity, dynamism, and imaginative power.

What is modern learned genius if not a powerful impression of nature in the present, that appears always new, like the Chinese garden? In so far as natural genius produces "Landskips without any certain Order or Regularity," it is arguably imbued with a putative Chinese aesthetics, as we have observed before. However, the learned modern genius could be said to be even closer to the Chinese garden that is invisibly "laid out" and "cut into Shape and Beauty by the Skill of the Gardener," in such a way as to preserve the sense of a natural rather than an artificial, imitative order (2: 129). The "extraordinary Figure" of these modern geniuses can be read in two senses, in terms of the conspicuous impact they make on society, and in terms of "Original" (irregular and altogether new) form. Carrying Addison's metaphors to their logical conclusion, we may postulate that the natural genius is a wild landscape, uncut and untrimmed, somewhat savage; the merely imitative and formally constricted modern writer is the formal garden of topiaries; and the inventive and original modern genius is the Chinese garden, where art and nature are fused into a self-renewing, self-renovating whole according to the 'double principle.' Speaking of Chinese gardens, Addison had spoken of the Chinese gardeners' "Genius in Works of this Nature," hinting at the ineffability of the "Art by which they direct themselves" and aligning it with poetic creativity (3: 552). He was being faithful to Temple's dictum that genius cannot be taught. But Addison, unlike Temple, planted the genius in the garden precisely to clear space for modern English geniuses like Milton. Temple had steered clear of Milton, no doubt for political reasons, reaching no farther than Spenser in his brief and decidedly derogatory discussions of English literary history. Similarly skirting Milton's politics and "fierce didactic aims," Addison nonetheless managed to reinvent him as "a Poet of the most unbounded Invention" and native genius (2: 587). *Paradise Lost* was for him simply equal to "the best invented Story I ever met with" (2: 543), a story "filled ... with so many surprising Incidents" (2: 543) and characters "more new than any Characters either in *Virgil* or *Homer*, or indeed in the whole Circle of Nature" (2: 563). The critical overemphasis on Addison as a theorist of the sublime, especially in his reading of Milton, is a romantic legacy that obscures Addison's equal attention to the novelty and modernity of Milton's epic.[91]

It may seem foolhardy to argue that Addison's vindication of modern English poetic genius as surprising and new had anything to do with Chinese porcelain and gardens. I have tried to show, however, that the

Spectator papers amply show that the "cultural milieu of Addison's literary criticism," to borrow Lee Elioseff's apt phrase, was globalized, mercantile, and defiantly modern, and that Addison used China as a potent sign of all of the above. As Trevor Ross has pointed out, Addison's emphasis on Milton's 'beauties' attests to the shift he engineered "from production to consumption, from codifying the rules of poetic practice to specifying the conditions for receiving works of English literature." In the process, Addison managed to transform "the labour of reading into spectacle, into conspicuous consumption."[92] When we ponder the process by which Addison arrived at Milton as the supreme example of English literary modernity and the representative purveyor of literary 'beauties,' we must note that it was via a series of linked reflections on the social and economic contexts of modern pleasures, which were being powerfully redefined in light of new patterns of consumption. Taking Temple as his guide, Addison nonetheless found a dramatically different use for Chinese aesthetics, which he mined for a "distinctly 'modern' psychological" criticism "unsubordinated to the consideration of art as moral discourse, imitation of nature, or formal structure"[93] – a criticism acutely in touch with mercantile practices, novel pleasures, and a globalized imaginary. With Addison and Defoe, China moves out of the rarified discourse on antiquity and into modern English consciousness. It is Addison, however, who properly brings China home for a mainstream audience, registering its impact on modern mores and importing Chinese aesthetics into national literary history.

CHAPTER 4

Oliver Goldsmith's Serial Chinaman

On January 24, 1760, two days after the Battle of Wandiwash in southern India, where the British troops led by Colonel Coote defeated the French and gained an upper hand in the Seven Years' War, an odd letter appeared on the front page of the recently launched *Public Ledger* (*Figure 4*). Dated October 21, 1759, it was addressed to an anonymous London merchant. The provenance of the letter was Amsterdam; the writer's name, like that of the addressee, had been politely left out of print. The letter announced that one of the two bills formerly sent to Amsterdam unfortunately had been "trifled with" and could not be "met with honour." The real business of the letter, however, lay elsewhere. It appeared that an English-speaking Chinese man had arrived in England.

> The bearer of this is my friend, therefore let him be yours. He is a native of Honan in China, and one who did me signal services when he was a mandarine, and I a factor at Canton. By frequently conversing with the English there, he has learned the language, though intirely a stranger to their manners and customs. I am told he is a philosopher, I am sure he is an honest man; that to you will be his best recommendation, next to the consideration of his being the Friend of, Sir, Yours, &c.

A copy of a letter signed "Lien Chi Altangi" and addressed to the same merchant in Amsterdam immediately followed this letter. In his letter, Altangi thanks this merchant friend profusely for the hospitality shown to him in Amsterdam, firmly returns a "sum of money ... privately conveyed into my baggage, when I was leaving Holland," and describes the turbulence of the sea as he voyaged from Rotterdam to England. After dwelling on his first impressions of London, he ends by requesting a favor. Would the Dutch friend mind forwarding some letters for him? Altangi will be writing to a Chinese friend and getting the letter to China is going to be no simple affair. He plans to address future letters to an acquaintance in Moscow, who will then be able to hand them to a Russian caravan to

Fig 4   Front page, *The Public Ledger, or, Daily Register of Commerce and Intelligence*,
January 24, 1760. Microform. *Early English Newspapers*, reel 1020.
Photograph courtesy of Firestone Library, Princeton University.

Peking where his Chinese friend lives. However, Altangi does not intend to make his merchant friend a mere conduit for an epistolary friendship destined elsewhere. He makes a startling offer: his friend can read all his letters and enjoy them equally. "I shall send them open," he writes, "in order that you may take copies or translations, as you are equally versed in the Dutch and Chinese languages." It is not clear that this is an authorization for his Amsterdam friend to hand translated copies of the letters to a newspaper, but that is what appears to have happened, for Lien Chi Altangi's letters addressed to "*Fum Hoam, first president of the ceremonial academy at Pekin in China*" would continue to appear periodically in the *Public Ledger* for eighteen more months.[1]

How the eighteenth-century English reader would have responded to this front-page item is difficult to tell. Certainly, a Chinese man on English shores at this time would have been big news, simply because of his sheer rarity. Very few Chinese travelers are on record as having traveled to Europe before the eighteenth century. The few who did make the long journey were all connected to the Jesuit missions and had been granted rare dispensations for their journeys.[2] The only Chinese person to make an appearance in England was a man named Shen Fuzong – or Michael Shen. Born in central China into a Christian family, Shen was brought to Europe in 1682 by the Flemish Jesuit Philippe Couplet and presented to a whole host of European dignitaries, including Louis XIV. With his considerable fluency in both written and spoken Latin, Shen was a living and speaking advertisement for the success of the Jesuit mission in China. In addition, he was clearly a highly interesting and entertaining act. Shen performed his Chineseness before a rapt European audience who wanted to see how he held a chopstick and wrote Chinese characters. He usefully buttressed Couplet's own authority as a translator from the Chinese, helping him secure necessary funds for the publication of *Confucius Sinarum philosophus* (1686).[3] By the time Shen arrived in England in 1687 he was able to attract the attention of notable scholars, artists, and even James II, who was so pleased with Sir Godfrey Kellner's portrait of Shen that he had it "hanging in his roome, next to the bed chamber." Jonathan Spence has reconstructed the story of how Thomas Hyde, librarian of the Bodleian Library in Oxford, first met Shen and wrote a letter of introduction for him to the celebrated Robert Boyle. Hyde also conversed with James II who personally inquired after Shen.[4]

It is tempting to speculate that, at least initially, some readers might have fallen for Lien Chi Altangi, though this is not very likely. By the mid-eighteenth century, the figure of the Chinese man in England had

become highly problematic chiefly due to George Psalmanazar's imposture of Formosan identity earlier in the century. As Chi-ming Yang notes,
Shen's performance of "the Chinese convert" paved the way for the success
of Psalmanazar's ethnographical writings and dramatized "spectacle of a
fake East."⁵ Unlike Shen or Psalmanazar, however, Altangi is not a figure
of conversion or cross-cultural learning, even though he is identified as a
scholar and philosopher. He is primarily associated with Canton and represents a very different set of Chinese–English relations. The English East
India Company had established a trading post in Canton in 1711; by mid-
century, England was inundated with Chinese goods – so much so, in fact,
that papers in the *Spectator* (1711–12), *Rambler* (1750–52), *Adventurer* (1752–
54), *World* (1753–56), and *Connoisseur* (1754–56), had all found it necessary to rail against the raging Chinese fad. It was alarming that Chinese
jars, tea dishes, and "odd Figures in *China* ware" were overtaking ladies'
drawing rooms and libraries (*Spectator* 37, April 12, 1711); that not only
women but also men were decorating their dressing rooms and toilettes
in "the *Chinese* taste" (*Connoisseur*, April 24, 1755); that "the Greek and
Roman architecture are discarded for the novelties of China" (*Adventurer*
139, March 5, 1754); and that whole estates and their gardens were being
redone with pagodas, serpentine walks, groves "perplexed with errors and
crooked walks," and other irregularities imported from China (*World* 15,
April 12, 1753). A letter from a frustrated husband in the *World* reported on
his marriage to "a lady of quality" who had turned his country house over
to a Chinese upholster named "Mr. Kifang."

> In short, sir, by the indefatigable zeal of this Chinese upholsterer, in about
> four months my house was entirely new-furnished; but so disguised and
> altered, that I hardly knew it again. There is not a bed, a table, a chair, or
> even a grate that is not twisted into so many ridiculous and grotesque fig-
> ures, and so decorated with the heads, beaks, wings and claws of birds and
> beasts, that Milton's *Gorgons, and hydra's and chimoera's dire* are not to be
> compared with them. (*World* 38, September 20, 1753)

But in fact part of the fun of chinoiserie was that there were so few authorities who could judge its authenticity – that there were, precisely, no Mr.
Kifangs who could say just what was Chinese and what was not. For both
the consumers and critics of the Chinese fashion, then, a Chinese mandarin from Canton with experience dealing with English traders would have
been good news. Lien Chi Altangi was free of Jesuit ties. He needed not
be suspected of working for the French, with whom they were at war in
several places around the world. Could he be the cultural arbiter they had
all been waiting for?

Improbably, the English would eventually meet this Chinese man, though Altangi would not be he. In 1769, seven years after Altangi's letters first appeared in the *Public Ledger*, a man who became known as Chitqua surfaced in England. His resemblance to Altangi is uncanny. Like Altangi, Chitqua came from Canton and was associated with the East India Company, on whose ship *Horsendon* he had voyaged. Like Altangi, he became "the fashion in London" during the three years he stayed in London. Fan Cunzhong notes that his "lodging at Mr. Marr's in the Strand was much frequented by savants, connoisseurs and artists."[6] A skilled clay modeler who had apparently kept "a shop for making figures" in Canton, he became popular by making small portrait figurines of prominent men.[7] According to David Clarke, two surviving examples of his work that can be attributed to him with reasonable safety are a clay portrait of Dr. Anthony Askew currently held in the collection of the Royal College of Physicians in London, and a small sculpture (ca. 1770) of a Dutch merchant, possibly Andreas Everardus van Braam Houckgeest, now housed in the Rijksmuseum in Amsterdam.[8] Chitqua's work was included in the 1770 exhibition of the Royal Academy and he can still be seen "peeping over the shoulders of Benjamin West and Jeremiah Meyer" in Johann Zoffany's *The Life School in the Royal Academy*.[9] Thomas Percy, who had published two important miscellanies on China, *Hau Kiou Choaan* (1761) and *Miscellaneous Pieces Relating to the Chinese* (1762), reported spending an evening with "Chetqua a Chinese from Canton" and William Chambers in 1770.[10] In 1773, a year after Chitqua left England to return to China, William Chambers prefaced his new edition of *Dissertation on Oriental Gardening* with *An Explanatory Discourse, by Tan Chet-qua, of Quang-Chew-fu, Gent.*[11] Chitqua's saga, like that of Altangi, challenges the imagination. All kinds of questions come to mind. How did he communicate? How did he manage to survive in England? The change in diet must have been challenging, to say the least. What did he wear? And what did he really think of the English? The answers to these questions can only be imagined, because the only testimony Chitqua left behind is a letter written in choppy English addressed to three Oxford ladies.[12]

The fact that Oliver Goldsmith, the author behind the elaborate ruse of Altangi's letters, was able to anticipate Chitqua's arrival in England suggests that for some time England had been readying itself for another close encounter with China. England was awash with Chinese things. Was it not time for the English to meet another *bona fide* Chinaman? But that is not exactly what Goldsmith gives his readers. In a rhetorical move diametrically opposite that of George Psalmanazar, whose fakery of Formosan identity had depended on a systematic performance of "antipodal" differences, Goldsmith turns Altangi into an English *semblable*. In this way, Goldsmith sidesteps the "crisis of authenticity" that was associated with China.[13] Altangi walks around in European clothes and appears to have no difficulty communicating in England. He is happy to eat English beef with English utensils in lieu of Chinese chopsticks, and shows little interest in performing his Chineseness for the benefit of English eyes. Indeed, he roams around London with enviable energy and curiosity, writing voluminously to his friend in Peking about what a curious and often foolishly absurd people the English are. Even the first credulous readers of Goldsmith's letters surely would have caught on quickly: Altangi was their own exoticizing gaze reflected accurately back at them. Experienced readers would have recalled other examples of this ruse: Marana's *Turkish Spy* (1684–94), Montesquieu's *Persian Letters* (1721), and, closer to home, George Lyttelton's *Letters from a Persian in England, to his friend in Ispahan* (1735). The joke was becoming an old one. However, Goldsmith's way of telling it was daring and new. By serializing Altangi's letters in the *Public Ledger*, he had taken a popular literary trick to a new level.

This chapter is an attempt to recuperate the original publishing context of Goldsmith's Chinese letters.[14] The reason why these letters have never managed to occupy center stage in any discussion of Goldsmith's works has much to do with the unclassifiable nature of this work. Originally serialized in the *Public Ledger*, the first and oldest continuously published daily newspaper in England (today it is published as a commercial gazette), then later collected and published in one volume under the title *The Citizen of the World*, the letters fail to conform strictly to any established genre. Nonetheless, the most extended and serious studies of this work have approached it basically as a single-genre work: an oriental tale in imitation of Montesquieu's *Persian Letters*, or an extended review or periodical essay. Following Martha Conant's lead in *The Oriental Tale in England in the Eighteenth Century* (1908), Ros Ballaster has recently analyzed Goldsmith's work in the context of the oriental pseudo-letter tradition.[15] Working from a different angle, Frank Donoghue's study *The Fame Machine* places *The Citizen of the World* in the context of review criticism, interpreting it as Goldsmith's "most cynical assault on the institutional influences on the production and consumption of literature."[16] These contrasting approaches point to a central divide in Goldsmith criticism: scholars who attend to Goldsmith's oriental or orientalist content have little or nothing to say about the journalistic form of his work;[17] meanwhile, those who emphasize the journalistic context of Goldsmith's work cannot account successfully for the Chinese or pseudo-Chinese content.[18] How can we begin to connect content and form in Goldsmith's *Citizen of the World*? This chapter proposes that we simply start where Goldsmith's work begins: with the letter in the newspaper.

The Foreign Correspondent

John Newbery launched *The Public Ledger, or, Daily Register of Commerce and Intelligence* on January 12, 1760. Published in the standard four-column, four-page format, its main fare was commercial news and advertising. Goldsmith's first Chinese letter appeared on January 24, 1760. A total of 119 letters were published.[19] The last letter in the series was followed by a note that announced the imminent publication of the letters in book form. The book edition was brought out on May 1, 1762, printed by John Newbery. Reviews of *The Citizen of the World* appeared in the *Critical Review* and *Monthly Review*, both of which Goldsmith had written for prior to being hired by Newbery. The remarks published in the *Critical Review* deserve close notice. After remarking that Goldsmith's letters as a whole may not score high according to "the standard of originality," the reviewer notes that the letters were originally published in a newspaper where a different standard must apply.

> These letters, if we mistake not, made their first appearance in a daily newspaper, and were necessarily calculated to the meridian of the multitude … This circumstance alone would sufficiently plead the author's excuse, had he need of an apology; that genius must be fruitful, indeed, which can supply such a variety of tastes with daily entertainment.[20]

It is not easy to gauge the reviewer's tone here, but by emphasizing the letters' "first appearance in a daily news-paper" and the demands of "daily entertainment," he clearly points out that we must take very seriously the terms and conditions of the "first appearance" of Goldsmith's *The Citizen of the World*. Any account of Goldsmith's work that ignores the newspaper format in which it first appeared risks misjudging its original conditions of meaning.

The *Public Ledger* was by no means a pioneer in the competitive world of eighteenth-century newspapers. It was a latecomer and made no pretensions to originality. The letter "To the Public" (signed by the "Proprietors") that was reprinted several times in the initial numbers self-consciously justified the launching of yet another newspaper by stressing the practical "Difficulty, and … Time and Expence" necessary to find the information one needed in a veritable glut of information. Arguing that "Intelligence, however copious, is confused," and "that as the Number of Particulars is greater, that which is sought will be less easily found," the "proprietors" defended the paper as a necessary addition to the market not on the basis of its original or rare content, but rather its utility as an economical index or "register" to content that already existed in the public realm. The *Public Ledger* thus devoted one full page to a "complete INDEX to all ADVERTISEMENTS, PROPOSALS, SCHEMES, DESIGNS, PROJECTS, ORDERS, MEETINGS, SUBSCRIPTIONS, TRANSACTIONS, INVITATIONS, and AMUSEMENTS, published in the *Daily*, *Evening* and *Weekly* Papers through the Kingdom."[21] In this appeal to an advertising-reading audience – an appeal, we should note, that does not so much allay as provoke anxiety about information one might be missing – the paper gambles that the reader will be seduced by the idea of obtaining for the price of one paper the advertisements in ten or more. The surfeit of information has created the need for a digest or "ledger" of other papers.

If we examine the January 24, 1760 issue of the *Public Ledger*, where the first letter in Goldsmith's letter series first appeared, we find on the first page, in addition to the first letter signed by "Lien Chi Altangi to *******, Merchant in Amsterdam," a continuation of an essay series entitled "Life," and a letter from "PROBUS" to the proprietors of the *Public Ledger* on the subject of the Seven Years' War. The second page consists of an index to recent advertisements in the *Public Ledger* (the previous issue of January 23, 1760), *Public Advertiser*, *Daily Gazetteer*, *Daily Advertiser*, *Lloyd's Evening Post*, *Newcastle Courant*, *Newcastle Journal*, *Salisbury Journal*, *Bath Journal*, *Sherborne Mercury*, and *Gloucester Journal* (in this order). The third page, which is visually dominated by a list of ships for sale, provides a veritable hodgepodge of information: a call for volunteers to join the "ROYAL WELCH VOLUNTEERS" in the service of King George; an advertisement for services wanted (a surveyor for turnpikes, a journeyman apothecary); notices about rental property (an estate, farms, a grist mill), stray horses, mislaid banknotes, and eloped servants (as well as a note warning against "Advertisements of an indecent Nature" that purportedly make it difficult for families to place some newspapers in the hands of children or female friends); announcements for recently published books (*The Child's Delight; or Little Master and Miss's Instructive and Diverting Companion*, a sermon preached by James Townley, M.A., *A Description of the Maritime Parts of France*, *The Natural and Civil History of the French Dominion in North and South America*), one magazine (*Royal Female Magazine; Or the*

Ladies General Repository of Pleasure and Improvement), and one serial publication (*A New and Complete Collection of Voyages and Travels*, to "be completed in One Hundred and Sixty Numbers"); a subscription notice for a proposed book (*The Ruins of the Emperor Dioclesian's Palace at Spalatro in Dalmatia*); advertisements for ships on sale; a notice about an upcoming sale of coffee, sugar, indigo, and "Fifty Puncheons fine flavour'd Jamaica Rum" at "Garraway's Coffee-house in Exchange-Alley." It is only on the last page of the paper that we see references to the news in the form of letters from foreign correspondents from "Leipsic" and "Dantzick"; one-sentence announcements about weather on the continent; notices about newly arrived and departed ships, political appointments, and petitions; short one-sentence notices covering marriage, murder, theft, sports (a boxing match), theater (announcements for two plays by Arthur Murphy, *The Desert Island*, and *The Way to Keep Him*, playing at Drury Lane); a list of letters waiting to be picked up at the general post office; and, finally, a short listing of stock prices. In addition, there are two slightly dated items: (i) an unsigned "Extract of a letter from Rome, Dec. 12" reporting on the Portuguese Jesuits in Rome and their plans for a seminary to teach young missionaries Chinese and Japanese in preparation for missionary activity in the Far East, and (ii) a short account, dated November 3, 1979, of a violent encounter between a British captain and a French privateer near Jamaica. Clearly, the hectic eclecticism of this issue of the *Public Ledger* cannot be accounted for solely by the terms announced in the proprietor's letter to the public.[22]

The cultural meaning of the disparate information collected and conveyed by the *Public Ledger* is conditioned, first and foremost, by the growing connection between the early press and maritime commerce. Michael Warner's observation that, in the colonial American newspaper, "print discourse derived its authority and material from the shipping trade" also holds true for the *Public Ledger* where, more than any other commodity, it is the ship that holds center stage. The thumbnail images of ships that adorn the ship advertisements on the third page of the *Public Ledger* are a visual index of this economic and discursive centrality. Warner writes, "The normal errands of maritime commerce were the only channels for transoceanic news, and papers announced ship arrivals more than any other kind of news."[23] The ship is much more than the central commodity on sale. It is the material base that mobilizes the global economy of goods and information. It is also the stage for a collective imaginary of the mobile, traveling self whose errant energies cannot be explained by the interests of commerce alone. We can glimpse this figure, made so familiar to us by

Defoe's protagonists, everywhere in the January 24, 1760 issue of the *Public Ledger*: in the advertisements for "Several Surgeons for the West-Indies and Coast of Africa, and two Maids for the East-Indies" and "A Valet de Chambre to go to Jamaica"; in the publication announcement of a serialized *New and Complete Collection of Voyages and Travels*; in the references to the missionaries bound for East Asia. The paper freely references the world at large with its reports on warfare and freezing weather on the continent; Portuguese Jesuits in Rome; ships arriving from Malaga, Jamaica, "Gottenburgh" (today Gothenburg in Sweden), Virginia, and New York, and others landing at Gibraltar, New York, and Carolina; encounters with privateers in Port-Royal, Jamaica; coffee, sugar, and indigo newly arrived from St. Domingo, Hispaniola (today's Haiti). As Richard Taylor notes, the *Public Ledger* was a predominantly "serious and topical newspaper, which was concerned with foreign intelligence dominated by accounts of military operations, port and domestic news, and advertisements."[24] How do Goldsmith's pseudo-letters, allegedly written by a Chinese philosopher traveling in London, fit into this mélange of information? What is this obviously fictional piece doing in this newspaper consisting largely of foreign news and classified ads?

It is important not to forget the strangeness of what Goldsmith is doing here as we reconstruct the eighteenth-century context for his extended literary joke in the commercial press. Although critics have been quick to point to Montesquieu and d'Argens as Goldsmith's predecessors, a key difference is that Goldsmith's joke in the *Public Ledger* depends on, and is authorized by, two conventions of serial publication in his time: the central role played by the foreign correspondent's letter in the newspaper, and the convention of the periodical eidolon, the main character in the periodical essay series.[25] The preponderant use of personal letters in the *Public Ledger* harkens back to the origin of the newspaper in newsletters – written or printed letters from correspondents who delivered news in the first person, often from abroad.[26] Goldsmith's Lien Chi Altangi is one of many foreign correspondents whose writings appear in the *Public Ledger*. In this regard, Goldsmith's Chinese philosopher does not immediately stand out. He is in rather good company with the unnamed correspondent from Rome and the anonymous suppliers of foreign intelligence from Leipzig and Danzig. The difference, of course, is that, compared to these other foreign correspondents, Altangi is more individuated, as befits his simultaneous role as an eidolon, or the authorial persona and main character of the periodical essay series. He is given a name; is vouched for by a reference (supplied to a Mr. *****, merchant in London); and is ornamented with a past, along with various specific references to dates and places. At the same time, he remains a flagrantly fictional, anonymous, and artificial personality. All this is, of course, part of Goldsmith's humor. On the one hand, he is poking fun at the way supposedly objective news is constructed out of "derivative, anonymous, and impersonal" sources that newspapers in his time made no effort to authenticate.[27] At the same time, he is making a joke about the periodical eidolon who is often very different from its creator, as Manushag Powell shows in *Performing Authorship*: higher-born, either much younger or older, unmarried, detached from society though not marginalized, and not writing for pay.[28] Altangi fits the bill in all ways but one: he is a Chinaman.

These jokes work partly at Goldsmith's own expense. Taylor suggests that Goldsmith's use of the Chinese philosopher can be read as a reference to his own personal experience as a foreign correspondent for Griffiths's *Monthly Review* and later Smollett's *Critical Review*. Goldsmith frequently used the traveler as his narrative persona, as when he impersonated an English traveler returning home after wandering in barbarous lands to extol the virtues of English laws, customs, and climate in his essay serial *A Comparative View of Races and Nations* published in June–September 1760 in *Royal Magazine; or Gentleman's Monthly Companion*.[29] By portraying himself extravagantly as a foreign traveler from China, in other words, Goldsmith may have been satirizing his own, marginalized, and "compromised" role as an Irish newspaper writer and a periodical essayist writing in "the world of professional writing in the metropolitan center" of London.[30] Without downplaying the importance of Goldsmith's own self-understanding as a marginal traveler and foreigner in the metropolis, however, I wish to suggest that much more than autobiographical self-reference is at stake in Goldsmith's rhetorical strategy here. The textual equivalent of the ship is the letter, the traveling text. Letters could travel because of ships; letters imitate the transcontinental, transoceanic mobility of ships and activate an imaginary of the mobile English self. Besides gesturing toward the history of the newspaper and its paradoxical dependence on 'foreign' correspondents for news, Goldsmith's Chinese letters thus support, through their very form, the outward-looking, global vision of the world in the *Public Ledger*. As Hannah Barker notes in her study of late-eighteenth-century English newspapers, the prominence of foreign news throughout the eighteenth century attests to the "absence of a narrow provincialism amongst the newspaper readership."[31] This was due, in her view, not only to England's constant involvement in war during this period, or the preoccupation with commerce at a national and global level, but also to a strongly held belief in the enabling role of the newspaper in wide-ranging, open political debate. Barker notes that published letters, "almost always anonymous," often provided the material for such debate. The anonymity of these letters was not seen as an obstacle. On the contrary, anonymity was seen as a way of protecting contributors, guaranteeing participation from a wide social and political pool, and creating a sense of "immediacy felt between a paper and its readership."[32]

Goldsmith has great fun with all of these ideas in Altangi's first letters in the *Public Ledger* where he satirizes the peculiar English way of producing, circulating, and consuming news:

> This universal passion for politics is gratified by Daily Gazettes, as with us at China … You must not, however, imagine that they who compile these papers have any actual knowledge of the politics, or the government of a state; they only collect their materials from the oracle of some coffee-house, which oracle has himself gathered them the night before from a beau at a gaming table, who has pillaged his knowledge from a great man's porter, who has had his information from the great man's gentleman, who has invented the whole story for his own amusement the night preceding. (Letter 4, 29–30)

There are multiple jokes going on here. There is a class joke embedded in the assertion that the daily news in England is in fact an invention of the lower classes for their own amusement. What turns the innocent private joke of the "great man's gentleman" into an exposure of the English nation is the complicitous system of collecting, gathering and pillaging, in the course of which hearsay is transformed into "knowledge of the politics, or the government of a state." This system is complicitous because it implicates not only the porter, beau, and coffee-house oracle who participate in this relay of the news, but also the wider public whose "universal passion for politics" supplies the demand that keeps the circle going. A darker version of this English game of Chinese whispers appears in the very next letter where Goldsmith lampoons the system of foreign correspondents:

> An English dealer in this way, for instance, has only to ascend to his workhouse, and manufacture a turbulent speech averred to be spoken in the senate; or a report to be dropt at court; a piece of scandal that strikes at a particular Mandarine; or a secret treaty between two neighboring powers. When finished, these goods are baled up, and consigned to a factor abroad, who sends in return, two battles, three sieges, and a shrewd letter filled with dashes – blanks and stars**** of great importance. (Letter 5, 32)

Here, news is not an accidental byproduct of a chain of conversations that link the great man's gentleman to the coffeehouse and to the public sphere of the newspaper. In this case, news is a deliberate and systematic "manufacture" – with all the multiple meanings of a hand-made good, a commodity related to a particular industry, and a deliberate fabrication of falsehood (*OED*) – produced in "work-houses" and exchanged between dealers and "factors abroad." The "dashes – blanks and stars**** of great importance" that decorate the foreign correspondent's missives are typographical clues to the "scandal" and the "secret" at the heart of modern news-making.

We should note that there is nothing original about Goldsmith's complaint. As Lennard J. Davis has pointed out, the charge that news was fictional and motivated mostly by money was coeval with the birth of news as a discursive genre.[33] The rhetorical insistence on recentness and factuality was something that eighteenth-century news shared with, rather than what distinguished it from, the novel. Like the novel, news in fact thrived on the unsubstantiated claims of shadowy characters whose identities could never be pinned down. As Davis puts it, news and the novel made up an "undifferentiated matrix": they shared "an insistence on recentness as well as on factuality," but their "claims to recentness and veracity" were not only often "falsely made" but also "unprovable"; "Readers of such works would be literally unable to say whether what they were reading was true or not."[34] The newspaper's strategy of dealing with the problem of the referential particularity of the speaker, however, is the very opposite of that of the novel. Whereas the novel intently ascribes minute particularities to its characters to flesh them out and endow them with verisimilitude, the newspaper refrains from mentioning anything at all about the speaker other than the geographical location from which he speaks.[35] It is not even clear that the speaker is aware that he is being publicly quoted. A whole confusion of private and public discourse appears to be taking place in the newspaper, where snippets of private correspondence appear on public pages with no explanation. If we take Goldsmith's *Citizen of the World* as his response to what Davis calls the "inherent doubleness or reflexivity" in news discourse, we can see that his strategy is a very complex one.[36] Altangi is a foreign correspondent re-engineered as an eidolon, treading a thin line between reportage and the periodical essay, and exploiting the ambiguous eighteenth-century divide between the exotic and the new, the openly fictive and the curiously newsworthy.

Wayne Booth's astute observation that readers of Goldsmith's letters "read on ... not to discover *what will happen* but to discover *what our hero's genius will reveal* when he turns to the next subject, and the next after that" underlines the formal challenge of his work – namely, the absence of "any particular known artistic form or established kind of unity" organizing the letter series apart from that of the eidolon's character.[37] In lieu of organic unity, Booth argues, Goldsmith offers the reader "a genuine 'art of the miscellaneous' " that is at home in the periodical.[38] We should note, though, that Goldsmith was also critical of the "curiosity" of the reader who might appreciate this art. After all, it was the desire to "gratify this curiosity" that had made possible not only the development of periodical literature but also its close cousin, the newspaper press (Letter 5, 31). Newspapers depend on the curious searching after today's news which are new only for a day, after which they turn into "a collection of absurdity or palpable falsehood" (Letter 5, 31). In lieu of this self-undermining novelty of the daily news, Goldsmith offers an alternative kind of novelty in his Chinese letters: the novelty that comes from a differential perspective. News is simply whatever one finds newsworthy. For Lien Chi Altangi, all of England is news because he is "a newly created being introduced into a new world," where "every object strikes with wonder and surprise" (Letter 3, 21). In Goldsmith's spin on Addisonian aesthetics, England is self-renewing news to the Chinaman. Goldsmith then takes this joke one step farther: England is the best kind of news also for the English if they can see it with Chinese eyes. Indeed, there is nothing stranger and more surprising than England. Why Goldsmith needed a fictional Chinese man to say this in a newspaper is the next question that we will need to answer.

Sequence, Serial, and the Orient

Goldsmith had a very real and pragmatic interest in the East. In his letter of August 31, 1758 to his brother-in-law Daniel Hodson, he mentions his plan to find employment as a surgeon on an East India Company ship bound for India:

> I suppose you have heard of my intention of going to the East Indies. The place of my destination is one of the factories on the coast of Coromandel and I go in quality of Physician and Surgeon for which the Company has sign'd my warrant which has already cost me ten pounds. I must also pay 50 Lb for my passage ten pound for Sea stores, and the other incidental expences of my equipment will amount to 50 or 70 Lb more.[39]

Having studied medicine at the University of Edinburgh and the Netherlands in 1752–54 in an effort to reinvent himself after an unhappy experience as sizar at Trinity College in Dublin, Goldsmith had tried unsuccessfully to set up a medical practice in Southwark in 1756.⁴⁰ Goldsmith frankly admits to Hodson that the attraction for him is financial. He calculates that as an East India Company surgeon he can look forward to "one thousand pounds per annum" which, together with various advantages attendant upon indirect involvement in colonial trade, will allow him to "separate" himself "from the vulgar." Faced with this prospect, Goldsmith determines that neither "the fatigues of sea the dangers of war and the still greater dangers of climate," nor "friends and esteem and ... all the conveniences of life" should stop him from embarking on his adventure.⁴¹ The reason why his plans fell through is unclear. John Dussinger speculates that he failed to qualify as a ship's surgeon; Katharine Balderston believes that it was news of military conflict with France on the Coromandel coast that had complicated the negotiations.⁴² French troops had been laying siege to former English footholds in India between April 1758 and February 1759. The English were not able to regain their control until the French surrendered at Pondicherry in January 1760 after losing the Battle of Wandiwash, a mere two days before the *Public Ledger* started serializing Goldsmith's Chinese letters. Whether it is Goldsmith who came short, or the East India Company had "simply postponed his sailing with evasions," it is clear that the East was a real destination for Goldsmith and not just a fictional location.⁴³ It was, most of all, an attractive commercial prospect.

Other letters demonstrate a more playful and imaginative identification with the East based on literary familiarity. In a 1753 letter to his uncle Thomas Contarine, who was providing financial support for his medical studies in Edinburgh, Goldsmith describes his feelings of isolation and estrangement in Scotland in the language of the oriental pseudo-letter novel: "here as recluse as the Turkish Spy at Parriss I am almost unknown to Every body."⁴⁴ Goldsmith repeats this self-orientalizing gesture in his letter of August 14, 1758 to his childhood friend Robert Bryanton, a school friend from Patrick Hughes's school at Edgeworthstown and also his Trinity College days:

> If ever my works find their way to Tartary or China, I know the consequence. Suppose one of your Chinese Owanowitzers instructing one of your Tartarian Chianobacchi – you see I use Chinese names to show my erudition, as I shall soon make our Chinese talk like an Englishman to show his. This may be the subject of the lecture:–"Oliver Goldsmith flourished in the eighteenth and nineteenth centuries. He lived to be an hundred and

three years old, [and in that] age may justly be styled the sun of [literature] and the Confucius of Europe."[45]

Written only two weeks before his letter to Hodson, this jocose letter shows Goldsmith imagining for himself a global identity of a very different kind, based not on his medical or financial success as a globe-trotting member of the colonial elite but rather on worldwide literary renown. The Turkish spy and the Confucian philosopher are figures that represent two different ways of understanding and conceptualizing eastern difference – as well as two different ways in which Goldsmith understood his role in society. Strikingly, Goldsmith updates the familiar figures of Turkish spy and Chinese sage by making them speak to topics he was to face continually throughout his life: the displacement of the individual in modern society and the role of the writer in a rapidly expanding public sphere. What I find distinctive about Goldsmith's self-reflexive use of the conventions of the oriental tale is precisely this interest in updating or modernizing the genre to make it relevant to his own contemporary context. The most striking instance of this process can be seen in his redefinition of the oriental tale sequence. In this respect, Goldsmith operates outside the oppositional dynamic identified by Srinivas Aravamudan between "a national realism that renders the domestic novel as central," and "the oriental tale and its sister genres" that are "excluded by acts of enclosure around the novel."[46] Goldsmith eschews this opposition in his Chinese letters, where the oriental and the national, the fantastic and the real, the foreign and the domestic intermingle in the playful space of the serial newspaper.

As Ros Ballaster has pointed out, the oriental narrative is most commonly defined by "the long sequence of tales more or less loosely held together by a 'frame narrative.'"[47] The two most common ways to frame stories about the orient in the seventeenth and eighteenth centuries involved two different kinds of fictions: that of the politically endangered oriental male adrift in Europe, engaging in secret intelligence-gathering activities and reporting back home, and that of the sexually subjugated oriental female trapped in a harem, desperately telling stories to delay the despot's decision to kill her. These fictions are based on, and at the same time resist, what Alain Grosrichard identified as "the two key terms, the two driving elements, of despotic power in the Orient": the gaze and the letter.[48] The orient is imaged as the empire of the gaze and simultaneously the empire of signs. The oriental despot sees all, without being seen; "he is master of the signifier" (he can create meanings arbitrarily through his will) and "is master through the signifier" (he communicates through signs in the pure medium of silence).[49] Oriental tales of the seventeenth and eighteenth century write supposedly against this all-powerful, all-seeing oriental despot who immobilizes history as well as fiction, deploying the male spy or the loquacious female-in-a-seraglio as figures that thwart the despot by producing unending stories. However, these tales tend to perpetuate the myth of the oriental despot even as they attempt to undermine it. As Grosrichard puts it: "In place of history – of which it can have no conception, and which it cannot beget – the Orient substitutes *histories.*"[50] The male spy whose power to see and to be seen is constantly put on trial, and the female sexual slave whose only means of resistance is a limitless loquacity, function as both symptoms and inversions of despotism. These fictions entail different formal strategies. The vehicle of the male spy is the basis for the epistolary pseudo-letter format of the oriental tale; that of the female tale-spinner is the foundation of the *Arabian Nights* type of oriental sequence. The male spy writes in the form of a secret correspondence; the female raconteuse verbally narrates intimate stories. In Goldsmith's time, there were two outstanding models for these two types of oriental tales: Giovanni Paolo Marana's *Letters Writ by a Turkish Spy* (first French edition 1684, English trans. 1687) and Antoine Galland's *Arabian Nights* (1704–17).[51] Both are notoriously long texts: *Letters Writ by a Turkish Spy* extends to 600 letters over 8 volumes; Galland's *Arabian Nights* was originally issued in 12 volumes.[52]

The *Turkish Spy* and the *Arabian Nights* are both organized around the storytelling activities of the subjugated oriental subject whose political or sexual fidelity to the despot is put on trial. Not surprisingly, these characters tell rather different kinds of stories. The oriental spy who is sent on an intelligence-gathering mission to the west writes in an ethnographic mode, comparing the European and Turkish (or Persian) forms of government, marriage, religion, and civil institutions in a pseudo-factual style; the beautiful Scheherazade narrates fantastic stories about transgression and transmigration. The female narrator is the controlling figure behind linked romance tales; the male spy narrative veers on satire. Both types of narration, however, are extremely episodic and loose in structure. The central literary problem in both cases is that of sequencing: how to justify the logic behind the linking and ordering of the tales? The oriental sequence as a rule offers a weak frame devoid of significant plot; this is why its form can function as a trope for the oriental lack of history, reason, and progress. Thus, as Ballaster has shown, the oriental tale as exemplified by the *Arabian Nights* constructs a kind of verbal agency that is repetitive, self-repeating, and self-deferring. The oriental tale does not so much progress as it defers progress (and death): "The *Nights*, like the woman who tells them, transform the world around them by repetitive acts of simple accretion";[53] "The *Arabian Nights* generates a sequence of stories whose forward progress is directed towards maintaining a continuous static state, Scheherazade's continuing survival."[54] Ballaster explains how this literary device was identified in ideological terms as a clue to the "simulacrum and negation of history" in the orient, or the inability of the orient to move forward in time like the west. This is why the fantastic transmigrations, metamorphoses, the "perpetual alteration of forms" in the oriental tale can be read as precisely their opposite: "the identity and permanence of a structure, the repetitive dryness and rigid automaton of a machine."[55] The oriental spy narrative takes this conceit even farther. Unlike the *Arabian Nights*, where female storytelling ultimately achieves its goal of subduing the despot and reversing the despotic will to kill, the spy narrative never manages to 'return home.' In this sense, the spy whose stories produce little or no effect for their recipient is arguably an even less disenfranchised figure than the oriental female. Whatever effect the oriental spy can produce has to do with the doubleness of his gaze; he has the unusual and uncanny ability to inhabit two sets of eyes (western, eastern) and see double, as it were. This emphasis on perspective, however, is detrimental to the plot. For this reason, writers like Montesquieu who were inspired by Marana's model but worried about the weak link between the letters deliberately attempted to create a better narrative logic for the letter sequence by importing the seraglio scenario of the *Arabian Nights* into the spy novel. In this sense, the *Persian Letters* is a kind of double oriental tale – both spy letter-writing and seraglio storytelling.

Goldsmith's letters follow Montesquieu's 1721 *Persian Letters* in their weak attempt at a plot: Altangi's son Hingpo travels through Tibet, ends up a slave in Persia, escapes during a Tartar invasion, and makes his way to Europe via Russia. This plot, however, is nowhere as developed as in Montesquieu's *Persian Letters*. As Booth comments, neither plot nor character is chiefly responsible for holding the reader's interest in the Chinese letters. Neither does plot provide the internal logic of the letters' sequence. By writing a pseudo-letter series for a newspaper, Goldsmith in effect wittily sidesteps the problem of sequencing in the oriental tale, replacing sequence with seriality – an effect created by the form of the serial, diurnal newspaper. Serial oriental fiction, of course, was not an invention of Goldsmith's. On occasion publishers had taken advantage of the episodic structure of the oriental tale, giving it a serial look: *Arabian Nights*, for instance, was published in serial form in the early numbers of the *Churchman's Last Shift; or, Loyalist's Weekly Journal* and in its entirety in George Parker's *Parker's*

London News between 1723 and 1725.[56] However, these publications merely exploit the episodic nature of the oriental sequence for periodical publication, taking advantage of the association of the oriental sequence with novelty, or "the unusual, the quirky, the puzzling."[57] Goldsmith's letters, by contrast, attempt a kind of literary *trompe l'oeil*, masquerading as up-to-date foreign correspondence by a Chinese man who imaginatively, and literally in the form of print, inhabits the same space and time as the English reader. As Davis explains, "it was not until the appearance of the regularly occurring serial newspaper that printed narrative could literally keep up with the passage of time." As print technology developed, print took on the "capacity ... to contain recentness": the "emphasis on continuity, seriality, and recentness" prompted the invention of a journalistic time of a "median past tense," which implied that readers were reading about events that had very recently taken place. The rhetorical effect of this temporal "recentness," or modernity, was that readers were encouraged to relate to the news in a highly engaged and personal way: "The reader is brought within the frame of the discourse both spatially and temporally since his life is brought within the compass of print and his perception of the passage of time is taken on by the median past tense." For this reason, Davis believes that "news/novel discourse, as it develops, draws the reader within it in a way that is quite new to Western culture."[58] Altangi's letters would have given English readers the playful sense that a Chinaman was inhabiting the same spatial and temporal framework that they lived in, foreshortening the distance between them and China.

A close literary analogue for what Goldsmith was doing is Addison and Steele's *Spectator*, which owed its success in no small part to its ability to insert itself as an integral part in the daily lives of its readers. Addison and Steele were well aware that one rhetorical effect of seriality is familiarity, proximity, immediacy. What readers enjoyed about the *Spectator* papers is the sense of intimacy it gave them: it suggested the intimacy of a diary, a private conversation or correspondence, a coterie identity. Stuart Sherman points out that the *Spectator*'s "most surprising innovations – its timing and persona – gave it the salient features of a diary, but of a diary turned inside out."[59] The *Spectator* sets in motion a dialectic between private and public, between "containment" and "continuity." Its papers take on the quality of public drama precisely because they become part of the shared "diurnal rhythm" of experience. By constantly addressing the reader and drawing the reader into conversation, the *Spectator* creates a sense of identity in its readers, "a fiction of reciprocity between itself and its readers, in which each part not only mirrors the other but appears to occupy the other's place in space and over time."[60] Goldsmith's Chinese letters, which reenact the fiction of a private correspondence on public display in the manner of the *Spectator* and other periodicals, introduces a Chinese man into the quotidian, diurnal space of modern England. The reader is thus led to imagine, and acknowledge, the Chinese gaze not so much as the despotic gaze of an orient located outside of history but as the contemporary and surprisingly proximate gaze of a neighboring stranger. In this sense, I would argue that Goldsmith's project takes the oriental spy narrative to a new level. Indeed, I would argue that by serializing these letters Goldsmith mobilizes a complex, dialectical play of collective identification that Benedict Anderson has theorized as modern "seriality": "the formation of collective subjectivities in the modern world" by means of identification with numerous, anonymous others.[61]

Performing Seriality

In *Imagined Communities*, Anderson famously pointed to the newspaper as one of the "two forms of imagining which first flowered in Europe in the eighteenth century" and "provided the technical means" for representing new ideas of time and the nation. According to Anderson, the newspaper and the novel represent a new kind of "simultaneity" or togetherness in a new kind of time "marked not by prefiguring and fulfilment, but by temporal coincidence, and measured by clock and calendar."[62] This simultaneity is not given but rather "imagined" or constructed by the reader who understands the "literary convention" behind these new kinds of texts. The reader of the modern novel understands that "actors who may be largely unaware of one another" are nonetheless connected in that they are living in "the same clocked, calendrical time"; the newspaper reader similarly understands that the miscellaneous articles that look randomly and arbitrarily "juxtaposed" in the newspaper are in fact linked by the "essential connection" of "calendrical coincidence." Not only does the reader of these modern genres connect these variously represented actors and events in her mind as existing in a single, synchronous time; she also imagines herself as part of a much larger social body of individuals simultaneously engaged in the "extraordinary mass ceremony" of consuming these mass-produced texts.[63] For Anderson, crucial innovations in mass publication, as well as the reader's ready participation in the literary conventions of mass-produced texts, provide the minimal "structural condition" for the modern idea of the nation.[64] What particularly interests me in Anderson's formulation is the connection he makes between modes of temporality and collective identities. Anderson's claim that our political identities depend on ideas about time, which are in turn dependent on literary conventions, can be rewritten thus: modern forms of national belonging are critically conditioned by the idea of literary modernity – literary because our ideas of time are necessarily mediated by literary conventions (of the novel and the newspaper), and modern because these conventions represent a new understanding of time.

In an important essay entitled "Nationalism, Identity, and the Logic of Seriality," published subsequently in *The Spectre of Comparisons*, Anderson modified some of his earlier formulations in *Imagined Communities*, acknowledging that his earlier focus on temporal consciousness had led him to overlook other "principles of coherence" in modern newspapers: namely, the fact that newspapers represent not only a national community living in "calendrical simultaneity" but also a wider world of nations. As we have seen, the early English newspaper consisted largely of foreign, rather than domestic, news. Anderson writes, "It would be *contra naturam* for a newspaper to confine its reports to events within the political realm in which it is published"; "newspapers everywhere take 'this world of mankind' as their domain no matter how partially they read it."[65] The eighteenth-century newspaper indeed assumes that it can go beyond its own political realm and refer to the global world outside it; it also takes for granted, as Anderson claims all newspapers do, that it has a common vocabulary that can be used to analyze cultural and political differences throughout the world "no matter how vast the real differences between the populations, languages, beliefs and conditions of life."[66] Pheng Cheah glosses Anderson's claim thus: the newspaper constructs the nation as one in a larger series, where "each nation is necessarily imagined as part of a common world, and all nations are imagined as *equivalent* coinhabitants of this continuous global domain through the use of similar categories to describe their internal features" (emphasis in original).[67]

Anderson's word for this way of understanding one's existence as always profoundly connected to a larger, universal world of anonymous others is *seriality*. When Jean-Paul Sartre originally used the term in *The Critique of Dialectical Reason*, seriality described the peculiarly banal, modern form of group belonging, where one is passively united to a larger mass of people with whom one does not have any reciprocal relationship but merely a serial one; one relates to others merely statistically, as it were. In seriality, one is never alone, yet one is always solitary; one is always part of a larger social group, but is disconnected from it at the same time. Sartre's examples of modern seriality are standing in a line to wait for a bus and listening to the radio. As a particular number in a line, or as one of incalculably many auditors of a radio broadcast, my identity is always conditioned by others and has meaning in relation to those others; however, my relationship to these others is only formal, numerical, and abstract. As such, Sartre approached seriality as a form of "passive unity of multiplicity," a way of living constantly outside oneself, always determined in relation to others who nonetheless exist merely as abstract ideas of otherness rather than full-fledged others.[68] For Anderson, however, seriality as a modern way of relating to anonymous others need not always confine us to a "finite numerology." Seriality can bind us when we turn into countable data, as in the census and in elections, and we are utilized for "governmentality." However, seriality can also unbind us. When we understand ourselves as being one of many, a "modern imagining of collectivity" can take place, where we become members of universal series that are essentially open and thus unnumbered, unbound, and uncountable.[69] Anderson's term for this kind of belonging is *unbound seriality*.

These theorizations by Sartre and Anderson, I propose, help us identify the multiple ways in which Goldsmith mobilizes seriality in his Chinese letters. In the first place, by publishing Altangi's Chinese letters in a serial newspaper, Goldsmith turns Altangi into a serial subject, thereby formally naturalizing the idea that England and China can be discussed together, in a "profoundly homogenized manner."[70] Goldsmith argues China's contemporaneity with the 'now' time of the newspaper, so different from the deferred or repetitive time of the oriental sequence, by placing Altangi squarely in the midst of contemporary events. Altangi writes about the Seven Years' War of 1756–63 (Letter 17), the English subscription to clothe French captives imprisoned in London in January 1760 (Letters 11, 23), the trial and subsequent execution of Laurence Shirley, the fourth Earl Ferrers, in January–May 1760 (Letter 38), the false news of Voltaire's death in May 1760 (Letter 43), the mad dog epidemic of August 1760 (Letter 69), and the upcoming coronation of George III in September 1761 (Letter 105). Altangi protests when he finds that the English want him to perform "true exotic barbarity" and "the true eastern style" for them (Letter 33, 142, 144). He is a worldly traveler and a modern man, he points out. He has "travelled so many thousand miles," "conversed familiarly for several years with the English factors established at Canton, and the missionaries sent us from every part of Europe" (Letter 33, 147). Thus, whereas the orient lies outside of history in the oriental tale, the *Public Ledger* imports China into contemporary history, thereby encouraging the reader to think of the English and the Chinese as correlative, comparable, "anonymous series" of "collective subjectivities." When China becomes a part of a common world ruled by "the same clocked, calendrical time" that rules England, it becomes an integral part of English consciousness.[71] In this sense, Altangi performs the seriality of the newspaper, which is outward-looking, international, and as Pheng Cheah points out, essentially comparative: the newspaper shows us that "imagining the nation is essentially a comparative process in which the nation is always haunted by something that is one and the same time both spatially other or exterior to it, but also similar to it in the sense that it is part of it and inhabits the same frame of consciousness."[72] Anderson speaks of the "natural universality" of the newspaper.[73] Altangi's seriality is universalizing in this very precise sense of opening up a profoundly comparative perspective on English nationality and culture.

Secondly, by making Altangi prove his modernity by behaving like a modern citizen at home in the big city, Goldsmith simultaneously updates representations of China and critiques metropolitan forms of life. Altangi can be considered a serial Chinaman in this other, more Sartrean sense of being a representative modern metropolitan. He could not be more different from Mahmut in Marana's *Turkish Spy*, who hides in a tiny room in Paris – a room "so small that jealousy itself can scarce enter" – going out as little as possible and encountering only trouble when he does.[74] Altangi, in stark contrast, moves around London like a fashionable man about town. He goes shopping in bookshops and silk shops, dawdles in coffeehouses, watches plays at Covent Garden and Drury Lane, visits Westminster Abbey and St. Paul's, diverts himself in Vauxhall Gardens, and attends the races at Newmarket. Unlike Sartre's serial man who is problematized precisely because he is always only one of a large metropolitan multitude from which he is alienated, Goldsmith's Altangi delights in being part of an alien crowd. With this ironic portrayal of a confidently metropolitan Altangi, I suggest, Goldsmith simultaneously takes issue with representations of modern Chinese as well as English urbanity.

Thirdly, by drawing attention to the serial nature of the national imaginary, Goldsmith launches a self-reflexive critique of English newspaper readership and English nationhood. On the one hand, his Chinese letters perform seriality in the sense of interpellating "fellow-readers" who are "connected through print" to form an imagined community of English nationals. These readers, who recognize themselves as the anonymous, common objects of Altangi's comic satire, are united by belonging to the category of the English nation, which Altangi constantly refers to.[75] He is indeed passionate about "national vices" and "national virtues" (Letter 4, 27) and enjoys nothing so much as making comparisons between different nations, as when he writes "The English seem as silent as the Japonese, yet vainer than the inhabitants of Siam" (Letter 4, 27). In this way, I believe Goldsmith shows how the early newspaper abets national units of identification, precisely through literary and fictional techniques. What Goldsmith's satire effectively shows is that the rhetoric of national difference that is so central to the newspaper owes a great deal to the 'foreign correspondents' in oriental spy narrative as well as to older travel narratives that referred constantly to 'national' differences. What distinguishes Goldsmith's references as well as appeals to the English nation from these older references, however, is the sustained attention he pays to the way in which the English serial press addresses, invokes, constructs, and calls forth a national readership. This self-conscious and self-reflexive representation of the nation as constructed by means of a specific kind of modern readership is indeed what distinguishes Goldsmith's practice of pseudo-letter writing from that of the Marquis d'Argens, whose *Lettres chinoises* has long been identified as a key model and source text for Goldsmith.

When Goldsmith speaks of the English nation, it is very particularly as a nation of newspaper and gazette readers. In Letter 5, which we briefly examined in the previous section, Altangi speaks tellingly of "*An Englishman*" who exemplifies "the singular passion of this nation for politics" by reading every day "a leaf of political instruction" in the privacy of his home, then repairing to a coffee-house where he can "increase his collection" of the news, after which he visits the "ordinary, enquires what news, and treasuring up every acquisition there, hunts about all the evening in quest of more" still (Letter 5, 31; my emphasis). Anonymous, representative, serial, this indefinite Englishman is interchangeable with other similar Englishmen; all together, they make up what Anderson calls "a single category-series" that spans an entire multitude of anonymous Englishmen.[76] Altangi states that the English are characterized above all by their hunger for politics, which they satisfy by reading the news. Following Anderson's argument, I believe we can read this seemingly light-hearted jab at the English obsession with the news not merely as a symptom of a broad category of Englishness but as Goldsmith's very precise analysis of how the political category of modern English nationhood was being constituted through mass participation in the daily ritual of reading a daily newspaper. Altangi, who starts out as an ironic observer of this newspaper public sphere, becomes in the course of the serialization just as avid a reader of the English news. Drawn into the English newspaper despite himself, he thus turns "almost" an Englishman by the end of the serial. As he ironically says, "I am almost become an Englishman; I now begin to read with pleasure of their taking towns or gaining battles, and secretly with disappointment to all the enemies of Britain" (Letter 85, 345). Goldsmith leaves room for comedy here, but he shows a keen awareness of the power of the newspaper press to construct powerful forms of anonymous political identification. It is particularly in these self-reflexive references to the English newspaper press that we need to locate Goldsmith's achievement and originality. It is true that Goldsmith shows at times an "almost parasitic dependence on the writings of others," borrowing freely from earlier oriental narratives and indeed mimicking them closely.[77] We should note, though, that what he chooses to borrow and copy are precisely the conventional elements common to the spy narrative and the oriental tale: tales about transmigration, dream sequences, stock references to the subjugated state of Asian women.[78] What he does with these conventional elements, however, is very different. Above all, Goldsmith is interested in the serial effect of the Chinese letters and the role of the newspaper press in constructing not only national but also supranational forms of identity.

For instance, in Letter 23, where Altangi refers to English subscriptions for French prisoners held captive in England, Goldsmith shows that reading newspapers can lead to political activism that goes beyond narrowly national interests. Referring to a list of subscribers published in the *London Chronicle* in January 17–19, 1760, Altangi writes, "When I cast my eye over the list of those who contributed on this occasion, I find the names almost entirely English, scarce one foreigner appears among the number." He then adds, "I am particularly struck with one who writes these words upon the paper that enclosed his benefaction. '*The mite of an Englishman, a citizen of the world, to Frenchmen, prisoners of war, and naked*'" (Letter 23, 99). The list to which Altangi refers indeed contains numerous references to anonymous persons ("An unknown person," "No Name," "A Lady unknown," "Gentleman unknown," and so on) whose erased, but nonetheless publicized identities he takes as a proof that the English have overcome "national hatred" to shower "National benevolence" on their "enemies in distress" (Letter 23, 99). He reads them, in short, as representatives of anonymous individuals united in their public roles both as English nationals and as citizens of the world. The reason why "*an* Englishman" can also be "*a* citizen of the world" is precisely because Goldsmith understands national identity as being synchronous with a larger, global identity. That said, we should note that the indefinite articles "a" and "an," which Anderson reads as powerful signals of a new kind of serial self-understanding, can also be taken as reminders of the smallness of the series in question – the fewness, in other words, of true global citizens.

A final comparison between Altangi and Crusoe may help us understand just how different Goldsmith's project was not only from the project of the oriental spy narrative but also that of the early English novel. Although Anderson considers the novel to be just as important a literary genre in the construction of modern seriality, Defoe's Crusoe novels evince a strong resistance to the idea of nations as belonging to a larger series in which they exist side by side, in "homogeneous, empty time." Anderson argues that the ideas of modernity, comparative history, and human pluralism were intimately connected; that "Europe's 'discovery' of grandiose civilizations hitherto only dimly rumoured" challenged sacred genealogies and enabled a new sense of "synchronic novelty," "parallelism or simultaneity" that would have profound political and cultural repercussions.[79] China is a seriality in this precise sense of being another modernity and a "synchronic novelty" in Goldsmith's work. Whereas Goldsmith insists on making the reader reflect on the idea of an alternative Chinese modernity that might serve as a self-reflective mirror for modern England, however, Defoe's Crusoe trilogy is concerned to write it *out* of history. As Crusoe says in *Farther Adventures*, China is "not … worth naming, or worth my while to write of, or any that shall come after me to read" (2: 173). Goldsmith reverses the trajectory of Defoe's novels, bringing China home to England. As we have seen, Crusoe would have no truck with China: "I must confess," he declared, "it seem'd strange to me, when I came Home, and heard our People say such fine Things of the Power, Riches, Glory, Magnificence, and Trade of the *Chinese*"; "As their Strength, and their Grandeur, so their Navigation, Commerce, and Husbandry" he had found to be equally "imperfect and impotent, compar'd to the same things in *Europe*" (2: 174). In Goldsmith's neat reversal, Altangi arrives in England after "a journey of seven hundred painful days, in order to examine its opulence, buildings, sciences, arts and manufactures on the spot" only to discover "no signs of that opulence so much talk'd of abroad" (Letter 2, 19). Defoe's characters, ranging from Robinson Crusoe and Captain Singleton to Moll Flanders and Roxana, are thrust out of England into the global space represented by the newspaper. Variously set loose in Europe, Africa, the Americas, and Asia, Defoe's heroes signal their modernity above all by their inability to stay put. They are, as Mary Jo Kietzman puts it, "serial subjects" in the sense of being always on the move, constantly changing their minds, trying on different identities.[80] The seriality of Defoe's aggressively self-fashioning subjects, however, has little to do with unbound seriality in Anderson's – or Goldsmith's – sense.

The Serial Chinaman

One possible objection to the argument of this chapter is that China never achieves the status of a fully contemporary, coeval reality in Goldsmith's work. For instance, Tao Zhijian has argued that "the figure of Lien Chi Altangi … is but Goldsmith thinly disguised," and that China in *The Citizen of the World* is hardly contemporary: "the desolate and obsolete 'reality' of exotic China" in Goldsmith's work is "simply an invented reality," "fabricated by Europeans" and "further fabricated by Goldsmith." Tao writes, "Although, on one side of Goldsmith's satire, China as the Other is often frivolously appreciated as the ideal, on the other side, it is also tacitly the butt of criticism."[81] Similarly, Christopher Brooks has declared that in Goldsmith's work, "little, if anything, is actually learned about the China of the eighteenth century, save for the English fondness for and subsequent rejection of this Eastern fad." According to Brooks, in his Chinese letters Goldsmith mimicked "the depths of emulative silliness and the exploitative 'use' of the Orient," precisely to point out the foolishness of the orientalist craze for chinoiserie. In the process, Brooks believes, Goldsmith "victimizes Altangi and the Orient," using China as a "vehicle for ironic discourse" but not much more.[82] For Brooks, the fact that Goldsmith "chose China (rather than Morocco or Fez) indicates just how exploitable the 'projection' of China was to a logocentric Westerner."[83] These critical approaches to Goldsmith's Chinese letters, however, drastically simplify the richness and subtlety of his work. As I have suggested, the originality of Goldsmith's work needs to be assessed in light of, and in comparison with, the genres of oriental fiction that were available to him at the time, as well as the powerful meanings embedded within the serial form. Just as it would be a foolish to write off all oriental fiction for containing "armchair voyagings and vicarious imaginings that sometimes bore little relation to realities in those countries," it makes little sense to dismiss Goldsmith's Chinese letters solely for misrepresenting, exploiting, and 'victimizing' China.[84] Correlatively, while David Porter is certainly right to point out that Goldsmith's work unmasks "the stubborn illiteracy of the English" when it comes to Chinese signs, I believe that the object of his satire goes well beyond the English reaction to chinoiserie.[85]

In considering Goldsmith's treatment of Altangi's serial Chineseness, I would argue, we should not take the fact that China serves at times as the butt of his satire to mean that Goldsmith always approaches China as an object to be mocked. In the same vein, we should note that seriality in his Chinese letters needs to be approached both as its structural condition of meaning as well as, at times, the object of his satire. The complexity of Goldsmith's work has everything to do with this slippery satirical strategy of not sparing the satirical persona from the satire, thereby allowing the satire to turn in on itself. We have seen how this works in Goldsmith's treatment of the English newspaper. As I have shown, he was keenly aware that the serial form of the publication in which the Chinese letters appeared would condition their reception, influence, and meaning. He understood, in other words, that the Chinese letters would necessarily be read in the context of the readerly interests of a nation-based, urban, and modern newspaper audience. The Chinese letters cater very effectively to precisely those expansive, commercial, and global interests in the up-to-date and the modern. At the same time, however, Goldsmith's letters satirize the forms of seriality in which the English newspaper participates precisely to debunk some of the false claims of modernity and nationalism. Goldsmith's analysis of contemporary English culture, it seems to me, aims most of all at destabilizing – indeed, caricaturing – all forms of simplistic judgment about it. Similarly, Altangi's Chinese identity should be understood as both the vehicle and object of Goldsmith's satire. As Donna Isaacs Dalnekoff pointed out in her influential essay "A Familiar Stranger: The Outsider of Eighteenth-Century Satire," the "outsider in a foreign land," an old and familiar figure who dates back to antiquity, takes on new importance in the eighteenth century when he is reimagined as a traveler from either a much more highly developed or a very primitive society in a foreign land. Both kinds of societies provide ample opportunities for satire because they represent "contradictory principles": the orient, for instance, was "linked with despotism as well as tolerance, prejudices and superstitions as well as reason," while the new world was "associated with bestiality, decline, and the debilitation of man" as well as "a lost paradise inhabited by men of superior virtue."[86] Eighteenth-century satire would be far less destabilizing and less powerful if its vehicles were less contradictory. With a satirical vehicle whose meaning is always shifting, the satirist can multiply his objects of satire. Goldsmith indeed manages to target multiple, moving satirical objects through his portrait of a serial Chinaman wandering around London. Neither China, nor England, nor England's idea of China, not even the figure of the Chinese traveler in England escapes Goldsmith's satire.

We have already seen that Altangi is portrayed in significant contrast to Mahmut in the *Turkish Spy*. This satirical reversal of the oriental spy figure serves to call into question conventional portrayals of a backward and exotic orient. In Marana's work, the east and west cohabitate uncomfortably and suspiciously, trapped in a relationship of observer and observed without achieving much in the way of reciprocity. As Arthur Weitzman points out, "the Letter writer is a Moslem, a foreigner, and moreover, a spy who is not particularly comfortable in the Parisian milieu, but is resigned to his duty, which he stoically accepts."[87] His self-description is telling:

> Being of low stature, of an ill-favoured countenance, ill-shaped and by nature not given to talkativeness, I shall the better conceal myself. Instead of my name, Mahmut the Arabian, I have taken on me that of Titus the Moldavian; and with a little cassock of black serge, which is the habit I have chosen, I make two figures, being in heart what I ought to be, but outwardly and in appearance what I never intend.[88]

Mahmut describes himself not as one figure but "two figures" divided between heart and outward appearance; secretive, self-concealing, and silent. Multiple, divided, he is the interiorized version of the ongoing hostility between the European and the Arab. Short and ugly in person, he is not much to look at. Meanwhile, the black habit he wears to hide himself visualizes and allegorizes the inability of these cultures to look straight at each other, to occupy the same space and time in comfortable proximity. Most of Mahmut's letters show him as a solitary and unhappy figure, observing Parisian life and mores at a distance while surviving on a diet of "bread and water."[89] He is, as he says, as good as "buried alive" in Paris.[90] There is nothing more terrifying for him than to have someone call out his name, as once happens when his former Christian slavemaster accosts him in front of Notre Dame and almost brings a Parisian mob down on him. When he does become a participant in Parisian life, it is usually in the unfortunate form of being imposed on, tricked, threatened, stabbed at, falsely accused, even imprisoned. Neither can he look home for an easy escape. Accused of converting to Christianity by his enemies back home, he finds himself as little welcome back home as in Paris.

Comparing Mahmut with Goldsmith's Altangi, we cannot fail to be struck by the very different figure Altangi cuts in modern London. Most of all, he is from the very start openly identified as Chinese. Letters and recommendations pave the road for his entry into London society. And to judge by all the dinner invitations he quickly starts receiving, in very little time he bursts onto the London scene as a cultural celebrity. Neither Altangi's Chineseness nor his "person by no means agreeable" (Letter 8, 42) is a block to his sociability. On the contrary, his Chinese identity and his "broad face and flat nose" (Letter 8, 42) enhance his appeal in the eyes of the fashionable Londoners who are as eager to ogle at, feed, and receive him in their private homes as he is to converse with them. Goldsmith interprets this hospitality cynically, revealing that the real motivations for such openness are always tied to a form of self-interest: there is not that big a difference, in the end, between the prostitutes who accost him on the streets in order to steal from him and the "distinguished" ladies and gents who are eager to add him to their roster of chinoiserie collectibles. Altangi's desire to get to know the English is never fully reciprocated. Nonetheless, he is emphatically not a spy and is not treated as one. He is most certainly not buried alive. Hardly ever alone, he walks about London in the company of friends – most importantly, the Man in Black (a figure who is a stand-in for Goldsmith himself) and the comically gauche Beau Tibbs who makes many more social gaffes than him. As Altangi writes to his friend Fun Hom back in China, "Behold me then in London gazing at the strangers, and they at me" (Letter 3, 22). Unlike Mahmut, Altangi exists to be seen as much as to see, and he seems to enjoy being a public spectacle as much as he loves attending one.[91]

The openness and relish with which Altangi enters into and enjoys modern English cultural life at the level of both narrative and form is thus symptomatic of the eighteenth-century English perception of the Chinese as a much more coeval rival than other oriental nations. Not that the common Englishman could easily tell them apart. In letter 33, Altangi describes going to a dinner party where the guests expect him to "sweat by Alla, rail against wine, and behave, and talk, and write like a Turk or Persian" (Letter 33, 142). Altangi, who is more amused than angered by this confusion, speaks up, though not to great avail:

> Besides, Sir, you must not expect from an inhabitant of China the same ignorance, the same unlettered simplicity, that you find in a *Turk, Persian,* or native of *Peru.* The Chinese are versed in the sciences as well as you, and are masters of several arts unknown to the people of Europe. Many of them are instructed not only in their own national learning, but are perfectly well acquainted with the languages and learning of the west. (Letter 33, 146)

There is little that is new in the cultural clichés Altangi rehearses here, and it is difficult to gauge his defense of modern Chinese learning. Still, Altangi's words suggest that China posed a different kind of challenge to English valuations of other cultures. Goldsmith's biographer James Prior noted that Goldsmith had initially considered impersonating "a native of Morocco or Fez" but eventually dropped this idea after "reflecting on the rude nature of the people of Barbary"; "A Chinese was then chosen as offering more novelty of character than a Turk or Persian; and being equally advanced in the scale of civilization, could pass an opinion on all he saw better than the native of a more barbarous country."[92] In fact, Altangi goes one step farther. Not only is China as "equally advanced" as Europe and very different from other "barbarous" countries, as Prior puts it, "the Chinese used such arts" as "gunpowder, and the mariner's compass" before they became familiar instruments in Europe (Letter 108, 419); indeed, some of its modern arts and sciences are still "unknown to the people of Europe" (Letter 33, 146). In short, it is in some aspects even more modern than Europe. By contrast, Persian modernity has been stopped in its tracks by political oppression. This last point is argued by Altangi's son Hingpo who sets out to join his father, only to fall prey to a series of misfortunes. After crossing "the desarts of Thibet," Hingpo is captured by "wandering Tartars" who then sell him to "merchants from Mesched" (Letter 22, 95). He eventually ends up a slave in Persia, from whence he writes to his father: "Into what a state of misery are the modern Persians fallen! A nation once famous for setting the world an example of freedom, is now become a land of tyrants, and a den of slaves" (Letter 35, 152). Ironically, this argument ends up dragging Chinese political modernity also into question since Hingpo's travails were set in motion by the Chinese emperor's "displeasure" at Lien Chi Altangi's departure, so "contrary to the rules of our government, and the immemorial custom of the empire" (Letter 6, 38). This irony is lost on the unruly dinner guests, though, who can only relate to the orient as an exotic object of consumption. Altangi is a disappointing and false specimen to them: he carries no opium or tobacco on him, does not use chopsticks, declines "a plate of *Bear's Claws*, or a slice of *Birds nests*" (Letter 33, 143), speaks with no "eastern style" whatsoever, and does not even have "the true Chinese cut" in his "visage" (Letter 33, 144). He conforms neither to the exotic image of China circulated in travelogues and reports in this period, nor the fantastic image of China in oriental tales, where it is a land of fable, "of genii, magicians, rocks, bags of bullets, giants, and enchanters, where all is great, obscure, magnificent, and unintelligible" (Letter 33, 144). For Goldsmith, the joke is all on the English consumers of this exoticized China.

Unlike the English, who are interested in Altangi mostly as a curiosity on par with the supposedly Chinese "pea-green" jars, "sprawling dragons, squatting pagods, and clumsy mandarins" that stuff the interiors of their houses, Altangi the serial Chinaman is interested in English modernity, in the reports of its glorious modern wealth, arts and sciences (Letter 14, 64–65). Unfortunately, his expectations are quickly dashed upon first arrival. The "gloomy solemnity" of the streets, the puddles moving "muddily along" the pavements, the "heavy laden machines with wheels of unwieldy thickness" that block every passage and threaten to crush the pedestrians to pieces, the nondescript houses quite devoid of decoration, and the "dismal looks of the inhabitants" make London pale in comparison to the "streets of Nankin … sometimes strewed with gold leaf" (Letter 2, 19–20). However, this vision of London's sordid urban waste and congestion fails to produce anything as caustic as the excremental vision of "modern life as a sewer" in Swift's *Description of a City Shower* (1710) or Pope's *Dunciad* (1728, 1743).[93] In very little time, he begins to be "better reconciled to the people" and starts to "fancy" that he will "find them more opulent, more charitable, and more hospitable" (Letter 8, 42). Altangi's inborn good humor, his weakness for women, and his fondness for "pleasure" and "gay company" constantly lead him out into the streets where he delights in losing himself in the crowd (Letter 65, 225). The contrast with Mahmut could not be starker. Unlike Mahmut, who has "a natural aversion for great and populous cities," which he describes as "so many magnificent sepulchers of the living, where men are shut up, imprisoned and buried from all commerce with the elements," Altangi points to the crowd as his natural element:[94]

> From this motive I am often found in the centre of a crowd; and wherever pleasure is to be sold, am always a purchaser. In those places, without being remarked by any, I join in whatever goes forward, work my passions into a similitude of frivolous earnestness, shout as they shout, and condemn as they happen to disapprove. (Letter 65, 225)

This striking image of a Chinese man losing himself with pleasure in the anonymity of the metropolitan London crowd and mimicking its passions is an image of the experienced modern city-dweller who takes active pleasure in "the particular experiences of physical crowding, social indiscriminacy, and especially spatial mobility characteristic of the modern metropolis."[95] When Altangi goes to see pageants, he goes more for the experience of "being in the crowd which sees it" than to see the pageant itself. The crowd is the real show: "it is amusing to observe the effect which such a spectacle has upon the variety of faces, the pleasure it excites in some, the envy in others, and the wishes it raises in all" (Letter 65, 268). When he goes walking, he goes partly for the pleasure of watching other strollers, and likes to size up the women who pass by: "the beauty of such as were handsome, or the dresses of such as had nothing else to recommend them" (Letter 54, 225–26). Altangi is a flâneur, a mingler, a partygoer, a woman-watcher, a crowd-follower – in short, a serial metropolitan.[96]

Goldsmith, who had clearly done some homework on China, may have taken the idea of Altangi's representative urbanity from a number of sources.[97] Michael Adas notes that "The accounts of early travelers unanimously celebrate the great number of walled cities in China, whose size, broad and regularly laid-out streets, and crowded markets made Europe's largest urban centers seem like mere provincial towns."[98] The two most important sources in Goldsmith's day for information about China were Le Comte and Du Halde, both of whom underscored the spectacular number and size of China's cities, as well as the extraordinary crowds that moved about in them. Comparing the Chinese capital to Paris, Le Comte opined in *Memoirs and Observations Made in a Late Journey through the Empire of China* (1697) that Paris was "but a quarter as large as all *Pekin*," marveling especially at the giant crowds he saw in the Chinese capital.[99] In Du Halde's *A Description of the Empire of China and Chinese-Tartary* (1738–1741), China is likewise noted for its "great Number of splendid Cities, celebrated on account of their Situation and Extent; the Multitude of their Inhabitants; the extraordinary Concourse of the Chinese drawn thither for sake of Trade; the Beauty of the publick Buildings, and Plenty which reigns therein."[100] As Goldsmith would have well known, the stereotypical image of Chinese urbanity cut both ways. On the one hand, the Chinese city was celebrated for its geometrical and rational shape ("the Cities of *China* resemble one another so nearly, that to see one, is almost sufficient to give an Idea of them all"; they are "for the most Part square … and encompass'd with high Walls, defended by Towers") as well as the "perfect Tranquillity" and "excellent Order" reigning therein.[101] As reported by Du Halde, in Peking order was "observed with the greatest Exactness, that Peace, Silence and Safety reign thro' the City"; soldiers swept and kept the broad streets of Peking clean; night guards would "suffer none to walk in the Night."[102] At the same time, life in Peking was lively, diverting, and carnivalesque. While "All the Riches and Commodities of the Empire" kept flowing in, people would gather in "infinite Multitudes" on the streets, and a mighty "Confusion" would result,

> caused by the surprising Number of Horses, Mules, Asses, Camels, Carts, Waggons, and Chairs, without reckoning the various Crowds of Men, 100 or 200 in a Cluster, which one meets with every now and then, gathered about some Fortune-teller, or Players at Cups and Balls; or listening to Ballad Singers, and others who read or repeat certain comical Stories to make Diversion; or else gaping at a sort of Quacks, who distribute their Medicines, and display their admirable Effects with a great deal of Eloquence.[103]

Du Halde's passage appears to be based on a very similar one in Le Comte's *Memoirs and Observations*, where Le Comte interprets the crowd very differently. In Peking, he writes, "the multitude of People in the Streets is so great, that one is frightned at it."

> Even the widest Streets are not free from Confusion; and at the sight of so many Horses, Mules, Camels, Wagons, Chairs, and Rings of 100 or 200 Person who gather here and there round the Fortune-Tellers, one would judge that some unusual Shew had drawn the whole Country to *Pekin*.
> Indeed, to outward appearance our most populous Cities are Wildernesses in respect of this.[104]

Le Comte's description of frighteningly large Chinese crowds that appear to reduce Europe's most populous cities to "Wildernesses," however, turns out to be a false call. Peking only seems to be more populous than Paris "to outward appearance," he adds, because their streets are so wide, and their houses only "only Story high," where the Chinese "dwell very close together."[105] Nor is Peking as well-engineered as Du Halde suggests in his later *Description*. Le Comte scorned the houses in Peking for being "neither well built nor high enough," and "always pester'd with Mud or Dust." In both summer and winter, he noted, there was so much dust that "the City is always covered with a Cloud of it": "the Dirt spoils the silken Boots," "sticks to their Clothes, especially if they are made with Sattin," "gets into the House, and makes its way into the closest Closets, so that take what care you will, your Goods should ever be full of it."[106] Goldsmith shows his familiarity with both Du Halde's and Le Comte's versions of Peking: the image of the utopian, ultra-ordered Chinese city epitomized by the Imperial Court and its "prodigious Collection of great Buildings, vast Courts, and Gardens,"[107] and the contrasting image of a city overrun by dirt, chaos, and crowds.[108] In his Chinese letters, he skilfully exploits these dual registers in the meaning of the Chinese city. Indeed, his use of Du Halde and Le Comte shows us that the image of China as a nation stuck in the agricultural stage of history, often erroneously attributed to Adam Smith, was at best a partial one.[109] China was also strongly associated with urban planning, as well as a highly developed metropolitan lifestyle.

Altangi, who comes from Canton, is obviously used to living in a large urban city with large crowds. As befits a former citizen of Canton, a city distinguished by its "Harbor Shipping" and the ships that "arrive daily from All Quarters of the World, with all manner of Goods," Altangi is used to urban commerce.[110] The charm and convenience of Chinese shops was a commonplace by Goldsmith's time. Magalhães had earlier reported that "at *Pe Kim*, and in all the other Cities of *China*, there is everything to be sold at your Door for entertainment, subsistence or pleasure."[111] Du Halde had also concluded that while the grandeur of Chinese cities lay in their "vast Extent," their beauty lay in the shops that lined their streets: generally speaking, in the "large Squares, and long Streets, some very wide, others narrow, with Houses on Each Side, having only a Ground Floor, or one Story at most," he wrote, "one sees Shops adorn'd with *China* Ware, Silks, and varnish'd or japann'd Goods; before the Door of each, there is placed a Pedestal, on which is erected a Board 7 or 8 Food high, either painted or gilded, with three large Characters written thereon, such as the Shop-Keeper chuses for his Sign."[112] Describing Canton, Du Halde noted that it was "one of the most populous and opulent in *China*," with "long and straight" streets "paved with very hard hewn-Stone, and extremely neat," "wholly taken up with Shops."[113] Hailing from China where everything is "sold at your Door," Altangi is an experienced shopper and finds the "Shops of London are as well furnished as those of Pekin" – though this does not stop him from being talked into buying much more silk than he intends to at a mercer's shop (Letter 77, 318–20). Unlike Addison's Spectator, however, he does not visit the Royal Exchange or eulogize the "Metropolis [as] a kind of *Emporium* for the whole Earth." Altangi, like the Spectator, fancies himself "a Citizen of the World," but not because he enjoys London's "grand Scene of Business" (*Spectator* no. 69, May 19, 1711; 1: 294). Altangi's enjoyment of the city is not about the benefits of international trade.[114] He understands that living in a city in eighteenth-century England means sharing public space, accepting both geographic and social mobility, and living in the company of diverse social classes.[115] His delight in London has a Hogarthian edge to it. In London, Altangi is accosted by prostitutes, one of whom steals his watch from him (Letter 8); eavesdrops on a conversation taking place between a prisoner, a porter, and a soldier while passing by one of London's prisons (Letter 4); sups at a visitation dinner with priests (Letter 63); has his shoe torn by the crowd and mended by a poor cobbler (Letter 65); meets a pawnbroker's widow (Letter 71); and listens to the story of a disabled soldier with a wooden leg (Letter 119). In a village nearby, he watches an overexcited and drunken crowd at an election quarrel over the relative merits of brandy and gin (Letter 112). In this series of Hogarthian stills, Goldsmith debunks England's pretension to progressive modernity. At the same time, Goldsmith identifies his readership optimistically as an urban population whose different classes commingle in common public places, who speak the same political language of liberty, and read the same newspapers.

In this regard, it is significant that Altangi finds it difficult to determine people's class identities in London. For instance, in London, people's dress is *not* a reliable sign of either their wealth or their status. This "difficulty of distinguishing men by their appearance" (Letter 52, 219) in the urban space of London is connected, I believe, to an important characteristic of the English periodical press that differentiates it from that of France. As Stephen Botein, Jack Censer, and Harriet Ritvo point out, in the English periodical press "attention to ceremony relating to the grand national hierarchy was apt to be rather perfunctory," and the English press appealed in general to a much larger, and broader, clientele than the mid-century French press.[116] Whereas the French press depended on a wealthy, educated, and in many cases aristocratic authorship as well as readership, and was quite tightly controlled by the monarchy until late in the century, the English and by extension American "periodical press operative within an expansive communications system that made room for people of lower social origins," was in general less dominated by the elite, and "reinforced an image of society in which all productive people – not the least of whom were the craftsmen and small retailers – were joined together as active partners."[117] Goldsmith, whose own social origins in an impoverished Irish family had led him to work as a hack-writer for such publishers such as Newbery, is clearly interested in not only the middling orders but also the social outcasts whom he portrays Altangi conversing with. Altangi's London, where different classes mingle in confusion, presents an urban landscape that is both utopian and dystopian, both celebratory and monitory. Unlike Defoe and Addison, Goldsmith was suspicious of global commerce and the colonial policies pursuing it. A critic of luxury, he was suspicious of what the imperial metropole represented. Speaking through Altangi, he reflects caustically on recent victories in the Seven Years' War, which he interprets as a war over fur, a "necessary commodity" now suddenly "found indispensable for the happiness of the state" (Letter 17, 73). As to the American colonies, he ponders the wisdom of "peopling the desarts of America" with the so-called "waste of an exuberant nation" in order to build new colonies. Could there be any sense in exchanging "the laborious and enterprising, of such men as can be serviceable to their country at home," for the new-fangled colonial commodities of "raw silk, hemp, and tobacco"? Should "hardy veterans, and honest tradesmen … be truck'd for a box of snuff or a silk petticoat" (Letter 17, 75)? Altangi's astonishment at the state of affairs in England, where the English "have filled their houses with our furniture, their public gardens with our fire-works, and their very ponds with our fish" (Letter 110, 426), is clearly not meant as an endorsement of the China trade.[118]

Against the false mobility of colonialism and consumerism, Goldsmith mobilizes philosophical cosmopolitanism, which he defines primarily through the trope of voluntary and impartial traveling. The cosmopolite is a traveler who is neither tourist, topographer, nor sales merchant – not one "who goes from country to country, guided by the blind impulse of curiosity," nor one who will "cross seas and deserts merely to measure the height of a mountain, to describe the cataract of a river, or tell the commodities which every country may produce." The cosmopolite is, rather, "a man who leaves home to mend himself and others," one "who is desirous of understanding the human heart, who seeks to know the *men* of every country, who desires to discover those differences which result from climate, religion, education, prejudice, and partiality" (Letter 7, 40–41). Thus, for Goldsmith it is not physical travel per se but the ability to engage in imaginative departures from one's own prejudices that defines the cosmopolite. Margaret Jacob has pointed out that "Cities are, and were, the natural habitat of the cosmopolitan"; "Amid the cloak of anonymity and the mingling permitted by urban trade, men and some women in all these cities found themselves in situations with unprecedented possibilities for talking, card playing, drinking, clubbing, or just mixing with relative strangers."[119] Following many writers such as Hume who took the city to be the natural habitat of philosophical cosmopolitanism, Goldsmith locates his ideal cosmopolite Altangi in "the urbane pluralism of the city."[120] Goldsmith's attitude toward the city, however, is a great deal more ambivalent than that of Hume, who describes the social man as a cosmopolite – one who is not "contented to remain in solitude, or live with their fellow-citizens in that distant manner, which is peculiar to ignorant and barbarous nations," but willing to "flock into cities ... to receive and communicate knowledge; to show their wit or their breeding; their taste in conversation or living, in clothes or furniture."[121] Whereas Hume considered the city as the center of polite letters, and described himself in his autobiography as removing in 1751 "from the country to the town, the true scene for a man of letters,"[122] Goldsmith found the London "republic of letters" to be a cannibalistic, Hobbesian world where "critics eat up critics, and compilers rob from compilations," "the dunces hunt in full cry till they have run down a reputation, and then snarl and fight with each other about dividing the spoil" (Letter 20, 86). Far from promoting cosmopolitan understanding and attempting "to persuade men to become

citizens of the world," the French and English republics of letters think it
their duty to "be at war" in imitation of their armies (Letter 20, 86). This
Popean vision of the London press as a confederacy of dunces rather than
a cosmopolitan commonwealth of letters should be taken at least in part
as a citation rather than a full-fledged attack, since it was the milieu in
which Goldsmith made, however precariously, both his reputation and his
living.[123]

Nonetheless, Goldsmith's position was very different from that of
Pope, who was one of the greatest beneficiaries of the new literary system
and yet claimed a moral independence from it. Precisely for this reason,
Goldsmith's image of the writer was not that of the Popean speaker who,
in the *Essay on Man*, commands prospect views from a stable position on a
country hilltop. John Barrell notes that, by the 1730s when Pope wrote this
work, the gentlemanly "ideal of the comprehensive observer" who owned
the vantage point of the aristocratic rural estate was "no longer identifi-
able with any very considerable body within the society of England."[124] As
Ingrid Horrocks points out, Goldsmith figures the writer not as a proper-
tied gentleman but as a "wanderer or traveler" who is "imagined as moving
through the world, assembling a view of society from multiple fragmentary
sights and interactions."[125] After publishing the Chinese letters, Goldsmith
increasingly chose to discuss his central question of "how a poet could,
from a marginalized, de-centered position, still hope to claim a universal
voice or a new prospect of society" through the figure of a mobile but melancholy, homeless traveler in rural spaces.[126] In *The Traveller*, for instance,
the poet-speaker is described as "Remote, unfriended, melancholy, slow"
(*Traveller*, l. 1; *CW* 4: 248) – a cosmopolitan who is *not* at home anywhere in the world. In the Chinese letters, however, where the dominant
mode is social comedy, Altangi the friendly urban wanderer represents "the
emblematic modern subject" not so much because he occupies "an identi-
fiable elegiac position of remoteness from anywhere and everywhere" but
because lives in and stands lively witness to the serial time of the city.[127]

An incident reported in Pior's biography of Goldsmith should put to
rest the theory that his interest in China and the East was merely skin-
deep. Toward the end of 1761, Goldsmith appealed to Lord Bute, the new
political authority under George III, requesting funds for "a tour of the
East to study Oriental arts and sciences."[128] The letter that he sent Bute
may have been a version of letter 108 in the Chinese Letters, where Altangi
declares his amazement "at the ignorance of almost all the European travelers, who have penetrated any considerable way eastward into Asia" (Letter
108, 418) and proposes the utility of sending a philosopher (rather than a

"missioner" or merchant) to learn about the "useful knowledge" of the East (Letter 108, 420). The letter ends with an extended description of the ideal man to send on such a journey:

> He should be a man of a philosophic turn, one apt to deduce consequences of general utility from particular occurrences, neither swollen with pride, nor hardened by prejudice, neither wedded to one particular system, nor instructed only in one particular science; neither wholly a botanist, nor quite an antiquarian; his mind should be tinctured with miscellaneous knowledge, and his manners humanized by an intercourse with men. He should be in some measure, an enthusiast to the design; fond of travelling from a rapid imagination, and an innate love of change, furnished with a body capable of sustaining every fatigue, and an heart not easily terrified at danger. (Letter 108, 421)

Read in the context of Goldsmith's appeal to Bute, this description of the ideal traveler and ultimate cosmopolitan sounds impossibly narcissistic. Goldsmith would go on to exploit the comic potential of this traveler figure in *The Vicar of Wakefield*, and his more tragic potential in *The Deserted Village*. In Altangi, what Richard Helgerson calls Goldsmith's "two worlds" – the city and the country – are balanced precariously in favor of the city and the cosmopolitanism it represents.[129] We know from these later works that Goldsmith's focus would eventually move away from the cosmopolitanism of the urbanite to the sentimentalism of the villager in whom he would locate a new humanism. If Goldsmith's dream of "a tour of the East" had come true, the trajectory of his literary career might have looked very different indeed.

CHAPTER 5

Thomas Percy's Chinese Miscellanies and the
Reliques of Ancient English Poetry

The story of how Oliver Goldsmith and Thomas Percy struck up a friendship in the early years of their literary careers is recorded vividly in Percy's
diary and his posthumous *Life of Oliver Goldsmith* (1802). Percy called on
Goldsmith in the spring of 1759, shortly after being introduced to him
by the Scottish poet and physician James Grainger. Percy's diary entry
dated February 21, 1759 reads: "Br. At Grainger's, din'd at Tavern with Mr.
Johnson. Evg at Dr. Grainger's. Mr. Goldsmith there, author of the present
state of polite literature."[1] It may have been curiosity about Goldsmith's
forthcoming *Enquiry into the Present State of Polite Learning in Europe*,
soon to be published in April 1759, that led Percy to pay Goldsmith a call
a few weeks later at his lodgings in Green Arbour Court, in the Old Bailey.
Percy reports:

> He [Goldsmith] had removed thither early in that year; for a friend of his
> [Percy] paying him a visit at the beginning of March, 1759, found him in
> lodgings there so poor and uncomfortable, that he should not think it
> proper to mention the circumstance, if he did not consider it as the highest
> proof of the splendor of Dr. Goldsmith's genius and talents, that by the bare
> exertion of their powers, under every disadvantage of person and fortune,
> he could gradually emerge from such obscurity to the enjoyment of all the
> comforts and even luxuries of life, and admission into the best societies in
> London.
> The Doctor was writing his Enquiry, &c. in a wretched dirty room, in
> which there was but one chair, and when he, from civility, offered it to his
> visitant, himself was obliged to sit in the window. While they were con-
> versing, some one gently rapped at the door, and being desired to come in,
> a poor ragged little girl of very decent behavior, entered, who, dropping a
> curtsie, said, "My mama sends her compliments, and begs the favour of you
> to lend her a chamber-pot full of coals."[2]

The spectacle of Goldsmith eking out a living as a hack writer clearly made
a deep impression on Percy, who was living in markedly different circumstances. Comfortably set up in his sixteenth-century vicarage of Easton

Maudit and soon to be married to Anne Gutteridge, who would bring him a handsome dowry, Percy enjoyed the patronage of the neighboring Earl of Sussex who invited him to London on multiple occasions and introduced him to the "best societies in London."[3] The gulf in their personal fortunes, however, did not stop the two men from forming a lasting attachment to each other. With their life's best work ahead of them, what did they talk about, we may wonder?

They talked, perhaps, about Samuel Johnson in whose company they had first met and who would eventually include them both in his famous literary club; about who were the best London publishers to work with; and what their forthcoming publications were about. Percy was in town to find a publisher for his first book – an English translation of a curious Chinese novel that he had found at a neighbor's house in manuscript form.[4] In February 1758 Percy had borrowed the manuscript from a neighboring Captain Wilkinson, whose uncle James Wilkinson had been a representative of the English East India Company. Wilkinson's relatives were under the impression that James Wilkinson had "undertaken" the translation "as a kind of exercise" while learning the Chinese language in Canton. As Percy explained in the preface to *Hau Kiou Choaan, or the Pleasing History* (1761), three-fourths of the translation were done in English, with the rest done in a different hand in Portuguese. Bound in "four thin folio books or volumes of Chinese paper," "doubled in the fore-edge, and cut on the back" in the manner of the Chinese, the manuscript had been "first written with a black-lead pencil, and afterwards more correctly over-written with ink," as if it had been "drawn up under the direction of a Chinese master or tutor" (1761, 1: x). Impressed by these physical signs of authenticity, and keenly aware of the fact that the only samples of Chinese fiction currently available were the "short pieces" included in Du Halde's *Description of China* (1738–41), Percy had seized upon the opportunity to present the first full-length Chinese novel to the English reading public. Percy's introduction to Goldsmith took place during his active pursuit of Robert Dodsley as a publisher for his project. James Grainger first introduced him to Ralph Griffiths, who eventually backed out of a tentative offer. Bertram Davis speculates that Goldsmith, whose *Enquiry* was soon to be published by Dodsley, may have helped Percy secure Dodsley as a publisher.[5] Having worked with both Griffiths and Dodsley, Goldsmith no doubt was able to provide valuable publishing advice for Percy. In return, Percy may have provided Goldsmith with the idea behind the *Public Ledger* letters, later published under the title *The Citizen of the World; or Letters from a Chinese Philosopher, Residing in London, to his Friends in the East* (1762).[6] It is easy to imagine Goldsmith taking a keen interest in Percy's Chinese curiosity, given his longstanding interest in the English East India Company and his ambition to "study Oriental arts and sciences."[7] Percy no doubt found a sympathetic interlocutor in Goldsmith, who shared his interest in the East. We will never know with certainty what transpired during this meeting between Goldsmith and Percy in March 1759. What we do know, however, is that the literary careers of both men were built upon writings about China and the Chinese.

When Percy visited Johnson and Goldsmith in the spring of 1759, he had already been working for several years on the *Reliques*. Much as his *Hau Kiou Choaan* was based on a manuscript find, the *Reliques* derived from an old folio book of English ballads that he had salvaged at a Shropshire friend's house. Percy later described the dramatic scene of discovery in a note inscribed inside the cover of his folio manuscript of ballads. Dated November 7, 1769, the note reads:

> This very curious Old Manuscript in its present mutilated state, but unbound and sadly torn & c., I rescued from destruction, and begged at the hands of my worthy friend Humphrey Pitt Esq., then living at Shiffnal in Shropshire, afterwards at Priorslee … I saw it lying dirty on the floor under a Bureau in ye Parlour: being used by the Maids to light the fire. It was afterwards sent, most unfortunately, to an ignorant Bookbinder, who pared the margin, when I put it into Boards in order to lend it to Dr. Johnson.[8]

Percy discovered the manuscript around 1753, but it was apparently not until several years later when he was settled in Easton Maudit and was first introduced to Samuel Johnson by his friend James Grainger that he conceived the idea of publishing the folio.[9] It was Johnson, to whom he lent the folio after having it bound by an "ignorant Bookbinder," who encouraged him to publish it in 1757.[10] Percy would spend almost ten years on the folio, corresponding widely with scholars and writers, comparing different versions of the ballads, collecting supplementary material to include in his book, and developing a scholarly apparatus that would lend dignity to his songs. Percy's revision and editing of *Hau Kiou Choaan*, in other words, coincided with his work on the *Reliques*. The public reception of these two works, however, cannot have been more different. Dodsley published a thousand copies of *Hau Kiou Choaan* in 1761, but the work was ignored by the reviewers and repeatedly suspected of being a hoax.[11] There were enough unsold issues a decade later that Percy was able to persuade James Dodsley, who had succeeded his brother Robert in the publishing business, to reissue the book with its original publication date and an advertisement, dated 1774, with a lengthier explanation of the identity of James Wilkinson.[12] Even Percy's most important literary friends such as William Shenstone could not take *Hau Kiou Choaan* seriously as a piece of literature but only "as a *Curiosity*, or perhaps as an agreeable means of conveying to the generality / all they *wish* or *want* to know, of the Chinese manners and constitution."[13] When the *Reliques* was published in February 1765, on the other hand, 600 sets of the three-volume work were sold by the end of March; within five months, more than 1,100 sets had been sold. Four more editions would appear in Percy's lifetime (1767, 1775, 1794, 1811). The *Reliques* was favorably reviewed in the major reviews of its time, including *Critical Review, Monthly Review*, and *Gentleman's Magazine*.[14] Percy's decision to dedicate the *Reliques* to Lady Northumberland of the House of Percy won him the lasting patronage of one of the richest and most distinguished families in the country. In short, the *Reliques* established his scholarly reputation for life, earning him DD degrees from both Cambridge (1770) and Oxford (1793), and catapulting him into the company of the highest echelons of society.

There is little indication that Percy anticipated these vastly differing outcomes. The fact that Percy staked his early literary career on *Hau Kiou Choaan* and two other literary collections on Chinese material, *Miscellaneous Pieces Relating to the Chinese* (1762) and *The Matrons* (1762), suggests that he assumed his Chinese books would excite wider popular appeal. Surely the sheer novelty of a full-length Chinese novel would not fail to attract notice and bring him renown? The ballads collected in the *Reliques*, on the other hand, were "an imminent disaster," to borrow Nick Groom's colorful phrase.[15] The ballad was a low genre, identified with the trivial, popular, vulgar, and the oral.[16] The folio manuscript upon which the *Reliques* was based, a seventeenth-century commonplace book with transcriptions of ballads, metrical romances, and popular songs, was certainly a valuable source since it included material not found elsewhere. However, it was plagued with the same problems that trail all ballads: uncertain and anonymous authorship, a multitude of variants, lack of historical documentation, uneven aesthetic quality. Even without knowing a word of Chinese, Percy singlehandedly pulled together several books on Chinese material by mining the libraries of his acquaintances and undertaking, to the best of his ability, extensive research on the existing literature on China.[17] The lack of existing authorities on Chinese language and culture, he calculated, would work to his advantage. In order to turn his ballad manuscript into publishable text, however, Percy needed all the help he could get. He had received an excellent classical education at Oxford and was an accomplished poet with sensitive literary taste, but he was no expert in either Anglo-Saxon, balladry, or textual annotation.[18] He needed a scholarly framework, editorial principles, and a justification for publication. To his credit, Percy was not shy about asking for help or acknowledging his debt to others. His position toward his folio manuscript and the *Reliques* was always a self-deprecating one. Percy maintained to the end that that it was only at the "importunity of his friends" and the urging of "such judges as the author of the RAMBLER, and the late Mr. SHENSTONE" that he had been prevailed upon to publish his ballads.[19] With the same amiable deference he had shown to Goldsmith, Percy approached the leading writers, scholars, ballad collectors, philologists, and antiquarians of his day. His extensive debt to William Shenstone has been amply documented.[20] Additional help came from, among others, the Shakespeare scholar Richard Farmer; Thomas Warton, professor of poetry at Oxford and the future author of the monumental *History of English Poetry* (1774–81); Edward Lye, scholar of Old English and author of *Dictionarium Saxonico-et Gothico-Latinum* (1772, posthumous); the Welsh antiquary Evan Evans; the historian Thomas Birch; antiquary and paleographer Thomas Astle; and even the actor David Garrick, who gave him "free use" of his "curious collection of old plays" in which he found "many scarce pieces of ancient poetry" (1765, 1: xiii).[21]

Rather than regarding Percy's Chinese books as a diversion from the major work of Percy's career, in this chapter I propose to examine how they functioned in multiple ways as important preparatives for the *Reliques*.[22] Critics today agree that the publication of Percy's *Reliques* in 1765 permanently changed the way in which English literary history would be conceived. In Stuart Curran's words, *Reliques* is a seminal text that, along with Thomas Warton's *Observations on the Fairy Queen* (1754; rev. 1762) and Richard Hurd's *Letters on Chivalry and Romance* (1762), "indelibly altered Britain's sense of its literary heritage."[23] In the *Reliques*, Percy constructs a northern European genealogy for native Anglo-Saxon English poetry, drawing a direct line of descent from the northern Scalds to the Anglo-Saxon minstrels and harpers who arguably kept alive a popular tradition of national song.[24] The *Reliques* thus played a key role in popularizing "the idea of a native literary tradition … born out of an act of severance from the classical literary inheritance" formerly defined by Greece and Rome.[25] Percy's redefinition of English literary tradition along non-classical lines and his emphasis on the Gothic literary heritage in English literature contributed significantly to the rise of new "tides in English taste" in clear conflict with classical standards of formal beauty and rhetorical eloquence.[26]

As we shall see, Percy's Chinese books shed important light on both the editorial and theoretical strategies that shaped the *Reliques* and enabled it to become a lasting literary landmark. To see their relationship in a clear light, however, we will first need to assess the peculiarly ethnographic and antiquarian approach Percy took toward his ballad collection.

Relics for Readers: Translating (Gothic) English Antiquity

In the preface to the *Reliques*, Percy leans on "the opinion of no mean critics" who had recently argued that the "pleasing simplicity, and many artless graces" of English ballads could "compensate for the want of higher beauties." In a footnote, Percy points to Addison's *Spectator* no. 70 as an important example of the new critical approach to balladry (1765, 1: x). Albert Friedman, who declares that "Ballad criticism began in England with Addison's 'Chevy Chase' papers," has argued that the significance of Addison's criticism lies in its critique of a contrastive "Gothic Manner in Writing" which Addison associated with the false wit of the metaphysical poets.[27] In his landmark paper that defends "The old Song of *Chevy Chase*" as "the favourite Ballad of the common People of England," Addison writes:

> I know nothing which more shews the essential and inherent Perfection of Simplicity of Thought, above that which I call the Gothic Manner in Writing, than this, that the first pleases all Kinds of Palates, and the latter only such as have formed to themselves a wrong artificial Taste upon little fanciful Authors and Writers of Epigram. *Homer, Virgil,* or *Milton,* so far as the Language of their Poems is understood, will please a Reader of plain common Sense, who would neither relish nor comprehend an Epigram of *Martial* or a Poem of *Cowley:* So, on the contrary, an ordinary Song or Ballad that is the Delight of the common People, cannot fail to please all such Readers as are not unqualified for the Entertainment by their Affectation or Ignorance; and the Reason is plain, because the same Paintings of Nature which recommend it to the most ordinary Reader, will appear beautiful to the most refined. (1: 297–98)

The best kind of writing, Addison argues, appeals to our "plain common Sense" and is universally pleasing, both to "the most ordinary Reader" and "the most refined." For this reason, our appreciation of "an ordinary Song or Ballad" such as Chevy Chase is not essentially different from our delight in Homer, Virgil, and Milton. Like Homer, the balladeer is a painter of nature; his perfection lies in a sublime "Simplicity of Thought" that soars above "Gothic" affectation and artifice. In *Spectator* no. 74, Addison goes on to say that the balladeer of Chevy Chase shows "the same Kind of Poetical Genius" and "the same Copyings after Nature" as Virgil. The "Sentiments in that Ballad," he asserts, "are extremely natural and poetical, and full of the majestic Simplicity which we admire in the greatest of the ancient Poets" (2: 315–16). Friedman points out that Addison's attack on Gothic writing in his ballad papers links back to his papers on true and false wit in *Spectator* nos. 58–63 where, lamenting the fact that "the Taste of most of our *English* Poets, as well as Readers, is extremely *Gothick*," he argues against the false wit of Cowley, Waller, and Herbert (2: 269).

While Percy would follow Addison in defending the "pleasing simplicity" of the English ballads, he would diverge from Addison's criticism in significant ways. In his dedication and preface to the *Reliques*, Percy refers to his "reliques of antiquity" as "rude songs" and "barbarous productions of unpolished ages," and avows that they "will require great allowances to be made for them."[28] To "compensate for the want of higher beauties" in the poems, Percy pleads their "curious," "artless graces" and "pleasing simplicity" (1765, 1: lx–x), suggesting that they be regarded "not as labours of art, but as effusions of nature, shewing the first efforts of ancient genius, and exhibiting the customs and opinions of remote ages" (1765, 1: vi). Although the rhetoric of Percy's dedication and preface follows Addison in signaling to the "genius" of the ballads, it construes that genius in drastically altered terms. Indeed, Percy chooses not to argue for the intrinsic artistic or aesthetic merit of the ballads but ostensibly only for the light they shed on ancient customs, opinions, and manners. The "genius" of the *Reliques* is thus not poetic but cultural and ethnographic in character; it refers to the distinctive character of a remote age and people. Addison had argued for the appeal of the ballads based on their continuing ability to move the reader in powerful ways. Based on natural sentiments and arrayed in simple language, ballads embody "always simple, and sometimes exquisitely noble," heroic thoughts (1: 321) "founded upon some important Precept of Morality, adapted to the Constitution of the Country" to which the balladeer belongs (1: 299). Thus, the greatness of the ballad of Chevy Chase, according to Addison, lies in its sensitive and balanced portrait of an heroic, feudal past when "unnatural Contentions" between competing "petty Princes" caused "unspeakable Calamities to the Country" (1: 299). While the ballad "shews a laudable Partiality to his Country-men" in its treatment of the tragic battle at Chevy Chase between Lord Piercy of Nurthumberland and Earl Douglas of Scotland, it also "represents the *Scots* after a Manner not unbecoming so bold and brave a People" (1: 301). Percy, who took a highly personal, genealogical interest in this ballad that bore his own family name, likewise adopts an air of "studied antiquarian impartiality" toward the "ancient enmities" of English and Scottish history in "The Ancient Ballad of Chevy-Chase."[29] However, instead of defining this ballad as an exemplary exception to "the Gothic Manner in Writing" as Addison did (1: 297), he argues throughout the *Reliques* that ballads, alongside medieval metrical romances and other examples of ancient English song culture, are evidence of England's Gothic, or Germanic, literary and social prehistory. Indeed, England's ballads are the very embodiment of the "Gothic Manner in Writing."

The divergence between Addison and Percy, particularly on the issue of the Gothic, points to the different, even contradictory, meanings of the word in eighteenth-century usage. For Addison, Gothic is primarily an aesthetic term synonymous with various symptoms of false taste: excessive ornamentation, ostentation, lack of natural simplicity. The Gothic manner in writing, like that in architecture, operates meanly upon the imagination in his view. The "Greatness of the Manner" of the Roman Pantheon that fills the imagination "with something Great and Amazing" is not to be compared to the "Meanness" of "a *Gothick* Cathedral, tho' it be five times larger than the other" (3: 556). Addison deems "the Antients, especially among the Eastern Nations of the World, infinitely superior to the Moderns" in "*Greatness*, in the Works of Architecture" (3: 553), going so far as to instance the fabled Tower of Babel, the hanging gardens of Babylon, the Egyptian pyramids, and even "The Wall of *China*" as examples of "these Eastern Pieces of Magnificence" (3: 553–55). The falsity of Gothic taste is, in this sense, a modern deviation from these standards of sublimity. Percy, on the other hand, returns to the political meaning of the word as first established by seventeenth-century parliamentarians to denote the original Germanic forebears of the English nation. As Samuel Kliger points out in *The Goths in England*, the seventeenth-century crisis in English politics led parliamentarians to search for historical precedents for political authority that could check absolute monarchy. They found what they were looking for in the Germanic, barbarian invaders of Rome whom they called Goths, eliding the difference between this particular tribe and the Angles, Saxons, and Jutes. Combing through the writings of Tacitus, Saint Augustine, Jordanes, and Bede, they concluded that the tribal assembly of the Goths was the prototype of the English parliament and that the political foundations of the nation had been laid down by these vigorous, hardy, freedom-loving, and martial people.[30] According to this political myth, the ancient tradition of Gothic liberty was at the heart of the distinctive character of the English constitution.[31]

In his "Essay on the Ancient English Minstrels," Percy outlines his famous northern origins theory that traces the English lyric tradition back to the Gothic "scalds." In the first edition of the *Reliques*, he writes:

> The MINSTRELS seem to have been the genuine successors of the ancient Bards, who united the arts of Poetry and Music, and sung verses to the harp, of their own composing. It is well known what respect was shewn to their BARDS by the Britons: and no less was paid to the northern SCALDS by most of the nations of the Gothic race. Our Saxon ancestors, as well as their brethren the ancient Danes, had been accustomed to hold men of this profession in the highest reverence. Their skill was considered as something divine, their persons were deemed sacred, their attendance was solicited by kings, and they were every where loaded with honours and rewards. (1765, 1: xv)

Percy's description of the English as descendants of the Goths is not in and of itself original or unusual. William Temple, too, refers to "the antient *Western Goths* (our Ancestors)" in his essay *Of Poetry* (1690: 303). Following general seventeenth-century practice, Temple uses the term Goth in its generic as well as more specific sense in his essay *Of Heroick Virtue*, where he refers to the region of northern Scythia in general as "the Seat of the *Getae*" or "*Gothae*," a "vast Hive out of which issued so many mighty Swarms of Barbarous Nations, who under the several names of *Goths, Vandals, Alans, Lombards, Huns, Bulgars, Francs, Saxons,* and many others, broke in at several times and places upon the several Provinces of the *Roman* Empire" (1690: 224). The Goths were descendants of the original *Getae* who had been "led into the North-West parts of *Europe*" by their leader Odin whom Temple describes as endowed with heroic virtue. Odin gave the Goths their Runic writing and founded many Gothic laws and institutions (1690: 227, 231). Temple claims that "of all the Northern Nations, the *Goths* were esteemed the most civil, orderly, and virtuous"; "the Frame and Constitution of the Gothick Government … seems to have been invented or instituted by the Sages of the *Goths*, as a Government of Freemen, which was the Spirit or Character of the North-West Nations, distinguishing them from those of the South and the East" (1690: 243–44). "*Gaul* was subdued by the *Francs*, and *Britain* by the *Saxons*," he writes, "both which Nations are thought to have come from the more Northern Regions, and seated themselves in those parts of *Germany*, that were afterwards called by their Names" (1690: 225). In his 1695 *Introduction to the History of England*, he also speaks specifically of the Saxons as "one branch of those *Gothick* Nations, which swarming from the Northern Hive, had, under the Conduct of *Odin*, possessed themselves anciently of all those mighty tracts of Land that surround the Baltick Sea."[32]

Citing Temple's "Gothic erudition," Kliger asserts "there can be no question of the profound sympathy between his liberal conservatism and the account he drew from the Gothic literature of Gothic democracy."[33] We should note, however, that despite the admiration he showed for "Gothic democracy" and Gothic "heroic virtue," in Temple's long view of history the invasions of the Goths and "other Barbarous or Northern Nations" were linked to the destruction of Rome and the decay of Rome's "great Empire of Wit" (1690: 312, 310). In *Of Poetry*, Temple characterizes Gothic, runic poetry as part of the "Empire … of the modern, which was introduced after the Decays, or rather Extinction of the old, as if true Poetry being dead, an Apparition of it walked about" (1690: 311–12). The invasion of the barbarians brought out a "Cloud of Ignorance" and a corruption of the Roman tongue into the various Romance languages (basically Latin "vitiated with the base allay of their Provincial Speech") (1690: 314). In England, Latin was "wholly extinguish't," paving way for "the intire use of the *Saxon* Language" (1690: 315). Thus, "the antient Poetry was wholly lost" and a poetry of Runes arose in its stead, becoming "the most general among all the *Gothick* Colonies in *Europe*" and making "Rhymes or Runes pass for the modern Poetry, in these parts of the World" (1690: 315, 317). Runic poetry, in which Percy would take such great interest, was for Temple essentially a fallen poetry composed in runes, i.e. "the antient *Gothick* Letters or Characters" invented by "*Odin*, in the Colony or Kingdom of the *Getes* or *Goths*, which he planted in the *North-West* Parts" (1690: 315). It was a rhyming, jingling, "*Dithyrambick*" sort of poetry "of a raving or rambling sort of Wit or Invention, loose and flowing, with little Art or Confinement to any certain Measures or Rules." What it lacked in "the true Flame of Poetry" it tried to make up in the form of enchantment. Temple believed that "all those Trophees of Enchantment, that appear in the whole Fabrick of the old *Spanish* Romances" "were the Productions of the *Gothick* Wit," just as "all the visionary Tribe of *Fairies*, *Elves*, and *Goblins*, of *Sprites* and of *Bul-baggers*" were products of the superstitious culture of the Goths. Their poets were sorcerers who used magic to make up for the lack of the "Sublime and Marvellous" of the ancients (1690: 318–19).

This extended excursus on Temple throws into sharp relief Percy's markedly different approach toward the Gothic roots of English poetry. In its general outline, Percy's project appears to share many of Temple's basic assumptions. Like Temple, Percy refers to "Our Saxon ancestors" and aligns them with "the nations of Gothic race," in particular "their brethren the ancient Danes" (1765, 1: xv). In the expanded version of this essay in the second edition of the *Reliques*, Percy mentions the special veneration "our own Teutonic ancestors, particularly ... all the Danish tribes" had for their singers or "SCALDS" who "sung verses to the harp of their own composing":

> The origin of their art was attributed to ODIN or WODEN, the father of their Gods; and the professors of it were held in the highest estimation. Their skill was considered as something divine; their persons were deemed sacred; their attendance was solicited by kings; and they were every where loaded with honours and rewards. In short, poets and their art were held among them in that rude admiration, which is ever shown by an ignorant people to such as excel them in intellectual accomplishments.[34]

Percy's characterization of the Goths as generally "an ignorant people" chimes with Temple's references to their barbarian nature. Like Temple, Percy appears to take an ironic stance toward the "rude admiration" of the bards, interpreting the Goths' belief in the "sacred" and "divine" power of the bards as a function in part of their benightedness. Just as Temple described Gothic poetry as "chiefly imployed, upon the Records of bold and Martial Actions, and the Praises of Valiant Men that had Fought successfully or Dyed bravely" (1690: 319), Percy claims the medieval Saxon minstrels sang songs "to do honour to the ruling passion of the times, and to encourage and foment a martial spirit" (1767, 1: xix). However, whereas Temple held a rather low opinion of these Gothic singers of "Songs or Ballads" that "were usually sung at Feasts, or in Circles of Young or Idle Persons, and served to inflame the Humor of War, of Slaughter and of Spoils among them" (1690: 319), Percy elevates the Danish scald and Anglo-Saxon bard to members of the princely court and historians of their people. Their business, he claims, "was to record the victories of their warriors, and the genealogies of their Princes" (1767, 3: ii). And unlike Temple, who believed that the "More refined Honor or Love, had little part in the Writings" of the Goths "because it had little in the Lives or Actions of those fierce People and bloody Times" (1690: 319), Percy argues that "our old Romances of Chivalry may be derived in a lineal descent from the ancient historical songs of the Gothic bards and Scalds" (1767, 3: iii). Citing Paul-Henri Mallet's *Introduction à l'histoire du Danemarch* (1755, 1763), he even goes so far as to state that "the ideas of Chivalry ... may be discovered as in embrio in the customs, manners, and opinions, of every branch of that people," the Goths: "That fondness of going in quest of adventures, that spirit of challenging to single combat, and that respectful complaisance shewn to the fair sex, (so different from the manners of the Greeks and Romans), all are of Gothic origin, and may be traced up to the earliest times among all the northern nations" (1767, 3: iv).

Unlike Temple and Addison, then, Percy clearly aims at vindicating the Gothic inheritance of England in both ethnic and poetic terms. All evidence suggests that Percy developed his Gothic theory of English poetry in large part as a studied response to the sensational 1760 publication of James Macpherson's *Fragments of Ancient Poetry Collected in the Highlands of Scotland.* Inspired by the success of Macpherson's Celtic poems, Percy decided very quickly to prepare a collection of Icelandic poems known in Britain with the help of Edward Lye. Macpherson's *Fragments* was published in Edinburgh in June; by September Percy had sent Shenstone a translation of one of his Icelandic poems with an announcement of his project. "Inclosed I send you an ancient Celtic, (or rather Runic) Poem, translated from the Icelandic. I am making up a small Collection of Pieces of this kind for the Press, which will be about the Size of the Erse Fragments," he announced.[35] We can infer from this letter that even as late as 1760 Percy did not make a clear distinction between the Celtic and Gothic traditions. By the time he wrote the preface to *Five Pieces of Runic Poetry Translated from the Islandic Language* (1763), however, he had an argument in place about the "ancient inhabitants of Sweden, Denmark and Norway" as "Gothic tribes." Icelandic, he claimed, was "the mother of the modern Swedish and Danish tongues, in like manner as the Anglo-saxon is the parent of our English." "Both these mother-tongues," he added, "are dialects of the ancient Gothic or Teutonic" and "of so near affinity" that speakers of one tongue could understand the other without difficulty.[36]

Percy appears to have developed his Gothic literary theory while conducting research for the *Reliques.* From Mallet's *Introduction à l'histoire du Danemarch* (which he translated and published in 1770 under the title *Northern Antiquities*) he derived the idea that the achievements of modern European civilization could be traced directly back to ancient Norse culture, or the Gothic "Antiquities of the North." Setting aside the classical heritage of ancient Greece and Rome, Mallet had argued that it was the northern Goths who had laid the foundations of modern European culture.

Is it not well known that the most flourishing and celebrated states of Europe owe originally to the northern nations, whatever liberty they now enjoy, either in their constitution, or in the spirit of their government? For although the Gothic form of government has been almost every where altered or abolished, have we not retained, in most things, the opinions,

the customs, the manner which that government had a tendency to produce? Is not this, in fact, the principal source of that courage, of that aversion to slavery, of that empire of honour which characterize in general the
European nations; and of that moderation, of that easiness of access, and
peculiar attention to the rights of humanity, which so happily distinguish
our sovereigns from the inaccessible and superb tyrants of Asia?[37]

Percy uses Mallet to reconstruct ancient English history along Gothic
lines, but also reads him against the grain, arguing that Mallet committed
the error of "supposing the ancient Gauls and Germans, the Britons and
the Saxons, to have been all originally one and the same people; thus confounding the antiquities of the Gothic and Celtic nations."[38] Underscoring
this distinction allowed Percy to distinguish his project from Macpherson's
and implicitly criticize it for characterizing the bardic tradition as Celtic.
In the *Fragments*, Macpherson had ascribed his ancient poems to "the
Bards; a race of men well known to have continued throughout many ages
in Ireland and the north of Scotland."[39] Percy's counterargument is that
the bards were important not only in the Scottish and Irish traditions but
also to the Anglo-Saxon forebears of England. By tracing the bards directly
back to the northern scalds, Percy could argue against Macpherson's elevation of the Celts as the true poets of Britain as well as his characterization
of the Scandinavians as a "remarkably barbarous and fierce" people who
belonged to "a nation much less advanced in a state of civilization, than
the inhabitants of Britain were in the times of Ossian."[40] In his *Critical
Dissertation on the Poems of Ossian, the Son of Fingal* (1763), Hugh Blair
had similarly contrasted the representative Norse poem, the ninth-century
Epicedium of Ragnar Lodbrog, with the poems of Ossian, claiming that
the "wild, harsh and irregular" of the former expressed "a most ferocious
spirit" of "a barbarous nation," while praising Ossian's poems for their "ten-
derness, and even delicacy of sentiment, greatly predominant over fierce-
ness and barbarity."[41] Taking issue with these constructions of an ancient
Celtic civility defined in opposition to the Anglo-Saxon heritage, Percy
defines the Anglo-Saxons as a barbarous but also proto-chivalrous people,
composers of early romances that, despite being delivered "in a barbarous
unpolished language," were as "regular" in their "plan" and "conduct, as
any of the finest poems of classical antiquity" (1765, 3: xvi).

Percy's redefinition of the ancient Goths of England as poets and
romancers was supported by two important publications of 1762, Richard
Hurd's *Letters on Chivalry and Romance* and the second edition of Thomas
Warton's *Observations on the Faerie Queene* (1st edition, 1754). The importance of these works, as Percy quickly saw, lay in their reappraisal of the

romance tradition in English literature. Warton had proposed that, although Spenser's *Faerie Queene* might be "destitute of that arrangement and oeconomy which epic severity requires," "if the critic is not satisfied, yet the reader is transported" by the poem's imaginative power.[42] Hurd likewise had argued that the great works of English literature should be "read and criticized" under the idea of "a Gothic, not classical poem." Arguing that the great English writers Spenser and Milton had been "charmed by the Gothic Romances," Hurd made the literary genre of romance synonymous with "the singular institution" of "Gothic CHIVALRY." His claim that "the foundation of this refined gallantry was laid in the antient manners of the German nations" was meant to contravene the dominant theory that romances were essentially a French import and to reclaim the romance as an indigenous Anglo-Saxon product that the nation could take pride in.[43] Immediately recognizing that Hurd's book, which placed the old romances "in a very respectable light," would help him frame and theorize his metrical romances, Percy aligned the *Reliques* with Hurd's *Letters*.[44] However, he distrusted Hurd's breezy, epistolary style unencumbered by any scholarly apparatus. One reason why he declared that Hurd "is clever, but he is a Coxcomb" in a letter to Richard Farmer is perhaps because he realized that Hurd had borrowed his argument from the French writer Sainte Palaye and had not even troubled himself to read the old romances he was discussing.[45] Percy's strategy, by contrast, was to present himself as a serious scholar and antiquarian collector of textual artifacts. In this regard, he learned not only from Hurd's omissions and mistakes but also from Macpherson's cautionary tale.[46]

Macpherson had famously claimed that his *Fragments of Ancient Poetry* contained "genuine remains of ancient Scottish poetry" even though he could produce no authors, no dates, and no original texts. Referring the poems to "an aera of the most remote antiquity," Macpherson had tried to argue that this very lack of authenticating device was yet stronger proof of the poems' antiquity.[47] If they were not so ancient, the implied argument went, they would have come equipped with an authorial, historical, and textual apparatus characteristic of modern literary production. Macpherson thus built his argument ingeniously on internal rather than external evidence, blithely conflating poetic evidence with historical proof.[48] The storm of controversy that accompanied Macpherson's later Ossianic publications *Fingal, an Ancient Epic Poem* (1762) and *Temora* (1763) proved to Percy that his own attempt to revive an ancient song tradition could easily become embroiled in a similar dispute over the authenticity of his ballads. Like Macpherson, Percy was interested in the idea of ancient poetry as the "genuine remains" of past cultures, particularly in the idea of ancient poetry as preserved in oral tradition.[49] Unlike Macpherson, however, he could make no claim to a special linguistic expertise authorizing his 'translations' of the oral into the written. The concept of oral tradition, which was just being developed in the mid-eighteenth century, was vital to popular antiquaries who were interested in reconstructing pasts undocumented in official histories and often without physical record, and who therefore had to rely on non-textual lines of transmission and modes of authentication.[50] Antiquarianism in England was both an adaptation of and a reaction to an already established antiquarian tradition centered on the classic ancient civilizations of Greece and Rome. English antiquarianism distinguished itself from its predecessor by its fascination with indigenous prehistory and "patriotic desire to furnish England with an historical and cultural background second to none."[51] This patriotic motive was challenged historiographically by the lack of material records dating from pre-Roman Britain, and complicated culturally by the double origin of British culture in indigenous Celtic and nomadic Germanic peoples.[52] Percy managed to overcome these challenges through a series of diplomatic balancing acts. His defense of England's Gothic heritage was unmistakably critical of the Ossianic cult, but it was also cosmopolitan rather than simply narrowly ethnic in spirit in its embrace of a pan-European Gothic identity. In addition, as Philip Connell has pointed out, while defending England's Anglo-Saxon cultural roots Percy also carefully distanced himself from the Scotophobic politics of radical Saxonists such as John Wilkes.[53] Percy consistently employed a deflationary rhetoric even as he championed his antique poems, calling them artifacts of barbarism and arguing for their sheer historical interest rather than, as Macpherson had done, praising their aesthetic value. The Celtic oral tradition recreated by Macpherson was essentially heroic, full of improbably "disinterested and generous sentiments" of ancient Celtic warriors;[54] by contrast, the ancient English songs collated by Percy were by and large "merely written for the people" and often full of sensational content (1765, 1: ix). Percy in fact felt it necessary to note that he had taken "great care ... to admit nothing immoral and indecent" (1765, 1: xiv).

Importantly, Percy also steered clear of Macpherson's mystification of oral tradition, stressing the continuity between orality and textuality in England's Gothic literary tradition. When Macpherson stressed that his literal prose translation of the Ossianic poems, which gave them "an English dress," could only be an "imperfect semblance" of the "majesty" of "an original," he was cleverly equivocating between the original Gaelic tongue and the original Ossianic song.[55] His point was that his knowledge of the former gave him special access to the latter. Percy presented himself very differently, concentrating on his role as an interpreter of English textual remains rather than Anglo-Saxon oral tradition. Furthermore, whereas Macpherson argued for the fidelity and continuity of oral tradition, comparing the power of the Celtic tradition with that of the ancient Greeks and even the Incas of Peru, Percy stressed "the imperfect state of his materials" (1765, 1: xii).[56] The "old popular rhymes," he stated, had "been handed down to us with less care, than any other writings in the world" (1765, 1: xii). After all, he had fortuitously rescued his ballads from the hands of maids who were about to use it as fire fodder. There was admittedly a comic, even absurd element in this dramatic story of textual discovery, but it drew a helpful line between the unlettered, oral tradition of the Celts and the literate Gothic tradition. Percy alluded early on to the controversy surrounding the authenticity of Macpherson's poems in his preface to *Five Pieces of Runic Poetry* (1763), noting that "till the Translator of those poems thinks proper to produce his originals, it is impossible to say whether they do not owe their superiority, if not their whole existence entirely to himself." His point was that the solid textual basis of his Icelandic poems, by contrast, did not allow "such boundless field for licence."[57] Since all the runic poems existed in the original, alongside their Swedish and Latin translations, they could not possibly be forgeries. Percy used a parallel argument to defend his *Reliques*. His ballads and romances were admittedly derived from ephemeral texts riddled with problems of textual transmission. However, the physical reality of his manuscript proved that he was not concocting a literary tradition out of his own head.

Percy claimed no special linguistic or philological expertise for his role as editor of his ancient poems. He was in fact no more a scholar of Old English than he was of the original Norse runes, which he likewise translated not from the original but from their translations into other languages. Therefore, his role as amateur translator necessarily differed from that of Macpherson's. He was, as it were, merely an accidental editor, a translator of translations; he had stumbled upon his fate, which he fulfilled only with the help of his scholarly friends. As he puts it at the end of his preface to the *Reliques*, "the Editor hopes he need not be ashamed of having bestowed some of his idle hours on the ancient literature of our own country, or in rescuing from oblivion some pieces (tho' but the amusements of our ancestors) which tend to place in a striking light, their taste, genius, sentiments, or manners" (1765, 1: xiv). The elaborate courtly apologetics with which he refers to his collection, however, needs to be read against the latent

heroism of the claim that he is responsible for its rescue. The rhetoric of
retrieval, revival, and rescue was common in eighteenth-century antiquarianism, and was used to justify its obsession with relics, monuments, and
other ruins of time threatened with utter oblivion. Percy's studied humility
is thus a double mask hiding both his scholarly weakness and his ambition.
Ultimately, Percy's all too literal rescue of a book originally consigned to
a domestic pyre begs to be read as a monitory allegory about the fate of
poetry in the world. Poetry, too, has a physical body, and can die a violent, unredeemed death – just like the ephemeral world of which it sings.
Textuality imports the song into the material world, but the body it gives
to song bares it to the fate of all bodies – decay, degeneration, dying. It is
not clear whether a fiery death at the hands of illiterate maids is a comic or
yet more melancholic version of such a fate. Percy's story refuses to roman-
ticize illiteracy as Macpherson does; it also makes clear that, although his
songs and poems originate with the people, they are safe only with the
public who can bestow upon them the care they deserve. If we nonetheless cannot help reading the story comically, it is surely because the plot of
manuscript discovery has been made overly familiar through readings of
eighteenth-century novels, and because it is tempting to read the maids'
manuscript, if not as the burning object of Percy's displaced desire, at least
as a manifestation of what Susan Stewart has called the ballad's "erotic of
transgression."[58] The climactic transfer of the manuscript from the maids'
to Percy's hands – from private, domestic, feminized space to the masculine realm of public culture, and from a lower to an upper class – and the
subsequent metamorphosis of the manuscript from disposable waste to
objet d'art, cultural commodity, and finally national treasure play out a
remarkable narrative of transformative desire.

In his landmark *Orality and Literacy*, Walter J. Ong matter-of-factly
declares, "Written words are residue. Oral tradition has no such residue
or deposit."[59] Percy's argument, contra both Ong and Macpherson, is that
oral tradition only has written residue.[60] Building on his folio manuscript,
Percy gathered poems from a variety of textual sources, in manuscript or
printed form, from private collections and public archives. Stressing the
materiality and textuality of oral tradition was thus a complex, paradoxical
move on his part, a strategy necessitated by a frank appraisal of his own
talents and the nature of his textual sources. It was also a move that was
highly ambitious in its intellectual engagement with poetry not simply
as an oral, but also textual, phenomenon and as a material object rooted
in the objective world. If, as Katie Trumpener has persuasively argued,
the true subject of Macpherson's poems was "not epic heroism but the

vicissitudes of oral tradition," then Percy's subject was the historical drama of the written text as an integral part of the antiquarian aesthetics he was championing in the service of a national, Gothicized poetic trust.[61] This created a fundamental tension in his work: the search for authentic Saxon origins would be repeatedly compromised by the "crisis of authenticity" resulting in the fragmentary, ruined form of the poetic artifact – just as the voice of balladry, the song in time, would be undermined by "the spatiality and stasis of the document."[62] Percy's strategy was to move deliberately away from a cult of the oral origin, even as he gestured toward it. His project was a bookish one, saturated with the love of reading, though imaginatively committed to a vision of ancient English communities of song. He knew he was translating ancient poems for modern readers who would access them as texts rather than as songs, and who might approach them more as curiosities than as works of art. His emphasis was thus on public readership that alone would take the relics out of their dusty isolation, save them from irreparable ruin, and restore them to their rightful place in English cultural tradition.

Gendering China and Romance

Percy self-deprecatingly refers to his *Reliques* as a "little miscellany" (1765, 1: xii) – an ironic comment, considering it was published in three volumes and ran to hundreds of pages. This throwaway remark was meant to underscore his large debt to fellow scholars, antiquaries, and learned friends who responded to his requests for help in editorial matters; in turn, their eminence and collaboration were meant to reflect positively on his eclectic collection. Additionally, this seemingly slight remark provides an important clue to the literary genre in which Percy saw himself working. As Barbara Benedict has shown, miscellanies and anthologies were key sites of literary and cultural negotiation in the early modern period. Literally "a mixed dish," the miscellany contained mediated offerings of choice selections.[63] Miscellanies reflected the proliferation of options in the booming markets of culture and the concomitant need for standards of taste; they defined cultural literacy and cultural ambition; they also provided "one of the vehicles by which literary criticism becomes an arena of cultural self-examination."[64] Thus, these collections served as aids to reading as well as critiques of judgment. As expressions of collective cultural identity dependent on communities of readers, they were both portable cultural capital and sites of social cohesion and social change. Miscellanies were a good form for editors, who could bask in the reflected light of their literary choices. Because they were associated with the proliferation of print and the leveling of the reading audience, however, miscellanies also were accused of being print bastards and mere curiosities.[65]

Percy's reference to the *Reliques* as a "little miscellany" clearly relates it back to his earlier miscellanies, which were also designed to mediate between a distant culture and a polite readership: *Hau Kiou Choaan, or The Pleasing History. A Translation from the Chinese Language* (1761), *Miscellaneous Pieces Relating to the Chinese* (1762), and *The Matrons* (1762).[66] In the case of these Chinese miscellanies, however, the relevance of Chinese culture to the English cultural consumer, and Percy's own role as cultural mediator, may be less easy to make out. As in the case of the *Reliques*, Percy justified his editorship of *Hau Kiou Choaan* by claiming he had chanced upon the original text, this time a translation "found in manuscript, among the papers of a gentleman who had large concerns in the East-India Company, and occasionally resided much at Canton" (1761, I: ix). However, Percy's mere assertion that *Hau Kiou Choaan* had to be an authentic Chinese novel since the translator was "a gentleman whose province was trade, and who probably never designed it for the Public," did not sell well. Upon publication the novel was promptly accused of being a fake, and Percy later found it necessary to defend its authenticity by identifying the gentleman residing in Canton as a certain "Mr. James Wilkinson, an English merchant, equally respected for his abilities and his probity"[67] – though this alone could not answer successfully the charge of forgery, especially in the contemporary climate of ingenious literary hoaxes and fakes.[68]

The reason why *Hau Kiou Choaan* was published ultimately as a kind of miscellany rather than as a freestanding work of art has everything to do with Percy's need to defend its authenticity as well as his dubious authority as translator. To stave off accusations and misunderstandings, the novel was published as the centerpiece of a Chinese miscellany or authentic collection of Chinese literary culture.[69] Besides the novel of the same title, *Hau Kiou Choaan* contained "I. The Argument or Story of a Chinese Play, II. A Collection of Chinese Proverbs, and III. Fragments of Chinese poetry," as well as voluminous footnotes and even an index to subjects treated in the novel.[70] These additions frame and collect the novel as one of several Chinese cultural artifacts, all of which stand in need of guide, glossary, and key. *Miscellaneous Pieces*, Percy's second Chinese miscellany, is a direct outgrowth of *Hau Kiou Choaan* and primarily comprises translated excerpts from the Jesuit *Lettres édifiantes et curieuses* (1702–76). The assorted pieces in this second miscellany – ranging from translations and commentaries on Chinese literature to descriptions of Chinese gardens, palaces, and rites – read like extended footnotes to *Hau Kiou Choaan*, as if Percy had decided on afterthought that the reading and research he had done for his earlier work would make just as good a book.

When Percy discovered his Chinese novel, he must have been struck by the golden opportunity it gave him. As he notes in his preface to *Hau Kiou Choaan*, Chinese literature was known at that time only in the form of "abstracts and versions of several Chinese books" given in Jesuit compilations such as the "curious collection" of Jean-Baptiste Du Halde.[71] The "few novels" Du Halde had to offer, however, were "but short pieces," whereas Percy had a full-fledged, "long narration" to show (1761, 1: xi). It was a perfectly rare find and, if authenticated, surely of singular value. As he put it, "the grand merit of such a piece as this must consist in its peculiarities and authenticities" (1761, 1: xxiii). Yet without any access to the original Chinese text, and without any first-hand linguistic or cultural knowledge of the Chinese, how could Percy authenticate his find? His solution was to authenticate the novel by squaring its content with existing reports of Chinese culture – in short, to treat the problem as one perfectly soluble by cross-referencing data, as if the agreement of signs would clear away the lingering possibility of duplicitous invention. The problem was that, by this time, China already was a sign divided against itself.[72] Percy's insistence that the novel is surprisingly lacking in "extravagant absurdities" so common in the other "Eastern nations" (1761, 1: xiii), that it "hath less of the marvellous and more of the probable" (1761, 1: xiv), and that it pays "a greater regard to truth and nature" than is commonly expected of the "Asiatics" (1761, 1: xiv) exemplifies his attempt to turn *Hau Kiou Choaan* into an "anti-oriental tale."[73] His goal was not so much to correct existing stereotypical judgments about Chinese culture, however, as to reimagine the novel as a culturally transparent form. The subtitle of *Hau Kiou Choaan* identifies it as a "history": "a faithful picture of Chinese manners, wherein the domestic and political oeconomy of that vast people is displayed with an exactness and accuracy to which none but a native could be capable of attaining" (1761, 1: xv). Percy's trick was to silence doubt about the fidelity of the translation, on the one hand, by focusing on the faithfulness of the novel to its own culture, while, on the other, quelling suspicion about novelistic invention by claiming the novel as the best possible source of factual information about a nation's culture. "The whole system of the manners of a people can only be thoroughly known to themselves," he declares, thereby inferring that *Hau Kiou Choaan* contains a true Chineseness of manners that is simply impossible for a non-native to fake (1761, 1: xvii).

Today we know that *Hau Kiou Choaan* – or *Haoqiu zhuan* – is indeed an authentic Chinese work. It was printed around the mid-seventeenth century, during the early Qing period, and belongs to a genre of fiction called "the scholar-beauty romance" (*caizi jiaren*). Following Qing convention, the work was published anonymously and attributed to a mysterious Master of Proper Confucian Teachings (*Mingjiao zhongren*).[74] According to Kai-chong Cheung, the scholar-beauty romance is defined by its protagonists: "In works of this genre, the male protagonist is a representative of the dominant scholar-official class, has all the masculine virtues, especially courage and physical strength, while the female protagonist, a sheltered daughter of the nobility, possesses the feminine virtues, especially charm and forbearance." Together they embody "the most important virtue of all, complete subservience to Confucian morality, especially physical and intellectual chastity." The plot of the scholar-beauty romance thus rewards "purity over sensuality, fidelity over passion, and arranged marriages over free choice."[75] During the late Ming and early Qing period, scholar-beauty romances constituted a noteworthy subgenre of fiction. Judging from their publication numbers, transregional diffusion within the Ming and Qing dynasties, intra-Qing language translations, and inclusion within the canon of the "books of genius" (*caizi shu*), Patricia Sieber has argued that scholar-beauty romances indeed comprise a significant part of the eighteenth-century Chinese book trade.[76] When we consider that Canton (Guangzhou) and Foshan, two cities in Guangdong province, began to figure prominently as new publishing centers in the eighteenth century, and connect this fact to Canton's importance as an entry point into China for Europeans in this period, it seems highly plausible that Wilkinson, an English merchant stationed in Canton, would have come across *Hau Kiou Choaan*. However, Percy did not have access to this kind of information and was therefore not able to authenticate *Hau Kiou Chooan* during his lifetime, despite his various efforts to do so. The 1774 reissue of the book included an extract of a letter sent from Canton in which the writer affirmed that when he mentioned "the Hero of the Story of *Ty-chung-u*" to his Chinese acquaintances, "they immediately knew what I meant." Obviously, however, an anonymous letter was not going to do the trick. Percy apparently wrote to Lord Macartney requesting help with the authentication of *Hau Kiou Choaan* but Macartney was not able to help.[77] In the end, it was George Staunton, who accompanied his father on the Macartney mission as a twelve-year-old boy and learned the Chinese language, who provided the earliest authentication in 1810, less than ten years after Percy's death.[78]

Without external authenticating markers, Percy strategically proffered *Hau Kiou Choaan* to the reader as an artifact that presented an unprecedented window onto Chinese culture not only in its form – its novelization of cultural truth – but also in its subjective, "interiour" content (1761, 1: xix). By holding up *Hau Kiou Choaan* as an insider's report on the private, domestic, real China, Percy put it in a different league from the Jesuit or merchant writings that showed China only as a "dead resemblance" (1761, 1: xvi). Insinuating intimate depths and delicate disclosures, he suggests in the preface that the novel lets us peek into the famous "privacy and reserve" of the Chinese that "must prevent many of their domestic customs from transpiring to strangers" (1761, 1: xix). With *Hau Kiou Choaan* Percy thus offered the English reader the possibility of cultural as well as sexual exploration. Never designed for foreigners' eyes, he argues, the novel offers the best possible circumvention of Chinese hostility toward them. The English reader becomes an illicit voyeur, a Peeping Tom snooping in the house of China, and the novel turns into a site of cultural licentiousness. We see Percy returning here to the associations of the novel with heterodoxy, the curious and surprising, and locating the genre's special brand of truth in its domestic and sexual content.[79] His translation of the Chinese novel thus stages the reader's "desire to violate cultural boundaries."[80] China is consumed and collected in the reader's transgressive reading that turns this work of fiction into a probing miscellany of Chinese culture, customs, and manners. The delicate balance of distance and disclosure we see at work in Percy's annotations and index to *Hau Kiou Choaan* turns on upholding its aura of authenticity while promoting a satisfying sense of cultural possession. Ironically, however, *Hau Kiou Choaan* is a work that is notoriously averse to sex and romance, even as it narrates the fulfillment of both.

Hau Kiou Choaan centers on the romance between the male scholar Tieh-chung-u (*Tie Zhongyu* – literally, Jade-in-iron) and the beauty Shuey-ping-sin (*Shui Bingxin* – which literally means, as Percy notes in a footnote, "water, ice, heart" [1761, 1: 70]). Shuey-ping-sin, the only daughter of an exiled Board of War official, is described as a seventeen-year-old beauty "so exquisitely beautiful, that it would exceed the power of the most masterly pencil, to express the exactness of her proportion"; "She was no less distinguished for the rare endowments of her mind, and greatness of her capacity, in which she equaled the most eminent of the opposite sex" (1761, 1: 69–70). Her widower father is extremely devoted to her and gives her complete command of the household while he serves in court. Distanced from her disgraced father, Shuey-ping-sin falls prey to the machinations of her uncle who schemes to marry her off to Kwo-khé-tzu, the playboy son of a high official. Much of the fun of reading *Hau Kiou Choaan* consists of following the clever means Shuey-ping-sin finds to evade the increasingly violent attempts of her uncle and her unwelcome suitor to entrap her in marriage. At first, she easily outwits them by means of subtle tricks: she tampers with marriage documents and marries her suitor off to her cousin, then plants a dummy in her palanquin, evading her uncle's attempt to kidnap her. This only infuriates her would-be captors, however, and increases their determination to remove her from her father's house. Tieh-chung-u, the handsome young son of an imperial censor, who happens to be returning home from a visit to his father in the capital, crosses paths with her captors and, like a knight in shining armor, comes to her rescue. When Kwo-khé-tzu takes revenge by poisoning Tieh-chung-u, Shuey-ping-sin goes against Confucian decorum and secretly brings him to her father's house and nurses him back to health. The hero and heroine find themselves mutually attracted to each other, but Shuey-ping-sin's act of gratitude has the unfortunate consequence of dooming their relationship, as it causes them to fall under the suspicion of having had premarital sex. After many twists and turns in the plot, Shuey-ping-sin's father recovers his status and Shuey-ping-sin and Tieh-chung-u marry upon the repeated injunctions of their parents. But they do not consummate their marriage. It is only after the emperor orders an investigation into rumors of their premarital relations and a physical examination proves Shuey-ping-sin's virginity that the two finally feel justified to consummate their marriage.

Although critics are agreed that this work belongs to the genre of the "scholar-beauty" narrative, they have used different generic terms to categorize it. Thus, Patricia Sieber considers *Hau Kiou Choaan* an example of the "amatory novel"; Richard C. Hessney calls it "a popular comic romance"; and Kai-chong Cheung considers it as "The first Chinese Novel Translated in Europe."[81] Percy himself refers to it variously as an example of the "fictitious narratives … of the Asiatics" and "the compositions of the East"; "a curious specimen of Chinese literature" (1761, 1: xiv); "a faithful picture of Chinese manners" (1761, 1: xv); "a domestic history" (1761, 1: xvii); and a "Romance" (1761, 4: 199). Percy's vacillating terms are congruent with eighteenth-century British literary practice, in which the boundaries between history, novel, and romance were still being worked out. In the early eighteenth century, theorists defined romance in formal as well as thematic terms. Pierre-Daniel Huet's widely read *History of Romances* (1715; *Sur l'origine des Romans*, 1670), for instance, defined romances as "Fictions of Love Adventures, disposed into an Elegant Style in Prose, for the Delight and Instruction of the Reader." In romances, Huet argued, "Love ought to be the Principal Subject"; the author of romances "must present Virtue successful, and Vice in disgrace."[82] Huet believed that the French romances, exemplified especially by the romances of Tristram, Lancelot, Merlin, Arthur, and Perceval, among others, were the most perfect of their kind due to the culture of French "gallantry" or "the great Liberty which the Men of *France* allow to the Ladies."[83] The open and easy interaction between men and women in France, in other words, had made possible the flowering of this very particular literary genre. Huet's definition of romance makes a fluid transition between ideas of genre and gender. These are, as is well known, words connected at the root. The etymology of the word gender leads us to the Anglo-Norman and Middle French word *gendre*, meaning kind, sort, sex, quality of being male or female, or belonging to a race or people. In this sense, one could say that the idea of a genus, kind, or genre is, historically speaking, intimately linked to an idea of gender difference. Romance as a genre makes this connection particularly clear. Huet believed that the genre of romance was made possible by a particular set of gender conventions in turn made possible by political conditions favoring the "Liberty of women."

When Percy calls *Hau Kiou Choaan* a romance, he appears to be following Huet's generic definition of romance: it is composed in prose, contains fictions of love adventures, amuses the reader, and teaches virtue at the same time. However, when we examine Percy's voluminous footnotes in which he cites information from the existing literature on China to explain the content of the work and prove its authenticity, we see that he performs a deliberately gendered reading of the work to prove the impossibility of genuine romance in China. Percy read *Hau Kiou Choaan* for proof of the degraded status of Chinese women in comparison to European ladies. He found no gallantry in *Hau Kiou Choaan*. Citing Du Halde, he noted that Chinese men had numerous second wives or concubines; that daughters were little valued and often killed at birth (1761, 1: 70–71n); that women were kept "recluse," immured in their apartments, and segregated from men, including male relations, beginning at the age of twelve (1761, 1: 103–04n, 2: 48–49n); that they were covered "from head to foot, so that nothing is to be seen but their faces" (1761, 1: 189n); that they suffered foot-binding (1761, 1: 190n). In short, Percy concluded, the women in China enjoyed "no delicacy shewn to their Sex" (1761, 2: 128n). He contended that "Where the Women general are held so cheap, we must not wonder that the men should be backward to acknowledge a soft and respectful passion for any one of them: or that a nation in other respects civilized and refined, should in this resemble the most savage and unpolished" such as "the wild Nations of North America" (1761, 2: 129n).[84] How, then, should we interpret the fact that Percy's ethnological remarks on Chinese find a precise counterexample in the leading female character of Shuey-ping-sin, who is not a daughter "held cheap" but rather "the darling of her father, who loved her with an affection, equal to that he would have had for a son of the same accomplishments" (1761, 1: 70); who admittedly is the object of numerous ruses to trick her into a marriage "contracted without the consent of the Parties" but who manages to outwit her foes and marry only the man who is her equal in virtue and intelligence (1761, 2: 128n); who, allegedly "where the Women have no power of refusing," does not stop refusing until she can accept with her whole heart (1761, 2: 128n); who, where "the Women will be in low esteem as Women," is the most shining character of all (1761, 2: 128)? Although the male hero in *Hau Kiou Choaan* is defined over and over by his martial prowess, sexual modesty, and knack of saving damsels in distress, Percy nonchalantly denies that "there should be any such thing as Gallantry among a people, who admit of no intercourse between the two Sexes" (1761, 2: 127–28n). Percy's conclusion is that "The Chinese morals, notwithstanding their boasted purity, evidently fall short of the Christian, since they know not how to inspire that open and ingenuous simplicity, void of all guile, which more elevated principles of morality propose to our esteem and imitation" (1761, 1: 129n). This last citation shows us how Percy led his "fair Reader" through the novel's fictional Chinese landscape as though through a shop of Chinese curios, providing an alternate story altogether different from its narrative – as if the dialectic between meaning and truth, fiction and fact, had no place in this novelistic world of difference (1761, 2: 127n).[85]

Percy's insistent denial of Chinese gallantry and romance flies in the face of textual evidence. Ling Hon Lam has pointed out that a key character in the original Chinese text is *xia*, translatable as chivalry, knight-errantry, heroism, or valiance. This term, he notes, is "systematically ignored or radically mistranslated" in Percy's translation.[86] *Hau Kiou Choaan* is certainly a text that problematizes heterosexual love and challenges the conventions of courtship. However, it is clearly a work that celebrates the couple well matched both in looks and in virtue. As Keith McMahon explains, the Chinese scholar-beauty romance tends to rationalize and de-eroticize love. Indeed, "the beauty-scholar romances work toward a vision of man and woman who are not really male and female and who do everything they can to avoid having sex. The couple replaces sex with words: poems, letters, and engaging conversation." Evenly matched both in beauty and

intelligence, the hero and heroine share a "crossing of gender characteristics" that operates as "a major aspect of the lovers' complementarity."[87]
In Percy's hands, however, this stylized Chinese vision of evenly matched
lovers becomes an ethnographic tale about the degradation of women; its
male hero who has a knack of magically turning up at scenes of ladies'
distress is glossed as lacking in gallantry.

Although Percy praises *Hau Kiou Choaan* in his dedication to the
Countess of Sussex for its "strict regard to virtue and decorum," contrasting it to the "fictitious narratives of the most licentious and immoral
turn" so popular in England, he claims repeatedly in his annotations that
the Chinese lack virtue. The most striking instance of this editorial strategy can be seen in Percy's comments on the conceit of sexual denial so
central to *Hau Kiou Choaan*: Shuey-ping-sin and Tieh-chung-u spend a
night together without engaging in any physical contact; they refuse to
marry each other although they are deeply in love; and even when they are
forced to marry they choose not to consummate their marriage. Citing
a passage in Montesquieu's *Spirit of the Laws* that claims "In *China* 'it is
regarded, as a prodigy of virtue, to find one's self alone with a woman in
a remote apartment without offering violence to her,'" Percy perversely
suggests that the novel exaggerates the hero and heroine's sexual denial
precisely because it is so *unlikely* in Chinese culture. The Chinese, he
writes, "are to the highest degree greedy of gain, libidinous and vindic-
tive." It is for this very reason, his argument goes, that they deem the very
idea of not raping a woman even when given a chance to do so "a prodigy
of virtue" (2: 147n). This is hardly a reasonable reading of the scene in
which a minor official attempts unsuccessfully to persuade Tieh-chung-u
to marry Shuey-ping-sin by recalling an old Chinese saying, "A man and
woman that can be together in private and yet preserve their chastity,
can break no law" (2: 145–46). The most interesting drama in *Hau Kiou
Choaan*, as mentioned earlier, has to do with the central characters' refusal
to marry *despite* their having broken no laws. Tieh-chung-u and Shuey-
ping-sin's moral dilemma derives from the conviction that they *might as
well* have broken the laws, since they will always lie under the suspicion
of having done so. This is also Percy's point, of course, but for him there
is no real moral dilemma: Tieh-chung-u and Shuey-ping-sin are exemplary not of Chinese virtue but the improbability if not impossibility of
Chinese virtue. Percy's argument is all the more surprising considering the
fact that *Hau Kiou Choaan* bears "some resemblance to the sentimental
fiction" of the period, "Starting with scenes of virtue in distress and ending with scenes of virtue rewarded."[88]

Whenever confronted with a discrepancy between the novel and the existing ethnographic literature on China, Percy pointedly chooses to read the novel against the grain. It would be too easy and simple, however, to take Percy's determined anti-reading of the novel simply as a sign of his sinophobia or his ambivalence toward Chinese culture. The reason why Percy chooses to become such a bad reader of the novel, I suggest, is not simply because he is invested in denigrating Chinese culture per se. As David Porter has shown, Percy's attitude toward China was "complex, ambivalent, and even deeply conflicted," but it was never simplistic.[89] The key to this question may be found not in *Hau Kiou Choaan* but in Percy's theorization of romance and gallantry in the *Reliques of Ancient English Poetry*. In his essay "On the Ancient Metrical Romances" included in the third volume of his *Reliques*, Percy theorized that the English romance, "which so long celebrated feats of Chivalry, and which at first in metre and afterwards in prose, was the entertainment of our ancestors," were derived not from a French source, as was commonly supposed, but from the Gothic culture of the northern European nations of Scandinavia (1765, 3: iii). Percy was building on his theory that the Scandinavian scalds were the model for the ancient Britons' bards and minstrels who sang songs at court and served as oral historians of their nations. In time, the scalds' mission became less historical; "it became their business chiefly to entertain and delight," and so they began to poeticize history, turning it into "marvelous fictions" – "stories of adventures with giants and dragons, and witches and enchanters, and all the monstrous extravagances of wild imagination, unguided by judgment, and uncorrected by art" (1765, 3: iii). Percy's point was that these apparently silly stories, like the apparently childish songs and ballads he also collected in the *Reliques*, were in fact an important historical legacy that proved that English literary history had a Saxon, or Gothic, origin.

With this theory Percy attempted to rebut several other competing theories of romance circulating in his time, especially the common idea that romance was imported from France and that it had developed out of European contact with the Arab world during the medieval crusades. As we have seen, Percy disagreed with Richard Hurd's theory that romance was a product of the feudal constitution; he believed that romance antedated feudalism. Percy also took issue with the common theory that romance had developed out of contact with the Arab world. In this sense, he was also opposed to Thomas Warton's climactic theory that the "cold and barren" lands of northern Europe had been influenced by the "ideal tales of these eastern invaders, recommended by a brilliancy of description, a variety of imagery, and an exuberance of invention, hitherto unknown and unfamiliar" to Europe.[90] Percy considered ballads and romances products of a rude and barbarous age, full of superstition and primitive belief, and he also believed that a cultural revaluation of these genres of 'low literature' was in order. The ballads and romances of the ancient Britons, he believed, proved that they were a rude but artless, pleasingly simple, passionate, and martial people, gallant toward their women, full of fire and imagination.

By reimagining the genealogy of chivalry and gallantry in this way, Percy was claiming romance as an ur-*British*, fundamentally Gothic genre. At the same time, he was implying that modern European Gothic manners were more 'developed' than the manners of other civilizations, past or present. Committed as he was to a Gothic revision of British cultural heritage, Percy was loath to recognize gallantry as a cultural value or romance as a meaningful genre in China. His willful insistence on the profound, indeed insuperable gender divide in China is interesting precisely because it shows us how ideas about genre and gender were used in transcultural contexts. Percy's use of the condition of women as an "index of comparison for societies" was not unusual for his time. Jane Rendall has shown that, in the second half of the eighteenth century, ideas about the exceptional status of women in the British medieval past, based chiefly on readings of Tacitus's *Germania*, were used both to critique and to defend modern British civil society and the British state.[91] The reinterpretation of romance in the mid- to late eighteenth century as a preeminently British and Gothic genre, "the rise of chivalry" and the reinvention of the ideal male Briton as a gallant and chivalrous man, and the antiquarian rediscovery of the British medieval past are all part and parcel of this new national historiography.[92] In this sense, the rise of romance is part of a larger nationalist narrative centered on the exceptionalism of the British Isles, in particular their political liberties and progress in civilization. As Michèle Cohen points out, women were central to this narrative in so far as "the relations between the sexes and the respect accorded to women were the mark of a civilized and refined nation."[93] Adam Ferguson blandly summed up the romance ethos of the mid-eighteenth century when he wrote in *An Essay on the History of Civil Society* (1767) that "The system of chivalry, when completely formed, proceeded on a marvelous respect and veneration to the fair sex, on forms of combat established, and on a supposed junction of the heroic and sanctified character."[94] Percy's *Hau Kiou Choaan* and *Reliques* are prime examples of this cultural shift toward Gothicism, antiquarianism, and gendered nationalism. What Percy's work indeed shows is that, when the English began to theorize cultural difference on the basis of literary examples, they thought in categories that linked genre and gender in dramatic ways, and moreover used gender as a central category of analysis in the interpretation of culture.

However, Percy's grand narrative of a chivalrous, Gothicized national literary trust residing in the sung verse of anonymous, itinerant entertainers, balladeers, and romancers does not sit easily with the often gory, asocial, and amoral content of the ancient English songs and ballads, nor with the sexual excesses of the romances. As Susan Stewart has pointed out, Percy's grand narrative of a Gothicized national literary trust contrasts sharply with the content of the ballads, which are obsessed with "the psychological tensions of the family, the humor of social stratification, and the tragic dilemma of individual desire pitted against the social good."[95] In Groom's words, Percy's *Reliques* "welters in gore: the bloodiness of death and dismemberment incarnadines the entire three volumes, and if occasionally watered by humor or levity, it is more often deepened by a colossal amorality."[96] When we examine the poems that follow Percy's essay "On the Ancient Metrical Romances" in the third volume of the *Reliques*, it is difficult to find evidence of "that respectful complaisance shewn to the fair sex, (so different from the manners of the Greeks and Romans)" that purportedly distinguished the culture of the ancient Gothic minstrels (1765, 3: iii). Instead, moral and sexual deviation abound. Adultery, cuckoldry, and murder are favorite themes: 'gallant' knights and 'chaste' ladies (including Queen Guinevere) receive an equally humiliating public undressing by a magic mantle in "The Boy and the Mantle"; "Old Sir Robin of Portingale" punishes his adulterous young wife by killing her lover, then mutilating her dead body by cutting off her breasts and ears; when "Little Musgrave and Lady Barnard" are discovered in bed, Lord Barnard likewise "cut her pappes from off her brest" (1765, 3: 72). In "The Knight and Shepherd's Daughter," a young woman meets "by chance a knighte" who courteously declares, "Good morrow to you, beauteous maide," then promptly proceeds to rape her. The disconnection between romance theory and ballad text in the *Reliques* points to the ideological strains in Percy's project. It is a disconnection that is already in evidence in Percy's repudiation of Chinese romance. In order to foreground a national, English tradition, and reinvent literary historiography, Percy sacrificed, in effect, the literary text. His book would redeem the personal tragedies embodied in the ballads and songs as fragments of a larger national tale of memory and preservation. The mangled, shattered bodies of the *Reliques* refer to a transfiguration that takes place outside the poetic narratives in which they are encased; it is the miscellany or the anthology that redeems the personal tragedies in these lyric relics as fragments of a larger national tale of memory and preservation. For Chinese literature, on the other hand, there would be no such meta-narrative of recovery, restoration, and transfiguration.

Lyric Nation

Hau Kiou Choaan and the *Miscellaneous Pieces* are important precursors to Percy's *Reliques* because they show us not only how Percy trained himself as an editor of miscellanies and a translator of cultural artifacts, but also how his (mis)understanding of the Chinese language may have helped him define the distinctive orality and textuality of the British Isles. In "A Dissertation on the Language and Characters of the Chinese," which was the only section of *Miscellaneous Pieces* for which he was "more immediately responsible," Percy outlined a complex theory of the Chinese language in which his theorization of the native English voice was already richly implied.[97] His theory of Chinese was built on a rather free interpretation of his acknowledged Jesuit sources, the writings of Theophilus Siegfried Bayer and Nicolas Fréret. Although he pretended to defer to these sources in claiming that the "chief merit" of his "Dissertation" was that it "derived from originals equally curious and authentic," Percy was more interested in using bits of information he had gleaned from these Jesuit writings to argue for the limitations of Chinese literary culture.[98] In volume four of *Hau Kiou Choaan*, for example, he had already printed an excerpt from the writings of Nicolas Fréret originally published in *L'Histoire de l'Academie Royale des Inscriptions et Belles Lettres*, to which he had added his own comments.

Percy began this excerpt with Fréret's provocative claim that "The Chinese language is the most musical and harmonious of all we are acquainted with" (1761, 4: 203). But his reason for singling out this passage, it turns out, was not so much to support Fréret's claim about the exceptional beauty of the Chinese spoken language as to emphasize the gap between Chinese orality and the Chinese script. For Fréret went on to discuss the extreme formality of Chinese poetry, which was said to be entirely regulated by "invariable laws" governing syllable measure, rhyme, and verse number (1761, 4: 209). In his comments, Percy noted that Chinese verse was further constrained by rules governing the "signification and meaning" of the verses, all of which proved that "the more difficult and artificial their compositions are, the more highly are they valued" (1761, 4: 213–14). According to Percy, this was precisely why "the Reader of taste" would fail to find great merit in

Chinese poetry, lacking as it was in "that bold and daring sublimity, which we expect to find in compositions of that name," or "that noble simplicity, which is only to be attained by the genuine study of nature, and of its artless beauties" (1761, 4: 217). Instead, Chinese poetry was full of "quaintness and affections; a fondness for little conceits" (1761, 4: 217) and "those *difficiles nugae* which good taste and sound criticism have taught *Europeans* to neglect" (1761, 4: 216). The reason why Chinese poetry was so difficult to translate and to appreciate in translated form, Percy ventured, was precisely because it was so dependent on these artificial and unnatural rules, which in turn reflected the "most artificial" state of Chinese civilization:

> no people live under more political restraints than the *Chinese*, or have farther departed from a state of nature: it is upwards of four thousand years since they began to form a civilized policed state: their civil and religious ceremonies have in this time become infinitely complicated and numerous: and hence their customs, manners, and notions are the most artificial in the world. (1761, 4: 201)

Whereas Percy stressed the untranslatability of Chinese poetry in *Hau Kiou Choaan* – owing not so much to Europeans' lack of knowledge of Chinese and Chinese culture as to the unnaturalness of Chinese poetry – in *Miscellaneous Pieces* he developed a more complex theory of the Chinese language as essentially divided between an underdeveloped orality and an overdeveloped script. The charge that written Chinese poetry failed to reflect the richness of spoken Chinese was generalized into a larger and bolder claim that the Chinese language itself was "wholly addressed to the eye" and had "no affinity with their tongue, as spoken": "The *Chinese* tongue is barren and contracted, wholly consisting of a few undeclinable and uncompounded monosyllables: the *Chinese* characters, on the contrary, are amazingly numerous and complicated" (1762, 1: 10). The consequences of this divorce between oral and written language in China, according to Percy, were dire: without a written language to refine and cultivate it, Chinese oral culture could only remain barbarous and unrefined, "unfit for literature"; meanwhile, the prohibitive difficulty of mastering the "amazingly numerous and complicated" "arbitrary characters" of written Chinese was responsible for "the slow progress the sciences have made in *China*" (1762, 1: 10–12).

On the surface, there seems to be very little originality in Percy's dissertation on the Chinese language; the great gulf between spoken and written Chinese and the extreme difficulty of learning the Chinese script were time-honored commonplaces in the Jesuit literature. As David Porter has shown, however, it was precisely these three characteristics of the Chinese script – "its difficulty, its precedence over the spoken tongue, and its role as a shared medium of communication among a number of linguistic communities within and around China" – that had led figures as diverse as Juan González de Mendoza, Matteo Ricci, Francis Bacon, John Wilkins, and John Webb to endow the Chinese script with an unsurpassed universality, legitimacy, and authenticity.[99] What Percy reflects very clearly are two new developments taking place in eighteenth-century Europe at this time: on the one hand, a re-evaluation of alphabetic writing and, on the other, the invention of the concept of oral tradition. Long associated with the Egyptians and the Chinese, hieroglyphs represented antiquity, divinity, and occult, symbolic knowledge. For instance, T. S. Bayer, whose 1730 *Museum Sinicum* Percy cites in the *Miscellaneous Pieces*, had devoted his life to uncovering the "ancient symbolic code" embedded in the hieroglyphic Chinese script.[100] Yet, as Percy's references to "the savages of *America*" and "the writings of the *Mexicans*" show, by the mid-eighteenth century the reports from the New World had shown that hieroglyphic, pictorial representation was also characteristic of primitive people (1762, 1: 7–8). Percy's statement that "The first and most obvious kind of writing … must be by way of picture, or hieroglyphic" reflects this new conceptualization of the hieroglyph as a primitive sign prevailing among men living "in a state of wild nature" (1762, 1: 7). Percy understood the first "pictures" to be representations of "corporeal objects" (1762, 1: 7); with "mental development" there arose the need to express abstract ideas, for which "arbitrary signs" were invented; these signs in turn gave rise to "characters" (1762, 1: 8). If the writings of the native Americans and Mexicans exemplified the first stage of writing, those of the Egyptians exemplified the second hieroglyphic stage, and those of the Chinese the third stage where "arbitrary characters ha[d] entirely supplanted picture of hieroglyphics," though still exhibiting "some vestiges of that more ancient way of writing" (1762, 1: 8–9). The next step in this new conjectural history of writing systems was alphabetic writing, an achievement common to the European languages. The Chinese, however, had not been able to "hit upon an alphabet of letters expressive of their oral language" and, "ignorant of any other kind of writing," had simply "bestowed their whole attention to cultivate and improve" their characters (1762, 1: 9–10).

In defining the Chinese language in these terms, Percy was in many ways following the current of the times; what distinguished his approach was the unique way in which he combined a new appreciation of alphabetic writing with the new ethnographic ideal of the "native eloquence" of the preliterate primitive.[101] As Nicholas Hudson has shown, this ideal, developed in such texts as Joseph François Lafitau's *Moeurs des sauvages américains* (1724), was transposed in the mid-eighteenth century not only to the Western classical tradition – newly interpreted as an oral tradition of a much simpler age – but also to the native traditions of the British Isles. Indeed, the mid-century Ossian phenomenon was very much a product of this discovery of oral tradition, which idealized primitive, preliterate orality as more vigorous, impassioned, eloquent, and thus poetic than civilized speech. When Percy argues that the divorce between oral and written Chinese has given rise to a "peculiarly circumstanced" Chinese literature that cannot embody an impassioned, expressive orality because it lacks a proper alphabetic "vehicle" for its expression, it is difficult not to be struck by the way in which he makes alphabetic writing the very condition for a rich orality: "so long as the *Chinese* cultivate their written characters, they have no inducement to improve or adorn their oral tongue" (1762, 1: 14). Percy's theory of Chinese literature aligns him with such critics of Ossian as David Hume and Samuel Johnson, who likewise saw writing – particularly alphabetic writing – as a precondition for literary production.[102] Aligning the native ancient British with the illiterate pagan savages of the New World would seem an odd way to recuperate British literary tradition. However, this was precisely what Percy did when he referred to his "artless" bards and minstrels (1762, 1: x). Here he was both arguing his way out of the "invidious position" of British history in comparison to "Biblical or classical chronologies," and placing the ancient English at a comfortable remove from the eighteenth century.[103] By defining poetic value primarily in terms of "artless" voice, he was also giving native British antiquity an aesthetic and moral advantage over the artifices of Chinese antiquity. The celebration of the native pagan ancestry of Britain required a new theory of culture that privileged a non-classical, but also a non-Chinese antiquity, defined precisely in terms not of cultural achievement but of a proto-romantic notion of simplicity.

Why, then, did Percy's China books, despite the similarity of their aesthetic to that of the *Reliques*, not do well?[104] The latter's emphasis on orality, simplicity, authenticity, and curiosity were already there in the earlier works. One reason may be that it is all too evident that China operates as a counterexample for Percy's aesthetic; nobody loves a bad example. Percy's attitude toward the material he is editing is too ambivalent, indeed too belittling, to make for compelling reading. The most decisive reason, though, was probably that Percy was too obviously an amateur to be able to substantiate his claims. *Miscellaneous Pieces* indeed turned into an embarrassment. In its preface, Percy had referred enthusiastically to John Turberville Needham's theory that Chinese characters were derived from Egyptian writing – a theory supposedly proven by "a learned Chinese" at the Vatican who had deciphered the hieroglyphs on an Egyptian bust. Percy had welcomed Needham's "great discovery" as a strike against "all the pretences of the Chinese to that vast antiquity, which has been wont to stagger weak minds, and which has with so much parade been represented by certain writers as utterly incompatible with the history of the bible."[105] It was Percy, however, who ultimately felt the blow, for Needham's theory was soon discredited. In a 1763 letter to Richard Farmer, Percy wrote, "Dodsley thinks it better to take no further notice of Needham's Imposture till our Chinese Things arrive to the honour of a 2d Edition" – which indicates he was sufficiently mortified by the discovery of his own gullibility to want to make appropriate changes to the book.[106] Dodsley's response in turn suggests that the book was simply not deemed important enough to fix. The honor of a second edition in fact never arrived for either of Percy's Chinese books.[107] William Shenstone, with whom Percy had corresponded at length about his progress with *Hau Kiou Choaan*, limited his comments to the binding and the dedication.[108] Only the *Monthly Review* noted it as a new publication. However, the groundwork had been laid for a much greater success on the author's native soil.

After defining Chinese literature as peculiarly circumscribed, Percy proceeded to celebrate the unique advantages of the English poetic voice. On the title page of the *Reliques*, Percy indicated that the "Old Heroic BALLADS, SONGS, and other PIECES of our earlier POETS" collected in the *Reliques* were "(Chiefly of the LYRIC kind.)." With the anthologized poems of the *Reliques*, Percy indeed created a lasting image of the English nation as a lyric one, defined primarily by the oral songs in which its primal history was preserved. In the second edition of the *Reliques* published in 1767, he defined these songs as the oral "poems, songs, and metrical romances" of nameless poets who once sang for "a martial and unlettered people," the ancestors of England (1767, 1: ix). Percy's explicit emphasis on the lyric form begs the question of what this generic category means for him and his anthology. Anne Janowitz's comments in *England's Ruins* are enlightening in this regard. She writes, "The antiquarian lineage is … closely related to the tradition of the miscellany which, when it meets up with antiquarian fragments or textual ruins, lays the ground for the validation of poetic structure reduced to the shape of a brief lyric." In other words, "the anthologization of poetry … means, in turn, the fragmentation of narrative poetry into lyric form."[109] Janowitz's comments suggest that the lyric is constituted as much by its formal manner of textual presentation as by its content. Percy's anthology, which highlights the fragmentary and incomplete form in which the English poetic tradition has survived, theorizes poetic transmission as a process of fragmentation and ruin. Therefore, what makes Percy's songs, ballads, and romances lyrical is, in part, the ruined form in which they have been rediscovered. Each piece is a historical fragment and sediment – a lyric relic of its age.

Percy's collection was also lyrical in the more familiar sense of being sung verse. In his *Dictionary of the English Language*, Johnson defined lyrical as "pertaining to an harp, or to odes or poetry sung to an harp."[110] The *Reliques* collected songs whose origins could be traced back to the ancient English minstrels. As with his Chinese novel and poems, Percy made no claims as to the aesthetic quality of the minstrels' songs. His interest lay, rather, with the insight into the manners and mores of the Gothic ancestors provided by these songs. But his cultural revaluation of what had long been considered low literature had grave implications not only for the late eighteenth-century Gothic revival but also the proto-romantic redefinition of poetry in lyric terms. Percy's lyrics do not rule out narrative or drama; they are indeed eclectic in form, and are sometimes even lifted out of larger plays or romances. He introduces and presents his lyrics as the building blocks of these larger poetic texts that were inspired and influenced by these preexisting popular songs. The image of the English nation as constructed in Percy's *Reliques* is thus an "image of the nation as a set of lyric segments."[111] These songs, sung by anonymous, itinerant entertainers, balladeers, and romancers, were collected as artifacts of the voice of a Gothic English nation. The continuity between Percy's Chinese books and his *Reliques*, then, lies in the coherence of his nationalistic project of English cultural recovery. If the *Reliques* present to us a "cultural museum of Englishness and choice examples of the Gothic temperament," Percy's Chinese books present an image of China as Gothic England's cultural foil.[112] Whereas the Chinese are characterized by the "abjectness of their genius," "servile submission, and dread of novelty" (1761, 1: xiii), "quaintness and affectation," "a want of that noble simplicity, which is only to be attained by the genuine study of nature, and of its artless beauties," the English are presented as descendants of a rude but artless, pleasingly simple, passionate, and martial people (1761, 4: 217). The Chinese are afflicted with an overdeveloped artifice and an underdeveloped orality and lyricism; the Gothic ancestors of the English were artless lovers of song. Philip Connell has argued that this "patriotic Gothicism of the *Reliques* is unmistakable" but also "studiously diplomatic" and inclusive. Percy included many Scottish ballads in his miscellany and adopted an "air of studied impartiality" toward the Scots.[113] He was less impartial toward the Chinese, however. The Jesuit adulation of China, as well as the popular conflation of Gothic taste with chinoiserie, no doubt played an important role in shaping Percy's negative attitude toward China; his lyric nation was an un-Chinese nation.

The argument that lies implicit in Percy's *Reliques* would be voiced more openly by such contemporary historians as Catherine Macaulay, Obadiah Hulme, and John Pinkerton, who attributed to the Anglo-Saxon heritage "the most perfect constitution the world had ever seen" and "standards of political liberty and civilization which other peoples, including the Celts, could only emulate."[114] And yet, as we have seen, his theory was not simply on the side of the moderns and their belief in the progress of civilization. Percy's literary theory consisted instead of an uneasy combination of the arguments of both the ancients and the moderns. Percy was a modern to the extent that he adhered to the narrative of historical progress by means of which "barbarity was civilized, grossness refined, and ignorance instructed" (1765, 1: vii). At the same time, he spoke in the nostalgic voice of an ancient when he mourned the loss of the "curious," "artless graces," and "pleasing simplicity" of his poems (1765, 1: ix–x). Downplaying the aesthetic value of these artifacts of barbarism and arguing rather for the sheer historical interest of his antique poems was Percy's way of demanding a new kind of historical and literary sympathy for them without subverting the moderns' narrative. Even so, Percy managed in this way to complicate the modern notion of the "progress of life and manners" in history, in which by "gradations barbarity was civilized, grossness refined, and ignorance instructed" (1765, 1: vii). Percy rehearsed the narrative of historical progress, and in this sense could be regarded a representative modern, yet the compensatory "artless graces" he located in his "barbarous" poems suggest that they compensate for something that has gone missing in modern art. With diplomatic nods to both the ancients and the moderns, Percy's *Reliques* manages to redefine literary antiquity for modern purposes.

Notes

Introduction

1 Michael F. Suarez, S. J. provides a helpful overview of these historical changes in his introduction to *The Cambridge History of the Book in Britain*, vol. 5, 1695–1830, ed. Michael F. Suarez, S. J., and Michael L. Turner (Cambridge: Cambridge University Press, 2009), 1–35.

2 Kathleen Wilson, *The Island Race: Englishness, Empire and Gender in the Eighteenth Century* (London: Routledge, 2003), 30–31; italics in the original.

3 I am taking the phrase from Richard Helgerson's provocative essay, "Before National Literary History," *Modern Language Quarterly* 64.2 (2003), 171.

4 Alok Yadav, *Before the Empire of English: Literature, Provinciality, and Nationalism in Eighteenth-Century Britain* (New York: Palgrave Macmillan, 2004).

5 Ibid., 55–109.

6 See Robert Markley, *The Far East and the English Imagination* (Cambridge: Cambridge University Press, 2006); David Porter, *Ideographia: The Chinese Cipher in Early Modern Europe* (Stanford: Stanford University Press, 2001) and *The Chinese Taste in Eighteenth-Century England* (Cambridge: Cambridge University Press, 2010); Chi-ming Yang, *Performing China: Virtue, Commerce, and Orientalism in Eighteenth-Century England, 1660–1760* (Baltimore: Johns Hopkins University Press, 2011); Eugenia Zuroski Jenkins, *A Taste for China: English Subjectivity and the Prehistory of Orientalism* (Oxford: Oxford University Press, 2013). Ros Ballaster devotes a chapter to China in *Fabulous Orients: Fictions of the East in England, 1662–1785* (Oxford: Oxford University Press, 2005). Relevant journal special issues are the special issue on "Europe and Asia in the Long Eighteenth Century" in *The Eighteenth Century: Theory and Interpretation* 45.2 (2004) and the issue on "China and the Making of Global Modernity" in *Eighteenth-Century Studies* 43.3 (2010). The *Eighteenth-Century Studies* special issue was an outgrowth of a Radcliffe Exploratory Summer Seminar on "China and the Making of Global Modernity, 1600–1800," co-organized by myself and Robert Markley at the Radcliffe Institute for Advanced Study from July 31 to August 4, 2007.

7 Porter, *The Chinese Taste in Eighteenth-Century England*, 7.

8 Zuroski Jenkins, *A Taste for China*, 2.

9 Yang, *Performing China*, 3, 31.

10 Ibid., 2, 11. My emphasis.

11 Eun Kyung Min, "China between the Ancients and the Moderns," *The Eighteenth Century: Theory and Interpretation* 45.2 (2004), 115–29.

12 William Temple, *Essay upon the Ancient and Modern Learning*, in *Miscellanea. The Second Part* (London, 1690), 24.

13 See Clara Marburg, *Sir William Temple, A Seventeenth Century "Libertin"* (New Haven: Yale University Press, 1932), 56–60, and J. E. Spingarn's notes to his edition of *Sir William Temple's Essays* On Ancient & Modern Learning *and* On Poetry (Oxford: Clarendon Press, 1909).

14 William Wotton, *Reflections upon Ancient and Modern Learning* (London, 1694), 145.

15 Douglas Lane Patey, "Ancients and Moderns," *The Cambridge History of Literary Criticism*, vol. 4, ed. H. B. Nisbet and Claude Rawson (Cambridge: Cambridge University Press, 1997), 32.

16 Hans Robert Jauss, "Modernity and Literary Tradition," trans. Christian Thorne, *Critical Inquiry* 31.2 (2005), 330, 332. For accounts of the quarrel that focus on progressive history and experimental science, see J. B. Bury, *The Idea of Progress: An Inquiry into Its Origin and Growth* (London: Macmillan, 1920); Richard Foster Jones, *Ancients and Moderns: A Study of the Rise of the Scientific Movement in Seventeenth-Century England*, 2nd ed. (Berkeley: University of California Press, 1965); David Spadafora, *The Idea of Progress in Eighteenth-Century Britain* (New Haven: Yale University Press, 1990).

17 Paul O. Kristeller, "The Modern System of the Arts: A Study in the History of Aesthetics (I)," *Journal of the History of Ideas* 12.4 (1951), 525.

18 Dipesh Chakrabarty, *Provincializing Europe: Postcolonial Thought and Historical Difference* (Princeton: Princeton University Press, 2000), 7.

19 Trevor Ross, "The Emergence of 'Literature': Making and Reading the English Canon in the Eighteenth Century," *English Literary History* 63 (1996), 413. Ross cites Addison's *Spectator* no. 273. See *The Spectator*, ed. Donald F. Bond, 5 vols. (Oxford: Clarendon Press, 1965), 2: 565.

20 Patey, "Ancients and Moderns," 34.

21 Ibid., 34.

22 Trevor Ross, *The Making of the English Literary Canon: From the Middle Ages to the Late Eighteenth Century* (Montreal: McGill-Queen's University Press, 1998), 197.

23 Ibid., 181, 184.

24 *The Dunciad Variorum, The Poems of Alexander Pope*, ed. John Butt (New Haven: Yale University Press, 1963), 351.

25 Ross, *The Making of the English Literary Canon*, 198, 200.

26 J. Paul Hunter, *Before Novels: The Cultural Contexts of Eighteenth-Century English Fiction* (New York: W. W. Norton, 1990), 10.

27 Ibid., 12.

28 Ibid., 11, 16; Henry Fielding, preface to *Joseph Andrews* and *Shamela* (Oxford: Oxford University Press, 1980), 8.

29 Jonathan Brody Kramnick, *Making the English Canon: Print-Capitalism and the Cultural Past, 1700–1770* (Cambridge: Cambridge University Press, 1998), 17, 24, 29.

30 Ibid., 53.

31 The important omission of drama in this book is likewise due to the fact that, although some of these authors wrote in other genres such as poetry or drama in which there were certainly other kinds of literary innovations at work, their non-prose writings are less relevant for this study of their engagement with China. For instance, Oliver Goldsmith reviewed Arthur Murphy's 1759 play *The Orphan of China* in the *Critical Review* and was an important dramatist in his own right, but his primary literary engagement with China took place in the newspaper. I have previously discussed the representation of China in seventeenth- and eighteenth-century drama in "The Rise and Fall of Chinese Empires on the English Stage, 1660–1760," *The Journal of Eighteenth-Century English Literature* 3.1 (2006), 53–75.

32 Kirsti Simonsuuri, *Homer's Original Genius: Eighteenth-Century Notions of the Early Greek Epic (1688–1798)* (Cambridge: Cambridge University Press, 1979), 26.

33 Laura Hostetler, "A Mirror for the Monarch: A Literary Portrait of China in Eighteenth-Century France," *Asia Major* 3.19 (2006), 352.

34 Eric Hayot, Haun Saussy, and Steven G. Yao, "Sinographies: An Introduction," in *Sinographies: Writing China*, ed. Eric Hayot, Haun Saussy and Steven G. Yao (Minneapolis: University of Minnesota Press, 2008), xi.

35 Fabian, *Time and the Other: How Anthopology Makes Its Object* (New York: Columbia University Press, 1983), xxxix.

36 Benedict Anderson, *Imagined Communities: Reflections on the Origin and Spread of Nationalism*, revised ed. (New York: Verso, 1991), 24.

37 Walter Benjamin, "Theses on the Philosophy of History," *Illuminations*, ed. Hannah Arendt, trans. Harry Zohn (New York: Schocken Books, 1969), 264; cited in Anderson, *Imagined Communities*, 24.

38 As Anne Gerritsen and Stephen McDowall point out, luxury imports from China conveyed a very different message about the scientific achievements of the Chinese than the writings of 'modern' skeptics such as le Comte. See Gerritsen and McDowall, "Material Culture and the Other: European Encounters with Chinese Porcelain, ca. 1650–1800," *Journal of World History* 23.1 (2012), 87–113.

39 Fabian, *Time and the Other*, 31.

40 Matei Calinescu, *Five Faces of Modernity: Modernism, Avant-Garde, Decadence, Kitsch, Postmodernism* (Durham: Duke University Press, 1987), 36.

41 Arthur O. Lovejoy, "The Chinese Origin of a Romanticism," *Essays in the History of Ideas* (Baltimore: Johns Hopkins University Press, 1948), 100.

42 William Temple, "On the Gardens of Epicurus; or, of Gardening, In the Year 1685," in *Miscellanea. The Second Part* (London, 1690), 131–32. The terms in which Temple describes the Chinese garden have become powerful common-places still in circulation to this day. See Young-tsu Wong's study of the famed

imperial garden destroyed in the nineteenth century: "In contrast to the geometric formality of Renaissance gardens, Chinese garden art appreciates untrammeled beauty with an emphasis on free form, continuous flow, and unexpected twists and turns." *A Paradise Lost: The Imperial Garden Yuanming Yuan* (Honolulu: University of Hawaii Press, 2001), 10.

43 *The Spectator*, 2: 541.
44 Kramnick, *Making the English Canon*, 1, 3–4.
45 David Lowenthal, *The Past Is a Foreign Country* (Cambridge: Cambridge University Press, 1985), xvi.

Chapter 1: China between the Ancients and the Moderns

1 Jonathan Swift, *The Battel of the Books, The Cambridge Edition of the Works of Jonathan Swift*, ed. Marcus Walsh, vol. 1 (Cambridge: Cambridge University Press, 2010), 144. All subsequent references to this text appear parenthetically by volume and page number.
2 William Temple, *An Essay upon the Ancient and Modern Learning*, in *Miscellanea. The Second Part* (London, 1690), 60. The essay was written in 1689 and printed in the 1690 edition of the *Miscellanea*. An earlier essay collection containing other essays had been published in 1680. Subsequent citations of Temple's *Miscellanea* appear parenthetically by publication year and page number. For a good synopsis of the quarrel, see John F. Tinkler, "The Splitting of Humanism: Bentley, Swift, and the English *Battle of the Books*," *Journal of the History of Ideas* 49.3 (1988), 455–56.
3 The full title reads *Miscellanea. The Third Part. By the late Sir William Temple, Bar. Published by Jonathan Swift, A. M. Prebendary of St. Patrick's, Dublin* (London, 1701). All subsequent references to these works by Temple and Wotton appear parenthetically by publication year and page number.
4 See David Spadafora, *The Idea of Progress in Eighteenth-Century Britain* (New Haven: Yale University Press, 1990); Joseph M. Levine, *The Battle of the Books: History and Literature in the Augustan Age* (Ithaca: Cornell University Press, 1991); and Joan DeJean, *Ancients against Moderns: Culture Wars and the Making of a Fin de Siècle* (Chicago: University of Chicago Press, 1997). See also Stephen Gaukroger, ed., *The Uses of Antiquity: The Scientific Revolution and the Classical Tradition* (Dordrecht: Kluwer Academic Publishers, 1991).
5 Levine, *The Battle of the Books*, 2.
6 See G. V. Scammel, "The New Worlds and Europe in the Sixteenth Century," *The Historical Journal* 12.3 (1969), 389–412.
7 Michael T. Ryan, "Assimilating New Worlds in the Sixteenth and Seventeenth Centuries," *Comparative Studies in Society and History* 23.4 (1981), 519–38.
8 China plays no role in Levine's *Battle of the Books* or in the following discussions of the English quarrel: H. W. Garrod, "Phalaris and Phalarism," in *Seventeenth-Century Studies Presented to Sir Herbert Grierson* (Oxford: Clarendon Press, 1938), 360–71; Charles H. Hinnant, "Sir William Temple's Views on Science, Poetry, and the Imagination," *Studies in Eighteenth-Century Culture* 8 (1979),

187–203; Douglas Lane Patey, "Ancients and Moderns," *The Cambridge History of Literary Criticism*, vol. 4, ed. H. B. Nisbet and Claude Rawson (Cambridge: Cambridge University Press, 1997), 32–71; and John F. Tinkler, "The Splitting of Humanism," 453–72.

9 Edwin J. Van Kley, "Europe's 'Discovery' of China and the Writing of World History," *American Historical Review* 76.2 (1971), 362.

10 Ibid., 360.

11 Paolo Rossi, *The Dark Abyss of Time: The History of the Earth and the History of Nations from Hooke to Vico*, trans. Lydia G. Cochrane (Chicago: University of Chicago Press, 1984), 133. Rossi notes that, within a year of the appearance of Lapeyrère's *Praeadamitae*, there had been nineteen attempts to refute the book. See also Virgile Pinot, *La Chine et la formation de l'esprit philosophique en France* (Paris: P. Geuthner, 1932), 193–200 for a discussion of Lapeyrère.

12 "Hanc enim qua de scribo, extremam Asiam ante diluvium habitatem fuisse pro certo habeo." Martino Martini, *Sinicae historiae decas prima res a gentis origine ad Christum natum in extrema Asia* (Amsterdam, 1659), 12. First edition, Munich, 1658. Cited in Van Kley, "Europe's 'Discovery' of China and the Writing of World History," 363.

13 Pinot, *La Chine et la formation de l'esprit philosophique en France*, 202; Van Kley, "Europe's 'Discovery' of China and the Writing of World History," 363.

14 Van Kley, "Europe's 'Discovery' of China and the Writing of World History," 364.

15 Isaac Vossius, *Dissertatio de vera aetate mundi, qua ostenditur natale mundi tempus annis 1440 vulgarum anticipare* (The Hague, 1659). See Van Kley, "Europe's 'Discovery' of China and the Writing of World History," 363.

16 John Webb, *An Historical Essay Endeavoring a Probability that the Language of the Empire of China is the Primitive Language* (London, 1669). See Van Kley, "Europe's 'Discovery' of China and the Writing of World History," 366.

17 Rachel Ramsey, "China and the Ideal of Order in John Webb's *An Historical Essay*," *Journal of the History of Ideas* 62.3 (2001), 492; Chen Shouyi, "John Webb: A Forgotten Page in the Early History of Sinology in Europe," in *The Vision of China in the English Literature of the Seventeenth and Eighteenth Centuries*, ed. Adrian Hsia (Hong Kong: Chinese University Press, 1998), 94.

18 See Robert Markley, "'The destin'd Walls/Of *Cambalu*': Milton, China, and the Ambiguities of the East," *Milton and the Imperial Vision*, ed. Balachandra Rajan and Elizabeth Sauer (Pittsburgh: Duquesne University Press, 1999), 195–97.

19 See Porter's *Ideographia*, 34–49.

20 Thomas Burnet's *The Theory of the Earth* (more generally known as *The Sacred Theory of the Earth*) was first published in Latin in two volumes under the title *Telluris Theoria Sacra* in 1681 and 1689. The English versions of the two volumes appeared in 1684 and 1690 respectively.

21 John Gascoigne, "'The Wisdom of Egyptians' and the Secularisation of History in the Age of Newton," in *The Uses of Antiquity*, 175–78. On the quarrel over Egyptian history, see also Kenneth J. Knoespel, "Newton in the School

of Time: The Chronology of Ancient Kingdoms Amended and the Crisis of Seventeenth-Century Historiography," *The Eighteenth Century: Theory and Interpretation* 30.3 (1989), 19–41, and John Michael Archer's chapter "Antiquity and Degeneration: The Representation of Egypt and Shakespeare's *Antony and Cleopatra*," in *Old Worlds: Egypt, Southwest Asia, India, and Russia in Early Modern English Writing* (Stanford: Stanford University Press, 2001). Archer notes that "Early modern Europe rediscovered the ancient belief in Egypt's cultural precedence over Greece along with the rest of classical learning" (38).

22 See Clara Marburg, *Sir William Temple, A Seventeenth Century "Libertin"* (New Haven: Yale University Press, 1932), 56–60, and J. E. Spingarn's notes to his edition of *Sir William Temple's Essays* On Ancient & Modern Learning *and* On Poetry (Oxford: Clarendon Press, 1909). Alvaro Semedo's *Imperio de la China* (Madrid, 1642) was translated into English in 1655 as *The History of That Great and Renowned Monarchy of China*; Gabriel de Magalhães's *Doze excellencias da China* was translated into French as *Nouvelle relation de la Chine* (Paris, 1688) and appeared in English as *A New History of China* in 1688; Nieuhof's work first appeared in Dutch under the title *Het gezantschap der Neêlandtsche Oost-Indische Compagnie aan den grooten tartarischen cham, den tegenwoordigen Keizer van China* (Amsterdam, 1665), then subsequently in English in Ogilby's lavish folio edition of 1669. On the Portuguese texts, see Fernando Cristóvão, "Les livres portugais de voyages en Chine au XVIIe siècle," in Anna Balakian and James J. Wilhelm, eds., *Proceedings of the Xth Congress of the International Comparative Literature Association: New York, NY, 1982* (New York: Garland, 1985), 422–26.

23 *Confucius Sinarum philosophus* was translated into English, in abridged form, in 1691 as *The Morals of Confucius*. Bellum Tartaricum, *or the Conquest of The Great and most Renowned Empire of China, By the Invasion of the Tartars* (1655) was first published in Antwerp in 1654 in Latin as *De bello Tartarico historia*. The English translation serves as a source for Elkanah Settle's 1676 play, *The Conquest of China by the Tartars*. For a general survey of seventeenth-century European literature dealing with the fall of the Ming empire, see Edwin J. Van Kley, "An Alternative Muse: The Manchu Conquest of China in the Literature of Seventeenth-Century Northern Europe," *European Studies Review* 6 (1976), 21–32.

24 Felix Gilbert, *Machiavelli and Guicciardini: Politics and History in Sixteenth-Century Florence* (Princeton: Princeton University Press, 1965), 225. Cited in John F. Tinkler, "The Splitting of Humanism," 460.

25 Levine, *The Battle of the Books*, 17; Anthony Grafton, "Renaissance Readers and Ancient Texts: Comments on Some Commentaries," *Renaissance Quarterly* 38.4 (1985), 618–19.

26 Tinkler, "The Splitting of Humanism," 463, 460–61.

27 That strategy had already been tried by John Webb. Arguing that "China served as an effective means for political conservatives wishing to launch a mediated critique in the face of the erosion of their hopes for the restored monarchy," Rachel Ramsey reads John Webb's work as "a last-ditch effort by

Webb ... to curry favor with the Court and thereby realize his professional aspirations within the Office of the Works." See "China and the Ideal of Order in John Webb's *An Historical Essay*", 503.

28 See the diary entry for July 6, 1679: "There was now brought up to *Lond.* a Child ... who both read & perfectly understood Heb: Gr: Latine, Arab: Syriac, & most of the Modern Languages; disputed in Divinity, Law, all the Sciences, was skillfull in Historie both Ecclesiastical & Prophane, in Politic &c, in a word so universaly & solidly learned at 11 yeares of age, as he was looked on as a Miracle" and "in sum a(n) Intellectus Universalis beyond all that we reade of Picus Mirandula & other precoce witts." *The Diary of John Evelyn*, ed. E. S. de Beer, 6 vols. (Oxford: Clarendon Press, 1955), 4: 172–73. Cited in Levine, *The Battle of the Books*, 33.

29 Thomas Rhymer, *An Essay Concerning Critical and Curious Learning; In which are contained Some Short Reflectsion on the Controversie betwixt Sir William Temple and Mr. Wotton; And That betwixt Dr. Bentley and Mr. Boyl* (London, 1698), 47–49. R. F. Jones suggests that it was the Royal Society that engaged Wotton to answer Temple. See *Ancients and Moderns: A Study of the Rise of the Scientific Movement in Seventeenth-Century England*, 2nd ed. (St Louis: Washington University Press, 1961), 267.

30 Levine notes that the young Boyle was "ill equipped for the job" and Aldrich was not in a position to offer proper guidance or evaluation (50). The ill-fated commission was offered as a way to showcase the future aristocrat's learning and association with Christ Church. Boyle was clearly sufficiently confident in his social position to take on Wotton's friend Bentley, the royal librarian, whom he accused of refusing to lend him a manuscript. In the preface to the 1695 edition of Phalaris, he accused Bentley of showing "singular humanity" with this refusal. Swift alludes to this famous incident in the *Battel of the Books* when he makes Scaliger rail at Bentley: "*Thy* Learning *makes thee more* Barbarous, *thy Study of* Humanity, *more* Inhuman" (1: 161). See Levine, *The Battle of the Books*, 50 and Tinkler, "The Splitting of Humanism," 455. Howard Weinbrot has argued that the battle became violent because it was perceived as an attack on class and rank. See " 'He Will Kill Me Over and Over Again': Intellectual Contexts of the Battle of the Books," *Reading Swift: Papers from the Fourth Münster Symposium on Jonathan Swift*, ed. Hermann Josef Real and Helgard Stöver-Leidig (Munich: Fink, 2003), 239–47.

31 William Wotton, preface to *Reflections upon Ancient and Modern Learning* (London, 1694), n. pag.

32 For a lucid summary of the Chinese Rites Controversy in the 1630s, see Liam Brockey, *Journey to the East: The Jesuit Mission to China, 1579–1724* (Cambridge, Mass.: Belknap Press, 2007), 98–107.

33 Verbiest's letters were first published in French under the title *Voyages de l'empereur de la Chine dans la Tartarie* (Paris, 1685).

34 Harold John Cook provides a detailed account of Cleyer's troubled relationship with Willem ten Rhijne, another doctor in the service of the Dutch East India Company, who later claimed that he had been responsible for collecting

the texts that had later metamorphosed into the *Specimen*. Ten Rhijne accused Cleyer of doing little more than paying Philippe Couplet for the original translations and noted that the *Specimen* "without an Interpreter can do Little Good in Europe." See Cook, *Matters of Exchange: Commerce, Medicine, and Science in the Dutch Golden Age* (New Haven: Yale University Press, 2007), 368.

35 The *Huangdi Neijing* is an ancient Chinese medical text attributed to the legendary Yellow Emperor who conversed with his ministers about Chinese medicine. It is generally dated to the Warring States (475–221 BCE) or early Han (206 BCE–220 CE) period.

36 A discussion of Wotton's response to Chinese medicine can be found in Roberta E. Bivins, *Acupuncture, Expertise and Cross-Cultural Medicine* (Basingstoke: Palgrave, 2000), 76–78.

37 Levine, *The Battle of the Books*, 34. David Spadafora similarly describes Wotton's *Reflections* as "the most comprehensive and fair-minded contribution to the war that appeared in either France or England during the seventeenth century." See *The Idea of Progress in Eighteenth-Century Britain*, 25.

38 On this topic, see James Bono, *The Word of God and the Languages of Man: Interpreting Nature in Early Modern Science and Medicine* (Madison: University of Wisconsin Press, 1995); Lionel Jensen, *Manufacturing Confucianism: Chinese Traditions and Universal Civilization* (Durham: Duke University Press, 1997); Robert Markley, *Fallen Languages: Crises of Representation in Newtonian England* (Ithaca: Cornell University Press, 1993); David Porter, *Ideographia: The Chinese Cipher in Early Modern Europe* (Stanford: Stanford University Press, 2001); and Robert Stillman, "Assessing the Revolution: Ideology, Language, and Rhetoric in the New Philosophy of Early Modern England," *The Eighteenth Century: Theory and Interpretation* 35.2 (1994), 99–118.

39 *The Diary of John Evelyn*, 4: 172–73. Cited in Levine, *The Battle of the Books*, 33.

40 Thomas Burnet, *The Theory of the Earth, Containing an Account of the Original of the Earth, and of All the General Changes Which It Hath Already Undergone, or Is to Undergo, Till the Consummation of All Things*, 2 vols. (London, 1684), 1: 279. All subsequent references to this edition appear parenthetically by volume and page number.

41 Markley, *Fallen Languages*, 8.

42 J. E. Force, "Newton, the 'Ancients,' and the 'Moderns,'" *Newton and Religion: Context, Nature, and Influence*, ed. James E. Force and Richard Popkin (Dordrecht: Klewer, 1999), 238.

43 Markley, *Fallen Languages*, 145–69.

44 Force, "Newton, the 'Ancients,' and the 'Moderns,'" 256.

45 Ibid., 239.

46 Steven C. A. Pincus, *Protestantism and Patriotism: Ideologies and the Making of English Foreign Policy, 1650–1668* (Cambridge: Cambridge University Press, 1996), 447.

47 "I own my Apprehensions that the *Peace*, which is now in a manner concluded with *France*, may not produce those lasting good Effects, which all Honest

Men, who wish well to the *Protestant Religion*, and to *British Liberty*, desire they should"; "*France* will not, it cannot, unless it will abjure Popery, support the *Church of England*, or *Protestant Episcopacy*. The *Pretender* under any Disguize, and *British Liberty*, are inconsistent Things." Wotton, *Observations upon the State of the Nation, in January 1712/3*, 2nd ed. (London, 1713), 3, 26.

48 Wotton, *Observations*, 22.

49 The phrase "from China to Peru" also occurs in Temple's essay *Of Poetry*, where he writes: "What Honour and Request the antient Poetry has Lived in, may not only be Observed from the Universal Reception and Use in all Nations from *China* to *Peru*, from *Scythia* to *Arabia*, but from the Esteem of the Best and the Greatest Men as well as the Vulgar" (1690: 338).

50 Abraham Cowley wrote in his preface to the *Pindarique Odes* (1656): "I have in these two *Odes* of *Pindar* taken, left out, and added what I please; nor make it so much my aim to let the Reader know precisely what he spoke, as what was his way and manner of speaking" (cited in *The Cambridge Edition of the Works of Jonathan Swift*, 1: 483n78). William Davenant likewise claimed his right to stray from the ancient text in his preface to *Gondibert an Heroick Poem* (1650): "he [Homer] hath rather prov'd a Guide for those, whose satisfy'd witt will not venture beyond the track of others, then to them, who affect a new and remote way of thinking; who esteem it a deficiency and meanesse of minde, to stay and depend upon the authority of example." As Walsh points out, Temple rejected Davenant's view of Homer (cited in 1: 494n140).

51 Levine, *The Battle of the Books*, 44–45.

52 Howard D. Weinbrot, *Britannia's Issue: The Rise of British Literature from Dryden to Ossian* (Cambridge: Cambridge University Press, 1993), 27.

53 Temple's retort to this argument appears in *Some Thoughts upon the Essay*: "They allow indeed the Sweetness of the *Greek* Poetry to be inimitable, but attribute it wholly to the Language, and the Sounds and Syllables that compose it. They might as well say, the Excellence of Picture comes from the Beauty of the Colours; and of Statuary from the Fineness of the Marble" (1701: 249).

54 Thomas Sprat, *The History of the Royal-Society of London* (London, 1667), 114. Cited in Trevor Ross, *The Making of the English Literary Canon: From the Middle Ages to the Late Eighteenth Century* (Montreal: McGill-Queen's University Press, 1998), 147. Ross notes that the quarrel between the ancients and the moderns developed into "in its later phase a conflict between rhetorical and objectivist thinking, between orators and scholars, in which either side could barely comprehend the other's assumptions since these were formed according to two starkly opposed processes of thought (153).

55 Weinbrot, *Britannia's Issue*, 32.

56 Ibid., 32.

57 Charles Gildon, "To my Honoured and Ingenious Friend Mr. Harrington, for the Modern Poets against the Ancients," in *Miscellaneous Letters and Essays, On Several Subjects* (London, 1694), 223; John Denham, "The Epistle Dedicatory," *The Advancement and Reformation of Modern Poetry* (London, 1701), n. pag.

Both are mentioned in Walter Jackson Bate's *From Classic to Romantic: Premises of Taste in Eighteenth-Century England* (Cambridge, Mass.: Harvard University Press, 1946), 33–34. Bate describes Gildon as a "faithful but not quite comprehending English henchman of the French critics" and notes that Gildon believed in the moderns' greater judgment. Dennis also believed in the superiority of modern poetry, but not because of the moderns' greater fidelity to rules but rather because of their alleged ability to rouse greater passions with the help of revealed religion.

58 Pierre Motteux, "A Discourse concerning the Ancients and the Moderns," *Gentleman's Journal, or, The monthly miscellany* (March 1692), 23.

59 See Weinbrot's *Britannia's Issue*, 25–113, for an extended treatment of the process sketched here.

60 Henry Felton, *Dissertation on Reading the Classics and Forming a Just Style*, 2nd ed. (London, 1715), 148. Cited in Weinbrot, *Britannia's Issue*, 75.

61 *The Poems of Alexander Pope*, ed. John Butt (New Haven: Yale University Press, 1963), 146–47.

62 Kirsti Simonsuuri, *Homer's Original Genius: Eighteenth-Century Notions of the Early Greek Epic (1688–1798)* (Cambridge: Cambridge University Press, 1979), 26. Patey makes a similar point when he writes, "those who at first appeared friends were becoming foreigners: difference between past and present rendered problematic both the direct accessibility and continuing relevance of ancient texts." See Patey, "Ancients and Moderns," 50–51.

63 Simonsuuri, *Homer's Original Genius*, 87.

64 Following Temple, Pope portrayed these modern critics (such as Wotton) as lowly intruders who usurped authority and disrupted social order: "So modern *Pothecaries*, taught the Art / By *Doctor's Bills* to play the *Doctor's Part*, / Bold in the Practice of *mistaken Rules*, / Prescribe, apply, and call their *Masters Fools*" (*An Essay on Criticism*, lines 108–11). See *The Poems of Alexander Pope*, 147.

65 Hans Robert Jauss, "Modernity and Literary Tradition," trans. Christian Thorne, *Critical Inquiry* 31.2 (2005), 345.

66 The phrase is Douglas's. Patey writes: "the nascent historicism of the Ancients conflicts with that other Ancient premise, universal taste." See Patey, "Ancients and Moderns," 59.

67 Ibid., 34.

68 J. E. Spingarn, introduction to *Critical Essays of the Seventeenth Century* (Oxford: Clarendon Press, 1908), 1: lxxxviii. In his biography of Temple, Homer E. Woodbridge similarly points out that the quarrel was characterized by a "strange confusion through which Bentley, the greatest classical scholar of the time, was classed as a modern, and Temple, modern in many of his sympathies, as an ancient." See *Sir William Temple: The Man and His Work* (New York: Modern Language Association of America, 1940), 318.

69 See Clara Marburg, *Sir William Temple*, xv–xvii. A notable exception is René Wellek, who views Temple as a "half-hearted" ancient at best, and a pioneering modern in his "historical method": "Temple is a child of his age in remaining half-heartedly tied to the older tradition. He even, ironically enough, became

the champion of classical antiquity in the much discussed and overrated controversy between the Ancients and the Moderns. His ignorant contempt for scientific discoveries and his impatience with the complacent prophets of unlimited progress had driven him into a position which was really uncongenial to his modern mind. His part in the controversy and his unfortunate blunder about the Phalaris letters have hitherto obscured the position of Temple, who is among the chief heralds of the historical method." See Wellek, *The Rise of English Literary History* (Chapel Hill: University of North Carolina Press, 1941), 43–44.

70 Although it is likely that Temple read Fontenelle in French, the translation history of *Digression* suggests English interest in it was high and that Temple's knowledge of the text was potentially mediated by its English translators. Three rival English translations of the first 1686 edition of the *Digression* appeared in short order: William Donville's *A Discourse of the Plurality of Worlds* (Dublin, 1687), Aphra Behn's *A Discovery of New Worlds* (London, 1688) and John Glanvill's *A Plurality of Worlds* (London, 1688). For a discussion of these translations see Line Cottegnies, "The Translator as Critic: Aphra Behn's Translation of Fontenelle's *Discovery of New Worlds* (1686)," *Restoration* 27.1 (2003), esp. 23–24. On Behn's translation in particular, see, in addition to Cottegnies, Robert Markley, "Global Analogies: Cosmology, Geosymmetry, and Skepticism in Some Works of Aphra Behn," in *Science, Literature and Rhetoric in Early Modern England*, ed. Juliet Cummins and David Burchell (Aldershot: Ashgate, 2007), esp. 200–06.

71 Albert Salomon, "In Praise of the Enlightenment: In Commemoration of Fontenelle, 1657–1757," *Social Research* 24.2 (1957), 207; Douglas McKie, "Bernard Le Bovier De Fontenelle, F. R. S. 1657–1757," *Notes and Records of the Royal Society of London* 12.2 (1957), 194.

72 Herbert Dieckmann, "Philosophy and Literature in Eighteenth-Century France," *Comparative Literature Studies* 8.1 (1971), 28.

73 I quote from the most recent English translation of Fontenelle's work, *Conversations on the Plurality of Worlds*, trans. H. A. Hargreaves (Berkeley: University of California Press, 1990), 11. All subsequent references to this text will appear parenthetically.

74 A modern English translation of the *Digression* exists, but I have preferred to use my own translation in this case. The *Digression* appeared in the first French edition of *Poésies Pastorales* published in 1688. I have used the 1707 edition of the *Poésies Pastorales* which was published in French in London. All subsequent references to the *Digression* are to this 1707 French edition of the *Poésies Pastorales* and appear parenthetically.

75 The text in the original reads, "Les meilleurs ouvrages de Sophocle, d'Euripide, d'Aristophane, ne tiendront guere devant Cinna, Horace, Ariane, le Misantrope, & un grand nombre d'autres Tragedies & Comedies du bon temps; car il en faut convenir de bonne foy, il y a quelques années que ce bon temps est passé. Je ne croy pas que Theagene & Chariclée, Clitophon & Leucippe soient jamais comparez à l'Astrée, à Zayde, à la Princesse de Cleves"

(122–23). Theagenes and Charicleia are characters in Aethiopica, a Greek prose narrative by Heliodorus. Clitophon and Leucippe are characters in a romance by Achilles Tatius. See *The Continental Model: Selected French Critical Essays of the Seventeenth Century, in English Translation*, ed. Scott Elledge and Donald Schier (Minneapolis: University of Minnesota Press, 1960), 394n22.

76 In *Essay upon the Ancient and Modern Learning*, Temple tersely comments that the best proof against Fontenelle's claim here is the quality of his own poetry published in the same volume of *Poésies Pastorales* that his *Digression* appeared in: "For Grammar or Rhetorick, no Man ever disputed it with them [the ancients], nor for Poetry, that ever I heard of, besides the New *French* Author I have mentioned, and against whose Opinion there could I think, never have been given stronger Evidence, than by his own Poems, printed together with that Treatise" (1690: 44).

77 Florence C. Hsia's *Sojourners in a Strange Land: Jesuits and Their Scientific Missions in Late Imperial China* (Chicago: University of Chicago Press, 2009) contains a brief discussion of Fontenelle's skeptical attitude toward the Jesuit accounts of China. See 135–37.

78 Arthur O. Lovejoy, "The Chinese Origin of a Romanticism," *Essays in the History of Ideas* (Baltimore: Johns Hopkins University Press, 1978), 113.

79 Ibid., 100.

80 Patey, "Ancients and Moderns," 65.

81 Julian Martin, "Francis Bacon, Authority, and the Moderns," in *The Rise of Modern Philosophy: The Tension between the New and Traditional Philosophies from Machiavelli to Leibniz* (Oxford: Oxford University Press, 1993), 88.

82 Kristine Louise Haugen, *Richard Bentley: Poetry and Enlightenment* (Cambridge, Mass.: Harvard University Press, 2011), 277n45; Woodbridge, *Sir William Temple*, 318–19.

Chapter 2: Robinson Crusoe and the Great Wall of China

1 Defoe, *A General History of Discoveries and Improvements, In useful Arts, Particularly in the great Branches of Commerce, Navigation, Plantation, in all parts of the known World*, 4 nos. (London, 1725–26), 4: 233–38. All subsequent references to this text will appear parenthetically by number and page number.

2 See Ilse Vickers's *Defoe and the New Sciences* (Cambridge: Cambridge University Press, 1996), esp. 74–80 for a discussion of Defoe's position in the quarrel between the ancients and the moderns. Vickers argues throughout her book that Defoe shows "his conscious alignment" with Baconian science (76). She does not discuss Temple and Wotton, however, and does not refer to China in her discussion of the *Consolidator* (69–73).

3 The full title reads *The Consolidator: Or, Memoirs of Sundry Transactions from the World in the Moon. Translated from the Lunar Language, By the Author of The True-born English Man* (London, 1705). All subsequent references to this text will appear parenthetically by publication year and page number. Defoe clearly thought highly enough of this work to set his name to it, although

it appears to have attracted little attention. For a brief discussion of the reception of *Consolidator*, see Max Novak, *Daniel Defoe: Master of Fictions* (Oxford: Oxford University Press, 2001), 253–54. The most detailed treatment of Defoe's *Consolidator* in the context of the quarrel between the ancients and the moderns is Narelle L. Shaw's "Ancients and Moderns in Defoe's *Consolidator*," *Studies in English Literature, 1500–1900* 28.3 (1988), 391–400.

4 Michael Adas, *Machines as the Measure of Men: Science, Technology, and Ideologies of Western Dominance* (Ithaca: Cornell University Press, 1989), 52.

5 Tommaso Campanella, *La Città del Sole* (1623); *Hakluytus Posthumous, or Purchas his Pilgrimes, contayning a History of the World in Sea Voyages* (1623). Cited in E. H. Gombrich, "Eastern Inventions and Western Response," *Daedalus* 127.1 (1998), 199–200. Gombrich concludes his essay with a stunning recapitulation of the thesis advanced by Wotton in the late seventeenth century: "In the venerable civilizations of the East, custom was king and tradition the guiding principle. If change came it was all but imperceptible, for the laws of Heaven existed once and for all and were not to be questioned. That spirit of questioning, the systematic rejection of authority, was the one invention the East may have failed to develop. It originated in ancient Greece" (202).

6 We do not know if Defoe had a specific text in mind, but the kind of rhetoric he is mocking may be illustrated by the following passage in Magalhães's *A New History of China*: "The Kingdom is so Ancient that it has preserv'd its form of Government, and has continu'd during the Reign of Twenty Two Families, from whence have descended Two Hundred Thirty Six Kings for the space of Four Thousand and Twenty Five Years." Magalhães calculated that "should we rest satisfi'd with what they look upon to be very probable, it would be Four Thousand Six Hundred and Twenty to this present Year 1668" – a number he had difficulty accepting at face value, however (59).

7 Shaw points out that Temple expressed reservations about Harvey's 'discovery' of the circulation of the blood. See Shaw, "Ancients and Moderns in Defoe's *Consolidator*," 395.

8 Ibid., 391–92.

9 Max Novak, *Daniel Defoe: Master of Fictions*, 253–54. Novak summarizes Defoe's relationship to Swift in the following way: Defoe "was too much of a modern himself truly to enjoy the wickedness of Swift's satire on contemporary philosophical systems, and too much a religious enthusiast to appreciate Swift's negative attitude toward enthusiasm in religion" (254). Swift refers to "*Chinese* Waggons, which were made so light as to sail over Mountains" in section 4 of *A Tale of a Tub*, *The Cambridge Edition of the Works of Jonathan Swift*, 1: 77. Frances Wood writes, "It is probably that the reference originates in Mendoza and refers to the sails sometimes hauled up over wheelbarrows in China to help them move faster under favourable conditions, though not to sail over mountains." See Wood, *The Lure of China: Writers from Marco Polo to J. G. Ballard* (San Francisco: Long River Press, 2009), 30.

10 I cite the following editions: *The Life and Strange Surprizing Adventures of Robinson Crusoe*, ed. W. R. Owens, vol. 1 of *The Novels of Daniel Defoe*

(London: Pickering & Chatto, 2008); *The Farther Adventures of Robinson Crusoe*, ed. W. R. Owens, vol. 2 of *The Novels of Daniel Defoe*; *Serious Reflections during the Life and Surprising Adventures of Robinson Crusoe*, ed. G. A. Starr, vol. 3 of *The Novels of Daniel Defoe*. Subsequent references to the trilogy will be made by volume and page number and will appear parenthetically.

11 See Qian Zhongshu's bibliographic essays "China in the English Literature of the Seventeenth Century" and "China in the English Literature of the Eighteenth Century" in *The Vision of China in the English Literature of the Seventeenth and Eighteenth Centuries*, ed. Adrian Hsia (Hong Kong: Chinese University Press, 1998), 59, 119.

12 The phrase comes from Srinivas Aravamudan, "Defoe, Commerce, and Empire," in *The Cambridge Companion to Daniel Defoe*, ed. John Richetti (Cambridge: Cambridge University Press, 2008), 52.

13 Charles H. Parker, *Global Interactions in the Early Modern Age, 1400–1800* (Cambridge: Cambridge University Press, 2010), 3.

14 See Lucinda Cole's recent discussion of Crusoe's implausibly "ratless island economy" in *Imperfect Creatures: Vermin, Literature, and the Sciences of Life, 1600–1740* (Ann Arbor: University of Michigan Press, 2016), 147, 148. Cole takes the term "apparitional" from John Bender's *Ends of Enlightenment*, though she uses it in a new ecological context.

15 Roy S. Wolper, "The Rhetoric of Gunpowder and the Idea of Progress," *Journal of the History of Ideas* 31.4 (1970), 595, 593.

16 George Hakewill, *An Apologie or Declaration of the Power and Providence of God* (London, 1635), 320. Cited in Wolper, "The Rhetoric of Gunpowder and the Idea of Progress," 595.

17 Joseph Glanvill, *Plus Ultra* (London, 1668), 81–82. Cited in Wolper, "The Rhetoric of Gunpowder and the Idea of Progress," 596–97.

18 Wotton includes "*Chymistry*, and *Anatomy*" in this list, but I have omitted them here because they are not instruments in the same sense as the other items (1694: 170).

19 Wotton mentions gunpowder briefly in the preface to the 1694 *Reflections* when he suggests that the Turks were "taught" gunpowder by the Christians: "Are the *Turks* so barbarous, or so spightful to themselves, that they will not use Gun-powder, because it was taught them by *Christians*?" (n. pag.).

20 I borrow this phrase from Carlo M. Cipolla's *Guns and Sails in the Early Phase of European Expansion, 1400–1700* (London: Collins, 1965).

21 For a discussion of the novel as a modern adventure tale, see Martin Green, *Dreams of Adventure, Deeds of Empire* (New York: Basic Books, 1979).

22 Joan DeJean, "No Man's Land: The Novel's First Geography," *Yale French Studies* 73 (1987), 188–89.

23 Ibid., 181.

24 Ibid., 181–82.

25 Ibid., 182, 177, 181.

26 Ibid., 179.

27 Ibid., 181.

28 Ibid., 176–77, 179.
29 Robin Evans, "The Rights of Retreat and the Rites of Exclusion: Notes Towards the Definition of Wall," in *Translations from Drawing to Building and Other Essays* (London: Architectural Association, 1997), 36.
30 Ibid., 38. For this very reason, Evans finds it particularly interesting that it was the same Chinese king, Qin Shi Huang (259 BCE–210 BCE), who conceived of the Great Wall and ordered the famous burning of the books. See Evans, "The Rights of Retreat and the Rites of Exclusion," 40.
31 Ibid., 45, 40.
32 Patricia Seed, *Ceremonies of Possession in Europe's Conquest of the New World, 1492–1640* (Cambridge: Cambridge University Press, 1995), 21, 19.
33 In her interesting study of the publication history of the Crusoe trilogy, Melissa Free documents that the Crusoe books were almost always published in two- or three-volume form in the eighteenth century. The first two books continued to be published as a unit until the end of the nineteenth century, and it is not until after World War I that the second volume drops out of view. See "Un-Erasing *Crusoe*: *Farther Adventures* in the Nineteenth Century," *Book History* 9 (2006), 91–93.
34 Christopher Hill, "Robinson Crusoe," *History Workshop* 10 (1980), 20.
35 The massacre is prompted by the lynching of one of the shipmates by the natives as punishment for his offense of having "violated, or debauch'd" a young native woman (2: 139). The shipmen retaliate with a bloody and indiscriminate massacre of the natives.
36 "The Company consisted of People of several Nations, such as *Muscovites* chiefly, for there were above sixty of them who were Merchants or Inhabitants of *Moscow*, though of them, some were *Livonians*, and to our particular Satisfaction, Five of them were *Scots*, who appeared also to be Men of great Experience in Business, and Men of very good Substance" (2: 180).
37 Similarly, when Crusoe later visits the "City of *Naum*," "a Frontier of the *Chinese* Empire," he comments: "they call it fortify'd, and so it is, as Fortifications go there; for this I will venture to affirm, that all the *Tartars* in *Karakathie*, which I believe, are some Millions, could not batter down the Walls with their Bows and Arrows; but to call it strong, if it were attack'd with Cannon, would be to make those who understand it, laugh at you" (2: 188).
38 In her brief discussion of this scene, Julia Lovell notes that "Defoe's armchair fulminations against China and its wall ... could have come out of the mouth of any of nineteenth-century Britain's gunboat diplomats." See *The Great Wall: China Against the World, 1000 BC–AD 2000* (New York: Grove Press, 2006), 282. For a discussion of the connections between Defoe's mockery of Chinese military science and earlier European exponents of similar views such as Galeote Pereira, see Jonathan Spence, *The Chan's Great Continent: China in Western Minds* (New York: W. W. Norton, 1998), 20–21, 67–68.
39 Anthony Pagden, *European Encounters with the New World from Renaissance to Romanticism* (New Haven: Yale University Press, 1993), 51.

40 Crusoe's description of the Chinese reaction to the solar eclipse is clearly indebted to the following passage in Le Comte's *Memoirs and Observations Made in a Late Journey through the Empire of China* (London, 1697): "They have fancied that in Heaven there is a prodigious great Dragon, who is a professed Enemy to the Sun and Moon, and ready at all times to eat them up. For this reason, as soon as they perceive an Eclipse, they all make a terrible rattling with Drums and brass Kettles, till the Monster frightned at the noise has let go his Prey" (72).

41 Ian Watt, *The Rise of the Novel: Studies in Defoe, Richardson, and Fielding* (Berkeley: University of California Press, 1957), 29, 32.

42 Susan Stewart, *On Longing: Narratives of the Miniature, the Gigantic, the Souvenir, the Collection* (Baltimore: Johns Hopkins University Press, 1984), 71.

43 Ibid., 68.

44 Evans, "The Rights of Retreat and the Rites of Exclusion," 45, 38.

45 Cole, *Imperfect Creatures*, 165. On Defoe's repeated denial of native Caribbean technology as evinced in Defoe's 'invention' of the barbecue and canoe, see Peter Hulme, *Colonial Encounters: Europe and the Native Caribbean, 1492–1797* (London: Methuen, 1986), 210–11. In *Farther Adventures*, Defoe makes sure that basket-weaving skill is imparted to the native Caribbeans by the English.

46 Hulme, *Colonial Encounters*, 40.

47 Timothy Billings, "Visible Cities: The Heterotopic Utopia of China in Early Modern European Writing," *Genre* 30 (1997), 114–15.

48 Johann Nieuhof, *An Embassy from the East-India Company of the United Provinces, to the Grand Tartar Cham, Emperor of China* (London, 1669), 322.

49 Ibid., 7.

50 Paris manuscript (ca. 1370) of Mandeville's *Travels*, II. 349, cited in Billings, "Visible Cities," 114.

51 Billings, "Visible Cities," 113.

52 Semedo, *The History of That Great and Renowned Monarchy of China*, 3–4.

53 Magalhães, *A New History of China*, 133, 139, 142–43.

54 Daniel Defoe, *The Advantages of Peace and Commerce; With Some Remarks on the East-India Trade* (London, 1729), 17. All subsequent references to this text will appear parenthetically preceded by the year of publication.

55 *Atlas Maritimus & Commercialis; Or, A General View of the World So far as relates to Trade and Navigation* (London, 1728), 100. All subsequent references to this text will appear parenthetically preceded by the year of publication.

56 See Max Novak, *Economics and the Fiction of Daniel Defoe* (Berkeley: University of California Press, 1962), esp. 1–31.

57 See Peter C. Perdue, "Boundaries and Trade in the Early Modern World: Negotiations at Nerchinsk and Beijing," *Eighteenth-Century Studies* 43.3 (2010), 341–56.

58 The Treaty of Nerchinsk established the geographical boundaries between Russia and China and created a strategic allegiance between these empires, providing security to the Chinese and trade to the Russians. As Mark Mancall

notes, however, the Nerchinsk Treaty was basically a peace treaty and was "only vague and permissive" as to the future conduct of Sino-Russian relations, especially with regard to commerce. It left open to each state the question of how to regulate and develop the Sino-Russian trade. See Mark Mancall, *Russia and China: Their Diplomatic Relations to 1728* (Cambridge, Mass.: Harvard University Press, 1971), 163–87. See also Peter Perdue, "Boundaries and Trade in the Early Modern World: Negotiations at Nerchinsk and Beijing" and *China Marches West: The Qing Conquest of Central Eurasia* (Cambridge, Mass.: Belknap Press, 2005), esp. 161–73. For a summary of the provisions made by the Kyakhta treaty, see Mancall, *Russia and China*, 249–55.

59　The next trade treaty between China and Russia, the later Kyakhta Treaty, was established in 1727, and is thus not relevant to our reading of the novel. However, it is noteworthy that Defoe displays up-to-date knowledge of this later treaty in *Advantages of Peace and Commerce*.

60　Perdue, *China Marches West*, 161.

61　Mancall, *Russia and China*, 185.

62　Aparna Dharwadker, "Nation, Race, and the Ideology of Commerce in Defoe," *The Eighteenth Century: Theory and Interpretation* 39.1 (1998), 79.

63　Adam Brand's account appeared in a German edition published in Hamburg in 1698; it ran through four German editions before appearing in Dutch translation in 1698. An English translation was printed in the same year. Ides's own account was first published in Dutch in Amsterdam in 1704, then translated into English in 1706 and into German in 1707. A second Dutch edition appeared in 1710. In a letter written to Cuper, Witsen claimed that he had written the Ides book based on his notes: "The description of Isbrandts is composed by me, as it is published in papers which he had sent to me which were very confusedly written in Hamburgish or Lower-Saxon." See Johannes Keuning, "Nicolaas Witsen as a Cartographer," *Imago Mundi* 11 (1954), 107; Marion Peters, *De wijze koopman: Her wereldwijde onderzoek van Nicolaes Witsen (1641–1717), burgemeester en VOC-bewindhebber van Amsterdam* (Amsterdam: Bert Bakker, 2010), 118–22; Donald F. Lach and Edwin J. Van Kley, *A Century of Advance*, vol. 3, book 1 of *Asia in the Making of Europe* (Chicago: University of Chicago Press, 1993), 503–04. The importance of Ides's book as a source for Defoe is noted in Arthur Wellesley Secord, *Studies in the Narrative Method of Defoe* (Urbana: University of Illinois Press, 1924), 68–74, and Markley, *The Far East and the English Imagination*, 129–36. Subsequent to writing my chapter, I discovered that Richard Bridges identified Brand as a source for *Farther Adventures* back in 1979. See Bridges, "A Possible Source for Daniel Defoe's *The Farther Adventures of Robinson Crusoe*," *British Journal for Eighteenth-Century Studies* 2.3 (1979), 231–36. I would like to thank Martin Heijdra at Princeton's Gest Library for helping me uncover bibliographical material on Brand and Ides.

64　Mancall, *Russia and China*, 188.

65　Ides had been entrusted with the mission of negotiating the extradition of fugitives, the establishment of a Russian church in Beijing, and permission for

Chinese merchants to travel to Moscow. Because of the diplomatic *faux pas* of inscribing the tsar's name before the Chinese emperor's on official papers, however, Ides was not allowed to conclude any official political business. He was received nonetheless by the emperor and higher officials who treated them to banquets and entertainments, including Chinese plays, and was allowed to circulate freely in Beijing to gather commercial information and to trade privately. See Mancall, *Russia and China*, 190, 193.

66 Ibid., 193.

67 "An Account of a Large and Curious Map of the Great Tartary, lately Publish'd in Holland, by Mr. Nicholas Witsen, being an Extract of a Letter from the Author thereof, to the Honourable Sir Robert Southwell Knt. and President of the Royal Society," *Philosophical Transactions* 16 (1686–1692), 492.

68 Ides, The Author's Epistle Dedicatory, *Three Years Travels from Moscow Over-Land to China* (London, 1706), n. pag.

69 Defoe followed Brand's text for the names of the Russian cities. The Russian city names he gives in *Farther Adventures* (Nortzinskoy, Jarawena, Adinskoy, Janezay, Tobolski, Arch-Angel) follow closely (with minor variations) the names provided by Brand (Nartzinskoy, Jerawena, Jenessay, Tobolsko, Archangel). Ides uses longer, much more Russian-sounding names.

70 Brand, *A Journal of the Embassy from their Majesties John and Peter Alexievitz, Emperors of Muscovy &c. Over Land into China*, 112.

71 Ibid., 30.

72 Ides, *Three Years Travels from Moscow Over-Land to China*, 12–13, 19, 30, 34, 54.

73 I have benefited from Hans Turley's discussion of this scene in *Rum, Sodomy, and the Lash: Piracy, Sexuality, and Masculine Identity* (New York: New York University Press, 1999), 154–55.

74 Hans Turley, "The Sublimation of Desire to Apocalyptic Passion in Defoe's Crusoe Trilogy," in *Imperial Desire: Dissident Sexualities and Colonial Literature*, ed. Philip Holden and Richard J. Ruppel (Minneapolis: University of Minnesota Press, 2003), 16.

75 The story of Alexander's walls appears in *The Travels of Marco Polo* and *The Travels of Sir John Mandeville*.

76 Arthur Waldron, *The Great Wall of China: From History to Myth* (Cambridge: Cambridge University Press, 1990), 203–04.

77 This and many other maps mentioned in this section are beautifully reproduced in Kenneth Nebenzahl's *Mapping the Silk Road and Beyond: 2,000 Years of Exploring the East* (London: Phaidon, 2004).

78 The inscription was done in Latin; I use Nebenzahl's translation. See *Mapping the Silk Road and Beyond*, 130–31.

79 Kircher, "Some Special Remarks Taken out of Athanasius Kircher's Antiquities of China," 99. In his article "'That mighty Wall, not fabulous / China's stupendous mound!': Romantic Period Accounts of China's 'Great Wall,'" Peter Kitson notes that the prevailing adjective for the Great Wall in Romantic writings is not 'sublime' but 'stupendous' – a word with far more ambivalent connotations. One of my anonymous readers for Cambridge University Press

pointed out to me that it is possible that Martini is an important source for this use of the word. See Kitson's article in *New Directions in Travel Writing Studies*, ed. Paul Smethurst and Julia Kuehn (New York: Palgrave Macmillan, 2015), 83–96.

80 Ibid., 100.

81 See Lach and Van Kley, *A Century of Advance*, vol. 3, book 4 of *Asia in the Making of Europe*, 1646.

82 Nieuhof states: "This great Work was begun … two hundred years before *Christ's* Birth" as a defense against the Tartars by a Chinese emperor who "employ'd so great number of Workmen, that it was finish'd in five years"; "Through all *China* the Emperor commanded three Men out of ten to work upon this Wall, who is so well built, and so strong, that there is not the least crack in it. This Wall is admirable, not only for the length and breadth, but in regard of its durableness, having lasted for so many Ages without alteration, being as entire as when it was first built." *An Embassy from the East-India Company of the United Provinces, to the Grand Tartar Cham, Emperor of China*, 131.

83 Brand, *A Journal of the Embassy from their Majesties John and Peter Alexievitz, Emperors of Muscovy &c. Over Land into China*, 77, 102.

84 Ides, *Three Years Travels from Moscow Over-Land to China*, 161.

85 Ibid., 60–61.

86 D. E. Mungello, *Curious Land: Jesuit Accommodation and the Origins of Sinology* (Honolulu: University of Hawaii Press, 1985), 120–21; Nebenzahl, *Mapping the Silk Road*, 128, 136.

87 Hilde De Weerdt, "Maps and Memory: Readings of Cartography in Twelfth- and Thirteenth-Century Song China," *Imago Mundi* 61.2 (2009), 158–60.

88 Ibid., 161–63. On the increasing divergence between European and Chinese discourses on the Great Wall, see Carlos Rojas, *The Great Wall: A Cultural History* (Cambridge, Mass.: Harvard University Press, 2010), 92–125.

89 I am grateful to Paize Keulemans for sharing his reading of this frontispiece in his paper "Translating Empire: Vondel's *Zungchin* and the Fall of the Ming Dynasty," a paper delivered at a conference on *The Dutch Golden Age and the World* at Columbia University in March 2007.

90 Waldron, *The Great Wall of China*, 191.

91 Semedo, *The History of That Great and Renowned Monarchy of China*, 51.

92 Magalhães, *A New History of China*, 61–62.

93 Matthew H. Edney, "The Irony of Imperial Mapping," *The Imperial Map: Cartography and the Mastery of Empire*, ed. James R. Akerman (Chicago: University of Chicago Press, 2009), 13.

94 Ibid.

95 Christian Jacob, *The Sovereign Map: Theoretical Approaches in Cartography throughout History*, trans. Tom Conley (Chicago: University of Chicago Press, 2006), 134, 273.

96 Bernhard Klein, *Maps and the Writing of Space in Early Modern England and Ireland* (New York: Palgrave, 2001), 88.

97 Daniel Defoe, *The Compleat English Gentleman*, ed. Karl D. Bülbring (London: David Nutt, 1890), 225–26. I have preserved the original (mis) spelling of the words.

98 Ibid.

99 Compare Sir Thomas Elyot's praise of maps in *The Book Named the Governor*. See Bernhard Klein, *Maps and the Writing of Space in Early Modern England and Ireland* (New York: Palgrave, 2001), 85–86.

100 Robert J. Mayhew, *Enlightenment Geography: The Political Languages of British Geography, 1650–1850* (New York: St. Martin's Press, 2000), 26.

101 Dennis Reinhartz, *The Cartographer and the Literati: Herman Moll and His Intellectual Circle* (Lewiston, NY: E. Mellen Press, 1997), 88.

102 Mary Louise Pratt, *Imperial Eyes: Travel Writing and Transculturation* (London: Routledge, 1992), 29.

Chapter 3: China in *The Spectator*

1 This essay was published in the first *Miscellanea* (London, 1680). All subsequent references to this text will appear parenthetically, preceded by the year of publication.

2 See Martina Scholtens, "The Glorification of Gout in 16th- to 18th-Century Literature," *Canadian Medical Association Journal* 179.8 (2008), 805.

3 See Roberta Bivins, *Acupuncture, Expertise and Cross-Cultural Medicine* (Basingstoke: Palgrave, 2000), 72–73; Harold Cook, *Matters of Exchange: Commerce, Medicine, and Science in the Dutch Golden Age* (New Haven: Yale University Press, 2007), 350–51; Lisa Jardine, *Going Dutch: How England Plundered Holland's Glory* (London: Harper, 2008), 343.

4 Jardine, *Going Dutch*, 341–45. For a full account of the Royal Society's response, see Cook, *Matters of Exchange*, 371–77. The reference to moxa as an "Indian" cure is probably due to its initial discovery in the Dutch East Indies. As Linda Barnes notes in *Needles, Herbs, Gods, and Ghosts* (Cambridge, Mass.: Harvard University Press, 2005), it is not clear that Temple made the connection between moxibustion and Chinese medicine, but by the early 1680s Abraham Janusz Gehema had identified moxa as Chinese, and Willem ten Rhijne, a VOC doctor and botanist who was sent to Dejima, Japan, had described it as a Japanese and Chinese cure (111). I would like to thank Harold Cook for discussing this issue with me.

5 Rajani Sudan, *The Alchemy of Empire: Abject Materials and the Technologies of Colonialism* (New York: Fordham University Press, 2016), 41.

6 Woodbridge, *Sir William Temple: The Man and His Work*, 323–24. Woodbridge notes that Temple's style was praised by Swift, Hughes, Johnson, and Blair.

7 John Dunton later explained that he was "obliged by authority" to change his title to *The Athenian Mercury* after the first few numbers. *The Athenian Gazette* was apparently too similar to *The London Gazette*. See Walter Graham, *The Beginnings of English Literary Periodicals* (London: Oxford University Press, 1926), 16–17. J. Paul Hunter notes that *The Athenian Library* (1725), a later collection of items from *The Athenian Mercury*, was advertised as "a universal entertainment for the lovers of novelty." See Hunter, *Before Novels: The Cultural Contexts of Eighteenth-Century English Fiction* (New York: W. W. Norton, 1990), 359n21.

8 Graham, *The Beginnings of English Literary Periodicals*, 17.

9 Dunton loved to cite the following lines by Robert Wilde: "We are all tainted with the *Athenian itch* / News, and new Things do the whole World bewitch." See *Poems on Several Occasions* (London, 1683), 83. Cited in Hunter, *Before Novels*, 359n23.

10 *Athenian Gazette*, March 17, 1690. Cited in Gilbert D. McEwen, *The Oracle of the Coffee House: John Dunton's* Athenian Mercury (San Marino: Huntington Library, 1972), 23.

11 John Dunton, *The Life and Errors of John Dunton, Late Citizen of London* (London, 1705), 261. Cited in McEwen, *The Oracle of the Coffee House*, 46n2. This piece, which appeared in the December 22, 1691 issue of *The Athenian Mercury*, overlaps with Temple's gout essay in its concern with medical ailments and various superstitious responses to them.

12 J. H. Plumb, "The Acceptance of Modernity," in *The Birth of a Consumer Society: The Commercialization of Eighteenth-Century England*, ed. Neil McKendrick, John Brewer and J. H. Plumb (Bloomington: Indiana University Press, 1982), 316–34.

13 All references to Addison and Steele's *Spectator* are to Donald Bond's five-volume edition (Oxford: Clarendon Press, 1965). All subsequent references will be made parenthetically by volume and page number.

14 Scott Black, "Social and Literary Form in the *Spectator*," *Eighteenth-Century Studies* 33.1 (1999), 26. For the argument that "novelty is the central category" in Addison's aesthetics, see also Black's "Addison's Aesthetics of Novelty," *Studies in Eighteenth-Century Culture* 30 (2001), 269–88.

15 Addison writes in *Spectator* no. 249, "When I make Choice of a Subject that has not been treated of by others, I throw together my Reflections on it without any Order or Method, so that they may appear rather in the Looseness and Freedom of an Essay, than in the Regularity of a set Discourse" (2: 465).

16 Tony C. Brown, "Joseph Addison and the Pleasures of *Sharawadgi*," *English Literary History* 74 (2007), 171–72, 175, 179.

17 Ibid., 173. By making China stand in for "a kind of floating framework" for Addisonian aesthetics, Brown's deconstructive reading simultaneously empties China of all historical reference and universalizes its aesthetic significance (188). I believe Brown's reading runs the risk of overgeneralization and does not do justice to the specificity of the aesthetic experience of the *new*.

18 Hans Robert Jauss, "Modernity and Literary Tradition," *Critical Inquiry* 31.2 (2005), 332.

19 Matei Calinescu, *Five Faces of Modernity: Modernism, Avant-Garde, Decadence, Kitsch, Postmodernism* (Durham: Duke University Press, 1987), 3. Calinescu is speaking here about a fundamental change that occurred, in his estimation, in the late eighteenth and early nineteenth centuries. I am proposing that we can see an earlier version of this shift in Addison's eighteenth-century aesthetics.

20 Stacey Sloboda, *Chinoiserie: Commerce and Critical Ornament in Eighteenth-Century Britain* (Manchester: University of Manchester Press, 2014), 6, 9–10.

21 Hunter, *Before Novels*, 167.

22 Ibid., 167, 168.

23 Ibid., 15.

24 Cited in Sara Warneke, "A Taste for Newfangledness: The Destructive Potential of Novelty in Early Modern England," *The Sixteenth Century Journal* 26.4 (1995), 885. Warneke notes that critics resorted to England's island geography and changeable climate to explain this peculiarly English vice. Their primary focus was thus diagnostic rather than causal (climate and geography being constants that cannot be changed).

25 "The good Queen far from designing any injury to the country where she was so entirely belov'd, little thought she was in either of these laying a foundation for such fatal excesses, and would not doubt have been the first to have reform'd them had she lived to see it." Daniel Defoe, *A Tour through the Whole Island of Great Britain*, ed. P. N. Furbank and W. R. Owens (New Haven: Yale University Press, 1991), 65.

26 Defoe is referring here to the Calico Acts of 1700 and 1721. See Defoe, *A Tour through the Whole Island of Great Britain*, 380n37. On Defoe's economic views, see Max Novak, *Economics and the Fiction of Daniel Defoe* (Berkeley: University of California Press, 1962), esp. 1–31. On calico and silk imports, see K. N. Chaudhuri, *The Trading World of Asia and the English East India Company, 1660–1760* (Cambridge: Cambridge University Press, 1978), 277–81; Woodruff D. Smith, *Consumption and the Making of Respectability, 1600–1800* (London: Routledge, 2002), 46–62.

27 Defoe, *A Tour through the Whole Island of Great Britain*, 65.

28 On the importance of tea and the growing British empire, see Philip Lawson's "Tea, Vice and the English State, 1660–1784" in *A Taste for Empire and Glory: Studies in British Overseas Expansion, 1660–1800* (Aldershot, Hampshire: Variorum, 1997); Eugenia Zuroski Jenkins, "Tea and the Limits of Orientalism in De Quincey's *Confessions of an English Opium-Eater*," in *Writing China: Essays on the Amherst Embassy (1816) and Sino-British Cultural Relations*, ed. Peter Kitson and Robert Markley, 105–31. On porcelain, see Robert Finlay's "The Pilgrim Art: The Culture of Porcelain in World History," *Journal of World History* 9.2 (1998), 141–87.

29 Anna Somers Cocks, "The Nonfunctional Use of Ceramics in the English Country House During the Eighteenth Century," in *The Fashioning and Functioning of the British Country House*, ed. Gervase Jackson-Stops, Gordon

J. Schochet, Lena Cowen Orlin and Elisabeth Blair MacDougall (Washington, D.C.: National Gallery of Art, 1989), 195–215. For illustrated examples of tea and coffee sets, as well as dinner service plates and dishes, see David Howard, *The Choice of the Private Trader: The Private Market in Chinese Export Porcelain* (London: Zwemmer, 1994).

30 See James Walvin, *Fruits of Empire: Exotic Produce and British Taste, 1660–1800* (Basingstoke: Macmillan, 1997), 16; Romita Ray, "Storm in a Teacup? Visualising Tea Consumption in the British Empire," in *Art and the British Empire*, ed. T. J. Barringer, Geoff Quilley and Douglas Fordham (Manchester: Manchester University Press, 2007), 205–22. See also Elizabeth Kowaleski-Wallace, *Consuming Subjects: Women, Shopping, and Business in the Eighteenth Century* (New York: Columbia University Press, 1996), 19–36, and Philip Lawson's essay "Women and the Empire of Tea: Image and Counter-Image in Hanoverian England" in *A Taste for Empire and Glory.*

31 On the imbrication of femininity in the consumption of chinoiserie, see Porter, *The Chinese Taste in Eighteenth-Century England*, esp. 57–77, 133–53; Stacey Sloboda, *Chinoiserie*, esp. 108–58; Zuroski Jenkins, *A Taste for China*, esp. 52–58.

32 Kathryn Shevelow, *Women and Print Culture: The Construction of Femininity in the Early Periodical* (London: Routledge, 1989), esp. 132–40; Kowaleski-Wallace, *Consuming Subjects*, 20.

33 Amanda Vickery, *Behind Closed Doors: At Home in Georgian England* (New Haven: Yale University Press, 2009), 272.

34 Ibid., 290, 274.

35 James H. Bunn, "The Aesthetics of British Mercantilism," *New Literary History* 11.2 (1980), 302–09.

36 Ronald Paulson, *The Beautiful, Novel, and Strange: Aesthetics and Heterodoxy* (Baltimore: Johns Hopkins University Press, 1996), 49. For the changing meanings of novelty in the eighteenth century, see also Julie Park, *The Self and It: Novel Objects in Eighteenth-Century England* (Stanford: Stanford University Press, 2010).

37 Porter, *The Chinese Taste in Eighteenth-Century England*, 29.

38 See, for instance, Y. Z. Chang, "A Note on Sharawadgi," *Modern Language Notes* 45.4 (1930), 221–24; Qian Zhongshu, "China in the English Literature of the Seventeenth Century"; S. Lang and Nikolaus Pevsner, "Sir William Temple and Sharawadgi," *The Architectural Review* 106 (1949), 391–92; Takau Shimada, "Is Sharawadgi Derived from the Japanese Word Sorowaji?" *The Review of English Studies* 48: 191 (1997), 350–52; Ciaran Murray, "Sharawadgi Resolved," *Garden History* 26.2 (1998), 208–13. Chang and Qian propose different possible Chinese sources that have the disadvantage of being unrelated to actual usage; Shimada proposes that the word may be a garbled version of the archaic version of a Japanese word "sawaraji" meaning "leaving things as they are"; Murray suggests that Temple heard another Japanese word "sorowaji" meaning "not regular" from Dutch men who had visited the gardens of Kyoto. Lang and Pevsner believe that the word is Temple's invention.

39 *The Diary of John Evelyn,* 4: 288. See B. Sprague Allen, *Tides in English Taste (1619–1800): A Background for the Study of Literature,* 2 vols. (Cambridge, Mass.: Harvard University Press, 1937), 1: 202.

40 Dorothy Osborne to William Temple, February 19, 1654, *The Letters of Dorothy Osborne to William Temple,* ed. G. C. Moore Smith (Oxford: Clarendon Press, 1928), 148. In the passage immediately following this mention of "a China Trunke," Osborne goes on to tell Temple that she has been reading about China: "(by the way) (this putts mee in minde ont) have you read the Story of China written by a Portuguese, Fernando Mendez Pinto I think his name is? if you have not, take it with you, tis as diverting a book of the kinde as ever I read, and is as handsomly written. you must allow him the Priviledge of a Travellour & hee dos not abuse it, his lyes are as pleasant harmlesse on's as lyes can be, and in noe great number considering the scope hee has for them" (148). This letter illustrates the degree to which artifacts from and books about China were entering into learned conversation by the mid-seventeenth century.

41 Finlay, "The Pilgrim Art," 150–52.

42 S. A. M. Adshead, *Material Culture in Europe and China, 1400–1800: The Rise of Consumerism* (Basingstoke: Macmillan, 1997), 85.

43 James C. Y. Watt, introduction to *East Asian Lacquer: The Florence and Herbert Irving Collection,* ed. James C. Y. Watt and Barbara Brennan Ford (New York: The Metropolitan Museum of Art, 1991), 10.

44 Finlay, "The Pilgrim Art," 154–55.

45 Ibid., 157; H. A. Crosby Forbes, *Hills and Streams: Landscape Decoration on Chinese Export Blue and White Porcelain* (Milton, Mass.: The China Trade Museum, 1982), n. pag.

46 Christiaan J. A. Jörg and Jan van Campen, *Chinese Ceramics in the Collection of the Rijksmuseum, Amsterdam: The Ming and Qing Dynasties* (London: Philip Wilson, in association with the Rijksmuseum, Amsterdam, 1997), 55. The Dutch East India trade in Chinese porcelain was initiated after the successful capture and sale of Portuguese cargoes in 1602 and 1604. The porcelain was dubbed 'Kraak' after the type of Portuguese merchant vessel, 'caracca,' from which it was first seized.

47 Jörg and van Campen, *Chinese Ceramics in the Collection of the Rijksmuseum, Amsterdam,* 55, 74. Jörg and van Campen note that the term 'transitional porcelain' was coined by Soame Jenyns in his book *Later Chinese Porcelain* (1951) and that it covers porcelain produced during the reigns of the Tianqi (1621–27), Chongzhen (1628–44), Shunzi (1644–61) emperors, and the early period of emperor Kangxi's rule (1662–1722). Export supply diminished drastically during the 1640s, however, with the VOC ceasing to buy about 1650, after which private traders carried on an erratic and limited trade. Transitional ware was made of finer clay than Kraak porcelain and decorated very differently, "with running landscapes or river scenes with lively figures and animals in action beautifully painted in various shades of underglaze blue" (74). In general, these decorations were no longer confined to panels and struck

"a fine balance between an almost 'impressionistic' scheme and a detailed naturalism" (75).

48 Rosemary Crill, *Chintz: Indian Textiles for the West* (London: V&A, 2008), 21.

49 Julia Hutt, "Asia in Europe: Lacquer for the West," in *Encounters: The Meeting of Asia and Europe, 1500–1800*, ed. Anna Jackson and Armin Jaffer (London: V&A, 2004), 239–40.

50 Joanne Kosuda-Warner and Elizabeth Johnson, *Landscape Wallcoverings* (London: Scala Publishers in association with Cooper-Hewitt, National Design Museum, 2001), 19.

51 Robert Copeland, *Spode's Willow Pattern & Other Designs after the Chinese* (New York: Rizzoli, 1980), 33. The Staffordshire pottery maker Spode introduced underglaze blue transfer printing in English soft-paste porcelain that allowed him to imitate the appearance of Chinese blue-and-white Kraak porcelain that dominated the European market in late seventeenth and early eighteenth century.

52 Elizabeth Hope Chang, *Britain's Chinese Eye: Literature, Empire, and Aesthetics in Nineteenth-Century Britain* (Stanford: Stanford University Press, 2010), 87.

53 Allen, *Tides in English Taste*, 1: 206–07.

54 Ibid., 1: 198, 200.

55 Horace Walpole, *The History of the Modern Taste in Gardening*, in *Horace Walpole: Gardenist*, ed. Isabel Wakelin Urban Chase (Princeton: Princeton University Press, 1943), 17, 4, 9. Walpole attacks Temple with virulence, declaring, "how cold, how insipid, how tasteless is his account of what he pronounced a perfect garden. I speak not of his style, which it was necessary for him to animate with the colouring and glow of poetry. It is his want of ideas, of imagination, of taste, that I censure" (17). His attack ironically shows that Temple continued to be admired for his style and that his essay on gardening had become an influential founding text of garden theory.

56 John Brewer writes, "The country house, the landscaped park and home farm were the visible embodiment and celebration of 'improvement,' further instances of the landed proprietor's reworking and transformation of nature, of his power to command the landscape." As a character puts it in David Garrick's play *The Clandestine Marriage* (1766), "The chief pleasure of a country house is to make improvements." See John Brewer, *The Pleasures of the Imagination: English Culture in the Eighteenth Century* (New York: Farrar, Straus and Giroux, 1997), 627.

57 Peter de Bolla, *The Education of the Eye: Painting, Landscape, and Architecture in Eighteenth-Century Britain* (Stanford: Stanford University Press, 2003), 5.

58 Donald Bond notes Temple's use of the phrase "pleasures of imagination" in the preface to his *Observations upon the United Provinces of the Netherlands* (1673) to point out that Addison was not the inventor of the phrase around which he organized his theory of taste. Not only was he not the originator of the phrase; the introductory remarks Addison makes on the imagination recapitulate an old tradition of regarding the imagination as the mid-way point

between sense and reason, albeit updating this older understanding with a newer empiricist model of sensory impression. For comparisons with Temple, see *Spectator* 1: 536n1, 1: 538n2. For older understandings of the imagination, see 1: 536n3, 1: 537n3.

59 These are, of course, conceptual categories that are experienced in mixed forms. Our imagination, Addison emphasizes, is all the more pleased "the more it finds of these Perfections in the same Object" (3: 544).

60 Carole Fabricant, "The Aesthetics and Politics of Landscape in the Eighteenth Century," in *Studies in Eighteenth-Century British Art and Aesthetics*, ed. Ralph Cohen (Berkeley: University of California Press, 1985), 57. Fabricant argues that the implicitly egalitarian basis of Addison's aesthetic theory fails to issue in a democratic aesthetics, however, and that he ends up "with a defense of monopoly capitalism and class division," "one that justifies social distinctions by converting them into epistemological, aesthetic, even biological categories" (69–70). I believe this is too strongly put, for Addison constructs an alternative hierarchy of taste that can bring such categories into debate. Doubtless, his social vision is hardly radical, but his papers on the pleasures of the imagination constitute more than a defense of the English class system.

61 Commenting on the same passage in *Spectator* no. 414 (3: 552), Tony Brown writes: "Chinese taste exemplifies aesthetic experience in its immediacy, on the one hand, and in its indifference to cognition, on the other." Throughout his article, Brown emphasizes the immediate impact of Addison's Chinese garden, interpreting it as an allegory of "the aesthetic's acognitive aspect [that] remains outside historical or temporal development." According to Brown, Addison uses the Chinese garden as a figure for the immediate, pre-cognitive, and in this sense "primitive" component of aesthetic experience. My argument, in contrast, is that what interests Addison about the Chinese garden is the paradoxical idea that the most immediate aesthetic experience can simultaneously be deeply mediated and indeed illusory, and that cognitive indeterminacy, or surprise, is felt *over time*. See Brown, "Joseph Addison and the Pleasures of Sharawadgi," 186.

62 Lee Andrew Elioseff argues in *The Cultural Milieu of Addison's Literary Criticism* that Temple considered the beautiful disorder of the Chinese garden under the category of beauty, whereas Addison viewed it from the perspective of the sublime. He writes: "Temple, unlike Addison, considers this 'disorder' under the category of beauty, emphasizing the fact that order and harmony are obscured in, not absent from, the artificial naturalness of the Chinese garden, whose style is so difficult to imitate that Temple discourages any English attempts to do so. Addison, by removing this naturalness from the realm of the beautiful, strikes upon the similarity between the artificial naturalness of these gardens and the sublimity of physical nature, which it imitates" (117–18). Elioseff's point that Addison introduced a new aesthetic category other than the beautiful to theorize the Chinese garden is helpful. However, I believe that it is the category of the new, rather than the great, that Addison uses to explain the effect of the Chinese garden. Elioseff's neglect of Addison's category of the

new, uncommon, and strange is typical of modern literary criticism which views Addison in post-romantic terms, primarily as a theorist of the sublime, when it is in fact his writings on the new that are most original. See *The Cultural Milieu of Addison's Literary Criticism* (Austin: University of Texas Press, 1963), 117–18.

63 I am in agreement with Michael G. Ketcham's thesis that Addison's garden "is laid out to provide the visitor with changing perspectives and with a variety of psychological effects that both stimulate and mirror the mind." I do not agree, however, that Addison's "garden thus becomes an emblem of time not as continuity but as psychological expansion of a single moment." As Ketcham himself notes, the spectator does not experience the garden as a still object; he walks around in it. Addison's description of nature itself as new, I propose, makes the garden a moving, rather than a still, emblem of time. See Ketcham, *Transparent Designs: Reading, Performance, and Form in the* Spectator *Papers* (Athens: University of Georgia Press, 1985), 86–87.

64 See Robin Dix, "Addison and the Concept of 'Novelty' as a Basic Aesthetic Category," *British Journal of Aesthetics* 26.4 (1986), 383–84. Dix points out that it was Thomas Reid who originally objected to Addison's category of the new on the basis that it referred to a relation between the subject and the object, and therefore could not be considered a quality of the object. Arguing persuasively against Reid in this paper, Dix proposes that Addison's category of the new had to do with something more than merely the subjective experience of surprise, and that Addison was arguing that an object "in a process of continual change" had an independent aesthetic merit. The new and the strange both refer to this idea of a shifting, moving object.

65 See Clarence DeWitt Thorpe, "Addison and Some of His Predecessors on 'Novelty,'" *Publications of the Modern Language Association of America* 52.4 (1937), 1114–29. Thorpe downplays the originality of Addison's idea of novelty, arguing that novelty is considered an essential ingredient in aesthetic response in writers as diverse as Longinus, Hobbes, Dryden, and Dennis, although he does give credit to Addison's "attempt to rationalize this pleasure and to place it in proper relationship to other aesthetic pleasures." He also remarks that Addison's theory of novelty is notable for the "full attention" Addison gives to "novelty in nature" (1129).

66 Dix, "Addison and the Concept of 'Novelty' as a Basic Aesthetic Category," 385–86.

67 Neil Saccamano, "The Sublime Force of Words in Addison's 'Pleasures,'" *English Literary History* 58.1 (1991), 88.

68 My account of Addison's interpretation of the Chinese garden is indebted to William Youngren's essay "Addison and the Birth of Eighteenth-Century Aesthetics," *Modern Philology* 79.3 (1982), 267–83. Although Youngren does not discuss gardens, he emphasizes Addison's interest in the reader's temporal experience and argues that Addison's reading of Locke motivated him to trace "the ways in which the mind processes its experience through time" (282). According to Youngren, it is this interest in time that distinguishes

Addison's aesthetics of the new from earlier aesthetic accounts of wonder and admiration.

69 This doubling effect sounds like a recipe for anxiety – and Freud would certainly later analyze it as the anxiety-producing effect of the uncanny – but for Addison such double objects as camera obscuras and Chinese gardens are playful rather than scary because they momentarily, and pleasurably, suspend our sense of reality rather than, as in Freud's scenario, pulling away the very ground beneath our feet.

70 See Arthur O. Lovejoy, "'Nature' as an Aesthetic Norm," in *Essays in the History of Ideas* (Baltimore: Johns Hopkins University Press, 1948), 69–77.

71 "The juxtaposition of originals and copies in the representations of nature as well as the representations of the imagination creates a double landscape in which the lines between art and nature are increasingly blurred. The resemblance between works of art and works of nature makes it increasingly difficult to tell the difference between originals and copies." David Marshall, "The Problem of the Picturesque," *Eighteenth-Century Studies* 35.3 (2002), 417.

72 Osvald Sirén, *China and Gardens of Europe of the Eighteenth Century* (Washington, D.C.: Dumbarton Oaks Research Library and Collection, 1990), 11. This is an important point that complicates Lovejoy's argument that Addison supposed that Chinese gardens were "essentially similar" to natural landscapes. See "The Chinese Origin of a Romanticism," in *Essays in the History of Ideas*, 115.

73 Jean-Denis Attiret (1702–68) was a French Jesuit who traveled to China in 1737 and served in Emperor Qianlong's court. His description of the imperial gardens was first published in the *Lettres édifiantes et curieuses écrites des missions étrangères par quelques missionnaires de la compagnie de Jésus* (Paris, 1749), and subsequently translated into English by Joseph Spence (under the name Sir Harry Beaumont) in 1752. William Chamber's essay "Of the Art of Laying out Gardens among the Chinese" was first published at the end of his 1757 book *Designs of Chinese* Buildings, Furniture, Dresses, Machines and Utensils. The fact that Thomas Percy reprinted both essays in the second volume of his 1762 *Miscellaneous Pieces Relating to the Chinese* suggests that the association between China and gardening remained very strong through the mid-century. Percy provided his own translation.

74 Jean-Denis Attiret, *A Particular Account of the Emperor of China's Gardens Near Pekin*, trans. Joseph Spence (London, 1752).

75 William Chambers, *A Dissertation on Oriental Gardening* (London, 1772), 35–38. In his earlier essay "Of the Art of Laying Out Gardens Among the Chinese," Chambers uses a slightly different terminology: the "pleasing, horrid, and enchanted." See Chambers, *Designs of Chinese Buildings, Furniture, Dresses, Machines, and Utensils* (London, 1757), 14–19.

76 Chambers, *A Dissertation on Oriental Gardening*, 27.

77 Chase, ed., *Horace Walpole: Gardenist*, 22–23.

78 Chang, *Britain's Chinese Eye*, 24. See Porter's *The Chinese Taste* for an extended discussion of this topic.

79 See Le Comte, *Memoirs and Observations*, 296–98.

80 Joseph Addison, *The Freeholder*, ed. James Leheny (Oxford: Clarendon Press, 1979), 52–54. All *Freeholder* references are to *Freeholder* no. 4, January 2, 1716.

81 Chase, ed., *Horace Walpole: Gardenist*, 35.

82 Edmund Burke's *Philosophical Enquiry into the Origin of Our Ideas of the Sublime and Beautiful* (1757, 1759) famously begins by dismissing novelty as an elementary but also childish and short-lasting pleasure. "We see children perpetually running from place to place to hunt out something new," he writes, "But as those things which engage us merely by their novelty, cannot attach us for any length of time, curiosity is the most superficial of all the affections; it changes its object perpetually." See *A Philosophical Enquiry into the Origin of Our Ideas of the Sublime and Beautiful*, ed. Adam Phillips (Oxford: Oxford University Press, 2008), 29.

83 John Dixon Hunt, *The Figure in the Landscape: Poetry, Painting, and Gardening During the Eighteenth Century* (Baltimore: Johns Hopkins University Press, 1989), 67.

84 Saccamano, "The Sublime Force of Words in Addison's 'Pleasures,'" 92.

85 Ibid., 93–94.

86 Kirsti Simonsuuri, *Homer's Original Genius: Eighteenth-Century Notions of the Early Greek Epic (1688–1798)* (Cambridge: Cambridge University Press, 1979), 21.

87 Addison uses virtually the same phrasing in *Spectator* no. 279, where he discusses the "Sentiments" of *Paradise Lost*. He writes: "*Homer* has opened a great Field of Raillery to Men of more Delicacy than Greatness of Genius, by the Homeliness of some of his Sentiments. But, as I have before said, these are rather to be imputed to the Simplicity of the Age in which he lived, to which I may also add, of that which he described, than to any Imperfection in that Divine Poet" (2: 589).

88 I use A. C. Guthkelch's two-volume edition of *The Miscellaneous Works of Joseph Addison* (London: G. Bell and Sons, 1914) for these texts. All subsequent references to this edition appear parenthetically by volume and page number, preceded by *MW*.

89 Addison elaborates on this point in *Spectator* no. 285, where he discusses the language of Milton's *Paradise Lost*. Addison writes that "A Poet should take particular care to guard himself against Idiomatick ways of speaking," since "the most obvious Phrases, and those which are used in ordinary Conversation, become too familiar to the Ear, and contract a kind of Meanness by passing through the Mouths of the Vulgar" (3: 10). This gives the ancients a great advantage over the moderns, he suggests, since the ancient languages are "dead" to the "Modern Reader" who is simply unable to tell the difference between common and uncommon, vulgar and proper expressions (3: 11).

90 Jonathan Brody Kramnick, *Making the English Canon: Print-Capitalism and the Cultural Past, 1700–1770* (Cambridge: Cambridge University Press, 1998), 61.

91 On Milton as a sublime poet, see Leslie E. Moore, *Beautiful Sublime: The Making of* Paradise Lost, *1701–1734* (Stanford: Stanford University Press, 1990).
92 Ross, *The Making of the English Literary Canon*, 214, 218.
93 Elioseff, *The Cultural Milieu of Addison's Literary Criticism*, 6.

Chapter 4: Oliver Goldsmith's Serial Chinaman

1 *Public Ledger; or, Daily Register of Commerce and Intelligence*, January 24, 1760.
2 In 1702, another Chinese convert named Arcadio Huang briefly stopped in England on his way to France where, to the chagrin of the Jesuits, he renounced Catholicism before he could be presented to the pope. Huang made a heroic attempt at civilian life, cataloging Chinese books in the Royal Library and working on a series of publications, including a French–Chinese dictionary and a grammar of the Chinese language to earn his living. Had he stuck with the Jesuits' plans for him, his life would have been much easier, but he seems to have been determined to make his own way. He married a French woman named Marie-Claude Regnier but their marriage was tragically brief. After Marie-Claude's death shortly after the birth of their daughter, Huang appears to have lost heart. He died in 1716. The Jesuits found their success story in another Chinese man by the name of Fan Shouyi – or Luigi Fan (1682–1753) – who arrived in Europe in 1708 as a part of Kangxi's second embassy to Pope Clement XI and stayed eleven years in Europe, eventually returning to China in 1719. He apparently never made it to England, however.
3 In *Journey to the East: The Jesuit Mission to China, 1579–1724* (Cambridge, Mass: Belknap Press, 2007), Liam Brockey notes that "Couplet's tour was part theater, since his train included a Chinese assistant, Miguel Shen Fuzong (ca. 1658–1691), and an array of Asian curiosities" (152). Not everybody enjoyed his "staged exoticism," however. See Brockey, *Journey to the East*, 447n72 and Theodore N. Foss, "The European Sojourn of Philippe Couplet and Michael Shen Fuzong, 1683–1692," in *Philippe Couplet, S.J. (1623–1693): The Man Who Brought China to Europe* (Nettetal: Steyler Verlag, 1990), 12–27.
4 Jonathan Spence, "When Minds Met: China and the West in the Seventeenth Century," 2010 Jefferson Lecture in the Humanities, May 20, 2010 [www.neh. gov/about/awards/jefferson-lecture/jonathan-spence-lecture, accessed July 7, 2015]. Shen left England in 1688 to return to China but apparently died during the long journey home.
5 See Yang, *Performing China*, 77, 105–8. In *The Pretended Asian: George Psalmanazar's Eighteenth-Century Formosan Hoax*, Michael Keevak notes that Psalmanazar's forgery of Formosan identity was partially enabled by the relative obscurity of the island after it was abandoned by European traders and absorbed into the Chinese empire at the end of the seventeenth century. However, Keevak argues, what is most striking about Psalmanazar's imposture is the fact that he managed to override eyewitness accounts of the island amid a general "complex confusion" between real and hoax accounts of Asian lands. See *The Pretended Asian*, 17–34, esp. 33.

6 Fan Cunzhong, "Sir William Jones's Chinese Studies," *The Vision of China in the English Literature of the Seventeenth and Eighteenth Centuries*, ed. Adrian Hsia (Hong Kong: The Chinese University Press, 1998), 328n12. Fan notes that detailed accounts of Chitqua are found in the *Gentleman's Magazine* 91.1 (1771), 237–38 and J. Nichols's *Illustrations of the Literary History of the Eighteenth Century*, 8 vols. (London: Nichols, Son, and Bentley, 1817–58), 5: 318.

7 David Clarke, "Chitqua: A Chinese Artist in Eighteenth-Century England," *Chinese Art and Its Encounter with the World* (Hong Kong: Hong Kong University Press, 2011), 21. Clarke cites Richard Gough's letter of August 3, 1770 to the Rev. B. Forster in Nichols's *Illustrations*, 5: 318. Clarke's essay on Chitqua is the most recent and authoritative study of sculptures that have been attributed to this portrait modeller.

8 Ibid., 39–45.

9 Fan, "Sir William Jones's Chinese Studies," 329.

10 See [L. W. Hanson], "Johnson, Percy, and Sir William Chambers," *Bodleian Library Record* 4.6 (1953), 292–93. This information appears in a note dated 10 November 1770 and handwritten in Percy's hand in his own copy of *Miscellaneous Pieces Relating to the Chinese* (1762). In an earlier note, dated August 1, 1764, and written on the blank page before Chambers' essay "On the Art of Laying out Gardens among the Chinese" included in the *Miscellaneous Pieces*, Percy had expressed his suspicion of Chambers's claim that much of his information came from conversations with a Chinese painter named Lepqua. Percy noted that Samuel Johnson had confirmed this suspicion. "Mr Johnson suspected, and at length Mr Chambers confessed, that the conferences wth *Lepqua* were apocryphal. Mr Johnson even doubts whether Chambers was in China at all." After meeting Chitqua in the company of Chambers in 1770, however, Percy was apparently sufficiently impressed by Chambers's ability to communicate with the Chinese artist to change his mind. In the 1770 note he writes, "I am now convinced Mr Chambers has been at Canton & spent some time there."

11 See Richard E. Quaintance, Jr.'s useful introduction to the Augustan Reprint Society's reprint of *An Explanatory Discourse by Tan Chet-qua, of Quang-chew-fu, Gent.* (Los Angeles: William Andrews Clark Memorial Library, 1989), i–x.

12 A copy of this letter is printed in William T. Whitley's *Artists and their Friends, 1700–1800* (London and Boston: The Medici Society, 1928), 1: 269–70. On Chitqua's letter and return to Canton, see Clarke's *Chinese Art and Its Encounter with the World*, 80–81; "Chitqua's English Adventure: An Eighteenth-Century Source for the Study of China Coast Pidgin and Early Chinese Use of English," *Hong Kong Journal of Applied Linguistics* 10.1 (2005), 47–58.

13 See Susan Stewart's chapter on Psalmanazar in *Crimes of Writing: Problems in the Containment of Representation* (Oxford: Oxford University Press, 1991), esp. 35, 41. Stewart notes that, in his posthumously published *Memoirs*, Psalmanazar explains how he based his "pregnant invention" of a Formosan identity on the fact that China and Japan were generally regarded by Europeans

as "Antipodes" to them "in almost every respect." His strategy in *An Historical and Geographical Description of Formosa, an Island Subject to the Emperor of Japan* (1704) was to rise to this expectation of antipodal otherness. Stewart cites the second edition of Psalmanazar's *Memoirs of *****. Commonly Known by the Name of George Psalmanazar; a Reputed Native of Formosa* (1765), 113. The first edition of the *Memoirs* appeared in 1764.

14 I use this informal title to distinguish the serialized work from the one-volume collection that was later compiled under the title *Citizen of the World*.

15 Ros Ballaster, *Fabulous Orients: Fictions of the East in England, 1662–1785* (Oxford: Oxford University Press, 2005), esp. 204–07, 247–51.

16 Frank Donoghue, *The Fame Machine: Book Reviewing and Eighteenth-Century Literary Careers* (Stanford: Stanford University Press, 1996), 99.

17 Examples include Christopher Brooks, "Goldsmith's *Citizen of the World*: Knowledge and the Imposture of Orientalism," *Texas Studies in Literature and Language* 35.1 (1993), 124–44; Tao Zhijian, "Citizen of Whose World? Goldsmith's Orientalism," *Comparative Literature Studies* 33.1 (1996), 15–34; and James Watt, "Goldsmith's Cosmopolitanism," *Eighteenth-Century Life* 30.1 (2005), 56–75. Among these, Watt, who argues that "fictional orientals in early-eighteenth-century British writing … offered another means of addressing the experience of modernity," takes the most balanced view (56).

18 See, for example, Robert D. Mayo, *The English Novel in the Magazines, 1740–1815* (Evanston: Northwestern University Press, 1962) and Richard C. Taylor, *Goldsmith as Journalist* (Rutherford, NJ: Fairleigh Dickinson University Press, 1993).

19 See Arthur Friedman's introduction to *The Citizen of the World* in *Collected Works of Oliver Goldsmith*, 5 vols. (Oxford: Clarendon Press, 1966), 2: ix–xii. All citations of Goldsmith's works are taken from this edition. An average of 8–10 letters appeared each month through the end of 1760, with fewer letters published in 1761. The last letter was published in August 1761. All references to Goldsmith's Chinese letters are to this definitive edition and will appear parenthetically by letter number and page number.

20 Arthur Friedman, introduction to *Collected Works of Oliver Goldsmith*, 2: xii.

21 The papers indexed differed from number to number. In the early issues the *Public Ledger* "adopted the rather eccentric policy of devoting a quarter of the paper to an index of advertisements from 11 London and 32 provincial papers." See Bob Clarke, *From Grub Street to Fleet Street: An Illustrated History of English Newspapers to 1899* (Aldershot: Ashgate, 2004), 86.

22 Compare this description of the contents of another metropolitan newspaper issued in the same year. "The major metropolitan dailies and triweeklies offered the widest coverage. Typical was the jumbled assortment promised by London's *Gazetteer* in 1760: 'a Series of Letters and Essays, respecting the Progress of the useful and polite Arts'; 'Essays, or Letters, on miscellaneous Subjects' submitted by correspondents; 'the principal Department of a Newspaper… *Intelligence*,' 'including the usual foreign Advices' as well as news from a special correspondent and 'domestick Intelligence' in sufficient quantity

to make it unnecessary for a family or public house to take other papers; a 'Commercial Register' listing current prices of various commodities; prices of gold, silver, and stock; an account of goods imported and exported; arrivals and departures of British ships at ports around the world; a bill of mortality; a list of unclaimed letters at the post office; and a list of bankrupts. Finally, in abundance, there were the standard advertisements." See Stephen Botein, Jack R. Censer and Harriet Ritvo, "The Periodical Press in Eighteenth-Century English and French Society: A Cross-Cultural Approach," *Comparative Studies in Society and History* 23.3 (1981), 479.

23　Michael Warner, *The Letters of the Republic: Publication and the Public Sphere in Eighteenth-Century America* (Cambridge, Mass.: Harvard University Press, 1990), 18.

24　Taylor, *Goldsmith as Journalist*, 119.

25　For an extended discussion of the eighteenth-century eidolon, see Manushag N. Powell, *Performing Authorship in Eighteenth-Century English Periodicals* (Lewisburg: Bucknell University Press, 2012), esp. 13–48.

26　See Robert E. Park, "The Natural History of the Newspaper," *American Journal of Sociology* 29.3 (1923), 276; Michael Harris, *London Newspapers in the Age of Walpole* (Cranbury: Associated University Press, 1987), 156.

27　Jeremy Black, *The English Press, 1621–1861* (Thrupp, Stroud, Gloucestershire: Sutton, 2001), 11.

28　Powell writes: "Indeed, eidolons are often violently at odds with their creators. They tend to be higher born and of better economic status, quite young or more usually quite old compared to the author, and are almost always unmarried"; "The assumptions about authorship that appear through the convention of the eidolon imply that authorship was ideally imagined to be something managed by educated English men with no need of steady employment." See *Performing Authorship in Eighteenth-Century Periodicals*, 26, 35.

29　See Taylor, *Goldsmith as Journalist*, 87.

30　Michael Griffin discusses Goldsmith's *A Comparative View of Races and Nations* in these terms. His point is that Goldsmith's early journalistic writings are necessarily conflicted, compromising, and contradictory. At this early stage in his career, Goldsmith was not free to reveal his political views. Griffin regards Goldsmith as "a late Jacobite ironist writing for bread in the midst of a Grub Street environment where his oppositional politics are often obscured by professional requirements." See *Enlightenment in Ruins: The Geographies of Oliver Goldsmith* (Lewisburg: Bucknell University Press, 2013), 32, 14.

31　Hannah Barker, *Newspapers, Politics, and Public Opinion in Late Eighteenth-Century England* (Oxford: Clarendon Press, 1998), 36.

32　Ibid., 36–38.

33　Lennard Davis, *Factual Fictions: The Origins of the English Novel* (New York: Columbia University Press, 1983), 75.

34　Ibid., 67, 70.

35　See Ian Watt, *The Rise of the Novel: Studies in Defoe, Richardson, and Fielding* (Berkeley: University of California Press, 1957), esp. 9–30.

36 Davis, *Factual Fictions*, 70.
37 Wayne Booth, " 'The Self-Portraiture of Genius': *The Citizen of the World* and Critical Method," *Modern Philology* 73.4 (1976), S86. Emphasis in original.
38 Ibid., S85–S86. This is nonetheless a flawed paper that, in seeking to locate the "genius" of Goldsmith's method not in the "organic" unity of the structure but in the stylistic, rhetorical, and critical intelligence of the author, ends up dismissing Altangi as "a character in his own right" and reading him merely as "mask and sometimes as direct spokesman" for Goldsmith (S94–S95). As I will show in the next section, this reading entirely misses Altangi's significance as an oriental spy narrator.
39 Goldsmith to Daniel Hodson, August 31, 1758, *The Collected Letters of Oliver Goldsmith*, ed. Katharine Canby Balderston (Cambridge: Cambridge University Press, 1928), 49–50.
40 John A. Dussinger, "Goldsmith, Oliver (1728?–1774)," *Oxford Dictionary of National Biography*, Oxford University Press, 2004; online edn, January 2009 [http://oxforddnb.com/view/article 10924, accessed 10 July 2015]. To what degree Goldsmith was actually qualified as a physician is a vexed question. In "The Medical Education and Qualifications of Oliver Goldsmith," Ernest Clarke speculates that Goldsmith managed to obtain a Bachelor of Physic degree from Trinity College, Dublin, between 1756 and 1763, where he had also taken his Bachelor of Arts degree in 1749, on the basis of his medical studies in Edinburgh and Leiden. His Trinity medical degree, Clarke suggests, enabled Goldsmith to acquire an ad eundem degree of M.B. from Oxford in 1769. Goldsmith started signing his own works in 1764 with the publication of *The Traveller* and identified himself as "Oliver Goldsmith, M.D." See *Proceedings of the Royal Society of Medicine* 7, Section of the History of Medicine (1914), 88–97.
41 Goldsmith to Daniel Hodson, August 31, 1758, *The Collected Letters of Oliver Goldsmith*, 52.
42 See Dussinger's article on Goldsmith in *Oxford Dictionary of National Biography*; Balderston, introduction to *Collected Letters of Oliver Goldsmith*, xxx–xxxii.
43 Balderston, introduction to *Collected Letters of Oliver Goldsmith*, xxxii.
44 Goldsmith to Thomas Contarine, May 8, 1753, *Collected Letters of Oliver Goldsmith*, 5.
45 Goldsmith to Robert Bryanton, August 14, 1758, *Collected Letters of Oliver Goldsmith*, 39–40.
46 Srinivas Aravamudan, *Enlightenment Orientalism: Resisting the Rise of the Novel* (Chicago: University of Chicago Press, 2012), 34. I agree with Aravamudan's point that whatever "novelty" there was in the "world of the long eighteenth century" should be regarded as "inherently translational" and related to such transcultural fictions as *The Turkish Spy* and *Arabian Nights* rather than the national English novel (75). Certainly, Goldsmith's Chinese letters suggest that writers wrote across rather than within genres, and that the divide between the oriental tale, the periodical essay, and the novel was porous. However, I also

believe the polemical opposition Aravamudan sets up between the oriental tale and the novel may be exaggerated and outdated today. Even novel-centered literary histories acknowledge the dialectic relationship between earlier genres such as the romance and the more 'modern' novel.

47 Ballaster, *Fabulous Orients*, 32.
48 Alain Grosrichard, *The Sultan's Court: European Fantasies of the East* (London and New York: Verso, 1998), 56.
49 Ibid., 60–61.
50 Ibid., 79; my emphasis.
51 Antoine Galland's *Mille et une nuits* was published in France between 1704 and 1717. English translations began to appear in the first decade of the eighteenth century. By 1715, there was a third edition on offer. The first installment of Giovanni Paolo Marana's *L'espion du Grand-Seigneur, et ses relations secretes envoyées au Divan de Constantinople* appeared first in Italian and French in 1684. The English translation appeared in 1687 under the title *Letters Writ by a Turkish Spy*. Both of these texts have extremely complicated publication histories because they were published in installments, with pirate editions and translations sometimes appearing in print before the original texts. See William H. McBurney, "The Authorship of *The Turkish Spy*," *Publications of the Modern Language Association of America* 72.5 (1957), 915–35; Duncan B. Macdonald, "A Bibliographical and Literary Study of the First Appearance of the 'Arabian Nights' in Europe," *The Library Quarterly* 2.4 (1932), 397–420; Peter L. Caracciolo, "Introduction: 'Such a store house of ingenious fiction and of splendid imagery,' " in *The Arabian Nights in English Literature: Studies in the Reception of the Thousand and One Nights into British Culture* (Basingstoke: Macmillan, 1988).
52 Ballaster, *Fabulous Orients*, 146–47.
53 Ballaster, "Narrative Transmigrations: The Oriental Tale and the Novel in Eighteenth-Century Britain," in *A Companion to the Eighteenth-Century English Novel and Culture* (Oxford: Blackwell, 2005), 80.
54 Ballaster, *Fabulous Orients*, 11.
55 Grosrichard, *The Sultan's Court*, 79; cited in Ballaster, *Fabulous Orients*, 11.
56 R. M. Wiles, *Serial Publication in England before 1750* (Cambridge: Cambridge University Press, 1957), 38.
57 Davis, *Factual Fictions*, 72. Davis makes the point that printed news was close to "the tale or short story with which it shared its name etymologically"; "These accounts were 'novels' – they were written on the occasion of the unusual, the quirky, the puzzling."
58 Davis, *Factual Fictions*, 73–74.
59 Stuart Sherman, *Telling Time: Clocks, Diaries, and English Diurnal Form, 1660–1785* (Chicago: University of Chicago Press, 1996), 113.
60 Ibid., 115.
61 Benedict Anderson, *The Spectre of Comparisons: Nationalism, Southeast Asia, and the World* (London: Verso, 1998), 29.

62 Benedict Anderson, *Imagined Communities: Reflections on the Origin and Spread of Nationalism* (New York: Verso, 1991), 24–25.

63 Ibid., 33, 26, 35.

64 See Pheng Cheah's helpful discussion of Anderson's work in "Grounds of Comparison," *diacritics* 29.4 (1999), 8.

65 Anderson, *The Spectre of Comparisons*, 33.

66 Ibid., 33.

67 Cheah, "Grounds of Comparison," 9–10.

68 Jean-Paul Sartre, "Seriality: The Bus Queue and the Radio Broadcast," in *Modern Times: Selected Non-Fiction*, trans. Robin Buss, ed. Geoffrey Wall (New York: Penguin Books, 2000), 220.

69 Anderson, *The Spectre of Comparisons*, 42, 29, 40.

70 Ibid., 33.

71 Ibid., 32, 30, 26.

72 Cheah, "Grounds of Comparison," 9–10.

73 Anderson, *The Spectre of Comparisons*, 33.

74 Giovanni Paolo Marana, *Letters Writ by a Turkish Spy*, ed. Arthur J. Weitzman (New York: Columbia University Press, 1970), 1.

75 I am here adapting phrases from the following sentence in Anderson's *Imagined Communities*: "These fellow-readers, to whom they were connected through print, formed, in their secular particular, visible invisibility, the embryo of the nationally imagined community" (44).

76 Anderson, *The Spectre of Comparisons*, 31.

77 Seamus Deane, "Goldsmith's *The Citizen of the World*," *The Art of Oliver Goldsmith*, ed. Andrew Swarbrick (London: Vision, 1984), 33.

78 Goldsmith's borrowings from d'Argens are extensively discussed in Newell Richard Bush, *The Marquis D'Argens and his* Philosophical Correspondence: *A Critical Study of d'Argens'* Lettres juives, Lettres cabalistiques, *and* Lettres chinoises (Ann Arbor: Edwards Bros, 1953); Ronald S. Crane and Hamilton J. Smith, "A French Influence on Goldsmith's Citizen of the World," *Modern Philology* 19 (1921), 83–92; Arthur Friedman, "Goldsmith and the Marquis D'Argens," *Modern Language Notes* 53.3 (1938), 173–76; A. L. Sells, *Les Sources Françaises de Goldsmith* (Paris: E. Champion, 1924; Genève: Slatkine Reprints, 1977); and Hamilton Jewett Smith, *Oliver Goldsmith's The Citizen of the World: A Study* (New Haven: Yale University Press, 1926).

79 Anderson, *Imagined Communities*, 68–69, 188.

80 Mary Jo Kietzman, "Defoe Masters the Serial Subject," *English Literary History* 66.3 (1999), 677–705. Kietzman defines serial subjectivity in terms of the invention of a series of multiple identities and the serial subject as one who is adept at revising her "life-stories in response to changing circumstance" (678). Kietzman is interested in serial subjectivity as "a viable mode of self-fashioning in which the conventional opposition between the private and public, the unconscious and conscious, the personal/unknowable and the universal/comprehensible, is displaced and re-anchored in a new

conception of situation or context as both psychic and historical." Defoe mobilizes female serial subjectivity in *Moll Flanders*, she argues, if only to tame it "within the more inclusive autobiographical narration of a subject who finally represents herself as unified and readable: bourgeois" (678–79). Here I am proposing that Altangi's serial subjectivity must be approached very differently.

81 Tao, "Citizen of Whose World? Goldsmith's Orientalism," 19, 24, 21.

82 Brooks, "Goldsmith's *Citizen of the World*," 133, 139, 128.

83 Ibid., 130.

84 I cite a passage in Srinivas Aravamudan's *Enlightenment Orientalism* where he discusses Paul Hazard's book *La crise de la conscience européenne*. As Aravamudan notes, despite their distortions, oriental tales are important because they express "a strong desire to understand civilizational differences both relativistically and universally" (5).

85 Porter, *Ideographia*, 138.

86 Donna Isaacs Dalnekoff, "A Familiar Stranger: The Outsider of Eighteenth-Century Satire," *Neophilologus* 57 (1973), 121, 124. For a historical overview of "the ambivalent attributions of the stranger … deeply ingrained in the Western tradition," see David Simpson's recent book *Romanticism and the Question of the Stranger* (Chicago: Chicago University Press, 2013), esp. 16–39.

87 Arthur J. Weitzman, introduction to *Letters Writ by a Turkish Spy*, xi.

88 Marana, *Turkish Spy*, 1.

89 Ibid.

90 Ibid., 75.

91 For these reasons I disagree with Dalnekoff's assessment that "Goldsmith exploits the associations of China with extreme formality, pedantry, and ceremonialism to turn his philosopher into a figure of ridicule." On the contrary, Altangi is a highly likeable and sympathetic character. See Dalnekoff, "A Familiar Stranger," 124.

92 James Prior, *The Life of Goldsmith* (London: J. Murray, 1837), 1: 360. Cited in Friedman, *Collected Works*, 2: ix–x.

93 Laura Brown, *Fables of Modernity: Literature and Culture in the English Eighteenth Century* (Ithaca: Cornell University Press, 2001), 51.

94 Marana, *Turkish Spy*, 174.

95 Brown, *Fables of Modernity*, 29.

96 I am in agreement here with Brooks's assessment that Altangi's "tour of London represents an urban circuit walk, a moving from place to place of social importance and high visibility." However, I beg to differ with his description of Altangi as "asexual and undemanding" like Gulliver in Brobdingnag. See "Goldsmith's *Citizen of the World*," 137.

97 Griffin notes Goldsmith's familiarity with Le Comte and Du Halde in *Enlightenment in Ruins*, 92.

98 See Michael Adas, *Machines as the Measure of Men: Science, Technology, and Ideologies of Western Dominance* (Ithaca: Cornell University Press, 1989), 45.

99 Le Comte, *Memoirs and Observations*, 56.

100 Du Halde, *A Description of the Empire of China*, 1: iii.
101 Ibid., 1: 64.
102 Ibid., 1: 67.
103 Ibid., 1: 66.
104 Le Comte, *Memoirs and Observations*, 56–57.
105 Ibid., 56.
106 Ibid., 59.
107 Du Halde, *A Description of the Empire of China*, 1: 67.
108 Johan Nieuhof's account also contains a memorable and widely noted description of the unpaved streets and dust in Peking: "The Streets are not Paved, insomuch that in wet weather (which is seldom) they are hardly passable; but when the Northern winds blow, and the weather dry, the Soil which is of a light substance, makes a dust far more noysome to Passengers then the deep and Miry Streets; for such it is, that it blinds a Man as he goes along. The Inhabitants therefore to prevent this inconvenience, are fain to wear Silk Hoods over their Faces; and the extraordinary foulness of the way makes very many to keep Horses to keep them after a Rainy day; for the infinite number of common people that are continually up and down, turns this dusty Soil into Mire and Dirt after a little Rain." See Nieuhof, *An Embassy from the East-India Company of the United Provinces, to the Grand Tartar Cham, Emperor of China*, 136.
109 For a standard account of Smith's criticism of China, see Ulrike Hillemann, *Asian Empire and British Knowledge: China and the Networks of British Imperial Expansion* (New York: Palgrave Macmillan, 2009), 17. Giovanni Arrighi has argued, however, that this is an erroneous understanding of Smith. "China is repeatedly mentioned as the exemplar of a country that had followed the path to economic maturity that Smith calls 'the natural course of things' or 'the natural progress of opulence'" – i.e. capital moving first to agriculture, then to manufactures, and lastly to foreign commerce. Smith's criticism of China's refusal of foreign commerce was based on his view that China was not letting "the natural course of things" to take place. "But nowhere does Smith suggest that China could or should have followed the 'unnatural and retrograde' European path" where, he believed, the natural course had been inverted, capital flowing from foreign commerce to manufactures, and lastly to agriculture. See *Adam Smith in Beijing: Lineages of the Twenty-First Century* (London and New York: Verso, 2007), esp. 57–59.
110 Nieuhof, *An Embassy from the East-India Company of the United Provinces, to the Grand Tartar Cham, Emperor of China*, 36.
111 Magalhães, *A New History of China*, 267.
112 Du Halde, *A Description of the Empire of China*, 1: 64.
113 Ibid., 1: 114.
114 China was well known for its lack of foreign trade; "for the *Chinese*, finding among themselves all Things necessary for the Support and Pleasures of Life, seldom go far from home" (Du Halde, 1: 333). The comparison could not be starker: England's poor natural endowments cannot compare with China's

profuse bounty which makes foreign trade simply redundant. According to Du Halde, "The inland Trade of *China* is so great, that the Commerce of all *Europe* is not to be compar'd therewith" (1: 334); "the most frequented Fair affords but a faint Resemblance of the incredible Crowds of People to be seen in the Generality of Cities, who are busy in buying or selling all sorts of Commodities" (1: 334).

115 See Susan Whyman, "Sharing Public Spaces," in *Walking the Streets of Eighteenth-Century London: John Gay's Trivia (1716)* (Oxford: Oxford University Press, 2007), 43–61.

116 Botein, Censer, and Ritvo, "The Periodical Press in Eighteenth-Century English and French Society," 482.

117 Ibid., 474, 475, 486.

118 John Tchen has shown that eighteenth-century desire for Chinese goods was all about social emulation and class desire: "'things' Chinese had become one of the forms of currency for gaining cultural 'distinction.'" Thomas Kim points out that a mantel decorated with oriental objects continues to mark "a kind of modern modality." See John Kuo Wei Tchen, *New York before Chinatown: Orientalism and the Shaping of American Culture, 1776–1882* (Baltimore: Johns Hopkins University Press, 1999), 13; Thomas W. Kim, "Being Modern: The Circulation of Oriental Objects," *American Quarterly* 58.2 (2006), 387.

119 Margaret C. Jacob, *Strangers Nowhere in the World: The Rise of Cosmopolitanism in Early Modern Europe* (Philadelphia: University of Pennsylvania Press, 2006), 13.

120 Thomas J. Schlereth writes: "Although he transcended his national *polis* in numerous ways, the typical Enlightenment cosmopolite flourished in the urbane pluralism of the city as he moved from one country to another. He was eminently, almost incurably an urban man." See *The Cosmopolitan Ideal in Enlightenment Thought: Its Form and Function in the Ideas of Franklin, Hume, and Voltaire, 1694–1790* (Notre Dame: University of Notre Dame Press, 1977), 5.

121 David Hume, "Of Refinement in the Arts," in *Essays Moral, Political, and Literary*, ed. Eugene F. Miller (Indianapolis: Liberty Fund, 1985), 271. See also Schelereth, *The Cosmopolitan Ideal in Enlightenment Thought*, 6.

122 Hume, "My Own Life," in *Essays Moral, Political, and Literary*, xxxvi.

123 As Richard Taylor notes, Goldsmith's attitude toward the Grub Street milieu in which he made his living embodied a central paradox: he "tried to take advantage of the advantages it presented, while abhorring its lack of moral and aesthetic foundation; to appeal to the coffeehouse tribunal, while protesting its vulgarity and injustices; and to establish an enduring place in a belletristic tradition that seemed to be vanishing." See *Goldsmith as Journalist*, 125.

124 John Barrell's *English Literature in History, 1730–80: An Equal, Wide Survey* (New York: St. Martin's, 1983), 35. See also Ingrid Horrocks, "'Circling Eye' and 'Houseless Stranger': The New Eighteenth-Century Wanderer (Thomson to Goldsmith)," *English Literary History* 77.3 (2010), 665.

125 Horrocks, "'Circling Eye' and 'Houseless Stranger,'" 665–66.
126 Ibid., 675.
127 Ibid., 683.
128 James Prior, *Life of Oliver Goldsmith*, I: 383; cited in Richard Taylor, *Goldsmith as Journalist*, 121.
129 See Richard Helgerson, "The Two Worlds of Oliver Goldsmith," *Studies in English Literature, 1500–1900* 13.3 (1973), 516–34.

Chapter 5: Thomas Percy's Chinese Miscellanies

1 Cited in Alda Milner-Barry, "A Note on the Early Literary Relations of Oliver Goldsmith and Thomas Percy," *The Review of English Studies* 2.5 (1926), 51.
2 *Thomas Percy's Life of Dr. Oliver Goldsmith*, ed. Richard L. Harp (Salzburg: Institut für Englische Sprache und Literatur, Universität Salzburg, 1976), 60–61.
3 See Bertram H. Davis, *Thomas Percy: A Scholar-Cleric in the Age of Johnson* (Philadelphia: University of Pennsylvania Press, 1989), esp. 32–36 for an account of Percy's amicable relationship with the Earl of Sussex during his first years at Easton Maudit. Unfortunately, the earl succumbed to a fever and died in 1758. Percy would never form the same kind of friendship with the earl's younger brother who succeeded him, but he continued to serve as family chaplain and enjoy access to the manor house library.
4 The original Wilkinson manuscript has never been found. Percy claimed that the first three volumes of the translation were in English and that the fourth was in Portuguese, "written in a different hand from the former." See preface to *Hau Kiou Choaan; or, The Pleasing History. A Translation from the Chinese Language*, 4 vols. (London, 1761), I: x. All further references to this text will be made parenthetically by volume and page number, preceded by publication date. In the absence of the original manuscript, critics have reconstructed the process of Percy's translation and publication of *Hau Kiou Choaan* by combing through his correspondence and diary. A series of articles published many decades ago in *The Review of English Studies* is particularly helpful. See Milner-Barry, "A Note on the Early Literary Relations of Oliver Goldsmith and Thomas Percy," 51–61; L. F. Powell, "*Hau Kiou Choaan*," *The Review of English Studies* 2.8 (1926), 446–55; Alda Milner-Barry and L. F. Powell, "A Further Note on *Hau Kiou Choaan*," *The Review of English Studies* 3.10 (1927), 214–18; Vincent H. Ogburn, "The Wilkinson MSS. and Percy's Chinese Books," *The Review of English Studies* 9.33 (1933), 30–36; T. C. Fan, "Percy's *Hau Kiou Choaan*," *The Review of English Studies* 22.86 (1946), 117–25.
5 Davis, *Thomas Percy*, 57. Having worked with both Griffiths and Dodsley, Goldsmith was no doubt able to provide valuable publishing advice for Percy.
6 Alice Gaussen writes, "It was said that Goldsmith, encouraged by the interest that the Chinese novel of his 'dignified acquaintance, Mr. Percy,' had awakened in the affairs of China and the Far East, began a series of Chinese letters

in the 'Ledger' that were subsequently republished as 'The Citizen of the World, or Letters from a Chinese Philosopher in London to his Friend in the East.' But, as at the close of 1760 ninety-eight of these letters had been published, it seems more probable that the idea was suggested to him by reading the work of his friend, Thomas Percy, while it was still in manuscript." See *Percy: Prelate and Poet* (London: Smith, Elder, & Co., 1908), 24–25. Milner-Barry also proposes that "The Chinese framework of the *Citizen of the World* may have been suggested by Percy's *Hau Kiou Choaan*." See "A Note on the Early Literary Relations of Oliver Goldsmith and Thomas Percy," 60.

7 James Prior, *Life of Oliver Goldsmith*, 1: 383; cited in Richard Taylor, *Goldsmith as Journalist*, 121.

8 The note appears in *Bishop Percy's Folio Manuscript*, ed. John W. Hales and Frederick James Furnivall (London: N. Trübner & Co., 1867), lxxiv.

9 There is some disagreement as to when the first meeting between Percy and Johnson first took place. Davis dates the meeting to the summer of 1756. Nick Groom suggests the first meeting took place in May 1757. See Davis, *Thomas Percy*, 38; Groom, *The Making of Percy's* Reliques (Oxford: Clarendon Press, 1999), 111.

10 Davis, *Thomas Percy*, 44. Johnson was well known for his scorn for ballads. Arthur Friedman attempts to explain Johnson's unusual endorsement of Percy's project by suggesting that he was interested in the metrical romances in the folio MS more than the ballads. To Percy's dismay, Johnson indeed spoke disparagingly of the *Reliques* once it was published, though the two men maintained cordial relations. Johnson's dislike for William Shenstone, a major collaborator in the making of the *Reliques*, has been offered as another explanation for Johnson's final disapproval. See Albert Friedman, *The Ballad Revival: Studies in the Influence of Popular on Sophisticated Poetry* (Chicago: University of Chicago Press, 1961), 189–91; Davis, *Thomas Percy*, 132.

11 Davis, *Thomas Percy*, 91.

12 Milner-Barry and Powell, "A Further Note on *Hau Kiou Choaan*," 214–15. Wilkinson's name was not mentioned in the original preface.

13 William Shenstone to Percy, September 12, 1761. See *The Percy Letters*, 7: 114.

14 Davis, *Thomas Percy*, 130; Roy Palmer, "Percy, Thomas (1729–1811)," *Oxford Dictionary of National Biography*, Oxford University Press, 2004; online edn, May 2006 [http://oxforddnb.com/view/article/21959, accessed 25 June 2012]; Groom, *The Making of Percy's* Reliques, 7.

15 Groom, *The Making of Percy's* Reliques, 12.

16 Bailey's *Dictionary* (1730) defines 'ballad' as "a Song commonly sung up and down the streets." Samuel Johnson's *Dictionary* (1755–56) cites Isaac Watt, who notes that "Ballad once signified a solemn and sacred song, as well as trivial, when Solomon's Song was called the ballad of ballads; but now is applied to nothing but trifling verse." Thomas Dyche's *A New General English Dictionary*, completed by William Pardon (1740), defines it as "a song, but now commonly applied to the meaner sort, that are sung in the streets by

the vulgar." See Ralph Cohen, "Literary History and the Ballad of George Barnwel," *Augustan Studies: Essays in Honor of Irvin Ehrenpreis*, ed. Douglas Lane Patey and Timothy Keegan (Cranbury, NJ: Associated University Presses, 1985), 18; Groom, *The Making of Percy's* Reliques, 23n10.

17 Percy provides a bibliographic list of the books he consulted while editing and revising *Hau Kiou Choaan*. See *Hau Kiou Choaan*, 1: xxix–xxxi.

18 Percy published two sonnets in the May and July issues of the *Universal Visiter* in 1756. He also contributed two poems to Dodsley's *Collection of Poems in Six Volumes, by Several Hands* (1758). See Friedman, *The Ballad Revival*, 37, 47.

19 *Reliques of Ancient English Poetry: Consisting of Old Heroic Ballads, Songs, and other Pieces of our earlier Poets, (Chiefly of the Lyric kind.) Together with some few of later Date*, 3 vols. (London, 1765), 1: ix. Hereafter this edition will be cited parenthetically by volume and page number, preceded by its publication date.

20 See Friedman's chapter on "Percy's *Reliques*" in *The Ballad Revival* and chapters 4–5 in Groom's *The Making of Percy's* Reliques.

21 See Friedman, *The Ballad Revival*, 197–98.

22 My ideas on Percy were first presented in a paper entitled "Antiquarianism and the Serendipitous Reader: Thomas Percy's Chinese Miscellanies and *The Reliques of Ancient English Poetry* (1765)" at the 37th Annual Meeting of the American Society for Eighteenth-Century Studies (ASECS) in Montreal, 2006. There was very little critical literature that focused on Percy's Chinese writings at that time. Recently, however, many more scholars have started to attend to the connections between Percy's interest in China and British Gothicism (Watt) and Romantic sinology (Porter, Kitson). See Watt, "Thomas Percy, China, and the Gothic," *The Eighteenth Century: Theory and Interpretation* 48.2 (2007), 95–109; Porter, *The Chinese Taste in Eighteenth-Century England*, 154–83; Kitson, *Forging Romantic China: Sino-British Cultural Exchange, 1760–1840* (Cambridge: Cambridge University Press, 2013), 26–44.

23 Stuart Curran, *Poetic Form and British Romanticism* (Oxford: Oxford University Press, 1986), 129.

24 Percy defines the Scalds as the "bards" of the "ancient inhabitants of Sweden, Denmark and Norway" in his preface to *Five Pieces of Runic Poetry Translated from the Islandic Language* (London, 1763), n. pag.

25 Richard Terry, *Poetry and the Making of the English Literary Past* (Oxford: Oxford University Press, 2001), 287. Terry argues that "the literary historiographical legacy that the eighteenth century left" is "a bifurcated tradition ... divided unhappily between the classic and gothic" (287–88).

26 The reference is to the title of B. Sprague Allen's book *Tides in English Taste (1619–1800)*.

27 Friedman, *The Ballad Revival*, 87, 99. See also Leopold Damrosch, Jr., "The Significance of Addison's Criticism," *Studies in English Literature, 1500–1900* 19.3 (1979), 425–26.

28 The dedication to Elizabeth Northumberland, of the ancient Percy family, was in fact composed by Samuel Johnson, probably during his eight-week stay with Percy in Easton Maudit. See Groom, *The Making of Percy's* Reliques, 220–22. However, since Percy was actively involved in revising and preparing the dedication, I will here assume that it is in line with Percy's authorship.

29 Philip Connell, "British Identities and the Politics of Ancient Poetry in Later Eighteenth-Century England," *The Historical Journal* 49.1 (2006), 177.

30 See especially the introduction and chapter 1 of Samuel Kliger's *The Goths in England: A Study in Seventeenth and Eighteenth Century Thought* (Cambridge, Mass.: Harvard University Press, 1952).

31 See also Groom, *The Making of Percy's* Reliques, 68–69 for a discussion of the semantic complexities of the word 'gothic.'

32 William Temple, *An Introduction to the History of England* (London, 1695), 44. Also cited in Kliger, *The Goths in England*, 92. For brief discussions of Temple's view of the Goths, see *The Goths in England*, 7, 91–92, 194–96.

33 Kliger, *The Goths in England*, 196.

34 *Reliques of Ancient English Poetry*, 2nd ed., 3 vols. (London, 1767), 1: xix–xx. Subsequent references to the second edition of the *Reliques* will be made by publication year, followed by volume and page number. Percy revised his essays extensively in later editions of the *Reliques* in response to vigorous criticism from antiquarians such as Samuel Pegge and Joseph Ritson. See Robert Rix, "Romancing Scandinavia: Relocating Chivalry and Romance in Eighteenth-Century Britain," *European Romantic Review* 20.1 (2009), 9.

35 Percy to William Shenstone, September 1760 [no day given], *The Percy Letters*, 7: 70. Rix discusses this letter in light of the Celtic-Gothic distinction in his article "Thomas Percy's Antiquarian Alternative to Ossian," *Journal of Folklore Research* 46.2 (2009), 202.

36 Percy, preface to *Five Pieces of Runic Poetry Translated from the Islandic Language* (London, 1763), n. pag. See Rix, "Thomas Percy's Antiquarian Alternative to Ossian," 202.

37 Paul-Henri Mallet, "The French Author's Preface," *Northern Antiquities, or A Description of the Manners, Customs, Religion and Laws of the Ancient Danes, and other Northern Nations; Including those of Our Own Saxon Ancestors*, trans. Thomas Percy (London, 1770), liii.

38 Percy, "The Translator's Preface," *Northern Antiquities*, ii.

39 Preface to *Fragments of Ancient Poetry, Collected in the Highlands of Scotland, and Translated from the Galic or Erse Language* (Edinburgh, 1760), v–vi. This preface was ghost-written by Hugh Blair. See Groom, *The Making of Percy's* Reliques, 76.

40 Macpherson, *Temora, an Ancient Epic Poem* (London, 1763), 171. Robin Rix discusses this passage in "Thomas Percy's Antiquarian Alternative to Ossian," 212.

41 Hugh Blair, *A Critical Dissertation on the Poems of Ossian, the Son of Fingal* (London, 1763), 11.

42 Thomas Warton, *Observations on the Fairy Queen of Spenser*, 2nd ed. (London, 1762), 1: 16.

43 Richard Hurd, *Letters on Chivalry and Romance* (London, 1762), 56, 4, 1, 19.

44 Percy to Richard Farmer, September 9, 1762, *The Percy Letters*, 2: 7. Cited in Arthur Johnson, *Enchanted Ground: The Study of Medieval Romance in the Eighteenth Century* (London: The Athlone Press, 1964), 73.

45 See Groom, *The Making of Percy's Reliques*, 82n64. In Hurd's defense, we should note that he openly acknowledged that he had not himself "perused these barbarous volumes" of chivalry but derived his "information" from "a learned and very elaborate Memoir of a French writer." Hurd pointed to "the xx tom. of the *Memoirs of the Academy of Inscriptions and belles Lettres*" as his source (24–25). Hoyt Trowbridge shows that Hurd's reference is to Sainte Palaye who wrote two "memoires" in volumes XVII and XX of the *Histoire de l'Académie des Inscriptions et Belles-Lettres* (1743, 1746), and that Sainte Palaye was in turn indebted to Jean Chapelain's *De La Lecture des Vieux Romans*, composed before 1650. See Trowbridge, introduction to *Letters on Chivalry and Romance (1762)* by Richard Hurd (Los Angeles: William Andrews Clark Memorial Library, 1963), iii.

46 Groom opines that "Thomas Percy could never have achieved what he did in the *Reliques* without the cautionary tale of James Macpherson." See Groom, *The Making of Percy's Reliques*, 73.

47 Percy, preface to *Fragments of Ancient Poetry*, iii.

48 Macpherson argued in his preface to *Fragments of Ancient Poetry*, the "spirit and strain of the poems themselves," their poetic content ("those ideas, and … those manners, that belong to the most early state of society" [iii]), diction and style, allusions and references provided "full proof" that the poems predated the onset of clanship and Christianity in the Scottish Highlands (v). In his subsequent publication *Fingal* (1762), Macpherson further fleshed out his argument that ancient Scottish poetry originally had been composed and delivered by bards who served as oral historians of early Highland clans, when the "use of letters was not known in the North of Europe." See Macpherson, *Fingal, An Ancient Epic Poem* (London, 1762), xii.

49 Percy, preface to *Fragments of Ancient Poetry*, iii.

50 See Nicholas Hudson, "'Oral Tradition': The Evolution of an Eighteenth-Century Concept," in *Tradition in Transition: Women Writers, Marginal Texts, and the Eighteenth-Century Canon*, ed. Alvaro Ribeiro and James G. Basker (Oxford: Clarendon Press, 1996), 161–76.

51 Rosemond Tuve, "Ancients, Moderns, and Saxons," *English Literary History* 6.3 (1939), 172. Marilyn Butler has noted that the popular antiquaries of the eighteenth century were often polemic in their "emphasis on oral, popular experience, and minority or conquered experience." See Butler, "Antiquarianism (Popular)," in *An Oxford Companion to the Romantic Age: British Culture, 1776–1832*, ed. Iain McCalman (Oxford: Oxford University Press, 1999), 330.

52 Sam Smiles, *The Image of Antiquity: Ancient Britain and the Romantic Imagination* (New Haven: Yale University Press, 1994), 9.

53 I am here following Philip Connell's argument that the "patriotic Gothicism of the *Reliques* is unmistakable – but it is also studiously diplomatic." Connell

argues that Percy endeavored "to reconcile his Gothicist theories of English cultural identity with a Moderate, Butite agenda of Anglo-Scottish cultural rapprochement." See "British Identities and the Politics of Ancient Poetry in Later Eighteenth-Century England," 176.

54 Macpherson, preface to *Fingal, an Ancient Epic Poem*, x.

55 Ibid., xiv, xvi.

56 Macpherson, preface to *Fingal*, xiii.

57 Percy, preface to *Five Pieces of Runic Poetry*, n. pag.

58 Susan Stewart, *Crimes of Writing: Problems in the Containment of Representation* (Oxford: Oxford University Press, 1991), 125.

59 Walter J. Ong, *Orality and Literacy* (New York: Routledge, 1988), 11.

60 My argument here is indebted to Groom's discussion of the relationship between Percy and Macpherson in *The Making of Percy's Reliques*, 61–105.

61 Katie Trumpener, *Bardic Nationalism: The Romantic Novel and the British Empire* (Princeton: Princeton University Press, 1997), 75.

62 Stewart, *Crimes of Writing*, 105, 124.

63 Barbara Benedict notes that Samuel Johnson traces the word to its etymological roots in the Latin term for "a dish of mixed corn." *Making the Modern Reader: Cultural Mediation in Early Modern Anthologies* (Princeton: Princeton University Press, 1996), 7.

64 Ibid., 10.

65 For Shaftesbury, for instance, the miscellany was a mere mismatch, a "*Patchwork*" quilt of "*Cuttings* and *Shreds* of Learning, with various *Fragments*, and *Points* of Wit … drawn together, and tack'd in any fantastick form." Anthony Ashley Cooper, Third Earl of Shaftesbury, *Characteristicks of men, opinions, times*, 3 vols. (London, 1711), 3: 5.

66 In *The Matrons*, Percy collected stories about widows from different cultures, including China. See my essay "Master Zhuang's Wife: Translating the Ephesian Matron in Thomas Percy's *The Matrons* (1762)" in *Writing China: Essays on the Amherst Embassy (1816) and Sino-British Cultural Relations*, ed. Peter Kitson and Robert Markley, 32–55, for a full discussion of this book.

67 This explanation was added in an "Advertisement" included in a reissue of the novel in 1774. See Milner-Barry, "A Further Note on Hau Kiou Choaan," 215.

68 On the basis of Percy's 1756 diary entries referring to his working on a "Portuguese fable," Chen Shouyi speculates that Percy himself was doubtful that the work was Chinese. See "Thomas Percy and His Chinese Studies," in *The Vision of China in the English Literature of the Seventeenth and Eighteenth Centuries*, ed. Adrian Hsia (Hong Kong: The Chinese University Press, 1998), 302–03. T. C. Fan notes that Percy was still receiving inquiries about the authenticity of the work fifty years after it was published. When Edmond Malone wrote to Percy in 1805 asking about the authenticity of *Hau Kiou Choaan*, he could only repeat the information he had already provided. Percy had written to Lord Macartney to ask him to confirm that the novel existed in China, but Macartney failed to produce the proof. See Fan, "Percy's *Hau Kiou Choaan*," 117–18; and Powell, "*Hau Kiou Choaan*," 452.

69 Vincent H. Ogburn suggests that the "extraneous selections bound up with the novel seem oddly out of place," and that the Chinese proverbs and poetry in particular probably "were included with the novel only as a matter of temporary convenience." See Ogburn, "The Wilkinson MSS. and Percy's Chinese Books," *Review of English Studies* 9.33 (1933), 35. I am suggesting, on the other hand, that the miscellaneous packaging of *Hau Kiou Choaan* was nothing less than a deliberate publishing strategy on the part of Percy and Dodsley.

70 See title page of *Hau Kiou Choaan.*

71 There is evidence that Percy consulted both John Watts's 1736 and Edward Cave's 1738–41 editions of Du Halde's original 1735 text. See T. C. Fan, "Percy and Du Halde," *Review of English Studies* 21.84 (1945), 326–29.

72 The popularity of such works as Gueullette's facetious *Chinese Tales: or, the Wonderful Adventures of the Mandarin Fum-Hoam* (London, 1725) show how empty China could be as a sign, and therefore how easily it could be filled with utter invention and play.

73 T. C. Fan, "Percy's *Hau Kiou Choaan*," 123. Cited in James St. André, "Modern Translation Theory and Past Translation Practice: European Translations of the *Haoqiu zhuan*," in *One into Many: Translation and the Dissemination of Classical Chinese Literature*, ed. Leo Tak-hung Chan (Amsterdam: Rodopi, 2003), 47.

74 Patricia Sieber, "The Imprint of the Imprints: Sojourners, *Xiaoshuo* Translations, and the Transcultural Canon of Early Chinese Fiction in Europe, 1697–1826," *East Asian Publishing and Society* 3 (2013), 60.

75 Kai-chong Cheung, "The *Haoqiu zhuan*, the First Chinese Novel Translated in Europe: With Special Reference to Percy's and Davis's Renditions," in *One into Many*, 31.

76 Sieber, "The Imprint of the Imprints," 36.

77 Powell, "*Hau Kiou Choaan*," 452.

78 In the introduction to his translation of Chinese penal law, Staunton declared that "even under the disadvantage, in part, of a double translation, and the Editor's [Percy's] want of acquaintance with the language of the original," the novel "conveys a juster and more lively picture of the actual state or manners and society in China, than any other work which we possess in the English language." See George Thomas Staunton, introduction to *Ta Tsing Leu Lee: being the Fundamental Laws, and a Selection from the Supplementary Statues, of the Penal Code of China*, i–xxxv; cited in Cheung, "The *Haoqiu zhuan*, the First Chinese Novel Translated in Europe," 30. See also Kitson, *Forging Romantic China*, 100–06.

79 See Ronald Paulson, *The Beautiful, Novel, and Strange: Aesthetics and Heterodoxy* (Baltimore: Johns Hopkins University Press, 1996).

80 Benedict, *Making the Modern Reader*, 3.

81 Sieber, "The Imprint of the Imprints," 35; Richard C. Hessney, "Beyond Beauty and Talent: The Moral and Chivalric Self in *The Fortunate Union*," in *Expressions of Self in Chinese Literature*, ed. Robert E. Hegel and Richard C. Hessney (New York: Columbia University Press, 1985), 214; Cheung, "The *Haoqiu zhuan*, the First Chinese Novel Translated in Europe," 29.

82 Pierre-Daniel Huet, *The History of Romances, An Enquiry into their Original; Instructions for composing them; An Account of the most Eminent Authors; With Characters and Curious Observations upon the Best Performances of that Kind,* trans. Stephen Lewis (London, 1715), 3–4.

83 Huet, *The History of Romances*, 138.

84 After comparing these customs to those of the North American Indians, also described in the *Lettres édifiantes et curieuses*, Percy signals to the reader, lest the latter pass over his note: "N.B. The Reader is desired to bear the above Remarks constantly in mind throughout this and some of the following Chapters" (1761, 1: 129).

85 I am thinking here of Frank Kermode's essay, "What Precisely Are the Facts?" in Kermode, *The Genesis of Secrecy: On the Interpretation of Narrative* (Cambridge, Mass.: Harvard University Press, 1979), 101–23.

86 The Chinese term "*da xia*" or the "great knight-errant" is translated as "wisdom and courage"; "the wonderful man and woman in righteous chivalry" (*yixia qi nannü*) is rendered as "so virtuous a pair"; and the narrator's praise of Shuey-ping-sin's "chilly bones of knight-errantry" (*xia gu lingling*) is translated as "Her countenance bespeaks a disposition as sweet as the most odoriferous flowers." In the original text, *xia* or chivalry is a non-gender-specific trait denoting "great bravery in war or danger," a characteristic equally shared by the male and female heroines. In this sense, it is a very different conceptualization of virtue from the eroticized notion of male chivalrous gallantry that we find in the eighteenth-century European context. See Ling Hon Lam, "A Case of the Chinese (Dis)order? The *Haoqiu zhuan* and Competing Forms of Knowledge in European and Japanese Readings," *East Asian Publishing and Society* 3 (2013), 79, 83–84, 86.

87 Keith McMahon, *Misers, Shrews, and Polygamists: Sexuality and Male-Female Relations in Eighteenth-Century Chinese Fiction* (Durham: Duke University Press, 1995), 102–03, 108.

88 Fan, "Percy's *Hau Kiou Choaan*," 123.

89 Porter, *The Chinese Taste in Eighteenth-Century England*, 159.

90 Thomas Warton, "Of the origin of romantic fiction in Europe," in *The History of English Poetry, From the Close of the Eleventh to the Commencement of the Eighteenth Century*, vol. 1 (London, 1774), n. pag.

91 Jane Rendall, "Tacitus Engendered: 'Gothic Feminism' and British Histories, c. 1750–1800," *Imagining Nations*, ed. Geoffrey Cubitt (Manchester: Manchester University Press, 1998), 57. I am indebted to James Watt's essay "Thomas Percy, China, and the Gothic" in *The Eighteenth Century: Theory and Interpretation* 48.2 (2007) for this reference.

92 Michèle Cohen, "'Manners' Make the Man: Politeness, Chivalry, and the Construction of Masculinity, 1750–1830," *Journal of British Studies* 44.2 (2005), 315. Cohen has argued along lines very similar to mine that the revival of chivalry was connected to a shift away from classical or Augustan taste toward the Gothic, as well as an increase in antiquarian inquiry into British antiquity.

93 Ibid., 318.

94 Adam Ferguson, *An Essay on the History of Civil Society* (Cambridge: Cambridge University Press, 1995), 191–92. Cited in Cohen, "'Manners' Make the Man," 319.

95 Stewart, *Crimes of Writing*, 115.

96 Groom, *The Making of Percy's Reliques*, 45.

97 Thomas Percy, preface to *Miscellaneous Pieces Relating to the Chinese*, 2 vols. (London, 1762), n. pag. Hereafter cited parenthetically by publication year, followed by volume and page number.

98 Ibid.

99 Porter, *The Chinese Taste in Eighteenth-Century England*, 36.

100 Ibid., 64.

101 Hudson, "'Oral Tradition': The Evolution of an Eighteenth-Century Concept," 166.

102 Hume, for instance, had expressed his suspicion of Ossian on the basis that the Highlanders long lacked an alphabet: they were a people "who, during twelve centuries, at least, of that period, had no writing, no alphabet; and who, even in the other three centuries, made very little use of that alphabet." In *A Journey to the Western Isles of Scotland*, Johnson had also accused Ossian of forgery on the basis that "Earse never was a written language," and therefore was incapable of giving rise to the high achievement of epic poetry. Cited in Hudson, "'Oral Tradition': The Evolution of an Eighteenth-Century Concept," 170–71.

103 As Smiles puts it, "Given that the British people made a late entry into world history after centuries of unrecorded barbarism," there had long been a general feeling that "the primitive life of the Ancient Britons was uncomfortably close to recent to allow a disinterested scrutiny of such a culture to flourish." See Smiles, *The Image of Antiquity*, 15.

104 Judging by its publication record, Cheung's assessment that "Percy's edition of the *Haoqiu zhuan* enjoyed remarkable success in both England and the European continent" is probably too optimistic, though it is true that on the Continent numerous translations appeared: French and German in 1766, Dutch in 1767. See Cheung, "The *Haoqiu zhuan*, the First Chinese Novel Translated in Europe," 31.

105 Percy, preface to *Miscellaneous Pieces*, n. pag. Percy had referred to John Turberville Needham's *De inscriptione quadam AEgyptiaca Taurini inventa, et characteribus AEgyptiis, olim Sinis communibus, exarata, idolo cuidam antique in regia universitate servato* (Rome, 1761) after coming across a favorable reference to this publication in the *Critical Review*. Needham's "imposition was promptly exposed by Guignes and Bartoldi in the *Journal des Savants* (December 1761), and by Edward Wortley Montagu (1713–76) in a letter read before the Royal Society." Needham had "been made the dupe of a Chinese who pretended to be able to read the hieroglyphics upon an Egyptian bust." See *The Percy Letters*, 2: 32n4.

106 Percy to Richard Farmer, January 30, 1763, *The Percy Letters*, 2: 31–32.

107 There is some disagreement on this issue, as there are copies of *Hau Kiou Choaan* with the publication date 1761 but with an inserted "Advertisement"

dated 1774. I am here following the opinion of Milner-Barry and Powell, who conclude that these copies are not second editions in the usual sense but reissues of the novel, with cancels. See Powell, "*Hau Kiou Choaan*," 451; Milner-Barry, "A Further Note," 215.

108 Shenstone wrote: "I have received your Chinese-Novel, but have not yet had time to read it. Tis a neat edition, I see; and I wish you all success. Do you not suppose 'the *House* of Sussex['] a little too pompous in your Dedication; or do you *mean* it *should* be pompous, in Lieu of much *other* Panegyrick? – The six last words in your Dedication had surely better been omitted – I have hitherto read no farther." Shenstone to Percy, July 5, 1761, *The Percy Letters*, 7: 106–07.

109 Anne Janowitz, *England's Ruins: Poetic Purpose and the National Landscape* (Oxford: Basil Blackwell, 1990), 17.

110 Samuel Johnson, *A Dictionary of the English Language*, 2nd ed. (London, 1755–56).

111 Janowitz, *England's Ruins*, 17.

112 Ibid., 25.

113 Connell, "British Identities and the Politics of Ancient Poetry," 176–77.

114 Wilson, *The Island Race*, 85; cited in Connell, "British Identities and the Politics of Ancient Poetry," 166.

Bibliography

Primary Sources

Addison, Joseph. *The Freeholder*. Ed. James Leheny. Oxford: Clarendon Press, 1979.
The Miscellaneous Works of Joseph Addison. Ed. Adolph Charles Louis Guthkelch. 2 vols. London: G. Bell and Sons, 1914.

Addison, Joseph, and Richard Steele. *The Spectator*. Ed. Donald F. Bond. 5 vols. Oxford: Clarendon Press, 1965.

Attiret, Jean-Denis. *A Particular Account of the Emperor of China's Gardens Near Pekin*. Trans. Joseph Spence. London, 1752.

Blair, Hugh. *A Critical Dissertation on the Poems of Ossian, the Son of Fingal*. London, 1763.

Brand, Adam, and Heinrich Wilhelm Ludolf. *A Journal of the Embassy from their Majesties John and Peter Alexievitz, Emperors of Muscovy &c. Over Land into China*. London, 1698.

Burke, Edmund. *A Philosophical Enquiry into the Origin of Our Ideas of the Sublime and Beautiful*. Ed. Adam Phillips. Oxford: Oxford University Press, 2008.

Burnet, Thomas. *The Theory of the Earth Containing an Account of the Original of the Earth, and of All the General Changes which it Hath Already Undergone, or Is to Undergo, till the Consummation of all Things*. 2 vols. London, 1684.

Chambers, William. *Designs of Chinese Buildings, Furniture, Dresses, Machines and Utensils*. London, 1757.
A Dissertation on Oriental Gardening. London, 1772.
An Explanatory Discourse by Tan Chet-qua, of Quang-Chew-Fu, Gent. Los Angeles: William Andrews Clark Memorial Library, University of California, 1978.

Cleyer, Andreas. *Specimen medicinae sinicae, sive, Opuscula medica ad mentem sinensium*. Frankfurt, 1682.

Couplet, Philippe, et al. *Confucius Sinarum philosophus, sive Scientia Sinensis*. Paris, 1687.

Dampier, William. *A New Voyage round the World*. London, 1697.

Davenant, William. *Gondibert: An Heroick Poem*. London, 1650.

Defoe, Daniel. *The Advantages of Peace and Commerce; With Some Remarks on the East-India Trade*. London, 1729.

Atlas Maritimus & Commercialis; Or, A General View of the World So far as relates to Trade and Navigation. London: James Knapton, 1728.

The Compleat English Gentleman. Ed. Karl D. Bülbring. London: David Nutt, 1890.

The Consolidator: Or, Memoirs of Sundry Transactions from the World in the Moon. Translated from the Lunar Language, By the Author of The True-born English Man. London, 1705.

A General History of Discoveries and Improvements, In useful Arts, Particularly in the great Branches of Commerce, Navigation, Plantation, in all parts of the known World. 4 nos. London, 1725–26.

The Novels of Daniel Defoe. 10 vols. London: Pickering & Chatto, 2008–09.

A Tour through the Whole Island of Great Britain. Ed. Philip Nicholas Furbank and W. R. Owens. New Haven: Yale University Press, 1991.

Denham, John. *The Advancement and Reformation of Modern Poetry.* London, 1701.

Dodsley, Robert, ed. *A Collection of Poems in Six Volumes, by Several Hands.* London, 1758.

Du Halde, J.-B. *A Description of the Empire of China and Chinese-Tartary, Together with the Kingdoms of Korea, and Tibet Containing the Geography and History (Natural as well as Civil) of those Countries.* 2 vols. London, 1738.

Dunton, John. *The Life and Errors of John Dunton, Late Citizen of London.* London, 1705.

Evelyn, John. *The Diary of John Evelyn.* Ed. E. S. de Beer. 6 vols. Oxford: Clarendon Press, 1955.

Felton, Henry. *Dissertation on Reading the Classics and Forming a Just Style.* London, 1715.

Ferguson, Adam. *An Essay on the History of Civil Society.* Cambridge: Cambridge University Press, 1995.

Fielding, Henry. *Joseph Andrews* and *Shamela.* Oxford: Oxford University Press, 1980.

Fontenelle, Bernard le Bovier de. *Conversations on the Plurality of Worlds.* Trans. H. A. Hargreaves. Berkeley: University of California Press, 1990.

A Discovery of New Worlds. Trans. Aphra Behn. London, 1688.

A Plurality of Worlds. Trans. John Glanvill. London, 1688.

Poésies Pastorales. London, 1707.

Gildon, Charles. *The Life and Strange Surprizing Adventures of Mr. D---- De F--, of London, Hosier, Who Has liv'd above fifty Years by himself, in the Kingdoms of North and South Britain.* London, 1719.

Miscellaneous Letters and Essays, On Several Subjects. London, 1694.

Glanvill, Joseph. *Plus Ultra.* London, 1668.

Goldsmith, Oliver. *The Collected Letters of Oliver Goldsmith.* Ed. Katharine Canby Balderston. Cambridge: Cambridge University Press, 1928.

Collected Works of Oliver Goldsmith. Ed. Arthur Friedman. 5 vols. Oxford: Clarendon Press, 1966.

Gueullette, Thomas-Simon. *Chinese Tales: or, the Wonderful Adventures of the Mandarin Fum-Hoam.* London, 1725.

Hakewill, George. *An Apologie or Declaration of the Power and Providence of God.* London, 1635.

Huet, Pierre-Daniel. *The History of Romances. An Enquiry into their Original; Instructions for composing them; An Account of the most Eminent Authors; With Characters and Curious Observations upon the Best Performances of that Kind.* Trans. Stephen Lewis. London, 1715.

Hume, David. *Essays, Moral, Political, and Literary.* Ed. Eugene F. Miller. Indianapolis: Liberty, 1987.

Hurd, Richard. *Letters on Chivalry and Romance.* London, 1762.

Ides, Evert Ysbrants. *Three Years Travels from Moscow Over-Land to China: Thro' Great Ustiga, Siriania, Permia, Sibiria, Daour, Great Tartary, &c. to Peking.* London, 1706.

Johnson, Samuel. *A Dictionary of the English Language.* 2nd ed. London, 1755–56.

Kircher, Athanasius. "Some Special Remarks Taken out of Athanasius Kircher's Antiquities of China." In *An Embassy from the East-India Company of the United Provinces, to the Grand Tartar Cham, Emperor of China Deliver'd by Their Excellencies, Peter de Goyer and Jacob de Keyzer, at His Imperial City of Peking*, by Johan Nieuhof. London, 1669.

Le Comte, Louis. *Memoirs and Observations Made in a Late Journey through the Empire of China.* London, 1697.

Nouveaux mémoires sur l'état présent de la Chine. 2 vols. Paris: 1696.

Macpherson, James. *Fingal, An Ancient Epic Poem.* London, 1762.

Fragments of Ancient Poetry, Collected in the Highlands of Scotland, and Translated from the Galic or Erse Language. Edinburgh, 1760.

Temora, an Ancient Epic Poem. London, 1763.

Magalhães [Magaillans], Gabriel de. *A New History of China.* London, 1688.

Mallet, Paul-Henri. *Northern Antiquities, or A Description of the Manners, Customs, Religion and Laws of the Ancient Danes, and other Northern Nations; Including those of Our Own Saxon Ancestors.* Trans. Thomas Percy. London, 1770.

Mandeville, Sir John. *The Voiage and Trauaile of Syr Iohn Maundeville Knight.* London: Oxford University Press, 1932.

Marana, Giovanni Paolo. *Letters Writ by a Turkish Spy.* Ed. Arthur J. Weitzman. New York: Columbia University Press, 1970.

Martini, Martino. *Bellum Tartaricum, or the Conquest of The Great and most Renowned Empire of China, By the Invasion of the Tartars.* London, 1655.

Sinicae historiae decas prima res a gentis origine ad Christum natum in extrema Asia. Amsterdam, 1659.

Mendoza, Juan González de. *The Historie of the Great and Mightie Kingdome of China, and the Situation Thereof: Together with the Great Riches, Huge, Cities, Politike Gouernement, and Rare Inuentions in the Same.* Trans. R. Parke. London, 1588.

Moll, Herman. *The Compleat Geographer: or, The Chorography and Typography of all the Known Parts of the Earth.* 3rd ed. 2 vols. London, 1709.

Motteux, Pierre. "A Discourse concerning the Ancients and the Moderns." *Gentleman's Journal, or, The Monthly Miscellany.* March 1692.

Navarrete, Domingo Fernández. *An Account of the Empire of China, Historical, Political, Moral and Religious*. In *A Collection of Voyages and Travels*. Vol. 1. London, 1704.

Needham, John Turberville. *De inscriptione quadam AEgyptiaca Taurini inventa, et characteribus AEgyptiis, olim Sinis communibus, exarata, idolo cuidam antique in regia universitate servato*. Rome, 1761.

Nieuhof, Johan. *An Embassy from the East-India Company of the United Provinces, to the Grand Tartar Cham, Emperor of China Deliver'd by Their Excellencies, Peter de Goyer and Jacob de Keyzer, at His Imperial City of Peking*. London, 1669.

Osborne, Dorothy. *The Letters of Dorothy Osborne to William Temple*. Ed. G. C. Moore Smith. Oxford: Clarendon Press, 1928.

Percy, Thomas. *Bishop Percy's Folio Manuscript*. Ed. John W. Hales and Frederick James Furnivall. 3 vols. London: N. Trübner & Co., 1867.

Five Pieces of Runic Poetry Translated from the Islandic Language. London, 1763.

Hau Kiou Choaan, or The Pleasing History. A Translation from the Chinese Language. 4 vols. London, 1761.

The Matrons. London, 1762.

Miscellaneous Pieces Relating to the Chinese. 2 vols. London, 1762.

The Percy Letters. Ed. David Nichol Smith and Cleanth Brooks. 9 vols. Baton Rouge: Louisiana State University Press, 1944–57; New Haven: Yale University Press, 1961–88.

Reliques of Ancient English Poetry: Consisting of Old Heroic Ballads, Songs, and other Pieces of our earlier Poets, (Chiefly of the Lyric kind.) Together with some few of later Date. 3 vols. London, 1765.

Thomas Percy's Life of Dr. Oliver Goldsmith. Ed. Richard L. Harp. Salzburg: Institut für Englische Sprache und Literatur, Universität Salzburg, 1976.

Pope, Alexander. *The Poems of Alexander Pope*. Ed. John Butt. New Haven: Yale University Press, 1963.

Psalmanazar, George. *An Historical and Geographical Description of Formosa, an Island Subject to the Emperor of Japan*. London, 1704.

Memoirs of ****. Commonly Known by the Name of George Psalmanazar; a Reputed Native of Formosa. London, 1764.

Rapin, René. *Observations on the Poems of Homer and Virgil: A Discourse Representing the Excellencies of Those Works; and the Perfections in General of All Heroick Action*. Trans. John Davies. London, 1672.

Rhymer, Thomas. *An Essay Concerning Critical and Curious Learning; In which are contained Some Short Reflectsion on the Controversie betwixt Sir William Temple and Mr. Wotton; And That betwixt Dr. Bentley and Mr. Boyl*. London, 1698.

Semedo, Alvaro. *The History of That Great and Renowned Monarchy of China*. London, 1655.

Shaftesbury, Earl of (Anthony Ashley Cooper). *Characteristicks of Men, Opinions, Times*. 3 vols. London, 1711.

Shebbeare, John. *Letters on the English Nation: By Batista Angeloni, a Jesuit, who resided many years in London. Translated from the Original Italian*. London, 1755.

Sprat, Thomas. *The History of the Royal-Society of London for the Improving of Natural Knowledge*. London, 1667.

Staunton, George Thomas. *Miscellaneous Notices Relating to China, and Our Commercial Intercourse with That Country, Including a Few Translations from the Chinese Language.* London, 1822.

Ta Tsing Leu Lee: Being the Fundamental Laws, and a Selection from the Supplementary Statues, of the Penal Code of China. London, 1810.

Swift, Jonathan. *The Cambridge Edition of the Works of Jonathan Swift.* Vol. 1. Ed. Marcus Walsh. Cambridge: Cambridge University Press, 2010.

A Tale of a Tub. To which is added, An Account of a Battel between the Antient and Modern Books in St. James's Library. London, 1704.

Temple, William. *An Introduction to the History of England.* London, 1695.

Miscellanea. The Second Part. 2nd ed. London, 1690.

Miscellanea. The Third Part. By the late Sir William Temple, Bar. Published by Jonathan Swift, A. M. Prebendary of St. Patrick's, Dublin. London, 1701.

Observations upon the United Provinces. London, 1673.

Trigault, Nicolas. *De Christiana Expeditione Apud Sinas.* Augsburg, 1615.

Verbiest, Ferdinand. "A Voyage of the Emperor of China into the Eastern Tartary, Anno. 1682." *Philosophical Transactions* 16 (1686): 39–62.

Vossius, Isaac. *Dissertatio de vera aetate mundi, qua ostenditur natale mundi tempus annis 1440 vulgarum anticipare.* The Hague, 1659.

Walpole, Horace. "The History of the Modern Taste in Gardening." In *Horace Walpole: Gardenist*, ed. Isabel Wakelin Urban Chase. Princeton: Princeton University Press, 1943. 3–52.

Warton, Thomas. *The History of English Poetry, From the Close of the Eleventh to the Commencement of the Eighteenth Century.* 3 vols. London, 1774–1781.

Observations on the Fairy Queen of Spenser. 2nd ed. London, 1762.

Webb, John. *An Historical Essay Endeavoring a Probability that the Language of the Empire of China is the Primitive Language.* London, 1669.

Wotton, William. *Reflections upon Ancient and Modern Learning.* London, 1694.

Reflections upon Ancient and Modern Learning. 2nd ed. London, 1697.

Reflections upon Ancient and Modern Learning To which is now added a defense thereof, in answer to the objections of Sir W. Temple, and others. With observations upon the Tale of a Tub. London, 1705.

A Defense of the Reflections upon Ancient and Modern Learning, In Answer to the Objections of Sir. W. Temple, and Others. With Observations upon The Tale of a Tub. London, 1705.

Observations upon the State of the Nation, in January 1712/3. 2nd ed. London, 1713.

Secondary Sources

Adas, Michael. *Machines as the Measure of Men: Science, Technology, and Ideologies of Western Dominance.* Ithaca: Cornell University Press, 1989.

Adshead, Samuel Adrian M. *Material Culture in Europe and China, 1400–1800: The Rise of Consumerism.* Basingstoke: Macmillan, 1997.

Akerman, James R., ed. *The Imperial Map: Cartography and the Mastery of Empire.* Chicago: University of Chicago Press, 2009.

Allen, B. Sprague. *Tides in English Taste (1619–1800): A Background for the Study of Literature*. 2 vols. Cambridge, Mass.: Harvard University Press, 1937.

Anderson, Benedict. *Imagined Communities: Reflections on the Origin and Spread of Nationalism*. Rev. ed. New York: Verso, 1991.

The Spectre of Comparisons: Nationalism, Southeast Asia, and the World. London: Verso, 1998.

Appleton, William Worthen. *A Cycle of Cathay: The Chinese Vogue in England during the Seventeenth and Eighteenth Centuries*. New York: Columbia University Press, 1951.

Aravamudan, Srinivas. "Defoe, Commerce, and Empire." In *The Cambridge Companion to Daniel Defoe*, ed. John Richetti, 45–63.

Enlightenment Orientalism: Resisting the Rise of the Novel. Chicago: University of Chicago Press, 2012.

Archer, John Michael. *Old Worlds: Egypt, Southwest Asia, India, and Russia in Early Modern English Writing*. Stanford: Stanford University Press, 2001.

Arrighi, Giovanni. *Adam Smith in Beijing: Lineages of the Twenty-First Century*. London: Verso, 2007.

Backscheider, Paula R., and Catherine Ingrassia, eds. *A Companion to the Eighteenth-Century English Novel and Culture*. Oxford: Blackwell, 2005.

Ballaster, Rosalind. *Fabulous Orients: Fictions of the East in England, 1662–1785*. Oxford: Oxford University Press, 2005.

"Narrative Transmigrations: The Oriental Tale and the Novel in Eighteenth-Century Britain." In *A Companion to the Eighteenth-Century English Novel and Culture*, ed. Paula R. Backscheider and Catherine Ingrassia, 48–96.

Barker, Hannah. *Newspapers, Politics, and Public Opinion in Late Eighteenth-Century England*. Oxford: Clarendon Press, 1998.

Barnes, Linda. *Needles, Herbs, Gods, and Ghosts*. Cambridge, Mass.: Harvard University Press, 2005.

Barrell, John. *English Literature in History, 1730–80: An Equal, Wide Survey*. New York: St. Martin's, 1983.

Bate, Walter Jackson. *From Classic to Romantic: Premises of Taste in Eighteenth-Century England*. Cambridge, Mass.: Harvard University Press, 1946.

Bender, John. *Ends of Enlightenment*. Stanford: Stanford University Press, 2012.

Benedict, Barbara M. *Making the Modern Reader: Cultural Mediation in Early Modern Literary Anthologies*. Princeton: Princeton University Press, 1996.

Benjamin, Walter. *Illuminations*. Ed. Hannah Arendt. Trans. Harry Zohn. New York: Schocken Books, 1969.

Berg, Maxine. *Luxury and Pleasure in Eighteenth-Century Britain*. Oxford: Oxford University Press, 2005.

Billings, Timothy. "Visible Cities: The Heterotopic Utopia of China in Early Modern European Writing." *Genre* 30 (1997): 105–34.

Bivins, Roberta E. *Acupuncture, Expertise and Cross-Cultural Medicine*. Basingstoke: Palgrave, 2000.

Black, Jeremy. *The English Press, 1621–1861*. Thrupp, Stroud, Gloucestershire: Sutton, 2001.

Black, Scott. "Addison's Aesthetics of Novelty." *Studies in Eighteenth-Century Culture* 30 (2001): 269–88.

"Social and Literary Form in the *Spectator.*" *Eighteenth-Century Studies* 33 (1999): 21–42.

Bono, James. *The Word of God and the Languages of Man: Interpreting Nature in Early Modern Science and Medicine.* Madison: University of Wisconsin Press, 1995.

Booth, Wayne. "'The Self-Portraiture of Genius': *The Citizen of the World* and Critical Method." *Modern Philology* 73.4 (1976): S85-S96.

Botein, Stephen, Jack R. Censer, and Harriet Ritvo. "The Periodical Press in Eighteenth-Century English and French Society: A Cross-Cultural Approach." *Comparative Studies in Society and History* 23.3 (1981): 464–90.

Brewer, John. *The Pleasures of the Imagination: English Culture in the Eighteenth Century.* New York: Farrar, Straus and Giroux, 1997.

Bridges, Richard M. "A Possible Source for Daniel Defoe's *The Farther Adventures of Robinson Crusoe.*" *British Journal for Eighteenth-Century Studies* 2.3 (1979): 231–36.

Brockey, Liam Matthew. *Journey to the East: The Jesuit Mission to China, 1579–1724.* Cambridge, Mass.: Belknap Press, 2007.

Brook, Timothy. *Vermeer's Hat: The Seventeenth Century and the Dawn of the Global World.* New York: Bloomsbury Press, 2008.

Brooks, Christopher. "Goldsmith's *Citizen of the World*: Knowledge and the Imposture of 'Orientalism.'" *Texas Studies in Literature and Language* 35.1 (1993): 124–44.

Brown, Laura. *Fables of Modernity: Literature and Culture in the English Eighteenth Century.* Ithaca: Cornell University Press, 2001.

Brown, Tony C. "Joseph Addison and the Pleasures of 'Sharawadgi.'" *English Literary History* 74.1 (2007): 171–93.

Bunn, James H. "The Aesthetics of British Mercantilism." *New Literary History* 11.2 (1980): 303–21.

Bury, J. B. *The Idea of Progress: An Inquiry into Its Origin and Growth.* London: Macmillan, 1920.

Bush, Newell Richard. *The Marquis d'Argens and his Philosophical Correspondence. A Critical Study of d'Argens' Lettres juives, Lettres cabalistiques and Lettres chinoises.* Ann Arbor: Edwards Bros, 1953.

Butler, Marilyn. "Antiquarianism (Popular)." In *An Oxford Companion to the Romantic Age: British Culture, 1776–1832,* ed. Iain McCalman (Oxford: Oxford University Press, 1999), 328–38.

Calinescu, Matei. *Five Faces of Modernity: Modernism, Avant-Garde, Decadence, Kitsch, Postmodernism.* Durham: Duke University Press, 1987.

Chakrabarty, Dipesh. *Provincializing Europe: Postcolonial Thought and Historical Difference.* Princeton: Princeton University Press, 2000.

Chan, Leo Tak-hung, ed. *One into Many: Translation and the Dissemination of Classical Chinese Literature.* Amsterdam: Rodopi, 2003.

Chang, Elizabeth Hope. *Britain's Chinese Eye: Literature, Empire, and Aesthetics in Nineteenth-Century Britain.* Stanford: Stanford University Press, 2010.

Chang, Y. Z. "A Note on Sharawadgi." *Modern Language Notes* 45.4 (1930): 221–24.
Chaudhuri, K. N. *The Trading World of Asia and the English East India Company, 1660–1760.* Cambridge: Cambridge University Press, 1978.
Cheah, Pheng. "Grounds of Comparison." *diacritics* 29.4 (1999): 3–18.
Chen, Jeng-Guo S. "The British View of Chinese Civilization and the Emergence of Class Consciousness." *The Eighteenth Century: Theory and Interpretation* 45.2 (2004): 193–205.
Chen, Shouyi. "John Webb: A Forgotten Page in the Early History of Sinology in Europe." In *The Vision of China in the English Literature of the Seventeenth and Eighteenth Centuries*, ed. Adrian Hsia, 87–114.
"Thomas Percy and His Chinese Studies." In *The Vision of China in the English Literature of the Seventeenth and Eighteenth Centuries*, ed. Adrian Hsia, 301–24.
Cheung, Kai-chong. "The *Haoqiu zhuan*, the First Chinese Novel Translated in Europe: With Special Reference to Percy's and Davis's Renditions." In *One into Many*, ed. Leo Tak-hung Chan, 29–38.
Cipolla, Carlo M. *Guns and Sails in the Early Phase of European Expansion, 1400–1700.* London: Collins, 1965.
Clarke, Bob. *From Grub Street to Fleet Street: An Illustrated History of English Newspapers to 1899.* Aldershot: Ashgate, 2004.
Clarke, David. *Chinese Art and Its Encounter with the World.* Hong Kong: Hong Kong University Press, 2011.
"Chitqua's English Adventure: An Eighteenth-Century Source for the Study of China Coast Pidgin and Early Chinese Use of English." *Hong Kong Journal of Applied Linguistics* 10.1 (2005): 47–58.
Clarke, Ernest. "The Medical Education and Qualifications of Oliver Goldsmith." *Proceedings of the Royal Society of Medicine* 7, Section of the History of Medicine (1914): 88–97.
Cocks, Anna Somers. "The Nonfunctional Use of Ceramics in the English Country House During the Eighteenth Century." In *The Fashioning and Functioning of the British Country House*, ed. Gervase Jackson-Stops et al., 195–215.
Cohen, Michèle. "'Manners' Make the Man: Politeness, Chivalry, and the Construction of Masculinity, 1750–1830." *Journal of British Studies* 44.2 (2005): 312–29.
Cohen, Ralph. "Literary History and the Ballad of George Barnwel." In *Augustan Studies: Essays in Honor of Irvin Ehrenpreis*, ed. Douglas Lane Patey and Timothy Keegan (Cranbury, NJ: Associated University Presses, 1985), 13–31.
Cohen, Ralph, ed. *Studies in Eighteenth-Century British Art and Aesthetics.* Berkeley: University of California Press, 1985.
Cole, Lucinda. *Imperfect Creatures: Vermin, Literature, and the Sciences of Life, 1600–1740.* Ann Arbor: University of Michigan Press, 2016.
Connell, Philip. "British Identities and the Politics of Ancient Poetry in Later Eighteenth-Century England." *The Historical Journal* 49.1 (2006): 161–92.
Cook, Harold John. *Matters of Exchange: Commerce, Medicine, and Science in the Dutch Golden Age.* New Haven: Yale University Press, 2007.

Copeland, Robert. *Spode's Willow Pattern & Other Designs after the Chinese.* New York: Rizzoli, 1980.

Cottegnies, Line. "The Translator as Critic: Aphra Behn's Translation of Fontenelle's *Discovery of New Worlds* (1688)." *Restoration* 27.1 (2003): 23–38.

Crane, Ronald S., and Hamilton J. Smith. "A French Influence on Goldsmith's *Citizen of the World.*" *Modern Philology* 19 (1921): 83–92.

Crill, Rosemary. *Chintz: Indian Textiles for the West.* London: V&A, 2008.

Cristóvão, Fernando. "Les livres portugais de voyages en Chine au XVII siècle." In *Proceedings of the Xth Congress of the International Comparative Literature Association* (1985): 422–26.

Curran, Stuart. *Poetic Form and British Romanticism.* Oxford: Oxford University Press, 1986.

Curtis, Julia B. "Markets, Motifs and Seventeenth-Century Porcelain from Jingdezhen." In *The Porcelains of Jingdezhen*, ed. Rosemary E. Scott (London: School of Oriental and African Studies, University of London, 1993), 123–49.

Dalnekoff, Donna Isaacs. "A Familiar Stranger: The Outsider of Eighteenth Century Satire." *Neophilologus* 57.2 (1973): 121–34.

Damrosch, Leopold, Jr. "The Significance of Addison's Criticism." *Studies in English Literature, 1500–1900* 3 (1979): 421–30.

Davis, Bertram Hylton. *Thomas Percy: A Scholar-Cleric in the Age of Johnson.* Philadelphia: University of Pennsylvania Press, 1989.

Davis, Lennard J. *Factual Fictions: The Origins of the English Novel.* New York: Columbia University Press, 1983.

Deane, Seamus. "Goldsmith's *The Citizen of the World.*" In *The Art of Oliver Goldsmith*, ed. Andrew Swarbrick (Totowa, NJ: Barnes & Noble, 1984), 33–50.

De Bolla, Peter. *The Education of the Eye: Painting, Landscape, and Architecture in Eighteenth-Century Britain.* Stanford: Stanford University Press, 2003.

DeJean, Joan. *Ancients against Moderns: Culture Wars and the Making of a Fin de Siècle.* Chicago: University of Chicago Press, 1997.

"No Man's Land: The Novel's First Geography." *Yale French Studies* 73 (1987): 175–89.

De Weerdt, Hilde. "Maps and Memory: Readings of Cartography in Twelfth- and Thirteenth-Century Song China." *Imago Mundi* 61.2 (2009): 145–67.

Dieckmann, Herbert. "Philosophy and Literature in Eighteenth-Century France." *Comparative Literature Studies* 8.1 (1971): 21–41.

Dix, Robin. "Addison and the Concept of 'Novelty' as a Basic Aesthetic Category." *British Journal of Aesthetics* 26.4 (1986): 383–90.

Donoghue, Frank. *The Fame Machine: Book Reviewing and Eighteenth-Century Literary Careers.* Stanford: Stanford University Press, 1996.

Dharwadker, Aparna. "Nation, Race, and the Ideology of Commerce in Defoe." *The Eighteenth Century: Theory and Interpretation* 39.1 (1998): 63–84.

Dussinger, John A. "Goldsmith, Oliver (1728?–1774)." *Oxford Dictionary of National Biography.* Oxford University Press, 2004; online edn, January 2009 [http://oxforddnb.com/view/article/10924, accessed 10 July 2015].

Edney, Matthew H. "The Irony of Imperial Mapping." In *The Imperial Map: Cartography and the Mastery of Empire*, ed. James R. Akerman, 11–45.
Elioseff, Lee Andrew. *The Cultural Milieu of Addison's Literary Criticism*. Austin: University of Texas Press, 1963.
Elledge, Scott, and Donald Stephen Schier, eds. *The Continental Model: Selected French Critical Essays of the Seventeenth Century, in English Translation*. Minneapolis: University of Minnesota Press, 1960.
Elliott, John Huxtable. *The Old World and the New, 1492–1650*. Cambridge: Cambridge University Press, 1970.
Evans, Robin. *Translations from Drawing to Building and Other Essays*. London: Architectural Association, 1997.
Ezell, Margaret J. M. *Social Authorship and the Advent of Print*. Baltimore: Johns Hopkins University Press, 1999.
Fabian, Johannes. *Time and the Other: How Anthropology Makes Its Object*. New York: Columbia University Press, 1983.
Fabricant, Carole. "The Aesthetics and Politics of Landscape in the Eighteenth Century." In *Studies in Eighteenth-Century British Art and Aesthetics*, ed. Ralph Cohen, 49–81.
Fan, Cunzhong [Fan, T. C.]. "Percy and Du Halde." *The Review of English Studies* 21.84 (1945): 326–29.
"Percy's *Hau Kiou Choaan*." *The Review of English Studies* 22.86 (1946): 117–25.
"Sir William Jones's Chinese Studies." *The Review of English Studies* 22 (1946): 304–14. Reprinted in *The Vision of China in the English Literature of the Seventeenth and Eighteenth Centuries*, ed. Adrian Hsia, 325–37.
Finlay, Robert. *The Pilgrim Art: Cultures of Porcelain in World History*. Berkeley: University of California Press, 2010.
"The Pilgrim Art: The Culture of Porcelain in World History." *Journal of World History* 9.2 (1998): 141–87.
Foerster, Donald Madison. *Homer in English Criticism: The Historical Approach in the Eighteenth Century*. New Haven: Yale University Press, 1947.
Forbes, H. A. Crosby. *Hills and Streams: Landscape Decoration on Chinese Export Blue and White Porcelain*. Milton, Mass.: The China Trade Museum, 1982.
Force, James E. "Newton, the 'Ancients,' and the 'Moderns.'" In *Newton and Religion: Context, Nature, and Influence*, ed. James E. Force and Richard H. Popkin (Dordrecht: Kluwer, 1999), 237–57.
Forman, Ross G. *China and the Victorian Imagination: Empires Entwined*. Cambridge: Cambridge University Press, 2013.
Foss, Theodore Nicholas. "The European Sojourn of Philippe Couplet and Michael Shen Fuzong, 1683–1692." In *Philippe Couplet, S. J. (1623–1693): The Man who Brought China to Europe*, ed. Jerome Heyndrickx (Nettetal: Steyler Verlag, 1990), 121–40.
Frank, Andre Gunder. *ReOrient: Global Economy in the Asian Age*. Berkeley: University of California Press, 1998.
Free, Melissa. "Un-Erasing *Crusoe: Farther Adventures* in the Nineteenth Century." *Book History* 9 (2006): 89–130.

Friedman, Albert B. *The Ballad Revival: Studies in the Influence of Popular on Sophisticated Poetry*. Chicago: University of Chicago Press, 1961.

Friedman, Arthur. "Goldsmith and the Marquis D'Argens." *Modern Language Notes* 53.3 (1938): 173–76.

Fumerton, Patricia, Anita Guerrini, and Kris McAbee, eds. *Ballads and Broadsides in Britain, 1500–1800*. Farnham: Ashgate, 2010.

Ganse, Shirley H. *Chinese Export Porcelain: East to West*. San Francisco: Long River Press, 2008.

Garrod, H. W. "Phalaris and Phalarism." In *Seventeenth-Century Studies Presented to Sir Herbert Grierson*, ed. Logan Pearsall Smith and John Dover Wilson (Oxford: Clarendon Press, 1938), 360–71.

Gascoigne, John. " 'The Wisdom of Egyptians' and the Secularisation of History in the Age of Newton." In *The Uses of Antiquity: The Scientific Revolution and the Classical Tradition*, ed. Stephen Gaukroger (Dordrecht: Kluwer Academic Publishers, 1991), 171–212.

Gaussen, Alice. *Percy: Prelate and Poet*. London: Smith, Elder, & Co, 1908.

Gerritsen, Anne, and Stephen McDowall. "Material Culture and the Other: European Encounters with Chinese Porcelain, ca. 1650–1800." *Journal of World History* 23.1 (2012): 87–113.

Gilbert, Felix. *Machiavelli and Guicciardini: Politics and History in Sixteenth-Century Florence*. Princeton: Princeton University Press, 1965.

Gombrich, E. H. "Eastern Inventions and Western Response." *Daedalus* 127.1 (1998): 193–205.

Grafton, Anthony. "Renaissance Readers and Ancient Texts: Comments on Some Commentaries." *Renaissance Quarterly* 38.4 (1985): 615–49.

Graham, Walter James. *The Beginnings of English Literary Periodicals: A Study of Periodical Literature, 1665–1715*. New York: Oxford University Press, 1926.

Green, Martin. *Dreams of Adventure, Deeds of Empire*. New York: Basic Books, 1979.

Griffin, Michael. *Enlightenment in Ruins: The Geographies of Oliver Goldsmith*. Lewisburg: Bucknell University Press, 2013.

Groom, Nick. *The Making of Percy's Reliques*. Oxford: Clarendon Press, 1999.

Grosrichard, Alain. *The Sultan's Court: European Fantasies of the East*. London: Verso, 1998.

Harris, Michael. *London Newspapers in the Age of Walpole: A Study of the Origins of the Modern English Press*. Cranbury, NJ: Associated University Presses, 1987.

Haugen, Kristine Louise. *Richard Bentley: Poetry and Enlightenment*. Cambridge, Mass.: Harvard University Press, 2011.

Hayot, Eric, Haun Saussy, and Steven G. Yao, eds. *Sinographies: Writing China*. Minneapolis: University of Minnesota Press, 2008.

Hazard, Paul. *La crise de la conscience européenne, 1680–1715*. Paris: Fayard, 1961.

Helgerson, Richard. "Before National Literary History." *Modern Language Quarterly* 64.2 (2003): 169–79.

"The Two Worlds of Oliver Goldsmith." *Studies in English Literature, 1500–1900* 13.3 (1973): 516–34.

Hessney, Richard C. "Beyond Beauty and Talent: The Moral and Chivalric Self in *The Fortunate Union*." In *Expressions of Self in Chinese Literature*, ed. Robert E. Hegel and Richard C. Hessney (New York: Columbia University Press, 1985), 214–50.

Hill, Christopher. "Robinson Crusoe." *History Workshop* 10 (1980): 6–24.

Hillemann, Ulrike. *Asian Empire and British Knowledge: China and the Networks of British Imperial Expansion*. Houndmills: Palgrave Macmillan, 2009.

Hinnant, Charles H. "Sir William Temple's Views on Science, Poetry, and the Imagination." *Studies in Eighteenth-Century Culture* 8 (1979): 187–203.

Hodgen, Margaret T. *Early Anthropology in the Sixteenth and Seventeenth Centuries*. Philadelphia: University of Pennsylvania Press, 1964.

Holmes, Geoffrey. *The Making of a Great Power: Late Stuart and Early Georgian Britain, 1660–1722*. London: Longman, 1993.

Honour, Hugh. *Chinoiserie: The Vision of Cathay*. London: J. Murray, 1961.

Horrocks, Ingrid. "'Circling Eye' and 'Houseless Stranger': The New Eighteenth-Century Wanderer (Thomson to Goldsmith)." *English Literary History* 77.3 (2010): 665–87.

Hostetler, Laura. *Qing Colonial Enterprise: Ethnography and Cartography in Early Modern China*. Chicago: University of Chicago Press, 2001.

"A Mirror for the Monarch: A Literary Portrait of China in Eighteenth-Century France." *Asia Major* 3.19 (2006): 349–76.

Howard, David Sanctuary. *The Choice of the Private Trader: The Private Market in Chinese Export Porcelain Illustrated from the Hodroff Collection*. London: Zwemmer, 1994.

Hsia, Adrian, ed. *The Vision of China in the English Literature of the Seventeenth and Eighteenth Centuries*. Hong Kong: Chinese University Press, 1998.

Hsia, Florence C. *Sojourners in a Strange Land: Jesuits and their Scientific Missions in Late Imperial China*. Chicago: University of Chicago Press, 2009.

Hudson, Nicholas. "'Oral Tradition': The Evolution of an Eighteenth-Century Concept." In *Tradition in Transition: Women Writers, Marginal Texts, and the Eighteenth-Century Canon*, ed. Alvaro Ribeiro and James G. Basker, 161–76.

Hulme, Peter. *Colonial Encounters: Europe and the Native Caribbean, 1492–1797*. London: Methuen, 1986.

Hunt, John Dixon. *The Figure in the Landscape: Poetry, Painting, and Gardening During the Eighteenth Century*. Baltimore: Johns Hopkins University Press, 1976.

Hunter, J. Paul. *Before Novels: The Cultural Contexts of Eighteenth-Century English Fiction*. New York: W. W. Norton, 1990.

Hutt, Julia. "Asia in Europe: Lacquer for the West." In *Encounters: The Meeting of Asia and Europe, 1500–1800*, ed. Anna Jackson and Amin Jaffer (London: V&A, 2004), 234–49.

Impey, Oliver R. *Chinoiserie: The Impact of Oriental Styles on Western Art and Decoration*. London: Oxford University Press, 1977.

Israel, Jonathan. *Enlightenment Contested: Philosophy, Modernity, and the Emancipation of Man, 1670–1752*. Oxford: Oxford University Press, 2006.

Jackson-Stops, Gervase, Gordon J. Schochet, Lena Cowen Orlin, and Elisabeth Blair MacDougall, eds. *The Fashioning and Functioning of the British Country House*. Washington, D.C.: National Gallery of Art, 1989.

Jacob, Christian. *The Sovereign Map: Theoretical Approaches in Cartography throughout History*. Trans. Tom Conley. Chicago: University of Chicago Press, 2006.

Jacob, Margaret C. *Strangers Nowhere in the World: The Rise of Cosmopolitanism in Early Modern Europe*. Philadelphia: University of Pennsylvania Press, 2006.

Jacobsen, Stefan Gaarsmand. "Chinese Influences or Images? Fluctuating Histories of How Enlightenment Europe Read China." *Journal of World History* 24.3 (2013): 623–60.

Jacobson, Dawn. *Chinoiserie*. London: Phaidon, 1993.

Janowitz, Anne. *England's Ruins: Poetic Purpose and the National Landscape*. Oxford: Blackwell, 1990.

Jardine, Lisa. *Going Dutch: How England Plundered Holland's Glory*. London: Harper Press, 2008.

Jarry, Madeleine. *Chinoiserie: Chinese Influence on European Decorative Art, Seventeenth and Eighteenth Centuries*. New York: Vendome Press, 1981.

Jauss, Hans Robert. "Modernity and Literary Tradition." Trans. Christian Thorne. *Critical Inquiry* 31.2 (2005): 329–64.

Jensen, Lionel. *Manufacturing Confucianism: Chinese Traditions and Universal Civilization*. Durham: Duke University Press, 1997.

Johnston, Arthur. *Enchanted Ground: The Study of Medieval Romance in the Eighteenth Century*. London: Athlone Press, 1964.

Jones, Richard Foster. *Ancients and Moderns: A Study of the Rise of the Scientific Movement in Seventeenth-Century England*. 2nd ed. St. Louis: Washington University, 1961.

Jörg, Christiaan J. A., and Jan van Campen. *Chinese Ceramics in the Collection of the Rijksmuseum, Amsterdam: The Ming and Qing Dynasties*. London: Philip Wilson, in association with the Rijksmuseum, 1997.

Kalter, Barrett. *Modern Antiques: The Material Past in England, 1660–1780*. Lewisburg: Bucknell University Press, 2012.

Keevak, Michael. *The Pretended Asian: George Psalmanazar's Eighteenth-Century Formosan Hoax*. Detroit: Wayne State University Press, 2004.

Kermode, Frank. *The Genesis of Secrecy: On the Interpretation of Narrative*. Cambridge, Mass.: Harvard University Press, 1979.

Ketcham, Michael G. *Transparent Designs: Reading, Performance, and Form in the Spectator Papers*. Athens: University of Georgia Press, 1985.

Keulemans, Paize. "Translating Empire: Vondel's *Zungchin* and the Fall of the Ming Dynasty." Paper presented at a conference on *The Dutch Golden Age and the World* at Columbia University in March 2007.

Keuning, Johannes. "Nicolaas Witsen as a Cartographer." *Imago Mundi* 11 (1954): 95–110.

Kidd, Colin. *British Identities before Nationalism: Ethnicity and Nationhood in the Atlantic World, 1600–1800*. Cambridge: Cambridge University Press, 1999.

Kietzman, Mary Jo. "Defoe Masters the Serial Subject." *English Literary History* 66.3 (1999): 677–705.

Kim, Thomas W. "Being Modern: The Circulation of Oriental Objects." *American Quarterly* 58.2 (2006): 379–406.

Kitson, Peter J. *Forging Romantic China: Sino-British Cultural Exchange, 1760–1840.* Cambridge: Cambridge University Press, 2013.

"'That mighty Wall, not fabulous / China's stupendous mound!': Romantic Period Accounts of China's 'Great Wall.'" In *New Directions in Travel Writing Studies*, ed. Paul Smethurst and Julia Kuehn (New York: Palgrave Macmillan, 2015), 83–96.

Kitson, Peter J., and Robert Markley, eds. *Writing China: Essays on the Amherst Embassy (1816) and Sino-British Cultural Relations.* Cambridge: D. S. Brewer, 2016.

Klein, Bernhard. *Maps and the Writing of Space in Early Modern England and Ireland.* New York: Palgrave, 2001.

Kley, Edwin J. Van. "Europe's 'Discovery' of China and the Writing of World History." *American Historical Review* 76.2 (1971): 358–85.

Kliger, Samuel. *The Goths in England: A Study in Seventeenth and Eighteenth Century Thought.* Cambridge, Mass.: Harvard University Press, 1952.

Knoespel, Kenneth J. "Newton in the School of Time: The Chronology of Ancient Kingdoms Amended and the Crisis of Seventeenth-Century Historiography." *The Eighteenth Century: Theory and Interpretation* 30.3 (1989): 19–41.

Kosuda-Warner, Joanne, and Elizabeth Johnson. *Landscape Wallcoverings.* London: Scala Publishers in association with Cooper-Hewitt, National Design Museum, 2001.

Kowaleski-Wallace, Elizabeth. *Consuming Subjects: Women, Shopping, and Business in the Eighteenth Century.* New York: Columbia University Press, 1996.

Kramnick, Jonathan Brody. *Making the English Canon: Print-Capitalism and the Cultural Past, 1700–1770.* Cambridge: Cambridge University Press, 1998.

Kristeller, Paul O. "The Modern System of the Arts: A Study in the History of Aesthetics (I)." *Journal of the History of Ideas* 12.4 (1951): 496–527.

Lach, Donald F., and Edwin J. Van Kley. *Asia in the Making of Europe.* 3 vols. Chicago: University of Chicago Press, 1965–93.

Lam, Ling Hon. "A Case of the Chinese (Dis)order? The *Haoqiu zhuan* and Competing Forms of Knowledge in European and Japanese Readings." *East Asian Publishing and Society* 3.1 (2013): 71–102.

Latour, Bruno. *We Have Never been Modern.* Cambridge, Mass.: Harvard University Press, 1993.

Lawson, Philip. *A Taste for Empire and Glory: Studies in British Overseas Expansion, 1660–1800.* Aldershot, Hampshire: Variorum, 1997.

Levine, Joseph M. *The Battle of the Books: History and Literature in the Augustan Age.* Ithaca: Cornell University Press, 1991.

Lipking, Lawrence. "Literary Criticism and the Rise of National Literary History." In *The Cambridge History of English Literature, 1660–1780*, ed. John J. Richetti (Cambridge: Cambridge University Press, 2005), 471–97.

Liu, Lydia H. "Robinson Crusoe's Earthenware Pot." *Critical Inquiry* 25.4 (1999): 728–57.

Liu, Yu. *Seeds of a Different Eden: Chinese Gardening Ideas and a New English Aesthetic Ideal.* Columbia: University of South Carolina Press, 2008.

Lovejoy, Arthur O. *Essays in the History of Ideas.* Baltimore: Johns Hopkins University Press, 1948.

Lovell, Julia. *The Great Wall: China Against the World, 1000 BC–AD 2000.* New York: Grove Press, 2006.

Lowenthal, David. *The Past Is a Foreign Country.* Cambridge: Cambridge University Press, 1985.

Mackenzie, Eileen. "Thomas Percy and Ballad 'Correctness.'" *The Review of English Studies* 21.81 (1945): 58–60.

Mancall, Mark. *Russia and China: Their Diplomatic Relations to 1728.* Cambridge, Mass.: Harvard University Press, 1971.

Marburg, Clara. *Sir William Temple, A Seventeenth Century "Libertin."* New Haven: Yale University Press, 1932.

Markley, Robert. "'The destin'd Walls/Of Cambalu': Milton, China, and the Ambiguities of the East." In *Milton and the Imperial Vision*, ed. Balachandra Rajan and Elizabeth Sauer (Pittsburgh: Duquesne University Press, 1999), 191–213.

Fallen Languages: Crises of Representation in Newtonian England, 1660–1740. Ithaca: Cornell University Press, 1993.

The Far East and the English Imagination, 1600–1730. Cambridge: Cambridge University Press, 2006.

"Global Analogies: Cosmology, Geosymmetry, and Skepticism in Some Works of Aphra Behn." In *Science, Literature and Rhetoric in Early Modern England*, ed. Juliet Cummins and David Burchell (Aldershot: Ashgate, 2007), 189–212.

Marshall, David. "The Problem of the Picturesque." *Eighteenth-Century Studies* 35.3 (2002): 413–37.

Martin, Julian. "Francis Bacon, Authority, and the Moderns." In *The Rise of Modern Philosophy: The Tension Between the New and Traditional Philosophies from Machiavelli to Leibniz*, ed. Tom Sorell (Oxford: Clarendon Press, 1995), 71–88.

Maurer, Shawn L. *Proposing Men: Dialectics of Gender and Class in the Eighteenth-Century English Periodical.* Stanford: Stanford University Press, 1998.

Mayhew, Robert J. *Enlightenment Geography: The Political Languages of British Geography, 1650–1850.* New York: St. Martin's Press, 2000.

Mayo, Robert Donald. *The English Novel in the Magazines, 1740–1815. With a Catalogue of 1375 Magazine Novels and Novelettes.* Evanston: Northwestern University Press, 1962.

McBurney, William H. "The Authorship of the Turkish Spy." *Publications of the Modern Language Association of America* 72.5 (1957): 915–35.

McCalman, Iain, ed. *An Oxford Companion to the Romantic Age: British Culture, 1776–1832.* Oxford: Oxford University Press, 1999.

McEwen, Gilbert D. *The Oracle of the Coffee House: John Dunton's Athenian Mercury.* San Marino: Huntington Library, 1972.

McMahon, Keith. *Misers, Shrews, and Polygamists: Sexuality and Male-Female Relations in Eighteenth-Century Chinese Fiction*. Durham: Duke University Press, 1995.

Milner-Barry, Alda. "A Note on the Early Literary Relations of Oliver Goldsmith and Thomas Percy." *The Review of English Studies* 2.5 (1926): 51–61.

Milner-Barry, Alda, and L. F. Powell. "A Further Note on Hau Kiou Choaan." *The Review of English Studies* 3.10 (1927): 214–18.

Min, Eun Kyung. "China between the Ancients and the Moderns." *The Eighteenth Century: Theory and Interpretation* 45.2 (2004): 115–29.

———. "Master Zhuang's Wife: Translating the Ephesian Matron in Thomas Percy's The Matrons (1762)." In *Writing China: Essays on the Amherst Embassy (1816) and Sino-British Cultural Relations*, ed. Peter J. Kitson and Robert Markley, 32–55.

———. "Novel/Topograph: Robinson Crusoe and the Great Wall of China." *Horizons: Seoul Journal of Humanities* 1.2 (2010): 251–75.

———. "The Rise and Fall of Chinese Empires on the English Stage, 1660–1760." *The Journal of Eighteenth-Century English Literature* 3.1 (2006): 53–75.

———. "Thomas Percy's Chinese Miscellanies and the *Reliques of Ancient English Poetry* (1765)." *Eighteenth-Century Studies* 43.3 (2010): 307–24.

Moore, Leslie E. *Beautiful Sublime: The Making of Paradise Lost, 1701–1734*. Stanford: Stanford University Press, 1990.

Mungello, D. E. *Curious Land: Jesuit Accommodation and the Origins of Sinology*. Honolulu: University of Hawaii Press, 1989. Reprint of *Studia Leibnitiana Supplementa* 25 (1985).

Murray, Ciaran. "Sharawadgi Resolved." *Garden History* 26.2 (1998): 208–13.

Nebenzahl, Kenneth. *Mapping the Silk Road and Beyond: 2,000 Years of Exploring the East*. London: Phaidon, 2004.

Nichols, John. *Illustrations of the Literary History of the Eighteenth Century*. 8 vols. London: Nichols, Son, and Bentley, 1817–58.

Nisbet, H. B., and Claude Rawson, eds. *The Eighteenth Century*. Vol. 4 of *The Cambridge History of Literary Criticism*. Cambridge: Cambridge University Press, 2008.

Novak, Maximillian E. *Daniel Defoe: Master of Fictions*. Oxford: Oxford University Press, 2001.

———. *Economics and the Fiction of Daniel Defoe*. Berkeley: University of California Press, 1962.

———. *Realism, Myth, and History in Defoe's Fiction*. Lincoln: University of Nebraska Press, 1983.

Nussbaum, Felicity A., ed. *The Global Eighteenth Century*. Baltimore: Johns Hopkins University Press, 2003.

O'Brien, Karen. "The History Market in Eighteenth-Century England." In *Books and Their Readers in Eighteenth-Century England*, ed. Isabel Rivers, 105–34.

Ogburn, Vincent H. "The Wilkinson MSS. and Percy's Chinese Books." *The Review of English Studies* 9.33 (1933): 30–36.

Ong, Walter J. *Orality and Literacy*. New York: Routledge, 1988.

Pagden, Anthony. *European Encounters with the New World from Renaissance to Romanticism.* New Haven: Yale University Press, 1993.

Palmer, Roy. "Percy, Thomas (1729–1811)." *Oxford Dictionary of National Biography.* Oxford University Press, 2004; online edn, May 2006 [http://oxforddnb. com/view/article/21959, accessed 25 June 2012].

Park, Julie. *The Self and It: Novel Objects in Eighteenth-Century England.* Stanford: Stanford University Press, 2010.

Park, Robert E. "The Natural History of the Newspaper." *American Journal of Sociology* 29.3 (1923): 273–89.

Parker, Charles H. *Global Interactions in the Early Modern Age, 1400–1800.* Cambridge: Cambridge University Press, 2010.

Patey, Douglas Lane. "Ancients and Moderns." In *The Eighteenth Century,* ed. H. B. Nisbet and C. J. Rawson, 32–71.

Paulson, Ronald. *The Beautiful, Novel, and Strange: Aesthetics and Heterodoxy.* Baltimore: Johns Hopkins University Press, 1996.

"What Is Modern in Eighteenth-Century Literature?" *Studies in Eighteenth-Century Culture* 1 (1971): 75–86.

Perdue, Peter C. "Boundaries and Trade in the Early Modern World: Negotiations at Nerchinsk and Beijing." *Eighteenth-Century Studies* 43.3 (2010): 341–56.

China Marches West: The Qing Conquest of Central Eurasia. Cambridge, Mass.: Belknap Press, 2005.

Peters, Marion. *De wijze koopman: Het wereldwijde onderzoek van Nicolaes Witsen (1641–1717), burgemeester en VOC-bewindhebber van Amsterdam.* Amsterdam: Bert Bakker, 2010.

Pincus, Steven C. A. *Protestantism and Patriotism: Ideologies and the Making of English Foreign Policy, 1650–1668.* Cambridge: Cambridge University Press, 1995.

Pinot, Virgile. *La Chine et la formation de l'esprit philosophique en France (1640–1740).* Paris: P. Geuthner, 1932.

Plumb, J. H. "The Acceptance of Modernity." In *The Birth of a Consumer Society: The Commercialization of Eighteenth-Century England,* ed. Neil McKendrick, John Brewer and J. H. Plumb (Bloomington: Indiana University Press, 1982), 316–34.

Pollock, Anthony. "Neutering Addison and Steele: Aesthetic Failure and the Spectatorial Public Sphere." *English Literary History* 74.3 (2007): 707–34.

Porter, David. *The Chinese Taste in Eighteenth-Century England.* Cambridge: Cambridge University Press, 2010.

Ideographia: The Chinese Cipher in Early Modern Europe. Stanford: Stanford University Press, 2001.

Porter, David, ed. *Comparative Early Modernities, 1100–1800.* New York: Palgrave Macmillan, 2012.

Potvin, John, and Alla Myzelev, eds. *Material Cultures, 1740–1990: The Meanings and Pleasures of Collecting.* Burlington, VT: Ashgate, 2009.

Powell, L. F. "*Hau Kiou Choaan.*" *The Review of English Studies* 2.8 (1926): 446–55.

Powell, Manushag N. *Performing Authorship in Eighteenth-Century English Periodicals.* Lewisburg: Bucknell University Press, 2012.

Pratt, Mary Louise. *Imperial Eyes: Travel Writing and Transculturation.* New York: Routledge, 1992.

Prior, James. *The Life of Oliver Goldsmith, M. B., from a Variety of Original Sources.* 2 vols. London: J. Murray, 1837.

Qian, Zhongshu [Ch'ien, Chung-shu]. "China in the English Literature of the Eighteenth Century." *Quarterly Bulletin of Chinese Bibliography,* new series, vol. 2 (1941): 7–28; 113–52. Reprinted in *The Vision of China in the English Literature of the Seventeenth and Eighteenth Centuries,* ed. Adrian Hsia, 117–213.

"China in the English Literature of the Seventeenth Century." *Quarterly Bulletin of Chinese Bibliography,* new series, vol. 1 (1940): 351–84. Reprinted in *The Vision of China in the English Literature of the Seventeenth and Eighteenth Centuries,* ed. Adrian Hsia, 29–68.

Rajan, Balachandra, and Elizabeth Sauer, eds. *Milton and the Imperial Vision.* Pittsburgh: Duquesne University Press, 1999.

Ramsey, Rachel. "China and the Ideal of Order in John Webb's *An Historical Essay.*" *Journal of the History of Ideas* 62.3 (2001): 483–503.

Raven, James. "New Reading Histories, Print Culture and the Identification of Change: The Case of Eighteenth-Century England." *Social History* 23.3 (1998): 268–87.

Ray, Romita. "Storm in a Teacup? Visualising Tea Consumption in the British Empire." In *Art and the British Empire,* ed. T. J. Barringer, Geoff Quilley, and Douglas Fordham (Manchester: Manchester University Press, 2007), 205–22.

Reinhartz, Dennis. *The Cartographer and the Literati: Herman Moll and his Intellectual Circle.* Lewiston, NY: E. Mellen Press, 1997.

Rendall, Jane. "Tacitus Engendered: 'Gothic Feminism' and British Histories, c. 1750–1800." In *Imagining Nations,* ed. Geoffrey Cubitt (Manchester: Manchester University Press, 1998), 57–74.

Ribeiro, Alvaro, and James G. Baker, eds. *Tradition in Transition: Women Writers, Marginal Texts, and the Eighteenth-Century Canon.* Oxford: Clarendon Press, 1996.

Richards, Sarah. *Eighteenth-Century Ceramics: Products for a Civilised Society.* Manchester: Manchester University Press, 1999.

Richetti, John, ed. *The Cambridge Companion to Daniel Defoe.* Cambridge: Cambridge University Press, 2008.

The Cambridge History of English Literature, 1660–1780. Cambridge: Cambridge University Press, 2005.

Rivers, Isabel, ed. *Books and Their Readers in Eighteenth-Century England.* London: Leicester University Press, 2001.

Rix, Robert W. "Romancing Scandinavia: Relocating Chivalry and Romance in Eighteenth-Century Britain." *European Romantic Review* 20.1 (2009): 3–20.

"Thomas Percy's Antiquarian Alternative to Ossian." *Journal of Folklore Research* 46.2 (2009): 197–229.

Rojas, Carlos. *The Great Wall: A Cultural History*. Cambridge, Mass.: Harvard University Press, 2010.

Ross, Trevor Thornton. "The Emergence of 'Literature': Making and Reading the English Canon in the Eighteenth Century." *English Literary History* 63.2 (1996): 397–422.

The Making of the English Literary Canon: From the Middle Ages to the Late Eighteenth Century. Montreal: McGill-Queen's University Press, 1998.

Rossabi, Morris. "The 'Decline' of the Central Asian Caravan Trade." In *The Rise of Merchant Empires: Long-Distance Trade in the Early Modern World, 1350–1750*, ed. James D. Tracy (Cambridge: Cambridge University Press, 1990), 351–70.

Rossi, Paolo. *The Dark Abyss of Time: The History of the Earth and the History of Nations from Hooke to Vico*. Chicago: University of Chicago Press, 1984.

Ryan, Michael T. "Assimilating New Worlds in the Sixteenth and Seventeenth Centuries." *Comparative Studies in Society and History* 23.4 (1981): 519–38.

Saccamano, Neil. "The Sublime Force of Words in Addison's 'Pleasures.'" *English Literary History* 58.1 (1991): 83–106.

Salomon, Albert. "In Praise of the Enlightenment: In Commemoration of Fontenelle, 1657–1757." *Social Research* 24.2 (1957): 202–26.

Sartre, Jean-Paul. *Modern Times: Selected Non-Fiction*. Trans. Robin Buss and ed. Geoffrey Wall. New York: Penguin Books, 2000.

Scammell, G. V. "The New Worlds and Europe in the Sixteenth Century." *The Historical Journal* 12.3 (1969): 389–412.

Schlereth, Thomas J. *The Cosmopolitan Ideal in Enlightenment Thought, Its Form and Function in the Ideas of Franklin, Hume, and Voltaire, 1694–1790*. Notre Dame: University of Notre Dame Press, 1977.

Scholten, Martina. "The Glorification of Gout in 16th- to 18th-Century Literature." *Canadian Medical Association Journal* 179.8 (2008): 804–05.

Schonhorn, Manuel. *Defoe's Politics: Parliament, Power, Kingship, and Robinson Crusoe*. Cambridge: Cambridge University Press, 1991.

Secord, Arthur Wellesley. "Studies in the Narrative Method of Defoe." *University of Illinois Studies in Language and Literature* 9.1 (1924): 9–248.

Seed, Patricia. *Ceremonies of Possession in Europe's Conquest of the New World, 1492–1640*. Cambridge: Cambridge University Press, 1995.

Sells, A. L. *Les Sources Françaises de Goldsmith*. Paris: E. Champion, 1924; Genève: Slatkine Reprints, 1977.

Shaw, Narelle L. "Ancients and Moderns in Defoe's *Consolidator*." *Studies in English Literature, 1500–1900* 28.3 (1988): 391–400.

Sherman, Stuart. *Telling Time: Clocks, Diaries, and English Diurnal Form, 1660–1785*. Chicago: University of Chicago Press, 1996.

Shevelow, Kathryn. *Women and Print Culture: The Construction of Femininity in the Early Periodical*. London: Routledge, 1989.

Shimada, Takau. "Is Sharawadgi Derived from the Japanese Word Sorowaji?" *The Review of English Studies* 48 (1997): 350–52.

Sieber, Patricia. "The Imprint of the Imprints: Sojourners, *Xiaoshuo* Translations, and the Transcultural Canon of Early Chinese Fiction in Europe, 1697–1826." *East Asian Publishing and Society* 3 (2013): 31–70.

Simonsuuri, Kirsti. *Homer's Original Genius: Eighteenth-Century Notions of the Early Greek Epic (1688–1798)*. Cambridge: Cambridge University Press, 1979.

Simpson, David. *Romanticism and the Question of the Stranger*. Chicago: University of Chicago Press, 2013.

Sirén, Osvald. *China and Gardens of Europe of the Eighteenth Century*. Washington, D.C.: Dumbarton Oaks Research Library and Collection, 1990.

Sloboda, Stacey. *Chinoiserie: Commerce and Critical Ornament in Eighteenth-Century Britain*. Manchester: Manchester University Press, 2014.

Smiles, Sam. *The Image of Antiquity: Ancient Britain and the Romantic Imagination*. New Haven: Yale University Press, 1994.

Smith, Charles Saumarez. *Eighteenth-Century Decoration: Design and the Domestic Interior in England*. New York: H. N. Abrams, 1993.

Smith, Hamilton Jewett. *Oliver Goldsmith's The Citizen of the World: A Study*. New Haven: Yale University Press, 1926.

Smith, Woodruff D. *Consumption and the Making of Respectability, 1600–1800*. London: Routledge, 2002.

Spadafora, David. *The Idea of Progress in Eighteenth-Century Britain*. New Haven: Yale University Press, 1990.

Spence, Jonathan D. *The Chan's Great Continent: China in Western Minds*. New York: W. W. Norton, 1998.

"When Minds Met: China and the West in the Seventeenth Century." 2010 Jefferson Lecture in the Humanities, May 20, 2010 [www.neh.gov/about/awards/jefferson-lecture/jonathan-spence-lecture, accessed 7 July 2015].

Spingarn, Joel Elias, ed. *Critical Essays of the Seventeenth Century*. 3 vols. Oxford: Clarendon Press, 1908.

Sir William Temple's Essays On Ancient & Modern Learning *and* On Poetry. Oxford: Clarendon Press, 1909.

St. André, James. "Modern Translation Theory and Past Translation Practice: European Translations of the Haoqiu zhuan." In *One into Many: Translation and the Dissemination of Classical Chinese Literature*, ed. Leo Tak-hung Chan, 39–65.

Stewart, Keith. "Ancient Poetry as History in the 18th Century." *Journal of the History of Ideas* 19.3 (1958): 335–47.

"The Ballad and the Genres in the Eighteenth Century." *English Literary History* 24.2 (1957): 120–37.

Stewart, Susan. *Crimes of Writing: Problems in the Containment of Representation*. Oxford: Oxford University Press, 1991.

On Longing: Narratives of the Miniature, the Gigantic, the Souvenir, the Collection. Baltimore: Johns Hopkins University Press, 1984.

Stillman, Robert. "Assessing the Revolution: Ideology, Language, and Rhetoric in the New Philosophy of Early Modern England." *The Eighteenth Century: Theory and Interpretation* 35.2 (1994): 99–118.

Suarez, S. J., and Michael, F. "The Production and Consumption of the Eighteenth-Century Poetic Miscellany." In *Books and Their Readers in Eighteenth-Century England: New Essays*, ed. Isabel Rivers, 217–51.

"Trafficking in the Muse: Dodsley's Collection of Poems and the Question of Canon." In *Tradition in Transition: Women Writers, Marginal Texts, and the Eighteenth-Century Canon*, ed. Alvaro Ribeiro and James G. Basker, 297–313.

Suarez, S.J., Michael F., and Michael L. Turner, eds. *The Cambridge History of the Book in Britain*. Vol. 5. 1695–1830. Cambridge: Cambridge University Press, 2000.

Sudan, Rajani. *The Alchemy of Empire: Abject Materials and the Technologies of Colonialism*. New York: Fordham University Press, 2016.

Sutherland, Kathryn. "The Native Poet: The Influence of Percy's Minstrel from Beattie to Wordsworth." *The Review of English Studies* 33.132 (1982): 414–33.

Tao, Zhijian. "Citizen of Whose World? Goldsmith's Orientalism." *Comparative Literature Studies* 33.1 (1996): 15–34.

Taylor, Richard C. *Goldsmith as Journalist*. Rutherford, NJ: Fairleigh Dickinson University Press, 1993.

Tchen, John Kuo Wei. *New York before Chinatown: Orientalism and the Shaping of American Culture, 1776–1882*. Baltimore: Johns Hopkins University Press, 1999.

Terry, Richard. *Poetry and the Making of the English Literary Past*. Oxford: Oxford University Press, 2001.

Thorpe, Clarence DeWitt. "Addison and Some of His Predecessors on 'Novelty.'" *Publications of the Modern Language Association of America* 52.4 (1937): 1114–29.

Tinkler, John F. "The Splitting of Humanism: Bentley, Swift, and the English *Battle of the Books*." *Journal of the History of Ideas* 49.3 (1988): 453–72.

Trowbridge, Hoyt. Introduction to *Letters on Chivalry and Romance (1762)* by Richard Hurd. Los Angeles: William Andrews Clark Memorial Library, 1963. i–ix.

Trumpener, Katie. *Bardic Nationalism: The Romantic Novel and the British Empire*. Princeton: Princeton University Press, 1997.

Turley, Hans. "Protestant Evangelicalism, British Imperialism, and Crusonian Identity." In *A New Imperial History: Culture, Identity, and Modernity in Britain and the Empire, 1660–1840*, ed. Kathleen Wilson, 176–93.

Rum, Sodomy, and the Lash: Piracy, Sexuality, and Masculine Identity. New York: New York University Press, 1999.

"The Sublimation of Desire to Apocalyptic Passion in Defoe's Crusoe Trilogy." In *Imperial Desire: Dissident Sexualities and Colonial Literature*, ed. Philip Holden and Richard J. Ruppel (Minneapolis: University of Minnesota Press, 2003), 3–20.

Tuve, Rosemond. "Ancients, Moderns, and Saxons." *English Literary History* 6.3 (1939): 165–90.

Van Kley, Edwin J. "An Alternative Muse: The Manchu Conquest of China in the Literature of Seventeenth-Century Northern Europe." *European Studies Review* 6 (1976): 21–43.

"Europe's 'Discovery' of China and the Writing of World History." *The American Historical Review* 76.2 (1971): 358–85.

"News from China: Seventeenth-Century European Notices of the Manchu Conquest." *The Journal of Modern History* 45.4 (1973): 561–82.

Vickers, Ilse. *Defoe and the New Sciences*. Cambridge: Cambridge University Press, 1996.

Vickery, Amanda. *Behind Closed Doors: At Home in Georgian England*. New Haven: Yale University Press, 2009.

Waldron, Arthur. *The Great Wall of China: From History to Myth*. Cambridge: Cambridge University Press, 1990.

Walvin, James. *Fruits of Empire: Exotic Produce and British Taste, 1660–1800*. Basingstoke: Macmillan, 1997.

Warneke, Sara. "A Taste for Newfangledness: The Destructive Potential of Novelty in Early Modern England." *The Sixteenth Century Journal* 26.4 (1995): 881–96.

Warner, Michael. *The Letters of the Republic: Publication and the Public Sphere in Eighteenth-Century America*. Cambridge, Mass.: Harvard University Press, 1990.

Watt, Ian. *The Rise of the Novel: Studies in Defoe, Richardson, and Fielding*. Berkeley: University of California Press, 1957.

Watt, James. "Goldsmith's Cosmopolitanism." *Eighteenth-Century Life* 30.1 (2005): 56–75.

"Thomas Percy, China, and the Gothic." *The Eighteenth Century: Theory and Interpretation* 48.2 (2007): 95–109.

Watt, James C. Y., and Barbara Brennan Ford, eds. *East Asian Lacquer: The Florence and Herbert Irving Collection*. New York: The Metropolitan Museum of Art, 1991.

Weinbrot, Howard D. *Britannia's Issue: The Rise of British Literature from Dryden to Ossian*. Cambridge: Cambridge University Press, 1993.

" 'He Will Kill Me Over and Over Again': Intellectual Contexts of the Battle of the Books." In *Reading Swift: Papers from the Fourth Münster Symposium on Jonathan Swift*, ed. Hermann Josef Real and Helgard Stöver-Leidig (Munich: Fink, 2003), 225–48.

Wellek, René. *The Rise of English Literary History*. Chapel Hill: University of North Carolina Press, 1941.

Wheeler, Roxann. *The Complexion of Race: Categories of Difference in Eighteenth-Century British Culture*. Philadelphia: University of Pennsylvania Press, 2000.

Whitley, William T. *Artists and Their Friends in England, 1700–1799*. 2 vols. London: The Medici Society, 1928.

Whyman, Susan E. "Sharing Public Spaces." In *Walking the Streets of Eighteenth-Century London: John Gay's Trivia (1716)*, ed. Clare Brant and Susan E. Whyman (Oxford: Oxford University Press, 2007), 43–61.

Wiles, R. M. *Serial Publication in England before 1750*. Cambridge: Cambridge University Press, 1957.

Wills, John E. *Embassies and Illusions: Dutch and Portuguese Envoys to K'ang-hsi, 1666–1687*. Cambridge, Mass.: Council on East Asian Studies, Harvard University, 1984.

Wilson, Kathleen. *The Island Race: Englishness, Empire and Gender in the Eighteenth Century*. London: Routledge, 2003.

Wilson, Kathleen, ed. *A New Imperial History: Culture, Identity, and Modernity in Britain and the Empire, 1660–1840*. Cambridge: Cambridge University Press, 2004.

Wolper, Roy S. "The Rhetoric of Gunpowder and the Idea of Progress." *Journal of the History of Ideas* 31.4 (1970): 589–98.

Wong, Young-tsu. *A Paradise Lost: The Imperial Garden Yuanming Yuan*. Honolulu: University of Hawaii Press, 2001.

Wood, Frances. *The Lure of China: Writers from Marco Polo to J. G. Ballard*. San Francisco: Long River Press, 2009.

Woodbridge, Homer Edwards. *Sir William Temple, the Man and His Work*. New York: Modern Language Association of America, 1940.

Yadav, Alok. *Before the Empire of English: Literature, Provinciality, and Nationalism in Eighteenth-Century Britain*. New York: Palgrave Macmillan, 2004.

Yang, Chi-ming. *Performing China: Virtue, Commerce, and Orientalism in Eighteenth-Century England, 1660–1760*. Baltimore: Johns Hopkins University Press, 2011.

Youngren, William H. "Addison and the Birth of Eighteenth-Century Aesthetics." *Modern Philology* 79.3 (1982): 267–83.

Zhijian, Tao. "Citizen of Whose World? Goldsmith's Orientalism." *Comparative Literature Studies* 33.1 (1996): 15–34.

Zimmerman, Everett. "Robinson Crusoe and No Man's Land." *The Journal of English and Germanic Philology* 102.4 (2003): 506–29.

Zuroski Jenkins, Eugenia. *A Taste for China: English Subjectivity and the Prehistory of Orientalism*. Oxford: Oxford University Press, 2013.

"Tea and the Limits of Orientalism in De Quincey's Confessions of an English Opium Eater." In *Writing China: Essays on the Amherst Embassy (1816) and Sino-British Cultural Relations*, ed. Peter J. Kitson and Robert Markley, 105–31.

Index

Adas, Michael, 157
Addison, Joseph, 7, 11, 13, 44, 95, 96–102,
    106–24, 138, 160, 169–71
    A Discourse on Ancient and Modern Learning,
        7, 121–22
    "Chevy Chase", 169–71
    "Pleasures of the Imagination", 13, 93,
        100–02, 106–11
    The Freeholder, 114
    The Spectator, 92–94, 96–99, 100–02, 116–20,
        128, 143–44, 159, 169–71
    "To Mr. Dryden", 120–21
Aesop, 16, 17, 33
Allen, B. Sprague, 105
alphabetic writing, 195–96
Anderson, Benedict, 12, 144–46, 147, 148,
    149, 150
Anglo-Saxons, 168, 174, 176, 177, 178, 199
Anson, George, 53
antiquarianism, 171, 177, 178, 180, 181, 191, 197
antiquity, 11, 18, 19, 35, 36, 37, 49, 124, 152, 170,
    177, 195
    Chinese, 4, 19, 20, 21, 26, 51, 113, 196, 197
    classical, 14, 176
    English, 14, 168, 171, 175, 198
    northern, 175
    pagan, 19
Aravamudan, Srinivas, 140
Argens, Jean-Baptiste de Boyer, marquis d',
    134, 148
    Lettres chinoises, 148
Aristotle, 36, 51
Astle, Thomas, 168
Attiret, Jean-Denis, 112

Bacon, Francis, 92, 195
Balderston, Katharine, 139
ballads, 14, 166, 167–71, 177–79, 192–93, 197–98
Ballaster, Ros, 130, 140, 141, 142
Barbuda, Luis Jorge de, 80
Barker, Hannah, 135

Barrell, John, 162
Bayer, Theophilus Siegfried, 193, 195
    Museum Sinicum, 195
Behn, Aphra, 210
Benedict, Barbara, 181
Bentley, Richard, 16, 17, 33, 46
biblical chronology, 4, 19, 22, 196
biblical history, 3, 21, 29
Billings, Timothy, 72
Birch, Thomas, 168
Bivins, Roberta E., 207
Black, Scott, 93
Blaeu, Joan, 81
Blair, Hugh, 176
Booth, Wayne, 137, 142
Boyle, Charles, 17, 25
Boyle, Robert, 17, 127
Boym, Michael, 28
Brand, Adam, 76–77, 78, 81
    A Journal of the Embassy, 76
Brooks, Christopher, 151
Brown, Tony, 94
Bunn, James, 100
Burke, Edmund, 228
Burnet, Thomas, 20, 21, 29, 30, 39
Busschoff, Hermann, 90
Butler, Samuel, 36

Calinescu, Matei, 13
Campanella, Tommaso, 50
Canton, 128, 129, 146, 158–59, 165, 182, 184
Celts, 175–76, 177–79, 199
    and bards, 176
    and poetry, 177–79
Chakrabarty, Dipesh, 5
Chambers, William, 44, 112, 129
    A Dissertation on Oriental Gardening,
        112–13, 129
Chang, Elizabeth, 105
Chaucer, Geoffrey, 10, 45
Cheah, Pheng, 145, 147

Cheung, Kai-chong, 184, 186
China
 aesthetic modernity, 115
 and antiquity, 4, 19, 20, 21, 26, 51, 113,
  196, 197
 and astrology, 27, 28
 and book trade, 184
 and chronology, 19
 and cities, 65, 157–59
 and diet, 73
 and export art, 103–05
 and export trade, 103
 and flowering tree motif, 104
 and government, 23, 27, 67
 and Great Wall, 26, 54, 58, 62, 71, 79–84, 171
 and history, 23
 and idea of beauty, 13, 44, 94, 102–03, 105, 124
 and lacquer, 73, 103
 and language, 20, 29, 193–96
 and literature, 183–89, 196, 197
 and manners, 183, 186, 198
 and map, 79–85
 and medicine, 28, 29
 and poetry, 193–94
 and porcelain, 67, 73, 97–99, 103–04, 105
 and science, 27–31, 49–51, 54, 57
 and script, 193–96
 and shops, 158–59
 and taste, 94–95, 106, 128
 and wallpaper, 105, 110
 and women, 114, 187–89
Chinese gardens, 13, 44, 102–03, 105, 106, 109,
  110, 111, 112–13, 116, 118, 123
Chinese Rites Controversy, 27
chinoiserie, 2, 95, 102, 105, 128, 151, 154, 199
Chitqua, 129
chivalry, 174, 190–92
Clarke, David, 129
classic(s), 7, 10, 19, 22, 37, 38, 40, 94, 104, 119
classical, 9, 10, 11, 14, 18, 19, 23, 34–35, 36, 37, 38,
  41, 47, 94, 105, 121, 122, 168, 175, 176, 196
classicism, 7, 9
*Clavis medica ad Chinarum doctrinam de
  pulsibus*, 28
Cleyer, Andreas, 28
Cocks, Anna Somers, 99
Cohen, Michèle, 191
Cole, Lucinda, 54, 70
Conant, Martha, 130
Confucius, 23, 25, 27, 44, 53, 140
Connell, Philip, 178, 198
Cook, Harold, 219
cosmopolitanism, 163
Couplet, Philippe, 22, 27, 127
 Confucius Sinarum philosophus, 22, 27, 127

Cowley, Abraham, 33, 34, 36, 169
Cruz, Gaspar da, 80
Curran, Stuart, 168

Dalnekoff, Donna Isaacs, 152
Dampier, William, 85, 86, 87
Davenant, William, 33, 34
Davis, Bertram, 165
Davis, Lennard J., 137, 143
De Bolla, Peter, 106
Defoe, Daniel, 11, 47–71, 72–79, 85–88, 96, 98,
  99, 113, 134, 150, 160
 *A General History of Discoveries and
  Improvements*, 48–49, 57
 A New Voyage round the World, 47
 *A Tour through the Whole Island of Great
  Britain*, 86, 98
 Atlas Maritimus & Commercialis, 73
 *Serious Reflections during the Life and
  Surprising Adventures of Robinson
  Crusoe*, 79
 The Advantages of Peace and Commerce, 72,
  74–75, 76
 The Compleat English Gentleman, 85
 The Consolidator, 49–52
 The Farther Adventures of Robinson Crusoe,
  47, 53, 57, 60–61, 63–71, 75–79, 86–88,
  96, 150
 *The Life and Strange Surprizing Adventures
  of Robinson Crusoe*, 47, 54–55,
  58–59, 63
 *The Life, Adventures, and Pyracies, of the
  Famous Captain Singleton*, 47
DeJean, Joan, 59–60, 61, 69
Denham, John, 33, 34, 37
Dennis, John, 36
Descartes, René, 33, 34, 40, 109
Dharwadker, Aparna, 76
Dieckmann, Herbert, 40
Dix, Robin, 109
Dodsley, James, 166
Dodsley, Robert, 165, 166, 197
Donoghue, Frank, 130
Dryden, John, 33, 34, 36, 109, 121
Du Halde, Jean-Baptiste, 157, 165, 183
 A Description of the Empire of China,
  157, 165
Dunton, John, 9, 92
 Life and Errors of John Dunton, 92
 The Athenian Mercury, 92
Dussinger, John, 139

Edney, Matthew, 85
eidolon, 134, 135, 137, 138
Elioseff, Lee, 124

Elliott, John, 18
English East India Company, 53, 64, 128, 129,
    138, 139, 165, 166
Evans, Evan, 168
Evans, Robin, 61, 70
Evelyn, John, 24, 103

Fabian, Johannes, 12, 13
Fabricant, Carole, 108
Fan, Cunzhong, 129, 230
Fan, Shouyi, 229
Fan, T. C., *see* Fan, Cunzhong
Farmer, Richard, 168, 177, 197
Felton, Henry, 37, 209
Ferguson, Adam, 191
flowering tree motif, 105
Fontenelle, Bernard le Bovier de, 20, 33, 39
    Digression sur les anciens et les modernes, 20,
        39, 42–43
    Entretiens sur la pluralité des mondes,
        20, 39–41
Fréret, Nicolas, 193
Friedman, Albert, 169, 170

Galland, Antoine, 141
    Arabian Nights, 141, 142
Garrick, David, 168
gender, 98–99, 100, 114–15, 187, 188, 189, 191
genius, 7, 33, 44, 45, 46, 95, 117, 120, 123,
    170, 179
Gildon, Charles, 36
Glanvill, John, 210
Glanvill, Joseph, 56
Góis, Bento de, 80
Goldsmith, Oliver, 7, 11, 12, 129–31, 134–40, 144,
    146–50, 158–63, 164–65, 168
    A Comparative View of Races and Nations, 135
    *An Enquiry into the Present State of Polite
        Learning in Europe*, 164
    The Citizen of the World, 125–27, 130–38,
        146–50, 153–63, 165
    The Deserted Village, 163
    The Traveller, 162
    The Vicar of Wakefield, 163
Gothic, 34, 35, 46, 169–79
    and poetry, 173, 174, 175, 177
    and romance, 177
    and taste, 169, 170, 171, 199
Goths, 171–79
    and bards, 176, 190, 196
    and chivalry, 177
    and government, 172, 175
    and liberty, 171

and manners, 191
and scalds, 172, 174, 176, 190
Grainger, James, 164, 165, 166
Griffiths, Ralph, 135, 165
Groom, Nick, 167, 192
Grosrichard, Alain, 140, 141
Gueullette, Thomas-Simon, 245

Hakewill, George, 56, 213
Hakluyt, Richard, 20
Harris, John, 52
Harvey, William, 51
Haugen, Kristine Louise, 46
Hayot, Eric, 12
Helgerson, Richard, 163
Hessney, Richard C., 186
Heylyn, Peter, 20
hieroglyphs, 195, 197
Hill, Christopher, 63
historicism, 5, 6, 31, 38
Hobbes, Thomas, 33, 34, 109
Hodson, Daniel, 138
Homer, 6, 33, 35, 37, 118, 119, 120, 123, 169
Horrocks, Ingrid, 162
Hostetler, Laura, 11
Huang, Arcadio, 229
Huangdi Neijing, 28
Hudson, Nicholas, 196
Huet, Pierre-Daniel, 186
Hulme, Obadiah, 199
Hume, David, 7, 161, 196
Hunt, John Dixon, 116
Hunter, J. Paul, 9, 11, 92
Hurd, Richard, 168, 176–77, 190
Huygens, Constantijn, 89, 90, 91
Hyde, Thomas, 127

Ides, Evert Ysbrants, 76–77, 78, 81
    *Three Years Travels from Moscow Over-Land
        to China*, 76

Jacob, Christian, 85
Jacob, Margaret, 161
Janowitz, Anne, 197
Jauss, Hans Robert, 38, 94
Johnson, Samuel, 33, 165, 166, 196, 198

Keevak, Michael, 229
Kietzman, Mary Jo, 150
Kircher, Athanasius, 20, 71, 81
    China Illustrata, 81, 84
Kitson, Peter, 241
Kliger, Samuel, 171, 173

Kowaleski-Wallace, Elizabeth, 100
Kramnick, Jonathan, 10, 14, 45, 122
Kristeller, Paul O., 5
Kyakhta Treaty, 74–75

La Curne de Sainte Palaye, Jean-Baptiste de, 177
Lafitau, Joseph François, 196
landscape, 107–08, 110, 111, 116–19
Lapeyrère, Isaac, 19
Le Comte, Louis, 113, 114, 157
    Memoirs and Observations, 113, 157, 158
Lettres édifiantes et curieuses, 43, 182
Levine, Joseph, 23, 29, 35
Lam, Ling Hon, 188
literary modernity, 1, 2, 3, 10, 12, 13, 14, 38, 96,
    119, 120, 124, 145
Liu, Lydia, 73
Lovejoy, Arthur, 44, 211
Lowenthal, David, 14
Lye, Edward, 168, 175
lyric, 197–99
Lyttelton, George, 130

Macartney, George, 184
Macaulay, Catherine, 199
Macpherson, James, 175–79, 180
    Fingal, an Ancient Epic Poem, 177
    Fragments of Ancient Poetry, 175, 176, 177
    Temora, 177
Magalhães, Gabriel de, 4, 22, 72, 85, 158
    A New History of China, 4, 22
Mallet, Paul-Henri, 174, 175
Mancall, Mark, 76, 77
Manchu invasion, 70
Mandeville, John, 72
maps, 41, 47, 82–88
Marana, Giovanni Paolo, 130, 141, 147, 152
    Letters Writ by a Turkish Spy, 141,
        147, 152–53
Marburg, Clara, 39
Markley, Robert, 2, 31, 53
Marshall, David, 111
Martini, Martino, 4, 19, 22, 27, 29, 80, 81, 87
    Bellum Tartaricum, 4, 22
    Novus Atlas Sinensis, 80, 81, 82
    Sinicae historiae decas prima, 19, 20
McMahon, Keith, 188
Mendoza, Juan González de, 20, 80, 195
mercantilism, 74, 100
    aesthetics of, 100, 102
Milton, John, 33, 34, 36, 118, 122–23, 169, 177
    Paradise Lost, 122–23
miscellany, 181–83

modernity, 2, 6, 12, 14, 30, 50, 55, 57, 85, 88, 92,
    115, 123, 150, 152
    aesthetics of, 13, 94, 115
    alternative, 50, 150
    and seriality, 150
    and time, 143
    and tradition, 14
    and transience, 13
    Chinese, 115, 147, 150, 155
    English, 4, 36, 38, 53, 155, 159
    literary, *see* literary modernity
    polite, 10
    politics of, 6
    vs. modernization, 14
Modernity
    and time, 12
Moll, Herman, 86, 87
Montaigne, Michel de, 91
Montesquieu, Charles-Louis de Secondat,
    baron de, 130, 134, 142, 189
    Persian Letters, 130, 142
    Spirit of the Laws, 189
More, Thomas, 72
Motteux, Pierre , 36, 209
Mundy, Peter, 52
Murphy, Arthur, 133, 202

Needham, John Turberville, 197
Nerchinsk Treaty, 74–76
Newbury, John, *see The Public Ledger*
news, 93, 131, 136, 137, 138
newspaper, 131–38, 140, 142, 143, 144–49, 159
Newton, John, 31
Nieuhof, Johan, 4, 22, 71, 81
    *An Embassy from the East-India Company of
        the United Provinces, to the Grand Tartar
        Cham, Emperor of China*, 4, 22, 81
novels, 10, 59, 69, 137, 140, 143, 144–45, 150, 185
novelty, 9, 13, 92, 93, 102, 108, 109, 112, 113,
    115, 150

Ong, Walter J., 180
oral tradition, 178–81, 190, 195
oriental spies, 140–42, 144, 148, 150, 152
oriental tale, 140–42, 149, 155, 183
Ortelius, Abraham, 80
Osborne, Dorothy, 103
Ossian, 176, 177, 178, 196
Ovid, 119

Pagden, Anthony, 67
Parker, Charles H., 53
Parker, George, 142

Patey, Douglas Lane, 4, 6, 38, 45
Paulson, Ronald, 101
Peking, 65, 157–58
Percy, Thomas, 11, 129, 164–69, 170–72, 173–99
  "A Dissertation on the Language and
    Characters of the Chinese", 193
  "Essay on the Ancient English Minstrels",
    172, 173–76
  Five Pieces of Runic Poetry, 175, 179
  Hau Kiou Choaan, or the Pleasing History,
    165–67, 182–89
  Life of Dr. Oliver Goldsmith, 164
  Miscellaneous Pieces Relating to the Chinese,
    167, 182, 193–97
  Northern Antiquities, 175
  "On the Ancient Metrical Romances", 190, 192
  Reliques of Ancient English Poetry, 166–69, 181
  The Matrons, 167, 182
Perdue, Peter, 215
periodical, 91–93, 96, 138
periodical essay, 91, 130, 134, 135, 137
Perrault, Charles, 33
Phalaris, 16, 17, 25
Philosophical Transactions, 28, 77
Pinkerton, John, 199
Pior, James, 162
Plato, 33, 107, 118
Pocock, J. G. A., 7
Pope, Alexander, 7, 10, 37, 162
  An Essay on Criticism, 37
  An Essay on Man, 162
  The Dunciad, 9, 156
Porter, David, 2, 20, 151, 190, 194
Powell, Manushag, 135
Pratt, Mary Louise, 87
Prior, James, 154
Psalmanazar, George, 128, 129
Purchas, Samuel, 20

quarrel between the ancients and the moderns,
  3–7, 9, 11, 15–46, 50, 54, 57, 94, 199

Ralegh, Walter, 20
realism, 52, 54, 59, 67, 71, 140
Rendall, Jane, 191
Rhymer, Thomas, 24
Ricci, Matteo, 84, 195
  Kunyu Wanguo Quantu, 84
Rogers, Woodes, 85, 86, 87
romance, 14, 141, 173, 174, 176–77,
  186–87, 190–92
Ross, Trevor, 7, 11, 45, 124
Royal Academy, 129
Royal College of Physicians, 129
Royal Exchange, 159

Royal Society, 24, 25, 28, 31, 36, 91
runes, 34, 46, 173, 175, 179

Saccamano, Neil, 110, 117
Samuel Purchas, Samuel, 50
Sanson, Nicolas, 84
Sartre, Jean-Paul, 145–46, 147
satire, 49, 100, 141, 147, 148, 151–52
Saussy, Haun, 12
Schall, Adam, 84
scholar-beauty romance (*caizi jiaren*), 184, 188
Seed, Patricia, 62
Semedo, Alvaro, 4, 20, 22, 72, 84
  *The History of that Great and Renowned
    Monarchy of China*, 4, 22
seriality, 142–50, 151
Seven Years' War, 125, 146, 160
Shakespeare, William, 10, 45, 118
sharawadgi, 13, 102, 109, 116
Shaw, Narelle, 52
Shen, Fuzong, 127
Shen, Michael, *see* Shen, Fuzong
Shenstone, William, 167, 168, 175, 197
Sherman, Stuart, 143
Shevelow, Kathryn, 100
Sieber, Patricia, 184, 186
Simonsuuri, Kirsti, 11, 37
Sloboda, Stacey, 95
Smith, Adam, 158
Smollett, Tobias, 135
Southwell, Robert, 77
Specimen Medicinae Sinicae, 28
Spence, Jonathan, 127
Spencer, John, 21
Spenser, Edmund, 10, 34, 45, 123, 177
Spingarn, J. E., 38
Spode, Josiah, 105
Sprat, Thomas, 36, 56
Staunton, George, 184
Stewart, Susan, 69, 180, 192
Stubbes, Philip, 96
sublime, 37, 67, 94, 107, 108, 119, 120, 123, 169,
  171, 173
Sudan, Rajani, 91
Swift, Jonathan, 10, 32, 33, 34–35
  "A Description of a City Shower", 156
  A Tale of a Tub, 17, 34, 52
  Battel of the Books, 15–17, 32, 34

Tacitus, 171, 191
Tao, Zhijian, 151
taste, 2, 5, 6, 38, 93, 94, 95, 96, 99, 100, 101, 104,
  105, 113, 161, 168, 169, 179, 193, 194
  and relativization of, 6, 38
  and standard of, 7, 44, 181

Taste, 170
Taylor, Richard, 134, 135
tea, 49, 73, 76, 88, 99, 100
Temple, William, 4, 7, 20–24, 32–34, 38–46,
    120, 123, 124
    Essay upon the Ancient and Modern Learning,
      4, 20–23, 39, 47–48, 51
    Essay upon the Cure of the Gout by
      Moxa, 89–92
    Essay upon the Gardens of Epicurus, 106
    Introduction to the History of England, 172
    Of Heroick Virtue, 23, 26–27, 31, 33, 41–42, 172
    Of Poetry, 33–34, 45, 172, 173
    Some Thoughts upon Reviewing the Essay of
      Ancient and Modern Learning, 32, 33
    Upon the Gardens of Epicurus, 13, 44, 103
The Adventurer, 128
The Connoisseur, 128
The Critical Review, 131, 135, 167
The Gentleman's Journal, 36
The Gentleman's Magazine, 167
The London Chronicle, 149
The Monthly Review, 131, 135, 167, 197
The Public Ledger, 125–27, 130, 131–38, 146, 165
The Rambler, 128
The Royal Magazine; or Gentleman's Monthly
    Companion, 135
The World, 128
Trigault, Nicolas, 20
Trumpener, Katie, 180
Turley, Hans, 53, 79

universal history, 4, 18

Van Kley, Edwin J., 18
Vauban, Sebastian Le Prestre de, 59, 61

Verbiest, Ferdinand, 28
Vickery, Amanda, 100
Virgil, 33, 35, 118, 119, 123, 169
Voltaire, 42, 146
Vossius, Isaac, 20, 33
Van Braam Houckgeest, Andreas Everardus, 129

Waldron, Arthur, 80
Walpole, Horace, 44, 106, 113, 116
Warner, Michael, 133
Warton, Thomas, 168, 176, 190
Watt, Ian, 64, 69
Watt, James, 241
Webb, John, 20, 195
Weinbrot, Howard, 36
Weitzman, Arthur, 153
Wilkes, John, 178
Wilkins, John, 195
Wilkinson, James, 165, 182, 184
Wilson, Kathleen, 2
Witsen, Nicolaas, 77
Wolper, Roy, 55
Woodbridge, Homer, 46, 91
Wotton, William, 4, 24–31, 35–36, 48, 56
    Observations upon the State of the Nation, in
      January 1712/3, 31
    Reflections upon Ancient and Modern Learning,
      4, 24–31, 35, 48, 50, 56

Yadav, Alok, 2
Yang, Chi-ming, 3, 128
Yao, Steven G., 12
Young, Edward, 44

Zoffany, Johann, 129
Zuroski Jenkins, Eugenia, 2, 3